Advance Praise from the Experts for
Mastering Global Markets:
Strategies for Today's Trade Globalist

"An extremely practical guide for navigating the opportunities and reducing the risks of doing business abroad."

Philip Kotler, Ph.D.,
Northwestern University

"The U.S. Congress has greatly benefited from the knowledge and research of Professors Czinkota and Ronkainen. On more than one occasion, Professor Czinkota has given of his talents to help policymakers understand the complex issues surrounding international trade. In *Mastering Global Markets*, the authors present international marketing and its nexus with trade policy in light of global risk and unprecedented opportunity. Marketers, analysts and policymakers have much to gain by reading this book."

Hon. Donald A. Manzullo,
Chairman, Committee on Small Business,
Congress of the United States

"*Mastering Global Markets* provides a well-structured and pragmatic presentation of what it takes to survive and succeed in the new global marketplace. From would-be exporters to veteran globalists, this primer is recommended reading."

Suzanne Clark,
Executive Vice President and Chief Operating Officer,
U.S. Chamber of Commerce

"A book you want to read before your competitors do. Among the rewards the authors present for the new trade globalists are the ability to leverage economic risk, to extend product life, and to tap into new resources of creativity, product development and problem solving. The rules of international marketing in the new millennium have changed. Czinkota, Ronkainen and Donath know and share the rules that can set you on the right track."

Frank Calamita,
Chairman, Global Human Resources and Administration,
SONY Corporation

"In our fast changing world, Dr. Czinkota's latest book is the clearest guide for successfully accomplishing the high aim of its title: *Mastering Global Markets.* He challenges the best thinking of what is changing and what is not, and provokes us to consider what is working, and what is not. His compelling new insights will be extremely valuable for any business executive who is seriously focused on global markets in the new millennium."

Lew Cramer,
Director General (retired),
U.S. and Foreign Commercial Service,
Managing Director, Summit Ventures

"After the collapse of the Soviet Union, economic competition supplanted ideological competition. Today, markets are no longer national, but instead, global. From political risks and cultural nuances to unfair competition and industrial espionage, companies must address a host of new issues if they want to be successful in the global marketplace. Written for the executive rather than the academic, *Mastering Global Markets* is must reading for anyone desirous of doing business overseas."

Neil C. Livingstone, Ph.D.,
Chairman and Founder of GlobalOptions, Inc.

"This book argues convincingly that companies that become international grow appreciably faster than pure domestic companies. It explains why this is so, and how companies can become more international in orientation and business practice. A must read for people that are or want to be in the global business."

"With *Mastering Global Markets,* three top experts in international business combine their insights and experience to tell it like it is in the booming global marketplace, and how it's going to be for businesses who are smart enough and adventurous enough to dive into that market. Like global chefs, the authors peel the onion of foreign trade, starting with a comprehensive overview of the opportunities and perils of doing business abroad, then laying out the strategies for success and, finally, zeroing in on the tactics that really work. No global trader will want to leave home without this valuable book."

"The new realities of global business precisely identified: this book could not be more observant or applicable to our needs!"

"It is a thorough handbook with very pertinent examples which will be helpful to anyone with interests in the global market, no matter his origin, since it gives insights useful for professionals from everywhere. I compliment the authors on this useful effort."

"No one in today's world can escape the effects of globalization, least wise dynamic businesses seeking to expand markets and improve shareholder value. International transactions are almost becoming mundane for most companies in the 21st century, and mastering the right marketing techniques to expand overseas is a matter of survival. This book will provide the novice globalist, as well as the most seasoned international executive with the fundamental background and tools to compete successfully in markets, whether they be in Chicago or Bangkok, Los Angeles or Buenos Aires."

Alan J. Beard,
Managing Director,
Interlink Capital Strategies

"Mastering Global Markets is a crisp, clear guide to the new realties of international business. Instead of spinning theories about the impact on globalization, it serves up a compelling "to do" list for corporate decision-makers. Both seasoned international managers and new entrants to the global market will regard this book as a powerful tool for coping with the new political economy of trade."

Kevin G. Nealer,
Principal, The Scowcroft Group

"Globalization continues to be a critical aspect of strategy formulation. *Mastering Global Markets* provides a comprehensive, contemporary analysis of today's international business environments."

Bill Dannehl,
Vice President, Strategic Planning and Business Development,
Harley-Davidson Motor Company

"This book is a valuable resource for anyone working in international marketing. It effectively blends solid academic concepts with seasoned insights from practical marketing experiences."

Gene Cunningham,
Regional Director, Europe,
International Business Development, The Boeing Company

CZINKOTA • RONKAINEN • DONATH

Mastering Global Markets

Strategies for Today's Trade Globalist

Michael R. Czinkota
Georgetown University

Ilkka A. Ronkainen
Georgetown University

Bob Donath
Bob Donath & Co.

THOMSON
™
SOUTH-WESTERN

Australia · Canada · Mexico · Singapore · Spain · United Kingdom · United States

SOUTH-WESTERN

Mastering Global Markets: Strategies for Today's Trade Globalist
Michael R. Czinkota, Ilkka A. Ronkainen, Bob Donath

Vice President/ Editorial Director
Jack Calhoun

Vice President/Editor-In-Chief
Dave Shaut

Acquisition Editor
Steve Momper

Consulting Editor in Marketing
Richard Hagle

Channel Manager, Retail
Chris McNamee

Channel Manager, Professional
Mark Linton

Production Manager
Tricia Matthews Boies

Editor
Kim Kusnerak

Manufacturing Manager
Charlene Taylor

Compositor
Sans Serif Inc.

Design Project Manager
Stacy Jenkins Shirley

Cover Design
Trish Knapke

Printer
Phoenix Book
Technology
Hagerstown, MD

CONTENTS

PREFACE

You are about to begin a noble journey as a trade globalist. Along the way you will find substantial opportunities to enrich your business, make important contributions to world prosperity, and, most important from a personal perspective, travel to fascinating places both geographically and professionally. Learning and practicing international marketing is an exciting adventure unique in the business world because it combines the science and the art of commerce with many other disciplines. Knowledge from economics, anthropology, sociology and contemporary cultural studies, geography, history, linguistics, jurisprudence, statistics, demographics, and other fields unlocks the sometimes daunting mysteries of marketing in foreign lands. By reading this book, you will possess the keys to success in global markets and get a comprehensive head start on a rewarding process of discovery. International marketing has been compared by many who have been active in the field to mountain climbing: challenging, arduous, and exhilarating. And, yes, mistakes can be very costly.

International marketing is important because the world has become highly globalized. Globalization increasingly looms large in all walks of life, not only in our entertainment, our fashions, and the products we buy, but also in our morals, belief systems, and our very sense of being a single human species. World trade influences it all to one degree or another, with international marketing taking place all around us every day. Now, at the dawn of the twenty-first century, international marketing is poised to make its greatest contributions. Companies facing increasing competition and technological challenges are learning that international trade—abetted by e-commerce and rising standards of living worldwide—is not only a wise strategic option, trade might well be required for corporate survival.

The world ultimately is a single marketplace, difficult and dangerous, but impossible to avoid. "Safe" markets in "protected" industries are no longer safe or protected. Companies that intend to grow must expand to new markets despite the exotic linguistic, cultural, political, organizational, and financial challenges that the world presents. Failing to overcome fear of the unknown, while understandable, dooms a company to go the way of the dinosaurs.

Trade is also becoming essential to social and cultural survival. Constant improvements in the economic, regulatory, and political environment for world trade have helped to reduce poverty and starvation in underprivileged lands, and have promoted freedom and democracy in developed nations that had earlier waged devastating wars on each other. Now, as the new century unfolds, the United States and its business community have an additional, special role to play on the world stage. As the only true superpower, American military, technological, and economic strength—along with cultural preeminence—has prompted many to hail a period of American "empire," a *Pax Americana* of superior world influence that includes the responsibility to exercise leadership with sensitivity and humility. World prosperity is the burden, the treasure, and the obligation of the United States, especially since the September 11 attacks on the World Trade Center and the Pentagon. Effectively waging war on terrorism includes eliminating the poverty and ignorance that breed hate and desperation. World trade and global marketing truly are key drivers of the planet Earth.

WHERE WE'RE HEADED

With that world view in mind, we prepared this book as an international marketing guide for managers ready to advance their careers and the fortunes of their firms by becoming trade globalists with an integrated world perspective. We approach international marketing in the way the manager of a firm does, stressing the hands-on application of international marketing processes with, we think, just enough theory and background to impart a rich understanding without distracting tangential musings.

Part One of this book, "The International Marketing Environment," provides an overview of the issues of world economy, commerce, law, politics, and culture that create the context for global trade and basic knowledge for international marketing success. Chapter 1, "Why Go International?" provides an overview of major trends influencing the role of international marketing in world affairs. Chapter 2 focuses on the economic environment for that role. Chapters 3, 4, and 5 take detailed looks at the financial institutions and methods of world trade, the foreign-market cultural contexts in which global marketers work, and the political and legal factors that help or hinder worldwide commerce.

Part Two emphasizes the strategic planning duties of the international marketer, ranging from initial foreign market entry through exporting in Chapter 6, to building thoroughly integrated global operations in Chapter 7. Then, in Chapter 8, we look closely at the special challenges of marketing services internationally, which can differ from the approaches supporting product-dominated offerings.

Part Three of the book discusses the marketing mix elements that provide the tactical follow-though that the trade globalist must master at each strategic stage, from exporting through multinational management. We start by reviewing the international research process and the information sources available for global marketing decision making in Chapter 9. Then the discussion moves to the "Four Ps" of marketing as they apply to a company's goods and services: the product (Chapter 10); the price (Chapter 11); the place (Chapter 12); and the promotion (Chapter 13).

Chapter 14, "Organizing for Global Marketing," pulls the previous chapters' concepts together by examining appropriate management structures for the international marketing firm. As the book concludes with Chapter 15, "Twenty-First Century Trade Globalists," we describe our vision for global trade as a tool for world prosperity.

COMPLETE PICTURE

This book offers research insights from around the globe and shows how corporate practices will be adjusting to the challenges suddenly looming before us. Specifically:

We cover the full spectrum of international marketing, from start-up operations to the formation of virtual alliances.

We discuss not only multinational corporations, but also the activities of small- and medium-sized firms, which are increasingly major players in the international market.

We examine international marketing from a truly global perspective rather than just from the U.S. point of view. By addressing, confronting, and analyzing the existence of different environments, expectations, and market conditions, we highlight the need for awareness, sensitivity, and adaptation.

This book also addresses the growing interaction between government and business, a critical dimension for all forms of global marketing.

We review the explosive growth of e-commerce which, despite the setbacks of overenthusiastic dot-com investing, promises to revolutionize international trade practices.

Along the way, we have referenced many of the insightful information sources and key thinkers that contribute to international marketing knowledge.

Our target reader

We are writing for the present and future trade globalist—the manager at any firm who plays a role in creating and implementing world trade strategies and who already understands and practices successful marketing domestically. If you head international marketing operations for a corporation, or might soon do so, this book is for you. However, our material should be of great interest to international marketing staff members seeking the "30,000-foot view" of their work, and to company chief executives pondering where and how to expand internationally.

Although much of our content applies largely to major corporations orchestrating a global presence, such knowledge is invaluable to readers in firms of any size. Not only does watching successful multinationals provide a critical perspective on what works, small companies that market adeptly become large organizations in time. Their managers must be ready to handle that growth. And finally, as a trade globalist of any size firm, you will also play a critical role in world development and the lives of other people everywhere, fulfilling a mission and a joy that we all share. As Socrates declared, "I am a citizen, not of Athens or of Greece, but of the world."

Maybe the whole idea of international marketing is enough to give you a headache. Language barriers! Cultural differences! Government regulations! Conflicting buying patterns! *Who needs it?*

The fact is, we *all* need it. The global marketplace is inevitable, inescapable, and here. It can be intimidating at first because it's new, strange, and exotic. But think instead that international marketing is the application of already familiar marketing principles, but with a twist that requires new knowledge and a broader view of strategy. This book is all about helping you make that transition efficiently and profitably for you and your company.

As we continue our involvement in international marketing, we hope to hear from you with feedback, new thoughts and directions. **We will pay attention!** If we can help clarify issues for you or your staff, let us know.

Michael R. Czinkota (czinkotm@georgetown.edu)
Ilkka A. Ronkainen (ronkaii@georgetown.edu)
Bob Donath (bob@bobdonath.com)

PART 1

THE INTERNATIONAL MARKETING ENVIRONMENT

Part One introduces the international trade framework and environment, highlighting the importance of international marketing in the twenty-first century. We look at the many global forces acting on companies today— whether they aggressively seek worldwide markets or choose to stick close to home—requiring marketers to adapt to foreign environments in response to political, cultural, and legal conflicts.

Chapter 1, "Why Go International?" is an overview of major trends, examining the role of international marketing in world affairs, the inevitability of global business involvement, and the strategic benefits to companies as they increase their commitment to international operations.

Chapter 2, "Trade's Economic Environment," reviews world economic trends and local market conditions confronting global traders today and tomorrow.

Chapter 3, "Trade's Financial Mechanisms," discusses the financial institutions and practices that guide and control international transactions.

Chapter 4, "Marketing within Cultural Contexts," concentrates on the cultural factors that influence customer preferences and behavior.

Chapter 5, "Trade, Politics, and Law," looks closely at international trade institutions and their interface with U.S. trade policy.

Why Go International?

It's no longer if, but when and how.

Except for the Postscript, this is one of the shortest chapters in this book. But don't ignore it. It sets the stage and frames the discussion for what follows. And what follows is about you—as entrepreneur, manager/executive, employee, and citizen of the world—and how you can capitalize on the opportunity at your doorstep if you know how.

The start of the twenty-first century brings with it the triumph of international marketing. We are seeing the rise of a "new old saying" (if there can be such thing). For several decades, people have said, "All politics is local." And as a corollary an increasing number of them are adding, "And all business is global." You can benefit on many levels.

The proof is in: The market approach to business works! More countries are opening their borders to the world market and enforcing rules and laws to ensure competitive market conditions. The fastest globalizing nations have enjoyed rates of economic growth up to 50 percent greater than those that have been integrating the world economy more slowly.[1] Citizens of these same countries have also gained more political freedom and faster increases in life expectancy, literacy rates, and the overall standard of living. All of this means more people with a greater ability to live more comfortably and more productively. It also means more customers for your goods and services—if you know how to reach them.

THE TANGIBLE BENEFITS OF GOING GLOBAL

Considering that you can become "international" by simply developing a Web site and waiting for unsolicited contacts from all over the world, why wouldn't an executive want to go global? Actually, many executives are hesitant to do so for several understandable reasons. It's easy to say "just put up a Web site." But then someone has to manage it. And when an order comes in, you have to do something—like worry about language differences and customs procedures, be certain not to offend the customer's cultural sensibilities, and make sure that exchange rates aren't sapping profits. Those distractions take time away from the "real" business. Besides, rosy forecasts associated with more serious (and expensive) startups have a way of getting dissipated by day-to-day business realities. In summary, the key reasons holding companies back are:

1. Lack of managerial talent.
2. Differences—in language, culture, and business and legal procedures.
3. Expense and risk.
4. Difficulty of serious market penetration.

In the face of such perceived obstacles, many executives are willing to avoid the issue completely or simply give such business to a broker who specializes in global marketing. The latter, as we will discuss later, is one way many companies initially get started in international markets.

But companies benefit substantially from global market expansion. Research has shown that firms of all sizes and in all industries engaged in international marketing outperform their strictly domestic counterparts. They grow more than twice as fast in sales and earn significantly higher returns on equity and assets.[2] With broader market reach and many more customers, firms marketing internationally produce more and do so more efficiently than their domestic-only counterparts.

As a result, these firms simultaneously realize lower costs and higher profits both at home and abroad. Market diversification and the stability arising from firms' lack of dependence on any particular market are other positive effects. Firms also learn from their competitors, which often makes their managers more sensitive and responsive to differing environments, preparing them for change. In addition, their recruiters can also find and develop the best talent from all nationalities.

World trade is also improving corporate processes. Ongoing global technological innovations in marketing have direct effects on the efficiency and effectiveness of all business activities. Products can be produced more quickly, obtained less expensively from sources around the world, distributed at lower cost, and customized to meet diverse clients' needs. For example, only a short while ago it would have been thought impossible for a firm to produce parts for a car in more than one country, assemble the car in yet another country, and sell it in still other nations. Today, such strategies are routine.

GLOBAL MARKETING MOTIVATIONS

As you would expect, companies with the most dynamic and better-educated senior managers tend to do better than others. Management attitude and commitment also tend to predict international marketing success, as do international work experience and multilingual skills. Managers of global activities have the ability and determination to handle risk and to persevere through setbacks. That same determination must percolate through all management ranks so that international marketing—whether for export-only or for full-blown global operations—becomes part of the firm's culture, universally accepted as "the way we do things around here."

Given the requisite management attitude, what other factors motivate firms to "go global"? Some companies globalize because they want to, some because they have to. Typically, a combination of push and pull considerations drive firms to the international marketing arena.

Going for Gold

Profit opportunities, not surprisingly, are primary. Of course, translating opportunities into realities is never simple, but several factors influence profitability. The following are key:

1. Having a unique technological advantage with goods or services or possessing exclusive market information not readily available from competitors helps to ensure profitability, at least as long as that advantage continues. The key question is, How long will that advantage last before competitors catch on?
2. Economies of scale can also be a source of greater profitability. Companies that go global can improve their efficiency in foreign and domestic markets alike by increasing output to spread fixed costs over larger unit volumes and by accelerating production learning curves. An economics rule of thumb says doubling output can reduce production costs up to 30 percent. Another rule of thumb states that higher volumes increase repetitions, which improve efficiency. Reaching for ever greater efficiencies is a powerful driver.
3. Tax benefits have historically also played a major motivating role. Many countries offer tax concessions to their local firms in order to encourage export activities. For example, some countries provide exporting firms with certain tax deferrals, thus making international marketing activities potentially more profitable. However, the rules of the World Trade Organization prohibit export

subsidies by all but the poorest countries. As of this writing, it appears that tax advantages for U.S. companies will be less attractive in the future.

Approaching Neighbors to Control Risk

Physical and psychological distance influence the degree of risk and ease or difficulty of market entry and certainly affect the decision to internationalize. Ease of transport influences management thinking about logistics, and being close to "foreign" customers who are one's neighbors can make export and investment decisions seem much less risky. Being close to foreign markets has long bred an internationalist outlook among, for example, European businesses, which share a must-do attitude toward cross-border trade generally not enjoyed by their American counterparts.

Then again, physical proximity does not necessarily reduce risk. Sometimes cultural variables, legal factors, and other societal norms make a geographically close market psychologically distant. U.S. firms tend to perceive Canada to be much closer psychologically than Mexico, research says. Even England seems closer because of language similarity despite the distance. Those attitudes are changing, of course, as the North American Free Trade Agreement (NAFTA) spurs intra-hemisphere trade and as the U.S. population with Latin American backgrounds grows.

Protecting Turf

Competitive threats—reflected in declining sales and saturated markets—might force a company into internationalization. For instance, competitors might be threatening a company's domestic markets and the firm's market share and, thus, its scale economies. In the face of such a threat, management might seek another outlet, a foreign outlet, for its products. Or the opposite might occur: Managers, fearful that they are losing ground to competitors who are growing stronger because of global market success, might rush into international markets without the proper preparation. That usually is a mistake.

Overproduction and excess capacity—two sides of the same coin that also relate to profitability—can impact pricing power negatively and create turf problems. They have traditionally led companies to look overseas for extra sales, particularly when domestic business slowdowns have not similarly affected foreign markets. Frequently, however, managers have treated such exports as a safety valve.

Rather than truly market their goods, they temporarily pump up overseas sales through price concessions.

These tactics don't work long for several reasons. First, many foreign customers are not interested in temporary or sporadic business relationships. So when the company comes back a second time, it might not find many takers. Second, managers expecting to "dump" goods on other markets by pricing them to cover only variable costs might trigger antidumping regulations in buyer markets. And, third, in the long run those low market-entry prices probably will not be sustainable.

Another motivator can be the product life cycle. Virtually every product has a natural life cycle in a market ranging from birth to growth, maturity, decline, and death. As a product reaches the end of its domestic market life cycle, it might still be popular in nondomestic markets and can still be manufactured efficiently for them. Shorter technology cycles and the rapid diffusion of technologies throughout advanced economies increasingly preclude selling obsolete goods to any but the less-developed, and almost certainly poorer, customers with less sophisticated needs.

Nevertheless, producing such goods super efficiently at home or shifting production to the low-wage environments of less-developed markets can be a viable strategy, particularly if the product is a well-respected brand. For example, think about how much good medical equipment that has been replaced in wealthy nations can do in developing countries where it is scarce. In addition, such a strategy enables the company to continue innovating in its more advanced markets (domestic and international) and profitably meeting real needs in less-developed economies.

On balance, we have found that just protecting turf is not the best motivator. Firms aggressively and proactively seeking international sales and expansion are more likely to be successful than are companies that merely react to external forces thrust upon them. Companies acting proactively are more likely to be customer service-oriented than are reactive firms.

GROWING GLOBAL MARKETING PROGRAMS

Some companies are "born global" with a core strategy of exporting or foreign investment, mostly due to either a small home market or lots of global demand. Typically, however, firms follow a more or less gradual process. If a firm has successfully filled a few unsolicited export orders, it steps cautiously into global marketing by registering with industry portals and online marketplaces. Then it approaches distributors and resellers in psychologically close markets to extend its downstream value chain across national borders for the first time. The firm's objective at the start is selling more of what it makes for the domestic market and achieving economies of scale with minimum additional investment. It can grow into fully integrated marketing investments spread across the globe.

As such modest experimentation continues, the nascent exporter begins to see that changes in marketing and perhaps even in product configuration or styling could easily improve foreign sales volume. More success emboldens management to start an export division that gives undivided attention to foreign markets. Focused management attention increases the visibility of export operations within the entire company. And having growth-minded managers with foreign sales as their only mission encourages the export division to cultivate closer ties with foreign distributors, resellers, and, eventually, foreign original equipment manufacturers.

But to win that international value chain support, the home company will have to prove it has the manufacturing capability and management commitment to be a reliable supplier to other than domestic markets. And, if a consumer product manufacturer, the company will have to mount its own consumer-oriented promotions and support the efforts of its channel partners to build a differentiated brand in target markets.

With new revenue streams rolling in and with the development of an increasingly effective export marketing staff, company management might well see ways to capture a larger share of the value it sells in foreign markets. A number of options will take the company beyond exporting into more advanced stages of global commitment. Rather than rely on a typical buyer-reseller relationship, the company will strengthen ties to foreign marketing partners through licensing, franchising, and other contractual arrangements. The company need not even ship domestically fabricated products but, instead, can sell franchises allowing foreign partners to use the originating company's business systems, technologies, trademarks, and copyrights. Licensing agreements can offer strong brands or logos worldwide. As the company succeeds with these options, its presence in target foreign markets becomes considerable.

In-depth Commitment

Now things get interesting. What was once the company's export department has grown to manage complex reseller and marketing partnership arrangements in target countries, working not only with products that might have been adapted to those markets but also with the trademarks, copyrights, technology rights, and other intellectual property that create and protect brands in foreign markets. With attractive sales forecasts, willing supply chain partners, and cultural and regulatory climates favoring local operations, the expansion of a foreign sales office into a manufacturing or assembly plant begins to look quite attractive. Production in the foreign market facilitates local R&D, makes product lines more tailored to local tastes, and benefits from local management talent.

Investing to become a local producer can thrill national hosts who focus on the manufacturing jobs created locally, and the possibility that the new plant on their soil might create exportable products. Less developed countries will see the multinational firm's plant as the source of much needed expertise, capital, and technology which is essential to convert their local commodity exports into differentiated and much more profitable finished goods. Everybody's happy, as long as politics, patronage, and cultural conflicts—not to mention the standard threats of competition and business cycles—don't get in the way.

With individual subsidiaries proliferating around the globe, the company's home office increasingly wrestles with the balance of local autonomy versus central control over country operations. Autonomy permits local responsiveness, while central control retains the integrity of the company's intellectual property and perhaps protects the size of its bottom line. Eventually, jet travel and Internet communications blur the boundaries that have been consigning customers and supply chains to neatly defined national or regional markets. Management realizes that expertise and technical skills need to be shared among country operations to keep the overall firm competitively efficient. Cross-pollination of talent makes local autonomy a less practical solution as ideas and capital need to be shared worldwide. Local laws and cultural tastes are recognized and accommodated as the multinational firm becomes a true global marketer, thinking globally while acting locally.

CRITICAL CHOICES: THE OPPORTUNITIES AND CHALLENGES AHEAD

Global trade has become an inexorable, if sometimes controversial, force at the start of the twenty-first century. During the three decades from 1970 to 2000, world trade expanded from $200 billion to $7.6 trillion. Trade growth on a global level has consistently surpassed the growth of domestic economies in the past few decades. Important trading blocs have emerged with the European Union in Europe, with NAFTA in North America, with Mercosur in Latin America and ASEAN in Asia. But linking markets around the world doesn't require governmental negotiations and formal treaties. It happens automatically, driven by humankind's eternal search for wealth and a better life.

We've described previously how companies and managers benefit from global marketing. But workers benefit as well. International firms of all sizes pay significantly higher wages than domestic-only firms.[3] Their employers' greater profitability and longevity improves workplace security for employees working in the plants of international marketers than for those working for local firms.[4]

Consumers are the greatest beneficiaries of all. They enjoy an unprecedented degree of product availability and choice. Furthermore, competition usually keeps the prices of internationally traded products low, offering a better quality and quantity of life to a broad spectrum of individuals. For the first time in history, international product and service availability has reached beyond the elite to become the reasonable expectation of the masses.

Exhibit 1.1: Dynamic Interdependence

- For the first 200 years of its history, the United States looked to Europe for markets and sources of supply. Today, U.S. two-way trade with Asia far outpaces U.S. trade with Europe.
- The United States accounted for nearly 25 percent of world merchandise exports in the 1950s, but by the turn of the century this share had declined to less than 13 percent.
- The way countries participate in world trade is shifting. In the past two decades the role of primary commodities in international trade has dropped precipitously, while the importance of manufactured goods has increased.
- Even more dramatic has been the increase in the volume of services trade. In a few decades, international services went from being an unmeasured activity to comprising a global volume of more than $1.5 trillion in 2002, according to the World Trade Organization.

But that is not to say that there are not risks as well as rewards on both the macro and micro levels—and some steep prices to be paid on the human level. Oil embargoes slow the entire world economy. In the 1990s the sudden decline of the Mexican peso affected markets in the United States and reverberated throughout Poland, Hungary, and the Czech Republic. From a national standpoint, economic isolationism has become impossible even as world trade threatens to disrupt established conditions. Foreign investment brings new industries to some communities while others lose their industrial base to regions with lower labor and production costs.

These risks and rewards can occur almost simultaneously in the same place. In South Carolina in the 1990s, for example, German carmaker BMW announced a $640 million direct investment in a new automotive plant in Spartanburg, thanks to generous tax, investment, and labor-training breaks offered by state and local authorities. Just 70 miles away in Iva, S.C., the aging Jackson Mills facility—a relic from the days when the textile industry employed 1.3 million people throughout the region—closed its doors in 1995. Despite technological advances and improved efficiency, mill operators found the cost of labor in the region had risen too high during the previous two decades for them to compete internationally. Much of the textile industry relocated to Latin America and Asia where labor costs are significantly lower.[5]

Such disruptions inevitably fan discontent among those who suffer dislocations and loss, even temporarily, because of global trade. The marketplace allows labor, land, technology, and capital to achieve their rightful and most productive uses. The best days of international marketing are still to come. To make use of the boundless and bountiful opportunities for market forces to help firms, individuals, and nations, managers must learn and understand. Global marketing is where the money is.

To prosper in a world of abrupt changes and discontinuities, governments, firms, and individuals need to respond aggressively with innovation, process improvements, and creativity. All parties concerned can forge cooperative agreements to bring their major strengths to the table and emerge with better products, services, and ideas than they could produce on their own. It requires an awareness of global developments, an understanding of their meaning, and an ability to accommodate change. Conditions and constraints around the world can differ substantially, as the article in Exhibit 1.2 points out.

Then again, in one respect the point is almost moot. Nearly every firm will be an international marketer, by default if not by design. As globalization expands, companies have no place to hide. New foreign competition in their own backyards forces them to think internationally if only defensively. Improving offerings to combat new rivals at home might well generate new demand for a firm's goods in foreign markets. As online marketplaces bring together buyers and

---

Exhibit 1.2: A Glimpse of the World in the New Century

One of the drivers behind the move toward global marketing strategies has been the notion that consumer needs are becoming more alike. Yet drastic differences in the development of the various regions of the world remain and are bound to continue existing well into the new century. Such differences warrant differentiation in both marketing and pricing strategies. Here are just a few examples of what a baby in the Western world and one in less developed countries may face upon birth in the new millennium.

THE WESTERN BABY:

- In Switzerland she will live to the age of 82, while he will live to the age of 75.
- In the Netherlands there is a 1 percent risk he will not see his fifth birthday and a 9 percent risk of not seeing his sixtieth.
- In the United States her family's income will likely exceed $21,541 per annum.
- In Canada he will share 1 square mile with eight other people.
- In Italy she will be living in a city, as 90 percent of the population does.

THE BABY OF THE LESS-DEVELOPED WORLD:

- In Sierra Leone she will live to the age of 39, while he will live to the age of 36.
- In Niger he will run a 9 percent risk of not seeing his fifth birthday and a 36 percent risk of not seeing his fortieth.
- In Uganda her family's annual income is likely to be about $602.
- In China he will share 1 square mile with 327 other people.
- In India she will be living in a rural area, as 72 percent of the population does.

SOURCE: "U.N. Human Development Report," Population Reference Bureau, World Almanac; *The Washington Post,* July 31, 1999, A15.

---

sellers from all over the world quickly and efficiently, Internet search engines lead prospective customers to company World Wide Web sites, even those designed for domestic buyers only.

Most firms will be exposed to new sales opportunities that should not—indeed cannot—be ignored. And size is virtually irrelevant. For example, hundreds of thousands of smaller sized firms have been fueling a U.S. export boom in times of limited domestic growth. The U.S. Department of Commerce indicates that between 1987 and 1999, the number of U.S. firms that export at least occasionally more than tripled to over 231,000. Almost 97 percent of these exporters were small or mid-sized companies.

Exhibit 1.3: Key Questions for the Would-Be Global Marketer

- How will my idea, good, or service fit into the international market?
- Should I obtain my supplies domestically or from abroad?
- What marketing adjustments are or will be necessary?
- What threats from global competition should I expect?
- How can I work with these threats to turn them into opportunities?
- What are my strategic global alternatives?

If you are starting out, consider the questions in Exhibit 1.3. You'll undoubtedly have more as you progress.

International operations are a critical strategic element in most industries. Growth requires at least an export program. Major corporations find that competition forces them to fully integrate autonomous multinational operations. Technology accelerates the trend, as does the overall integration of world economies through politically sophisticated mechanisms such as the World Trade Organization. From most perspectives, world trade conducted by savvy international marketers is the prerequisite to global growth, prosperity, and freedom for all peoples. And for companies themselves, the choice is clear: Have lunch or be lunch.

NOTES

1. Global Business Policy Council, *Globalization Ledger*, Washington, D.C.: A. T. Kearney, 2000, Introduction.
2. Charles Taylor and Witold Henisz. *U.S. Manufacturers in the Global Market Place.* Report 1058. New York: The Conference Board, 1994.
3. *Business America*, 117, 9, September 1996: 9.
4. J. David Richardson and Karin Rindal, *Why Exports Matter: More!* The Institute for International Economics and the Manufacturing Institute, Washington, D.C., February, 1996.
5. Chris Burritt, "Hit Hard by Textile Losses, S.C. Lifted by BMW Plant," *Atlanta Journal-Constitution*, April 8, 2001; Michael R. Czinkota and Peter Fitzmaurice, "Attracting Foreign Direct Investment: German Luxury Cars in the USA," Case study, 1999 Annual Meeting, Academy of International Business, Charleston, South Carolina; Sue Anne Pressley, "With Textile Jobs' Departure Goes a Way of Life," *The Washington Post*, March 28, 1999.

2

Trade's Economic
Environment

Assessing market potential starts with economic factors.

Sizing up any marketing opportunity begins with an assessment of size and potential, and assessing global market opportunities is no different. At the outset you will will have many possibilities to examine. What's most important is to keep an eye on the variables closely related to purchase and consumption of the products you want to sell. This chapter covers the trends and tools that will be most helpful isn making a sound assessment of potential, including the sources and uses of global market information, the key characteristics of emerging global trading blocs, and the likely shape of future international markets.

USING FOREIGN MARKET DATA

As a useful first step, divide countries into four basic categories (excluding whatever centrally planned economies still exist with their unique characteristics of strict governmental control and centralized procurement). This approach enables you to cover general country considerations—such as population, GDP, geography, manufacturing as a percentage of national product, infrastructure, and per capita income—relevant to a company's industry. Exhibit 2.1 describes four categories of general country conditions relevant to the use of electricity and electrical goods.

You can apply a finer evaluation screen to home in on the most promising markets within a group of countries that exhibit potential. Various international organizations, individual governments, and private organizations or associations provide data on the market variables that should be examined. For instance, *The Statistical Yearbook of the United Nations,* World Bank publications, and individual countries' Statistical Abstracts provide the starting point for market investigations. The more developed the market, the more data are

---

Exhibit 2.1: Basic Economic Development Categories: Electricity/Electrical Goods

- **Less developed:** These countries have primarily agrarian and/or extractive economies. High birth rates, along with limited infrastructures, account for the low per capita income and low use of electricity. Electrification is limited to the main population centers. Generally, basic electrical equipment is imported.
- **Early developing:** These countries have begun initial development of an infrastructure and have infant industries, especially mining and selected cottage manufacturesing. Target economic sectors may enjoy high growth rates even though per capita income and electricity consumption are still modest. Progressively more sophisticated electrical equipment is imported, frequently to achieve forward integration of extractive industries.
- **Emerging:** These countries have started an accelerated expansion of infrastructure and wide industrial diversification. Thus, per capita income and electricity consumption are growing rapidly. Increased discretionary income and electrification allow greater ownership of autos and electrical appliances among the expanding middle class. Larger quantities of high-technology equipment are imported.
- **Developed:** These countries enjoy well-developed infrastructures, high per capita income and electricity consumption, and large-scale industrial diversification. They are also characterized by low rates of population and economic growth, as well as shifts in emphasis from manufacturing to service industries—notably transportation, communication, and information systems.

SOURCE: Adapted from V. Yorio, *Adapting Products for Export* (New York: Conference Board, 1983), 11.

---

available. *Business International,* for example, annually compiles market-size indicators for more than 110 countries that account for more than 90 percent of the world's output in goods and services. Chapter 9 discusses how to use market research internationally and provides an extensive list of information sources.

Population and Demographics

The number of people in a particular market provides one of the most basic indicators of market size and, in itself, indicates the potential demand for certain staple items that have universal appeal and are generally affordable. Population size and concentration are not evenly divided among the major regions of the world. Asia holds over half the world's population, and Europe has high population density, making it a strategically located center of operation and one of the major markets of the world.

Population forecasts are critical to the marketer assessing future potential. United Nations projections,[1] for example, point to a population explosion mainly in developing countries. Northern Europe will show nearly zero population growth for the next thirty years, while the population of Africa probably will triple. But even in the low- or zero-growth markets, the news is not necessarily bad for the international marketer. Those in the 25-to-45 age group, whose numbers are increasing, are among the most affluent consumers of all, having formed family units that consume household goods in large quantities as they reach the peak of their personal earnings potential.

Population data can reveal specific characteristics of a market. Age distribution and life expectancy correlate strongly with levels of market development, for example. Industrialized countries, with their increasing median age and a larger share of the population above 65, offer unique opportunities for international marketers with new products and services. A number of companies in the United States, for example, are marketing an adult diaper. As life expectancy in foreign markets lengthen and new target markets become available, international marketers may be able to extend their domestic products' life cycles by marketing them abroad.

An important variable to consider is the size of the household. For example, the average household size in the European Union has shrunk from 2.9 to 2.7 persons since 1977 and is expected to decline further.[2] Divorce and an increase in sole-survivor households is one cause. These changes might lead marketers in the relevant areas to consider offering single-serving portions of frozen foods and smaller appliances to meet changing demand conditions.

Increased urbanization of many markets has distinctly changed consumption patterns. Urban populations as a percentage of the total will vary from a low of 6 percent in Burundi to a high of 97 percent in Belgium. The degree of urbanization often dictates the nature of the marketing task the international marketer faces, not only in terms of distribution but also in terms of market potential and buying habits. Urban areas provide larger groups of consumers who may be more receptive to marketing efforts because of their exposure to other consumers (the demonstration effect) and to communications media. In markets where urbanization is recent and taking place rapidly, the marketer faces additional responsibility as a change agent, especially when incomes may be low and the conditions for the proper use of the products may not be adequate. This is especially true in countries where rapid industrialization is taking place, such as Greece, Spain, and Portugal.

Interpreting demographics requires some experience and knowledge. For instance, which female age categories should be included in an estimate of market potential for a new contraceptive? The answer will vary from the very early teens in the developing countries to older age groups in developed countries where women mature later.

When using international information sources, the international marketer must recognize that data definitions might vary among different secondary sources. The concept of urbanization, for example, has different meanings depending on where one operates. In the United States, an urban area is defined as a place of 2,500 or more inhabitants; in Sweden, it is a built-up area with at least 200 inhabitants with no more than 200 meters between houses; in Mauritius, it is a town with proclaimed legal limits.

Income and Income Distributions

Beyond basic staple items, for which population figures provide a demand correlate, income is the most predictive market potential variable for most consumer and industrial products and services. The marketer using information such as gross domestic product data needs additional knowledge about income distribution. The wide use of GDP figures can be explained by their easy availability, but they should be used with caution. In industrialized countries, the richest 10 percent of the population consume 20 percent of all goods and services, whereas the respective figure for the developing countries may be as high as 50 percent.[3] In some markets, income distribution produces wide gaps between population groups. Major urban centers in developing countries may have income levels comparable to those in more developed markets, while rural areas may not have incomes needed to buy imported goods. The more developed the economy, the more income distribution tends to converge toward the middle class.

The following classification[4] is a good planning guide:

1. **Very low family incomes.** Subsistence economies tend to be characterized by rural populations in which consumption relies on personal output or barter. Some urban centers may provide markets. Example: Cameroon.
2. **Very low, very high family incomes.** Some countries exhibit

strongly bimodal income distributions. The majority of the population may live barely above the subsistence level, but there is a strong market in urban centers and a growing middle class. The affluent are truly affluent and will consume accordingly. Examples: India, Mexico.

3. **Low, medium, high family incomes.** Industrialization produces an emerging middle class with increasing disposable income. The very low and very high income classes tend to remain for traditional reasons of social class barriers. Example: Portugal.

4. **Mostly medium family incomes.** The advanced industrial nations tend to develop institutions and policies that reduce extremes in income distribution, resulting in a large and comfortable middle class able to purchase a wide array of both domestic and imported products and services. Example: Denmark.

Although national income figures provide a general indication of a market's potential, they suffer from various distortions. Data from secondary sources are often in U.S. dollars. The per capita income figures may not be a true reflection of purchasing power if the currencies involved are distorted in some way. Researchers sometimes use *purchasing power parities* (PPP) instead of exchange rates to overcome that problem. PPPs show how many units of currency are needed in one country to buy the amount of goods and services that one unit of currency will buy in another country.

Also, using a monetary measure may not be a proper and all-inclusive measure of income. For example, in developing economies where most consumption is either self-produced or bartered, relying on financial data alone seriously understates the standard of living. Several types of services commonly included in industrialized countries' national income figures (for example, protective services and travel) do not exist for markets at lower levels of development.

Although income data are useful in the initial screening of markets, they might not play a major role for predicting demand for some products, most notably products whose value is to some degree intangible. For example, Chinese consumers demand motorcycles and television sets despite the high prices of those goods in relation to wages because of their high prestige value. And, in general, foreign origin can increase the appeal of certain products, such as perfume or automobiles.

Also, while the lack of income in a market may preclude marketing a standardized product, the market might respond to an appropriately adjusted product. A packaged goods company, confronted with considerable disparity in income levels within the same country, adapted a deodorant product to fit two separate target income groups—the regular product version in an aerosol can and the less expensive one in a plastic squeeze bottle. By substituting cheaper parts and materials, successful international marketers can make both consumer and industrial products more affordable in less affluent markets and therefore reach a wider target audience.

Consumption Patterns

The availability of useful consumption data for a market often depends on the sophistication of its data collection systems. The share of income spent on necessities, for example, indicates the market's development level and implies how much money consumers have left for other purchases. The well-known "Engel's Curve" provides some generalization about consumers' spending patterns that are useful when precise data are not available. Ernst Engel, a nineteenth-century German statistician, stated that as a family's income increases, the percentage of income spent on food will decrease, the percentage spent on housing and household operations will be roughly constant, and the amount saved or spent on other purchases will increase.

Data on product saturation or diffusion—the percentage of households in a market that own a particular product—provide more market potential detail. Sources such as the data series *International Marketing Data and Statistics* and *European Marketing Data and Statistics* published by Euromonitor, and *The Statistical Abstract of the United States* by the U.S. Government Printing Office provide consumption information.

Product diffusion can indicate other conditions of interest to marketers. A large number of telephones and their uniform distribution throughout a population or target group suggest that marketing research surveys by telephone could be productive, barring cultural or other obstacles.

But marketers should use consumption information with discretion. The data might, for example, conceal critical differences in product forms, such as the generally smaller size of European household appliances compared to their U.S. counterparts. Low rates of diffusion should be approached cautiously because they might indicate a lack of marketing opportunity—due to low incomes levels, use of a substitute product, or lack of acceptance—rather than pent-up demand. For example, the timesaving feature of microwave ovens may not be as attractive in more tradition-bound societies as it is in the United States or the European Union. And even if a product's saturation levels in a market are high, robust demand for replacement, complementary, or ancillary products may well exist.

International economic conditions complicate consumption information and a marketer's response. Varying currency inflation rates might require changing a product (make it more economical without compromising quality), adjusting its promotion (add more rational appeals), and its distribution (build more customer involvement). And local government price controls might make it impossible to sell a product for an acceptable profit. Debt is another persistent international marketing problem: Many developing countries shoulder huge debts measured in trillions of dollars. Debt crises crush nations' buying power and force imports down and exports up to meet interest payments.

Nonetheless, savvy marketers wisely look at developing countries 10 to 15 years ahead. They might invest in market access by helping political leaders provide jobs and boost exports. For example, Hewlett-Packard launched an initiative called World e-Inclusion, which, through a range of global and local partners, will sell, lease, and donate a billion dollars' worth of satellite-powered computer products and services to the underdeveloped markets of Africa, Asia, Eastern Europe, and Latin America.[5] H. J. Heinz operates in many developing countries through joint ventures in which it holds 51 percent. To sell copiers and printers in Brazil, Xerox exports Brazilian steel to Europe and Brazilian venetian blinds to the United States.

Infrastructure

The availability and quality of a nation's infrastructure is critically important in evaluating marketing potential. As an international marketer you will rely heavily on services provided by the local market for transportation, communication, and energy as well as on those that facilitate marketing functions, such as marketing communications, distribution, information, and finance. Indicators such as steel consumption, cement production, and electricity production correlate to the overall industrialization of the market and the availability of suppliers you will need for support.

Transportation networks by land, rail, waterway, or air are essential for physical distribution. Expanded transportation infrastructure, for example, has contributed significantly to increased agricultural output in Asia and Latin America. One useful way to begin investigating transportation capabilities is to analyze rail traffic by freight tons per kilometer. The number of passenger cars as well as buses and trucks can be used to analyze the state of road transportation and transportation networks.

However, such figures may not always indicate the true state of the system. China's railway system carries five times as much freight as

India's, which is an amazing feat considering that only 20 percent of China's network is double-tracked and that it is shared by an ever-growing amount of passenger traffic. Thus, despite the higher use figures of China's railway system, if you were marketing in China, you probably would have to rely on other methods of distribution to expand beyond the major urban population centers of Guangzhou, Shanghai, and Beijing.

Communication is as important as transportation. Data such as the number of telephones, computers, broadcast media, and print media in use indicate how well a firm can communicate outside and within the market. But official figures might not reveal the quality of those services. For example, the telephone system in Egypt, especially in Cairo, is notorious for its frequent breakdowns and lack of capacity. Nor will today's data by themselves indicate whether a nation is investing properly in advanced communication technologies such as the Internet and wireless phone and data transmission.

Marketers must look for clues to the future. While 2 billion people in Asia are without electricity and only 16 in 1,000 have access to a telephone, the Asian market is the one most keenly watched by the telecommunications industry. China overtook the United States in pager use by late 1997, for instance, mainly because of the low cost of the needed infrastructure to support paging. The booming middle class in cities such as Bangkok will ensure that cellular phone sales continue at a record pace. With increasing affluence comes an increasing need for energy.

Data on the availability of commercial (marketing-related) infrastructure often are not readily available. Information on which to base an assessment may be provided by government sources, such as Overseas Business Reports; by trade associations, such as the Business Equipment Manufacturers' Association; and by trade publications, such as *Advertising Age*. The more extensive the firm's international involvement, the more it can rely on its existing support network of banks, advertising agencies, and distributors to evaluate new markets.

Quality of Life

Because of the close relationship between economic and social development, many economic data are social indicators as well. Consider the following factors and their significance: share of urban population, life expectancy, number of physicians per capita, literacy rate, percentage of income received by the richest 5 percent of the population, and percentage of the population with access to electricity. Other variables are cultural indicators: number of public libraries, registered borrowings, book titles published, and number of daily newspapers, for example. The Physical Quality of Life Index (PQLI) is a composite measure of the level of welfare in a country.[6] Its three components—life expectancy, infant mortality, and adult literacy rates—make the PQLI one of the few comparative social indicators covering all of the countries of the world.

Differences in the degree of urbanization in lesser-developed countries influence international marketers' product strategies. If products are sold only to urban areas, manufactured products usually need minimal adjustments, mainly to qualify them for market entry. However, when targeting national markets, firms may need to make extensive adaptations to match more closely the reduced expectations and narrowed consumption experiences of the rural population.

When infrastructure improves in rural areas, nonfarm enterprises such as shops, repair services, and grain mills appear and expand, and customs, attitudes, and values change. A World Bank study on the impact of rural roads of the Yucatán in Mexico found that roads increased women's access to new ideas, education, medical care, and economic alternatives to maize cultivation, changing their roles in society. In particular, women married later, had fewer children, and pursued more nondomestic activities. Radio and television have had similar effects on rural cultures when introduced, offering new opportunities to the international marketer.

The presence of multinational corporations, which by their very nature are change agents, will accelerate social change. If government control is weak, the multinational corporation bears the social responsibility for its actions. In some cases, governments add the environment to multinational marketers' responsibilities, restricting the freedom of multinational corporations to affect the environment. However, some trade agreements such NAFTA—the North American Free Trade Agreement—allow companies to sue governments in special tribunals over environmental regulations.

Local Acceptance of Investment

If you are interested in entering a particular foreign market, it is important to know how such entry, particularly direct investment, will be received. Analyze the degree of foreign direct investment by country and by industry in a given market, and examine the rules governing such investment. Restrictions might exist mainly by industry type or by origin of the investor. Many nations have established investment-screening agencies to assess foreign direct investment proposals. For example, in the United States, major foreign direct investments must be reviewed by the Committee for Foreign Investments in the United States (CFIUS).

Foreign direct investment tends to be driven by efficiency and the need to participate directly in international markets that cannot adequately be reached through exports and imports. Other important drivers are falling regulatory barriers, smaller costs in telecommunications and transportation, and freer domestic and international capital markets for acquisitions.[7] Companies from a growing number of countries are participating in foreign direct investment activities.. In the 1970s, half of all multinational corporations were U.S. or British; today, just less than half are from the United States, Japan, Germany, and Switzerland (with Britain coming in seventh).

The estimated total world stock of direct investment abroad reached $4.7 trillion in 2000.[8] The favored investment regions are: for U.S. companies, Europe and Canada; for Japanese companies, North America and Asia; and for German companies, Europe and North America. By 2000, the total number of multinational corporations—firms that own or control production or service facilities outside the country in which they are based—exceeded 59,900 with 508,000 affiliates around the world.[9] The largest 600 multinationals are estimated to generate between one-fifth and one-fourth of the value added in global production of goods and services.

MARKETING TO EMERGING TRADING BLOCS

Economic integration has been one of the main economic developments affecting world markets since World War II. Countries have wanted to engage in economic cooperation to use their respective resources more effectively and to provide larger markets for member-country producers. Some integration efforts have had quite ambitious goals, such as political integration; some have failed because of perceived inequities or political disagreements.

Regional Integration

Overall, regional groupings based on economics became increasingly important in the 1990s. Thirty-two such groupings are estimated to be in existence: 3 in Europe, 4 in the Middle East, 5 in Asia, and 10 each in Africa and the Americas. Trade within the three major blocs—the American, European, and Asian—has grown rapidly, while trading among these blocs or with outsiders is either declining or growing far more moderately.

The *free trade area* is the least restrictive and loosest form of economic integration among nations. In a free trade area, member countries remove all trade barriers to other members, but each member maintains its own trade barriers with respect to nonmembers. NAFTA is a prime example. The world's largest free market with 390 million consumers and a total output of $8.6 trillion at its formation,[10] NAFTA gives U.S. firms access to a huge pool of relatively low-cost Mexican labor at a time when demographic trends are resulting in labor shortages in many parts of the United States. At the same time, U.S. firms create many new jobs in Mexico, companies in both countries have access to millions of additional consumers, and liberalized trade promotes more economic growth in both countries. (See the latest NAFTA trade statistics at www. census.gov/foreign-trade/).

Overall, the corporate view toward NAFTA has been overwhelmingly positive, but critics of the pact complain about labor and environmental issues. Although NAFTA includes the formation of the North American Agreement on Labor Cooperation (NAALC) and the Commission on Environmental Compliance, those entities have had little impact, mainly because they have almost no enforcement power.[11] The good news for labor is that free trade creates higher-skilled and better-paying jobs—10 to 15 percent more—in the United States.

Other alliances in the Americas have been designed to help mostly small, developing countries open wider markets for the goods their fledgling industries produce to displace imports. Central America had its structure (the Central American Common Market, CACM), the Caribbean nations had theirs (CARICOM), and South America had its own different forms. Under more recent banners—the four-nation Mercosur and five-nation Andean Common Market (ANCOM)—Latin American nations are realizing that if they do not unite, they will become increasingly marginal in the global market. The ultimate goal is a free trade zone from Point Barrow, Alaska, to Patagonia under a framework called the Free Trade Area of the Americas (FTAA), slated for negotiations and an agreement by 2005.

The *customs union* is one step further toward economic integration. As in the free trade area, members of the customs union dismantle barriers to trade in goods and services among members. In addition, the customs union establishes a common trade policy with respect to nonmembers. Typically, this takes the form of a common external tariff, whereby imports from nonmembers pay the same tariff when sold to any member country.

The latest customs union formation occurred in Asia, driven by market forces as Asian nations seek to counterbalance European and

Western Hemisphere trading blocs. Future integration will most likely grow out of the most established arrangement in the region, the Association of Southeast Asian Nations (ASEAN), whose members formed a customs union called Asean Free Trade Area (AFTA). The Malaysians have pushed for the formation of the East Asia Economic Group (EAEG), which would add Hong Kong, Japan, South Korea, and Taiwan to the membership list—rapidly industrializing countries that should not be ignored. The big player in the region, Japan, has been cool toward all types of regionalization efforts, however, mainly because it has the most to gain from country-by-country free trade. But should the other trading blocs turn against Japan, its only resort may be to seek more formal trade arrangement in the region.

The *common market* amounts to a customs union covering the exchange of goods and services, the prohibition of duties in exports and imports between members, and the adoption of a common external tariff in respect to nonmembers. In addition, factors of production (labor, capital, and technology) are mobile among members. A common market abolishes restrictions on immigration and cross-border investment, enabling capital, labor, and technology to be employed in their most productive uses.

Despite the obvious benefits, members of a common market must be prepared to cooperate closely in monetary, fiscal, and employment policies. Although a common market will enhance the productivity of members in the aggregate, it is by no means clear that individual member countries will always benefit. Because of these difficulties, the goals of common markets have proved to be elusive in many areas of the world, notably Central and South America, and Asia.

The *economic union* requires integration of economic policies in addition to the free movement of goods, services, and factors of production across borders. Under an economic union, members harmonize monetary policies, taxation, and government spending. They either use a common currency—such as the euro in the European Community—or fix currency exchange rates among members. Joining an economic union requires surrendering a large measure of national sovereignty to supranational authorities in community-wide institutions such as the European Parliament. The final step would be a political union calling for political unification.

Producers within economic unions enjoy economies of scale as production facilities consolidate and competition grows among suppliers. Companies no longer face currency risks on intraunion trade, and they benefit from the elimination of transaction costs such as border patrols and customs procedures. Insiders can freely expand beyond their country borders. A borderless Europe opens access to about 380 million consumers, for example.

Additional regional integration efforts beyond those already mentioned include the Asia Pacific Economic Cooperation (APEC) forum proposed by Australia to maintain a balance in negotiations among ASEAN members plus Australia, New Zealand, Japan, South Korea, Canada, Chile, Mexico, and the United States. Originally, the model for APEC was not the European Union, with its Brussels bureaucracy, but the Organization for Economic Cooperation and Development (OECD), the Paris-based center for international research and high-level discussion. However, APEC has now established an ultimate goal of achieving free trade in the area among its twenty-one members by 2010.[12]

In South Asia, seven nations (India, Pakistan, Bangladesh, Sri Lanka, Nepal, Bhutan, and the Maldives) launched the South Asian Association for Regional Cooperation (SAARC) in 1985. Cooperation has been limited to relatively noncontroversial areas, such as agriculture and regional development.

Africa's economic groupings range from currency unions among European nations and their former colonies to customs unions between neighboring states. Many of those blocs have not been successful due to small memberships and insufficient ability to produce goods to trade among members. Sixteen West African nations attempted in 1975 to create a megamarket large enough to interest investors and reduce hardship, but many of the objectives of their Economic Community of West African States (ECOWAS) have not been realized.

Countries in the Arab world have made some progress in economic integration. The Gulf Cooperation Council (GCC) is one of the most economically powerful of any trade groups. Its six member states (Bahrain, Kuwait, Oman, Qatar, Saudi Arabia, and the United Arab Emirates) formed the GCC in 1980 mainly as a defensive measure due to the perceived threat from the Iran-Iraq war. Its aim is to achieve free trade arrangements with the European nations.

New regional integration plans are constantly being developed. In 1995 a new bloc was proposed between NAFTA and EU members. Called TAFTA (the Transatlantic Free Trade Area), this has not yet materialized. Since 1991, twelve former republics of the Soviet Union have tried to forge common economic policies, but to date only Belarus, Kazakhstan, Kyrgyzstan, Russia, and Tajikistan are signatories in the Customs Union.

Integration and the Global Marketer

Regional economic integration creates opportunities and potential problems for the international marketer. Integration might influence the market entry strategy by favoring direct investment to make the company a business citizen within the region. Larger markets do create favorable conditions for local production, more intraregional trade, and greater product standardization through regional standards harmonization. However, if you are going to market internationally, you must make integration assessments and decisions from four points of view.[13]

1. Envision the outcome of the change. Change in the competitive landscape can be dramatic if scale opportunities can be exploited in relatively homogeneous demand conditions. This could be the case, for example, for industrial goods, consumer durables such as cameras and watches, and professional services.
2. Consider the varying degrees of change readiness within the markets themselves. Governments and other stakeholders such as labor unions may oppose the liberalization of competition in all industries. For example, while plans have called for liberalization of air travel and automobile marketing in Europe, European Union members have found loopholes to protect their own companies.
3. Develop a strategic response to the new environment that will maintain a sustainable, long-term competitive advantage. Those companies already present in an integrated market should fill in gaps in European product and market portfolios through acquisitions or alliances to create a balanced pan-regional company. Those with a weak presence, or none at all, may have to create alliances with established firms.[14]
4. One additional option is to leave the market altogether if it cannot remain competitive because of new competitive conditions or the level of investment needed.

Of course, different companies have different strengths, market positions, and corporate goals when confronting regional trading blocs. John F. Magee's four scenarios suggest proposed courses of action:[15]

*   *Established multinational marketers,* such as H.J. Heinz and Colgate-Palmolive, will be able to take advantage of the new economies of scale, but they also face more intense competition. Many multinationals have developed pan-European strategies to exploit the European Union situation, for example. They are standardizing their

products and processes to the greatest extent possible without compromising local input and implementation.

- *Single-market firms* those with a foothold in only one union market, face the danger of competitors who can use the strength of multiple markets. Furthermore, eliminating trade barriers may impair their competitive advantages. For example, more than half of the 45 major European food companies have operated in just one or two of the individual European markets and seriously lag behind broader-based U.S. and Swiss firms. Similarly, automakers PSA and Fiat are nowhere close to the cross-manufacturing presence of Ford and GM. The smaller companies' courses of action include expansion through acquisitions, mergers, or strategic alliances, or concentrating only on business segments in which the company can be a leader across the integrated region.
- *Exporters* will need to worry about maintaining their competitive position and continued access to the market. Companies with a physical presence in the union may be in a better position, suggesting that direct investment in bloc countries can be good strategy.
- *Uninterested firms* do not see a reason either to approach the trading bloc at all or to change their approach from exporting to more involved modes of entry. They may fear barriers to outsiders, such as local content regulations or obstacles raised against foreign agricultural products.

The international marketer's response to these situations might require reorganizing global capabilities, such as centralizing authority to better execute regional programs. In staffing, management will have to focus on individuals who understand the subtleties of consumer behavior across markets and are therefore able to evaluate the similarities and differences between cultures and markets. In developing systems for the planning and implementation of regional programs, companies may even move corporate or divisional headquarters from the domestic market to be closer to the customer.

Lobbying Policymakers

Economic integration will create its own powers and procedures similar to those of the European Commission and its directives. Because policymakers often rely on the private sector to carry out their own work, influencing change will include providing industry information, such as test results, to policymakers. Many marketers consider lobbying a public relations activity and therefore go beyond the traditional approaches, as General Motors exemplified in Asia. (See Exhibit 2.2)

Lobbying will usually have to take place at multiple levels simultaneously; within the European Union, this means the European Commission in Brussels, the European Parliament in Strasbourg, or the national governments within the European Union. Marketers with substantial resources have established their own lobbying offices in Brussels, while smaller companies get their voices heard through joint offices or their industry associations. In terms of lobbying, U.S. firms have an advantage because of their experience in their home market. But for many European firms, lobbying is a new, yet necessary, skill to be acquired. At the same time, marketers operating in two or more major markets (such as the European Union and North America) can work to produce more efficient trade through, for example, mutual recognition agreements (MRAs) on standards.

FUTURITIES

The effects of closer global linkages will be dramatic in the future. Policymakers increasingly realize that it is very difficult to segregate domestic and international market events. Decisions that once were clearly in the domestic purview—such as interest rates and agricultural policies—are more vulnerable to revision by influences from abroad. Global market forces often counteract policies. For example, trade flows used to determine currency flows and therefore exchange rates. But now, the reverse is often true. Private sector financial flows vastly outweigh the financial flows governments can control, even when they act together. Similarly, continuous technological change and communications advances enable companies to quickly counteract carefully designed government plans.

Policymakers therefore will face increasing responsibilities with fewer and less effective tools to carry out them out. Governments have sought to restrict the impact of global trade and financial flows by erecting barriers, charging tariffs, designing quotas, and implementing other import regulations. However, these measures face growing restrictions by international agreements, particularly the World Trade Organization (WTO).

Governments, with the help of private enterprise, will have to undertake new social marketing tasks. These will range from promoting and providing incentives for larger families in Scandinavia, for example, to increased family planning efforts in Thailand. Nevertheless, current trends will accelerate the division of world markets into the "haves" and the "have-nots." Companies that want to sell in developing countries must adjust to the realities of reduced individual

Exhibit 2.2: Supporting Free Trade in Asia

General Motors—and all the major car makers—is driving into Asia. The world's largest industrial company has found challenges considerable despite the substantial market potential of a growing middle class. In addition to distribution challenges from aggressive competitors, the most daunting ones are free trade barriers. For example, in Indonesia, GM faces competition from a local model, the Timor, which costs substantially less due to government supports (that is, lower duties on imported components). Before President Suharto's resignation, the company was run by one of his sons.

To overcome distribution difficulties, GM invested $450 million in the mid-1990's in the Rayong Province manufacturing facility to build the specially designed Opel "Car for Asia" starting early this century. The Thai facility is the culmination of GM's buildup in Asia that started in 1990 with the establishment of a regional office in Hong Kong and representative offices in Bangkok, Jakarta, Kuala Lumpur, and Beijing. GM's Asia headquarters was moved from Detroit to Singapore. It established GM China in 1994 as a separate entity, and in Japan it bought a 37.5 percent equity stake in Isuzu and has been steadily increasing ownership in Suzuki to 20 percent by 2001. Due to the Asian economic crisis, GM scaled down the investment in Thailand and switched production from the Astra to a considerably cheaper model. GM has also recently shifted its strategy to the Suzuki YGM-I as its small car for Asia.

To combat protectionism and further the cause of free trade, GM has developed a three-pronged strategy. The first approach focuses on executives working with government representatives from the United States, European Union, and Japan to dismantle what GM regards as the largest flaws. The company uses its clout as a major investor, but it can also call on support from industries that follow it into a new market, such as component manufacturers. On the second level, GM works within existing frameworks to balance the effects of nationalistic policies. In countries such as Indonesia and Malaysia, it develops company-specific plans to preserve avenues of sales even under challenging circumstances. Finally, GM is also pursuing its business strategy in Asia's free-trade areas. Since it will be a long time before barriers are taken down in the Asia Pacific Economic Cooperation Forum (APEC), its immediate focus is on the ASEAN Free Trade Area (AFTA). GM is hopeful that the automotive sector will be a beneficiary of tariff reductions—provided that member governments can be persuaded that such cuts are in their best interests.

SOURCES: "U.S. Automakers Demonstrate Commitment to Thailand," U.S.-ASEAN Business Council press release, May 12, 1999, available at http://www.us-asean.org; "GM Delays Plans to Open Big Thai Plant," *The Wall Street Journal,* January 6, 1998, A2; and "GM Presses for Free Trade in Asia," *Crossborder Monitor,* January 15, 1997, 1, 9; "GM Lifts Stake in Suzuki," *Waikato Times,* September 22, 2000; "Global Manufacturing: GM Gets Flexible in Thailand, *Wards Auto World,* September 1, 2000, Katherine Zachary.

purchasing power and increased government participation in the markets for basic products.

Concurrently, demands for political solutions to other economic and financial problems are likely to increase. Some countries may consider migration as a key solution to population growth problems— a policy welcomed by firms, but only for skilled labor. Countries will also count on debt forgiveness on a broad scale and close collaboration with international financial institutions.

Emerging Markets

The emerging markets of Latin America and the Asia-Pacific region will fuel much of the global economy's future growth. In Latin America, the international business climate will improve due to economic integration, market liberalization, and privatization. Despite some inefficiencies, Mercosur continues to bring countries closer together and encourages their collaboration. Due to substantial natural resources and relatively low cost of production, an increased flow of foreign direct investment and trade activity from the United States, Europe, and Japan, is likely. Despite recession-induced economic crises such as appeared in Argentina, Brazil, and Uruguay in 2001–2, developed nations' recognition of the importance of short-term aid—evidenced by U.S. loan guarantees issued in mid-2002— auger well for eventual stability and growth. Still, Latin American economic institutions will have to learn how to manage through downturns as well as the boom times of the late 1990s.

The Asia-Pacific region will again become a hot spot for international marketers in the next decade. The area is predicted to grow into a massive economic, political, and technological power, with simultaneously increasing consumer demand. For the industrialized nations, this development will offer a significant opportunity for exports and investment, but it will also diminish, in the longer term, their superior status and influence in the world economy.

China's growth is likely to be the economic event of the early decades of the new millennium. Experts see Chinese pragmatism prevailing, and companies willing to make significant investments are likely to be the main beneficiaries of growth. Long-term commitment, willingness to transfer technology, and an ability to partner either with local firms through joint ventures or with overseas Chinese-run firms are crucial for success.

Among the other promising emerging markets are Korea and India. Korean firms must still improve their ability to adopt a global mindset. Also the possibility of reunification of North and South Korea raises many questions for the long term. India is considered more important for the size of its potential market, its significant natural wealth, and its large, highly educated middle class. While many experts believe that political conflict, nationalism, and class structure may temper the ability of Indian companies to emerge as a worldwide competitive force, the country's disproportionately large and specialized workforce in engineering and computer sciences make it a power to be reckoned with.

Africa's developing countries remain a relatively cool region for international marketing purposes. Continuing political instability and the resulting inability of many African firms to be consistent trading partners are the key reasons for such a pessimistic view. Concerns also exist about infrastructural inadequacies, both physical—such as transportation—and societal—such as legal systems.

In Eastern Europe, economic recovery and participation in world trade by Russia and the other nations of the former Soviet Union and the Warsaw Pact have been gradual. Slowness has been in part a function of self-imposed constraints caused by domestic fears of outsiders. For political reasons, financial inflows into the region will continue in the near future, yet if these investments are to make a difference, governments need to find market-oriented ways to reduce the flight of capital abroad. These nations will need to develop new trading and financing techniques in order to make business propositions viable and must ensure respect for property rights, contractual arrangements, and protection for investors from public and private corruption.

Many of the newly emerging democracies wrestle with major infrastructure shortages. Transportation systems, warehousing facilities, refrigeration facilities, housing stock, and communication systems are taking years to improve. Even though major efforts to improve are underway, infrastructure shortcomings will inhibit economic growth for years to come.

But change has occurred not just in these newly emerging democracies. The established market economies of the West must welcome the former socialist countries as partners in global trade. Providing open markets is much more valuable than the occasional transfer of aid funds. Meanwhile, changes in the nature of military threats confronting the world's industrialized democracies affect military budgets, military production, and defense sector jobs.

Last but not least in shaping the future economic landscape for international marketers, technology is likely to keep advancing at ever-faster rates, upsetting established relationships, rewarding the right investments, and penalizing nations and companies choosing the wrong bets or making none at all. The communications arena promises great changes in the way marketers work and their customers buy.

The diffusion of Internet technology into core business processes and the lifestyles of consumers has been rapid, especially in industrialized countries. The number of Internet hosts (computers through which users connect to the Internet) increased to 162.1 million by 2003, up from 72.3 million in 2000 and 43.2 million in 1999.[16] Given expected changes in the first years of the new century, current estimates of explosive growth may turn out to be too low.

NOTES

1. Thomas M. McDevitt, *World Population Profile: 1998* (Washington, D.C.: Government Printing Office, 1999), 1–2. See also http://www.census.gov.
2. *European Marketing Data and Statistics 1999* (London: Euromonitor, 1999), 395.
3. The World Bank, *World Development Indicators* (Washington, D.C., 2000), 85.
4. Philip Kotler, *Marketing Management* (Englewood Cliffs, NJ: Prentice-Hall, 1991), 405.
5. "B2-4B Spells Profits," *Marketing News,* November 5, 2001, 1, 11–12.
6. Ben Crow and Alan Thomas, *Third World Atlas* (Milton Keynes, England: Open University Press, 1984), 85.
7. "A Survey of Multinationals," *Economist,* March 27, 1993.
8. United Nations, *World Investment Report* (New York: United Nations, 2001), Promoting Linkages, preface.
9. United Nations, *World Investment Report* (New York: United Nations, 1999), xvii.
10. Raymond Ahearn, *Trade and the Americas* (Washington, D.C.: Congressional Research Service, 1997), 3–4.
11. "NAFTA's Do-Gooder Side Deals Disappoint," *The Wall Street Journal,* October 15, 1997, A19.
12. "Asia Free Trade Lags," *Export Today* (October 1999): 12.
13. Eric Friberg, Risto Perttunen, Christian Caspar, and Dan Pittard, "The Challenges of Europe 1992," *The McKinsey Quarterly* 21 (Number 2, 1988): 3–15.
14. John A. Quelch, Robert D. Buzzell, and Eric R. Salama, *The Marketing Challenge of 1992* (Reading, MA: Addison-Wesley, 1990), Chapter 13.
15. John F. Magee, "1992: Moves Americans Must Make," *Harvard Business Review* 67 (May–June 1989): 72–84.

3

Trade's Financial Mechanisms

Managing global marketing's financial environments and risks.

In the competitive international environment, a company cannot always expect to sell in its own currency and receive cash in advance. Most companies will have to expose themselves to new types of financial risk, recognizing that if they do not finance customers' international trade, their competitors or the competitors' governments probably will. Finance is a critical marketing tool.

CREDIT FINANCING

You cannot control the international financial environment. You need to analyze it carefully and understand your company's ability to operate within its demands. To state the issue positively, effective financial arrangements can significantly support your marketing program if your company's marketing department and finance operations work together.

Credit Policies

Offering favorable credit terms to buyers often wins sales. With large numbers of competent firms active in international markets, financing packages—often put together with the help of governments—have become more common. This is especially true in fields such as engineering and construction where superior technical capability and attractive cost may not be enough to secure a contract. Like buyers anywhere, customers abroad may be prepared to accept higher prices if they can obtain attractive credit terms.

To get the best assistance, most companies need to access either regional banks, with which exporters maintain day-to-day relationships, or money-center banks, which typically are larger and provide more sophisticated and broader services than regional banks can give. The larger banks provide a full range of finance, insurance, and advisory services available to all exporters through the correspondent relationships that regional banks have with the large banks. Many large companies have direct relationships with money-center banks.

Finance as a Marketing Tool. The seller's primary concern is to be paid for the goods shipped. Before receiving any orders the company should already have a policy on the acceptable degree of risk and preferable terms of international transactions. A good credit policy should:

- Help the exporting company determine the extent of risk it is willing to absorb.
- Allow the company to explore new ways of financing exports.
- Prepare the company for a changing environment.

In some cases, the marketing and financial departments of the firm will be at odds. Marketing may want to expand sales and move into new markets, whereas finance may want to minimize risk and, as a result, market selectively. These issues need to be addressed and resolved before, not after, the fact.

Developing a credit policy requires teamwork between the company's marketing and finance departments and its commercial banks. For their part, marketing executives should understand financing options and credit managers' concerns well enough to convincingly communicate the need for credit financing directly to banks. Marketers can, for example, hold regular roundtable discussions with bankers and set up trips abroad by teams of marketers and finance people working together to understand sales and financing packages from start to finish.

Types of Risk. Overseas political and commercial developments can destroy overnight even the most careful credit judgments and marketing programs. In addition to macro-developments causing non-payment, the buyer might go out of business before paying the seller. The major types of financial risk are commercial risk, political risk, foreign exchange risk, and other risks such as those related to inflation.

Commercial risk refers primarily to the insolvency of, or protracted payment default by an overseas buyer. Commercial defaults, in turn, usually result from deteriorated conditions in the buyer's market, fluctuations in demand, unanticipated competition either domestically or internationally, or technological change. The list of reasons for buyer default is virtually limitless but include loss of key personnel or key customers, sudden expenses, natural disasters, or slow payment from downstream creditors, such as a government. All these risks can emerge in the domestic environment as well, but the geographic and psychological distances to international markets make the risks more severe and more difficult to anticipate.

Noncommercial, or political, risk is beyond the direct control of either the buyer or the seller. As discussed in Chapter 5, the foreign buyer may be willing to pay, but the government may try to delay payment as far into the future as possible.

Foreign exchange risk derives from fluctuating exchange rates. The currency of quotation depends largely on the bargaining positions of the buyer and the seller as well as on accepted business practices in the industry. However, if the price quotation is not in the seller's currency, the seller firm must be prepared to protect itself against possible losses resulting from unfavorable changes in the value of the currency transaction.

Financing Sources

Except in the case of larger companies that may have their own financing sources, most international marketers help their customers abroad secure appropriate financing. Export financing terms can significantly affect the final price paid by buyers. In some cases, buyers will award a contract to the provider of cheaper credit and overlook differences in quality and price.

Financing assistance is available from both the private and the public sectors. The international marketer should assess not only domestic programs but also those in the buyers' countries. For example, Japan and Taiwan have import financing programs that provide exporters added potential in penetrating their significant markets.

Commercial Banks. Commercial banks the world over provide trade financing, depending on their relationship with the exporter, the nature of the transaction, the country of the borrower, and the availability of export insurance. Frequently, banks provide financing assistance only to first-rate credit risks, leading many U.S. exporters to complain about overly stringent credit criteria. Furthermore, some U.S. banks do not see international trade finance as part of their core competence. Although the situation has improved, exporters still complain about lack of export financing pertaining to developing countries, high technology sales, or lending against foreign receivables. Many exporters complain that banks will not deal with them without a guarantee from the Ex-Im Bank or rock-solid collateral, such as property and/or equipment.

However, as the value of international sales and reach of companies increases, banking relationships become all the more important, a fact also noted by banks themselves. Many banks offer enhanced services, such as electronic services, which help exporters monitor and expedite their international transactions to customers who do a certain amount of business with them. As with all suppliers, the more business done with a bank, the higher the level of service, usually at a better price. As the relationship builds, the bankers feel more comfortable about the exporter's business and the more likely they will go out of their way to help, particularly with difficult transactions.

In addition to using the types of services a bank can provide as a criterion of choice, an exporter should assess the bank's overseas reach. This is a combination of the bank's own network of facilities and correspondent relationships. While money-center banks can provide the greatest amount of coverage through their own offices and staff, they still use correspondents in regions outside the main banking or political centers of foreign markets. For example, Citibank has a worldwide correspondent network of 5,000 institutions in addition to its facilities in more than 100 countries.

Some banks have formed alliances to extend their reach to markets that their customers are penetrating. Wachovia, a super-regional bank from North Carolina, has developed relationships with global banks that have strong correspondent networks in place in emerging markets. Regional banks, such as Bank One, which have no intention of establishing branches abroad, rely only on strong alliances with foreign banks. Foreign banks can provide a competitive advantage to exporters because of their home country connections and their strong global networks.

Regardless of the arrangement, the bank's own branches or correspondents play an important role at all stages of the international transaction, from gathering market intelligence about potential new customers to actually processing payments. Additional services include reference checks on customers in their home markets and suggestions for possible candidates to serve as intermediaries.

Forfaiting. A trade financing technique that was developed in Europe has only become widely known in the United States over the past decade. *Forfaiting* was first used by European commercial banks in financing trade to Eastern European countries and has since spread to banks throughout the world. Forfaiting provides the exporter with cash at the time of the shipment. In a typical forfait deal, the importer pays the exporter with bills of exchange or promissory notes guaranteed by a bank in the importer's country. The exporter can sell them to a third party (for example, Citicorp) at a discount from their face value for immediate cash. The sale is without recourse to the exporter, and the buyer of the notes assumes all the risks. The discount rate takes into account the buyer's creditworthiness and country, the quality of the guaranteeing bank, and the interest cost over the term of the credit.[1]

The benefits to the exporter are the reduction of risk, simplicity of documentation (because the documents used are well known in the market), and 100 percent coverage. In addition, forfaiting does not involve either content or country restrictions, which many of the official trade financing sources may have.

The major complaints about forfaiting center on availability and cost. Forfaiting is not available where exporters need it most, that is, for high-risk countries. Furthermore, it is usually a little more expensive than public sources of trade insurance.

Factoring. Certain companies, known as factoring houses, may purchase an exporter's receivables for a discounted price (2 to 4 percent less than face value). Factors do not only buy receivables but also provide the exporter with a complete financial package that combines credit protection, accounts-receivable bookkeeping, and collection services to take away many of the challenges that come with doing business overseas. Arrangements are typically with recourse, leaving the exporter ultimately liable for repaying the factor in case of default. Some factors accept export receivables without recourse but require a large discount.

The industry is dominated by a dozen major players, most of which are subsidiaries of major banks. Leaders include the CIT Group and Bank of America Commercial Finance/Factoring, which has won the President's "E" Award for its excellence in export service.[2] However, with the increase in companies looking for factoring services, independent factors are also emerging. Factors can be found through the Commercial Finance Association or through marketing facilitators whose clients use factors.

Although the forfaiting and factoring methods appear similar, they differ in four significant ways:

- Factors usually want a large percentage of the exporter's business, while most forfaiters work on a one-time basis.
- Forfaiters work with medium-term receivables (over 180 days to 5 years), while factors work with short-term receivables.
- Factors usually do not have strong capabilities in the developing countries, but because forfaiters usually require a bank guarantee, most are willing to deal with receivables from these countries.

- Forfaiters work with capital goods, factors typically with consumer goods.[3]

OFFICIAL TRADE FINANCE

Official financing can take the form of either a loan or a guarantee, including credit insurance. In a loan, the government provides funds to finance the sale and charges the buyer interest on those funds at a stated fixed rate. The government lender accepts the risk of a possible default. In a guarantee, a private-sector lender provides the funds and sets the interest rate, with the government assuring that it will reimburse the lender if the loan is not paid. The government is providing risk protection, but not funds.

Guarantees

Guarantee programs have these advantages, according to the Export-Import Bank of the United States (Ex-Im Bank):

- Protection in the riskiest part of an exporter's business (foreign sales receivables);
- Protection against political and commercial risks over which the exporter does not have control;
- Encouragement to exporters to make competitive offers by extending terms of payment;
- Broadening of potential markets by minimizing exporter risks;
- The possibility of leveraging exporter accounts receivable; and
- The opportunity for commercial banks to remain active in the international finance arena through the government guarantee.

Because credit has emerged as an increasingly important component in export selling, governments of most industrialized countries have established mechanisms to insure export credit risks. Officially supported *export credit agencies* (ECAs) are organizations whose central purpose is to promote national trade objectives by providing financial support for national exports. Some ECAs are divisions of government trade missions. Other ECAs operate as autonomous or even private institutions, but most require a degree of recourse to national government support.

International marketers should monitor the export-import credit agencies of other countries to assess the structures, terms, and rates of import financing programs available for U.S. goods and services. Among them are the Export-Import Bank of Japan, the State Export-

Import Bank of Ukraine, and the Export Development Corporation of Canada.

The international union of export credit and investment insurers, or the "Berne Union," established a voluntary international understanding on export insurance terms by recommending loan coverage periods ranging from five years for capital goods to eighteen months for consumer durable goods. The Organization for Economic Cooperation and Development (OECD) Agreement on Guidelines for Officially Supported Export Credits came into force in 1978 as a nonbinding standardization of international financing. Despite the agreement, some countries tend to circumvent it by providing mixed credits—that is, a combination of commercial export financing funds and "soft" development aid funds. U.S. firms are estimated to lose hundreds of millions of dollars in annual export sales because of such aid provided by other countries.

Ex-Im Bank

The Export-Import Bank of the United States (www.exim.gov) became an independent U.S. government agency in 1945 "to aid in financing and facilitating exports." Since its inception, Ex-Im Bank has supported more than $300 billion in U.S. export sales. In September 1992, Ex-Im Bank acquired its former insurance agent, the Foreign Credit Insurance Association (FCIA). The short-term insurance programs formerly offered by the FCIA are now offered as Ex-Im Bank insurance.

Under its charter, Ex-Im Bank must have "reasonable assurance of repayment." Therefore, it conducts a careful analysis of the foreign buyer's creditworthiness and the project's viability. If necessary, Ex-Im might require government loan guarantees from the host country of the foreign buyer, although the guarantees of a commercial bank in the host country may be sufficient.

Exhibit 3.1 lists type of export products and services, their customary financing terms, and the appropriate Ex-Im Bank programs. The applicability of a particular program depends on the details of the specific transaction. Ex-Im Bank financing, as with ECA financing overall, is most important for exporters seeking business in "emerging markets" where economic growth rates are high, where there is high demand for capital goods imports to fuel economic growth, and where capital markets have not yet fully developed to provide the necessary financing. Growth in the developing world is approximately double growth in the industrialized world, a trend that is likely to continue.

Pre-export Support. One of the greatest impediments small businesses experience in attempting to fulfill export orders is a lack of adequate working capital to build the necessary inventory. Despite their creditworthiness, these exporters sometimes find their local bank is reluctant to make the necessary financing available. In some cases, exporters have already reached the borrowing limits set by the banks, while others do not have the amount or type of collateral their banks require. In response to this need, Ex-Im Bank created a Working Capital Guarantee Program (WCG). It is the only pre-export program offered by Ex-Im Bank. All other Ex-Im Bank programs finance exports after shipment or performance.

Under WCG, Ex-Im Bank guarantees the lender against default by the exporter. The guarantee is for 90 percent of the loan and interest up to 1 percent over the U.S. Treasury borrowing rate. The lender must retain 10 percent of the risk. Should the exporter default, only the commercial bank is covered. For example, if the foreign buyer of the U.S. goods defaults, only the exporter's outstanding loan with the commercial bank is covered under the WCG. For this reason, many exporters secure additional Ex-Im Bank insurance to protect themselves against failure of the foreign buyer to pay the obligation. Coverage can be comprehensive (covering both commercial and political reasons) or political only.

The WCG may be used for single sales or as a revolving line of credit. It may also be used for marketing and promotion purposes. However, most of the WCGs approved by Ex-Im Bank are for single-sale transactions. The exporter must put up collateral equal to 110 percent of the value of the loan. Ex-Im Bank takes a broad interpretation of acceptable collateral and will accept raw materials, fixed assets in certain cases, foreign receivables, or other collateral. Frequently, the personal guarantee of the exporting company's officers is also required. The exporter may approach Ex-Im Bank directly for a WCG or apply through its bank.

Export Credit Insurance. The ability to offer financing or credit terms is often the most critical element in competing for, and winning, export sales. Increasingly, foreign buyers of goods and services expect suppliers to offer "open account" or unsecured credit terms rather than requiring letters of credit, which may be expensive, or cash in advance. In general, the more secure the payment terms are for the exporter, the less attractive the terms are for the foreign customer. Yet for a small or medium-sized exporter, extending credit terms to foreign customers may represent an unacceptable risk and may be an undue financial burden, especially when the exporter's bank is

Exhibit 3.1: Selection Chart for Ex-Im Bank

Exports	Appropriate Programs	Example
Pre-Export	Working Capital Guarantee	Pragmatic Environmental Solutions of Roanoke, Virginia, received a $100,000 loan from Suntrust Bank that enabled it to make an export sale of pollution control equipment to Wren Oil Co. of Australia.
Short Term	Export Credit Insurance	Wildflower International of Santa Fe, New Mexico, expanded its export sales of software to Mexico, Israel, and Saudi Arabia by offering 90- and 180-day open account credit terms in insuring them with Ex-Im.
Medium Term	Guarantees	Senstar Capital Group provided a 4-year, $400,000 loan to Ecopreneur, S.A. of Buenos Aires to purchase water treatment equipment from six U.S. small-business water-treatment suppliers.
Long Term	Direct Loans	49.7 million loan to sponsor Ormat Leyte Co., Ltd. to build, own, and operate four geothermal plants in the Philippines with significant inputs from U.S. suppliers.

SOURCE: Examples courtesy of Craig O'Connor, Export-Import Bank of the United States.

unwilling to accept foreign receivables as collateral for working lines of credit.

Ex-Im Bank's Export Credit Insurance Program protects the exporter against political and commercial default by its foreign customers. The insurance provides the exporter with important advantages in competing for export business. First, the exporter can use extended credit terms as an offering feature along with the product itself, its technology, and related services. Second, the insurance lets the exporter expand sales with existing customers and prudently pursue higher-risk foreign markets. Third, the insurance gives the exporter and its bank greater flexibility in handling overseas accounts receivable. Because Ex-Im Bank covers the risk of default, banks are willing to lend against or "discount" an exporter's foreign sales receivables.

Any entity—including the U.S. exporter, a U.S. or foreign bank, or the foreign buyer—may apply to Ex-Im Bank for a premium quote, at no cost, to determine the availability and cost of export credit insurance. Ex-Im Bank offers eight standard policies, which fall into two basic categories: multibuyer and single-buyer types. These policies accommodate the special needs of various types of exporters and financing institutions, either of which can be an insured party. The insurance premiums charged are based on the buyer, the length of the repayment term, the country of importation, the experience of the insured, and the volume of business.

A combination of short- and medium-term insurance is available, used mainly to protect U.S. exporters who offer floor plans to overseas dealers and distributors. This option offers protection on parts and accessories sales on terms up to 180 days and capital equipment inventory financing for up to 270 days that can be converted to a medium-term receivable of up to three years.

The coverage offered under the policies may be comprehensive (covering both commercial and political risks of default) or political only. A comprehensive policy is advisable because of the difficulty in predicting events. Also, devaluation is not covered as a political risk but, if it causes default, may be covered as a commercial risk. Ex-Im Bank does not offer commercial risk coverage alone. The policies have U.S. content requirements in order to fulfill the basic mission of supporting U.S. jobs. Products or services sold by small businesses with short-term repayment periods must have at least 50 percent U.S. content. Products or projects sold by large U.S. exporters must have at least 85 percent U.S. content. No value may be added after shipment from the United States.

In addition, Ex-Im Bank will insure political risks for goods on consignment where payment is made to the exporter only after the goods have been sold. Should an exporter consummate a sale requiring payment in foreign currency rather than U.S. dollars, Ex-Im Bank will cover such transactions under all policies; however, coverage is limited to "freely transferable" currencies, and no exchange or transfer risk is insurable under this endorsement.

Claims may be submitted immediately upon default, or there may be a waiting period of up to eight months, depending on the provisions of the policy and the cause of the default. At the time of the

---

Exhibit 3.2: Example of Ex-Im Bank Insurance

(1) Contract value	$100,000
(2) Cash payment (15%)	15,000
(3) Financial portion (85%)	85,000
(4) Exporter commercial retention (10% in line 3)	8,500
(5) Ex-Im Bank commercial risk coverage (90% of line 3)	76,500
(6) Ex-Im Bank political risks (100% of line 3)	85,000

SOURCE: Example courtesy of Louis G. Guadagnoli, former vice president, Export-Import Bank of the United States.

---

claim, the exporter must submit certain documents, such as copies of bills of lading, the debt instrument, evidence of attempts to collect, and evidence of compliance with any special conditions imposed by Ex-Im Bank. The exporter must therefore retain all documents until the claim has been paid.

Single-buyer policies allow exporters to select the sales they desire to insure. There is no first-loss deductible. It may cover single or repetitive sales to one buyer.

Multibuyer policies may cover short- or medium-term sales or a combination of both. They require that the insured pay the premium on all, or a reasonable spread, of export credit sales. This requirement exists to prevent the insured from making an adverse selection of sales to be insured and increasing Ex-Im Bank's risk. Typically, it is used by an exporter for comprehensive coverage on worldwide short-term sales. Ex-Im Bank assigns an aggregate policy limit, which is the maximum dollar amount in claims that will be paid in a policy year. However, the insured must submit credit information to Ex-Im Bank and receive approval for each buyer whose receivables are to be insured. A discretionary credit limit may be granted to experienced insiders to relieve them from obtaining preapproval for sales under a certain dollar amount, provided they maintain a credit file on the buyer. A first-loss deductible for commercial risk claims is typical. The minimum premium is usually $500 per year paid up front, and the insured pays premiums monthly, based on shipments. A typical example is provided in Exhibit 3.2.

Other coverages available from Ex-Im Bank include several policies specifically designed for financing institutions such as banks. For example, the Bank Letter of Credit Policy covers the obligation of a foreign bank to remit funds to a bank that has confirmed a letter of credit opened by that foreign bank for the purchase of U.S. goods.

To insure against risks from the date of signing the sales contract instead of from the date of shipment, Ex-Im Bank offers comprehensive preshipment coverage. This coverage is necessary when goods are specially manufactured or require a long factory lead time. Nonacceptance coverage against the arbitrary refusal of the buyer to accept products that conform to the contract of sale may be offered at no extra cost in addition to the normal coverage except when greater-than-normal risk exists, such as with perishable items.

To encourage U.S. firms to expand their foreign business during a period when there is a strong overseas demand for services, Ex-Im Bank developed services coverage. Industries benefiting from this include management consultants, engineering service firms, transportation companies, architecture and design firms, and other firms offering the service of U.S.-based personnel to foreign buyers with repayment being made in U.S. dollars in the United States.

The New-to-Export Policy is for companies that have had little or no export sales experience. The policy gives added commercial risk protection of 95 percent to further cushion any potential losses. The applying company must have average annual export credit sales of less than $2 million during the preceding two years and prior direct coverage under any Ex-Im Bank insurance program.

Guarantees. Ex-Im Bank guarantees repayment protection for private sector loans to creditworthy buyers of U.S. goods and services exports. Guarantees are backed in full by the U.S. government. Both medium- and long-term guarantees are available.

Medium-term guarantees are available for export transactions usually up to $10 million, with a maximum repayment term not to exceed seven years. Most typically, they are used by commercial banks that do not want exposure in a certain country or that have reached their internal "exposure limit" in a given country. The Ex-Im Bank guarantee overcomes these limitations. The medium-term guarantee provides the lender 100 percent political and commercial risk protection. Under this guarantee, the foreign buyer is required to make a 15 percent cash down payment (as per OECD guidelines), so the guarantee covers the financed portion of 85 percent.

Ex-Im Bank's fee schedule is determined by country risk and the repayment terms of the transaction. Rates vary from the highest-rated "A" country to the lowest-rated "E" country. By having a rate schedule based on perceived risk assumption, Ex-Im Bank is able to remain open for business longer in more countries because it is compensated for the risk it is being asked to take.

Long-term guarantees are used for transactions in excess of $10 million and repayment periods of eight or more years. The commercial and political risk coverage is 100 percent. The fee structure is the same as under medium-term guarantees. One major difference is that loans made under the long-term guarantee may be denominated in foreign currencies acceptable to Ex-Im Bank. This enables foreign buyers with access to foreign currency earnings to use this currency to repay loans. A good example of this would be a foreign airline with earnings, through its flight routes, in Japanese yen. The airline wishes to buy U.S.-made airplanes but wants to borrow in yen and use its yen earnings to service the debt. An Ex-Im Bank long-term guarantee could be utilized for such a transaction.

Ex-Im Bank, by statute, does not compete with commercial banks. Rather, it provides *commercial bank complements and supplements* that support exports by assuming risks unacceptable to banks. As is well known, commercial banks will only rarely provide fixed interest rate loans for any type of commercial transaction. Yet today, in the highly competitive international marketplace, many foreign buyers can demand financial support as a precondition to their purchase of goods from abroad. These foreign buyers may require fixed-rate financing as a condition of their purchase.

A commercial bank extending a medium-term loan under the Ex-Im Bank guarantee may liquidate the transaction at any time by selling it to the Private Export Funding Corporation (PEFCO). This arrangement replaces a facility previously offered by the Ex-Im Bank wherein a commercial bank could borrow from the Ex-Im Bank at a discount and lend onward to the foreign buyer at a higher, fixed rate.

For fixed-rate loans in excess of $10 million and repayment periods of eight years or longer, Ex-Im Bank may act as a lender directly to the foreign buyer. This is so because most commercial banks simply do not extend loans beyond seven-year repayment terms. Often, these transactions are large ones, in excess of $100 million, and commercial banks do not want such large exposure for long periods of time in one country or exposure in a particular industrial sector. Because such major projects, or large product purchases, are often awarded through competitive international bidding, U.S. exporters would be unable to compete successfully without Ex-Im Bank participation.

Ex-Im Bank has eased its U.S. *content requirements* somewhat and is now prepared to finance up to a maximum of 15 percent foreign content in the export order. The rest of the export must be U.S.-produced goods and services. If the foreign content exceeds 15 percent of the shipment, then that foreign content will be excluded entirely from Ex-Im Bank support.

Payment *terms* are normally determined by studying cash flow projections from the proposed project or the useful life of the product. In any case, repayment rarely exceeds a 10-year term. Normally, if a project is involved, repayment begins six months after the project

Exhibit 3.3: Typical Financing Plan for a Turnkey Project

Costs (in millions)		Financing Plan (in millions)	
Hardware	$10.0	Ex-Im Bank credit/guarantee	$ 8.5
Infrastructure	5.0	U.S. banks—U.S. costs	1.5
Interest during construction	2.0	U.S. banks—infrastructure	5.0
Working capital requirements	2.0	Sponsor's equity	4.0
Total	$19.0	Total	$19.0

SOURCE: Example courtesy of Louis G. Guadagnoli, former vice president, Export-Import Bank of the United States.

commences commercial operations. For a product, such as a commercial jet aircraft, repayment begins six months after the plane goes into service.

An example of typical financing for a turnkey project is provided in Exhibit 3.3. Ex-Im Bank funds or guarantees 85 percent of U.S. costs at a fixed rate, with the rate varying by country classification. The bank financing for infrastructure is a separate transaction. To be involved, Ex-Im Bank and commercial banks must be satisfied that the project is technically and financially feasible. The balance of the financing requirements usually comes out of the project owner's resources.

Other Public Financing

OPIC. The Overseas Private Investment Corporation (OPIC) is a federal agency that offers investment guarantees to U.S. manufacturers that wish to establish plants in less-developed countries, either by themselves or as a joint venture with local capital. OPIC finances and/or insures only foreign direct investment through:

- Direct loans from $2 million to $10 million per project with terms of 5 to 15 years;
- Loan guarantees to U.S. institutional lenders of $10 million to $100 million; and
- Political risk insurance against currency inconvertibility, expropriation, or takeover, and physical damage resulting from political strife.

The importance of this activity is increasing rapidly because foreign direct investment enables firms to remain competitive in the world marketplace. It is difficult to maintain viable market share without presence as a producer, making trade more dependent on investment with time. Since its inception in 1971, OPIC has supported investments amounting to $121 billion, generated $58 billion in exports, and helped create 237,000 U.S. jobs. Currently, its programs are available in 140 countries worldwide.

AID and TDP. The Agency for International Development (AID) administers most of the foreign economic assistance programs for the U.S. government. Because many AID agreements require that commodities be purchased from the United States, exporters should use this support mechanism. AID estimates that 70 percent of all U.S. aid comes back in purchases of goods and services from U.S. companies. In the long term, the agency's objective is to increase potential for increased exports by follow-up sales and by creating potential in the market for other purchases.

As a companion agency to AID, the U.S. Trade Development Program (TDP) uses foreign assistance funds to increase U.S. exports by financing the planning of projects and dispersing grants for feasibility studies of development projects.

Additional Sources. In addition to these U.S. entities, you will find it worthwhile to monitor the activities of multilateral development banks (such as the World Bank Group), regional development banks (such as the Inter-American Development Bank and the Asian Development Bank), and many national development banks, as well as the United Nations. These banks specialize in financing investment activities and can provide valuable leads for future business activity. The United Nations has purchased $3 billion in goods and services annually with about 12 percent of the budget for procurement going to U.S. companies.

The World Bank Group has, since its inception, provided more than $313 billion in financing for more than 5,800 projects. In 2002, loans totaled $19.5 billion for more than 230 new operations. Projects cover a wide spectrum, including agriculture, industry, transportation, telecommunications, and population planning. Loans are at variable rates, based on the cost of borrowing, and for 15- to 20-year terms. All loans must be guaranteed by the government of the borrowing country. To get business from World Bank projects, international marketers have to closely monitor the entire process—from the identification of the project to the approval of the loan.

The Multilateral Investment Guaranty Agency (MIGA) encourages the flow of financial resources to its developing member countries. To accomplish this, MIGA is authorized to issue guarantees against noncommercial risks in host countries, so that investors may assess the benefits of projects on economic and financial grounds rather than political risk. By 2002, MIGA had facilitated investments worth $9 billion in 78 countries.

Overall, many businesses benefit from a new flow of funds being committed by multilateral banks to projects around the world.[4] From 1990 to 1995, the World Bank Group and the African, Asian, European, and Inter-American Development Banks committed nearly $200 billion in projects for agriculture, energy, industry, finance, transportation, and education. By the year 2000, they had committed $410 billion to developing countries in these sectors. With such large amounts at stake, some international marketing managers believe that these funds are out of reach or too big, bureaucratic, or difficult to obtain. While some funds are subject to competitive international bidding, others, at the lower end of the scale, are accessible and available via different methods of procurement, including direct negotiation.

Government-funded counseling and information services for foreign trade make finding and securing multilateral bank contracts easier. For example, AID's goals are to counsel small to mid-size companies on doing business with developing countries. The United Nations publishes *Development Business* twice a month, which offers information about projects to be launched in Africa, Asia, Latin America, and Eastern Europe.

Private Sector Insurance

The Private Export Funding Corporation (PEFCO) is a private corporation founded in 1970 for the purpose of making fixed-rate U.S. dollar loans to foreign importers to finance purchases of goods and services of U.S. manufacture or origin. PEFCO's stockholders consist of 55 commercial banks, including most of the major U.S. banks involved in export financing, investment banking firms, and manufacturing firms.

The Ex-Im Bank and PEFCO maintain an agreement whereby Ex-Im Bank guarantees the principal and interest on debt obligations that are issued by foreign purchasers of U.S. products and services by PEFCO. PEFCO thereby acquires a portfolio of Ex-Im Bank–guaranteed paper that can be used as the basis for raising funds in the private market. Because all of its loans are guaranteed, PEFCO itself does not evaluate credit risks, appraise economic conditions in foreign countries, or review other factors that might affect the collectibility of its loans.

The role of private export credit insurers has increased in recent years. For example, American International Underwriters, a division of American International Group, offers coverage of commercial credit and political risks similar to that offered by Ex-Im Bank. Other firms that offer limited forms of commercial and political risk coverage include Citicorp International Trade and American Credit Indemnity. Private underwriters offer political risk coverage for confiscation, expropriation, and nationalization risks—coverage that is similar to the programs provided by OPIC.

Proponents of the private insurers cite their faster processing time, lower rates because of selectivity, absence of U.S.-origin requirements, and ability to do business in countries embargoed by the U.S. government. The drawbacks, however, are that they require a minimal but substantial amount of business to be covered, they cater mainly to the large multinational corporations and are not as interested in smaller firms, and, the most important caveat, their insurance may not be as acceptable to commercial banks that will be providing the financing.

MANAGING INTERNATIONAL FINANCIAL RISKS

After financial risks have been assessed, you need to decide whether to do business in the particular environment. If you decide to do so, you need to minimize risk through actions by either the company itself or by support systems. The decision must be an informed one, based on detailed and up-to-date information on credit and country conditions.

Creditworthiness

In many respects, the assessment of a buyer's creditworthiness requires the same attention to credit checking and financial analysis as for domestic buyers. However, the assessment of a foreign private buyer is complicated by some of the following factors:

1. Credit reports may not be reliable.
2. Audited reports may not be available.
3. Financial reports may have been prepared according to a different format.
4. Many governments require assets to be annually reevaluated upward, which can distort results.
5. Statements are in local currency.
6. The buyer may have the financial resources in local currency but may be precluded from converting to dollars because of exchange controls and other government actions.

Exhibit 3.4: Sources of
International Credit Information

Source	Response Time	Cost	Comments
1. Dun & Bradstreet www.dnb.com	Same day to 40 days, depending on location	$100 to $375. Varies by geographic region	Standard in the industry. Data are often sketchy, since subjects are reticent to respond to a credit inquiry.
2. @rating www.cofacerating.com	Instantaneous	Free on-line	Launched late 1999; wishes to become a standard reference for e-commerce; supported by the EU Commission.
3. International Company Profiles www.ita.doc.gov	Variable; if known name, quick; otherwise, lengthy delays; 3 to 4 weeks	$100	If prominent name, comprehensive. Tendency to be out of date.
4. Local Credit Agency Report	Long, start from scratch	$100 to $200	Quality varies. International market perspective lacking.
5. Bank Reports	Slow	None	Limited in scope.
6. FCIB-NACM Corporation www.fcibnacm.com	Same day to 3 weeks	$66 to $310; members get 5% discount; membership $840	Network of 15 agencies worldwide.

SOURCE: Interviews with company and organization personnel, December 1999.

Exporters and investors should obtain more than one credit report and determine how each credit agency obtains its reports. Credit reporters may use the same correspondent agency, in which case it does the exporter no good to obtain the same information from two sources and to pay for it twice. Exhibit 3.4 summarizes the major sources of credit information.

Where private-sector companies (such as Dun & Bradstreet or Veritas) are able to provide the needed credit information, the services of the U.S. Department of Commerce's International Company Profiles (ICP) are not available. However, 50 countries currently are still served by the ICP. Local credit reporting agencies, such as Profancresa in Mexico, may also provide regional services (in this case, throughout Latin America). With the growth of e-commerce, a company may want to demonstrate its creditworthiness to customers and suppliers in a rapid and secure fashion. The Coface Group (www.cofacerating.com), of which Veritas is the information arm in the Americas, introduced the "@rating" system, available on the World Wide Web and designed to assess a company's performance in paying its commercial obligations.

Getting Paid. Beyond protecting yourself by establishing creditworthiness, you can match payment terms to the customer. In the short term, an exporter may require payment terms that guarantee payment. In the long term, the best approach is to establish a relationship of mutual trust, which will ensure payment even if complications arise during a transaction. Payment terms need to be stated clearly and followed up effectively. If prompt payment is not stressed and enforced, some customers will assume they can procrastinate.

Smaller exporters often feel that they can't afford the luxury of weighing risks and investigating the creditworthiness of foreign customers that big corporations have because they can't afford to lose the business. More often than not, exporters will do less checking on an international account than they will on a domestic customer.[5] For example, a U.S. fan blade manufacturer with less than $10 million in revenue was left with an overdue payment of $127,000 owed by an African customer. Before shipping the goods, the company had failed to call any of the customer's credit references. These turned out to be nonexistent—just like the company itself.

The simple guideline of selling only in countries where you are most likely to get paid may not be enough, given that collection periods for some of the more attractive markets may be long. However, in many cases, basic information about the economic and political conditions in markets may be enough to warrant caution. One U.S. manufacturer was still waiting for payment after two years from a buyer in a newly emerging market because the foreign bank it dealt with had trouble obtaining U.S. dollars despite the country's strengthening foreign reserve position.

Should a default occur despite those preparatory measures, the exporter's first recourse is the customer. Communication with the customer may reveal a misunderstanding or error regarding the shipment. If the customer has financial or other concerns or objections, rescheduling the payment terms may resolve the problem. Third-party intervention through a collection agency may be needed if the customer disputes the charges. For example, the Total Credit Management Group, a cooperative of leading credit and collection companies in 46 countries, can be employed. Use an attorney only when further amicable demands are futile.

Foreign Exchange Risk

When the international marketer is to receive payment in a currency other than that of his or her country, the risk exists of a decline (devaluation) in the foreign currency during the time between the signing of the contract and the receipt of the foreign currency. (Naturally, changes can also affect the marketer favorably.) Protection against foreign exchange risk cannot be secured from the same sources as for commercial and political risk. It must emerge from sound management practices.

A firm faces exposure to three kinds of foreign exchange risk:

- *Transaction exposure* refers to the effect of outstanding contracts (for example, payables and receivables).
- *Translation exposure* occurs if the financial statements of the marketer are affected as a result of having to report consolidated worldwide results in home country currency. Translation exposure for a U.S. firm is a function of the rules issued by the Financial Accounting Standards Board (FASB), in particular FASB 52 ("Foreign Currency Translation"), issued in 1981.
- *Economic exposure* arises if the long-term health of a business entity is affected by foreign exchange beyond transaction and translation exposure. Marketers can avoid unnecessary economic exposure by careful selection of target markets and prudent pricing and credit policies. Any firm with ongoing international marketing activities will have economic exposure.

Foreign Exchange Markets. The foreign exchange market is the market for currencies, that is, the physical and institutional structure through which the money of one country is exchanged for that of another country, the rate of exchange between currencies is determined, and foreign exchange transactions are physically completed. The participants in this market include banks, governments, and speculators as well as individuals and firms conducting transactions.

The price of one currency in terms of another is called the *ex-*

change rate, printed in financial newspapers and on Web sites daily. The marketer, however, has to contact a particular bank's foreign exchange trader for a firm quote.

Both spot and forward transactions are made in the market. The market for buying and selling on the current day is the spot market. The market for closing contracts on subsequent periods of 30, 60, or 90 days is called the forward market. If, for example, the forward quote for British pounds is less than spot, and the pound is said to be selling at a discount to the dollar. When the foreign currency is more expensive in the forward market than in the spot market, the foreign currency is said to be selling at a premium. Anything having an impact on the spot rate, such as balance-of-payments problems, will have the same impact on forward rates. Forward contracts for lesser-known currencies are not readily available, and for unstable currencies, they are quite expensive.

Forward contracts provide a form of protection, or *hedge,* against exchange risks. When a forward exchange contract is signed, the forward quote (such as the 90-day quote for Germany) is the rate that applies, although no payment is generally made until the settlement date of the contract. The user pays the price of foregoing possible gains in order to ensure protection against possible losses.

Managing Exchange Risk. The rate of exchange between two countries is the result of supply and demand (if the currency is in a free float) as well as governmental policy. For example, an increase in a country's exports or its interest rates would increase demand for its currency and thus lead to an increase in its currency value. In some cases, governments will establish an exchange rate for their currency and absorb and countermarket pressures (and thus accept foreign currency losses) up to a point before allowing the exchange rate to change. Some currencies move in and out of various types of "pegged" exchange rate relationships that tie one currency's rate to that of another one. For example, the Hong Kong dollar is tied to the U.S. dollar at a rate of 7.8. Occasionally, governments will coordinate their actions to rectify an imbalance in demand and supply conditions.

Three protections against currency-related risk have been proposed:

1. *Risk modifying,* such as manipulating prices or incurring local debt. For example, the firm borrows money in the market to which it exports its product. If the foreign currency depreciates relative to domestic currency, the loss in the operating cash flows is buffered by the reduction in debt.

2. *Self-insuring*, such as manipulating the leads and lags in terms of export and import payments in anticipation of either currency revaluations or devaluations.
3. *Risk shifting*, such as purchasing of options or futures.

With long-term exchange rate shifts, marketers may have to change their production bases and supply sources. Some marketers have focused on products that are far less sensitive to pricing changes. In addition, marketers that may not be able to shift production overseas have increased their production efficiencies.

Options and futures are a relatively new development in foreign exchange markets. An option gives the holder the right to buy or sell foreign currency at a prespecified price on or up to a prespecified date. The difference between the currency options market and the forward market is that the transaction in the options market gives the participant the right to buy or sell, whereas a transaction in the forward market entails a contractual obligation to buy or sell. If the exporter does not have enough much currency when the contract comes due, it would have to go into the foreign exchange markets to buy the currency, potentially exposing itself to major losses if the currency had appreciated in the interim.

The greater flexibility of the options contract makes it more expensive than the forward contract, but minimum transaction sizes are considerably smaller on the futures market. Forward quotes apply to transactions of $1 million or more, whereas on the futures market, transactions will typically be well below $100,000. This market, therefore, allows relatively small firms engaged in international trade to lock in exchange rates and reduce their risk. Forward contracts, options, and futures are available from banks, the Chicago Mercantile Exchange, and the Philadelphia Stock Exchange.

Finessing Financial Crises. A series of currency crises have shook all emerging markets during the 1990s and the early 2000s, each with its own complex causes and unknown outlooks. Crises can occur when international investors expect—due to a possibly wide range of causes—a country to default on debt or otherwise suffer sudden weakness in its currency. A crisis might have a domino effect within a region, such as Argentina's 2001 currency and debt crisis had on Brazil and Uruguay in 2002. In that instance, U.S. credits provided in mid-2002 were designed to tide over Brazilian and Uruguayan central banks until they negotiated longer-term IMF loans.

A crisis can affect trade worldwide, however. The 1997 Asian currency crisis quickly became a region-wide recession depressing world demand for many products, especially commodities. World oil markets, copper markets, and agricultural products all saw severe price drops as demand kept falling. These changes were immediately noticeable in declining earnings and growth prospects for other emerging economies. Recessions have an impact on consumer spending, retarding the sale of imports deemed luxuries as consumers switch to lower-cost local brands or generic products. Cars and other big ticket purchases may be put on long-term hold.

Some marketers abandon d markets; others substantially increase their efforts. While Daihatsu pulled out of Thailand during the Asian crisis, GM decided to stay, changing the car model it produced and reducing production volume. Returning to a market having once abandoned it can be difficult. For example, distribution channels may be blocked by competition, or local partners might suspect the depth of the returnee's commitment.

Using tools of the marketing mix is another response. Imported products usually are more expensive than local versions, so emphasizing the import's brand name, the country of origin, and other benefits may convince the consumer of a positive value-price relationship. If the perceived prices are still too high, the product and/or its packaging may have to be changed by making the product smaller or the number of units in a pack fewer.

While marketers from North America and Europe may face these challenges, companies in emerging markets hit by currency crises may have an advantage, not only at home but in international markets as well. Their lower prices give them an opportunity to expand outside their home markets or aggressively pursue expansion in new markets. Similarly, buying from suppliers in markets hit by currency crises may enable them to benefit from lower procurement costs.

The most interesting approach in the face of challenges is to invest more to build market share. During the 1994 peso crisis, a number of U.S. companies in Mexico such as Procter & Gamble decided to invest more as competitors (who left) decreased and local buying power increased. When the market rebounds, investments will be rewarded.

FUTURITIES

Financial crises will be periodic features of the global marketplace. Given the close linkages between financial markets, shocks in one market will quickly translate into rapid shifts in others and threaten to overpower the financial resources of individual governments. Even closely coordinated government fiscal and monetary policies are unlikely to be able to negate long-term market effects in response to changes in economic fundamentals.

Exhibit 3.5: Consumer and Marketer
Adjustment to Financial Crisis

Consumer Adjustment to Financial

*General reactions
  Reduce consumption and
    wastefulness
  More careful decision making
  More search for information

*Product adjustments
  Necessities rather than luxuries
  Switch to cheaper brands or generics
  Local rather than foreign brands
  Smaller quantities/packages

*Price adjustments
  Life-cycle costs—durability/value
  Emphasis on economical prices

*Promotion adjustments
  Rational approach
  Reduced attraction to gifts
  Information rather than imagery

*Shopping adjustments
  Increased window shopping
  Preference for discount stores
  Fewer end-of-aisle purchases

Marketer Adjustment Hardship

*Marketing-mix strategies
  Withdraw from weak markets
  Fortify in strong markets
  Acquire weak competitors
  Consider youth markets
  Resale market for durables

*Product strategies
  Prune weak products
  Avoid introducing new products
    in gaps
  Flanker brands
  Augment products with warranties
  Adaptive positioning

*Pricing strategies
  Improve quality while maintaining
    price
  Reduce price while maintaining
    quality
  Consider product life-cycle pricing

*Promotion strategies
  Maintain advertising budget
  Focus on print media
  Assurances through rational appeals
  Expert endorsements
  Advisory tone
  Customer loyalty programs
  Train sales force to handle objections

*Distribution strategies
  Location is critical
  Sell in discount and wholesale centers
  Prune marginal dealers
  Alternative channels

SOURCE: Compiled from Swee Hoon Ang, Siew Meng Leong and Philip Kotler, "The Asian Apocalypse: Crisis Marketing for Consumers and Businesses," Long Range Planning 33(February 2000): 97-119.

Certainly the financing terms of a transaction will continue to be important marketing tools. To help international marketers deal with financial risk, both the government and the private sector will strengthen risk management assistance programs.

Less-developed countries (LDCs) might not see the growth in financial aid they had been hoping for, however. Industrial-nation corporations are not likely to address the LDC's problems in a major way. Governments, multilateral institutions, and nongovernmental organizations (NGOs) will be needed. Periodic surges in the social conscience of industrialized nations may result in targeted investments but won't be enough to transform the economic future of LDCs, particularly without their own internal reforms. Nevertheless, global trade liberalization offers some hope to those regions by easing restrictions on their exports.

Among the emerging democracies of Central and Eastern Europe, capital shortages continue as a major constraint to catching up with the West. In addition, environmental consciousness will require large investments in environmentally sound energy generation and production facilities. Even though programs are being designed to draw hidden personal savings into the economies, these nations must rely to a large degree on attracting capital and hard currency from abroad. Recession, high demand for capital, and continued domestic uncertainties make this difficult. So does coping with the downside of market economies: lost jobs, bankruptcies, and the emergence of a wealthy entrepreneurial class. But in the optimistic view, an increase in ambivalence and uncertainty could produce rapid shifts in economic and political thinking that will lead to greater stability and long-term wealth accumulation.

NOTES

1. Louis G. Guadagnoli, *Practical Guide to Export Financing and Risk Management* (Arlington, VA: Government Information Services, 1989), III-33.
2. Ray Pereira, "International Factoring," *World Trade*, December 1999, 68–69.
3. Mary Ann Ring, "Innovative Export Financing," *Business America*, January 11, 1993, 12–14.
4. David DeVoss, "The $3 Billion Question," *World Trade*, September 1998, 34–39; Adrienne Fox, "Global Capitalists," *International Business* (March 1996): 50–54; Adrian Feuchtwanger, "The Search for Eldorado," *World Trade*, November 1993, 116–118; and Nicholas H. Ludlow, "Tapping Development Bank Lines of Credit," *Export Today* 9 (October 1993): 26–30.
5. "Congratulations, Exporter! Now about Getting Paid . . ."*Business Week,* January 17, 1994, 98; and "Small Firms Hit Foreign Obstacles in Billing Overseas," *The Wall Street Journal,* December 8, 1992, B2.

4

Marketing within Cultural Contexts

Understand your market's local concerns, special quirks, and homegrown idiosyncrasies.

There are many forces and influences involved in creating and defining culture and, thus, many possible definitions. Here we'll define *culture* as an integrated system of learned behavior patterns that are distinguishing characteristics of the members of any given society. It includes everything that a group thinks, says, does, and makes—its customs, language, material artifacts, and shared systems of attitudes and feelings.[1]

Global management embraces two schools of thought about cultural diversity. One is that business is business the world around, following the successful models of Pepsi and McDonald's. On the other hand, companies must tailor business approaches to individual cultures: "Think globally, market locally." Aligning worldwide strategies and local procedures in each country becomes akin to an organ transplant; the critical issue is acceptance or rejection. The major challenge to the international marketer is practicing patience, and avoiding the cultural myopia that causes rejection.

For decades, as Western cultural influences swept across the globe, marketers have predicted an emerging homogeneity embodied in "global customers" who would think and purchase alike the world over.[2] Universal marketing programs could appeal to their similarities.

But using that thinking to justify standardization could be a fatal mistake. Adaptability, not standardization, is the key to global marketing success. Marketers must recognize what drives customer behavior in different markets and detect the extent to which similarities exist or can be created through marketing efforts.

As you expand globally, you will acquire new customers and new partners—the agents, distributors, service suppliers (e.g., advertising agencies, law firms), and governments whose assistance is necessary for market development and penetration. Expansion also means new employees or strategic partners whose motivations can make or break marketing programs. Understanding the hot buttons of these groups becomes critical. Believing that concern about culture and its elements is a waste of time often proves disastrous. Understanding culture is critical to get strategies right and to ensure effective local implementation.

Cultural competence—the ability to detect similarities and to allow for differences—must be recognized as a key management skill. The marketing strategist transfers successful ideas across borders for efficiency and adapts them to local conditions for effectiveness.

Cultural knowledge can be defined by the way it is acquired. Objective or factual information is obtained from others through communication, research, and education. *Experiential knowledge* is acquired only by being involved in a culture other than one's own.[3] Both factual and experiential information can be general (e.g., understanding the implications of regional integration) or country-specific (e.g., factual knowledge about government rules, experiential knowledge about the best product appeals). The more a marketer becomes involved in the international arena, the more he or she is able to develop a metaknowledge about the ground rules that apply, whether in Kuala Lumpur, Malaysia, or Asunción, Paraguay.

BUILDING CULTURAL KNOWLEDGE

Market-specific cultural knowledge does not necessarily travel well, but the general variables do. Managers ranked eight sources of international business expertise in a survey, emphasizing the value of experience (Exhibit 4.1). They gave written materials an important but supplementary role, providing general or country-specific background information before operational decisions must be made. Many of today's international managers have pre-career experience in government, the Peace Corps, the armed forces, or missionary service. Travel that involves meetings with company personnel, intermediaries, facilitating agents, customers, and government officials—rather than general tourism—is what counts.

However, from the corporate point of view, developing a global capability requires the experience of heavy business involvement, such as foreign assignments and networking across borders via multicountry, multicultural teams developing strategies and programs. Developing the ability of a management team to understand and fully appreciate the nuances of different cultural traits and patterns—gaining interpretive knowledge—requires "getting one's feet wet" globally over a sufficient length of time.

Exhibit 4.1: Managers Rank Factors
Involved in Acquiring International Expertise

Factor	Considered Critical	Considered Important
1. Business travel	60.8%	92.0%
2. Assignments overseas	48.8%	71.2%
3. Reading/television	16.0%	63.2%
4. Training programs	6.4%	28.8%
5. Precareer activities	4.0%	16.0%
6. Graduate course	2.4%	15.2%
7. Nonbusiness travel	0.8%	12.8%
8. Undergraduate courses	0.8%	12.0%

SOURCE: Stephen J. Kobrin, *International Expertise in American Business* (New York: Institute of International Education, 1984), 38.

Nestlé, for example, shuffles its managers around a region, such as Asia or Latin America, at four- to five-year intervals, giving them intervening two- to three-year tours at headquarters. This has allowed those managers to pick up ideas and tools they can use in other markets. In Thailand, where supermarkets are revolutionizing consumer-goods marketing, Nestlé applied systems it perfected elsewhere. Its Thailand experience has helped Nestlé develop subsequent emerging markets in the same region, such as Vietnam.

Published sources and institutions provide a wealth of information to managers, expanding their knowledge of specific cultures. Most sources deal with the factual information that provides a necessary basis for market studies. Beyond the normal business literature with its tutorials and case examples, governments, private companies, and universities publish specific country studies:

- The U.S. Department of Commerce's *Country Commercial Guides* cover 133 countries. (www.ita.doc.gov)
- The Economist Intelligence Unit's *Country Reports* cover 180 countries. (www.eiu.com)
- *Culturegrams* detailing the customs of peoples in 174 countries are published by the Center for International and Area Studies at Brigham Young University. (www.culturegrams.com)

Many facilitating agencies—such as advertising agencies, banks, consulting firms, and transportation companies—provide background information on the markets they serve for their clients:

- Runzheimer International's international reports on employee relocation and site selection for 44 countries. (www.runzheimer.com)
- Hong Kong and Shanghai Banking Corporation's *Business Profile Series* for 22 countries in Asia-Pacific. (www.hsbc.com)
- *World Trade* magazine's "Put Your Best Foot Forward" series, which covers Europe, Asia, Mexico/Canada, and Russia. (www.worldtrademag.com)

CULTURAL ANALYSIS

A global marketing team can develop checklists and models for examining critical cultural elements, but any framework covering all cases inevitably shortchanges the unique characteristics that might be critical in a particular market. But organizing disparate cultural factors into one presentation provides a useful tool that focuses management attention on most of the critical issues.

One useful approach emphasizes the process cycles of innovation and change as the basis for market development: Exporters and multinational corporations transplant concepts and products from one culture to another where they are perceived to be new and different. Analysis focuses on the new-market culture's propensity to change as determined by the strength of cultural beliefs, the behavior of change agents (including the multinational marketer itself) and opinion leaders, and the nature of communications about change and innovation from government, social, and commercial sources.[4]

Hofstede identifies four major dimensions of cultural difference: individualism ("I" versus "we" consciousness); power distance (degree of equality in a society); uncertainty avoidance (the need for formal rules and regulations); and masculinity (attitudes toward achievement and the roles of men and women).[5] One could include a fifth dimension: long- versus short-term orientation, which distinguishes success based on a market share from short-term profit orientation.[6]

Knowing where a market shapes up on such dimensions can guide strategy. Examining all markets' positions can produce meaningful culture-based segmentation plans that are more reliable guides for addressing cultural similarities and differences than are geographic segmentations. For example, consider risk-reducing marketing programs offering extended warranties and return privileges in markets possessing high uncertainty avoidance.[7] Thus, a marketer would

Exhibit 4.2: Elements of Culture

—Language:
- Spoken (denotation and connotation)
- Nonverbal (Nonspoken): space, time, material possessions, friendship patterns, and business agreements

—Religion: defines the ideals for life reflected in the values and attitudes of societies and individuals and shapes their behavior.
- More than 10,000 distinct religions worldwide; 150 have a million or more followers
- Major religions influencing major world markets: Christianity, Islam, Hinduism, Buddhism, Sikhism, Judaism, and Confucianism.

—Values and attitudes:
- Values: shared beliefs or group norms that individuals have internalized.
- Attitudes: evaluations of alternatives based on one's values.

—Manners and customs: matters of habit and ways of conducting oneself. Some of the areas in which marketers need to prepare include:
- Fully understanding different ways of thinking.
- Giving sufficient attention to an adversary's need to save face.
- Strong knowledge and appreciation of host country history, culture, government, and attitudes toward foreigners.
- Adequate recognition of the decision-making styles and the role of personal relations and personalities.
- Need to allocate time for negotiations.

—Product consumption:
- What use benefits is the product competing against?
- Purchase patterns differ with societies.
- Usage habits are different in different societies.
- Package sizes need to be adapted to usage needs.

—Myths and legends: unsubstantiated but widely held beliefs about the efficacy or harm of certain conditions or practices.
- Folklore
- Superstitions
- Popular beliefs

—Aesthetics: popular taste in artistic expressions, reflected in color, form, and music.

—Education: both formal educational levels and qualitative aspects of education and skills, including loyalty to the corporate family.

—Social institutions: the mix of reference groups that provide the values and attitudes that help shape the behaviors and individual's concept of self.

SOURCES: David B. Barrett, George T. Kurian, Todd M. Johnson (eds.) *World Christian Encyclopedia: A Comparative Survey of Churches and Religions in the Modern World,* 2nd ed. (Oxford, U.K.: Oxford University Press, 2001) as cited on www.adherents.com accessed August 8, 2002; and Sergey Frank, "Global Negotiations: Vive Les Differences!" *Sales & Marketing Management* 144 (May 1992): 64–69.

position new products to those markets as continuous innovations that do not require radical changes in consumption patterns.[8]

Cultural analysis can also provide specific guidelines for marketing mix development. Because the United States prizes individualism, U.S. market promotional appeals should be relevant to the individual and informal and friendly to accommodate the reduced power distance in the market.[9] In opposite situations, marketing communications should emphasize that the new product is socially accepted. However, an imported product can sometimes use global or foreign cultural positioning, permitting an individualism appeal, which would be inappropriate for domestic products in low-individualism societies.[10]

Cultural factors also influence channel choices. Marketers in high-individualism markets are more likely to choose channel partners based on objective criteria, whereas firms at the opposite end of the dimension would prefer to deal with friends.[11] In Japan, a number of Western companies have run into obstructions in the Japanese distribution system, where great value is placed on established relationships. Everything is done on the basis of favoring the familiar and fearing the unfamiliar. In most cases, foreign companies can solve the problem by joint venturing with major Japanese entities having established contacts.

Business negotiating styles can differ markedly. In Germany, the emphasis is on efficiency. One can expect a counterpart who is thorough, systematic, very well prepared, but also rather dogmatic, lacking flexibility and compromise. In Mexico, however, the counterpart is much more likely to address problems on a personal and private basis rather than on a business level. This means more emphasis on socializing and conveying one's humanity, sincerity, loyalty, and friendship. Also, the differences in pace and business practices of the region have to be accepted.

On occasion, a company might be able to change existing customs

Exhibit 4.3: When and What to Give as Gifts

China	India	Japan	Mexico	Saudi Arabia
Chinese New Year (January or February)	Hindu Diwali festival (October or November)	Oseibo (Jan. 1)	Christmas/New Year	Id al-Fitr (December or January)
√ Modest gifts such as coffee table books, ties, pens	√ Sweets, nuts, and fruit; elephant carvings; candleholders	√ Scotch, brandy, Americana, round fruit such as melons	√ Desk clocks, fine pens, gold lighters	√ Fine compasses to determine direction for prayer; cashmere
X Clocks, anything from Taiwan	X Leather objects, snake images	X Gifts that come in sets of four or nine	X Sterling silver items, logo gifts, food baskets	X Pork and pigskin, liquor

√ recommended
X to be avoided

SOURCE: Kate Murphy, "Gifts without Gaffes for Global Clients," *Business Week*, December 6, 1999, 153.

rather than adjust to them. Initially, Procter & Gamble's traditional hard-selling style in television commercials jolted most Japanese viewers accustomed to more symbolic and subtle approaches. Now P&G ads are being imitated by Japanese competitors. However, this does not imply that Japanese advertising will necessarily adopt Western approaches. The Japanese still emphasize who speaks as well as what is spoken. Though P&G promotes only brand names in U.S. and European markets, it must also prominently promote its corporate name in Japan.[12]

TRAINING CHALLENGES

Cultural modeling can aid strategic planning by ensuring that all variables are considered, but the analyst must avoid judging cultures by his or her own values. James A. Lee reasoned that the natural self-reference criterion—unconscious reference to one's own culture—is the root of most international business problems.[13] However, recognizing and acknowledging such bias is often difficult. Controlling ethnocentrism—the belief that one's own culture is superior to others—can be achieved only by acknowledging it and properly adjusting to its possible effects in managerial decision making.[14]

Greater international trade increases the need for cultural sensitivity training at all levels of the organization. Some companies try to avoid the training problem by hiring only nationals or well-traveled executives for their international operations. This makes sense for the management of overseas operations but will not solve the training need, especially if transfers to a culture unfamiliar to the manager are likely. International experience may not necessarily transfer from one market to another.

A survey of European executives found that a shortage of international managers was considered the single most important constraint on expansion abroad.[15] To foster cultural sensitivity and the ability to adapt, companies must take charge of their own management training with programs emphasizing culture-specific data, cultural general information about the values, practices, and assumptions of countries other than one's own, and manager self-awareness of values, assumptions and perceptions of others.[16] The objective of formal training programs is to foster the four critical characteristics of preparedness, sensitivity, patience, and flexibility in managers and other personnel. These programs vary dramatically in terms of their rigor, involvement, and, of course, cost.

The activities of Korean multinationals in the last ten years are instructive. They embarked on a mission of *segyehwa*, or globalization, which meant preparing managers and employees who would be in charge of the program. At Kumho Group, the chairman required all airline and tire maker employees to spend an hour each morning studying a language or learning about foreign cultures. Cards taped up in bathrooms taught a new phrase in English or Japanese each day. Hyundai Motor Co. sent 25 managers in their thirties and forties to Cornell University for nearly a year to learn new disciplines and the less rigid U.S. management style.[17] Samsung formed several special interest groups to focus on issues such as Japanese society and business practices, the Chinese economy, changes in Europe, and the U.S. economy. In addition, groups also explored cutting-edge business issues, such as new technology and marketing strategies. And, in recent years, Samsung has been sending its brightest junior employees abroad for a year.[18]

Area studies, such as environmental briefings and cultural orientation programs, provide factual preparation for a manager to work in, or work with people from, a particular country. Area studies should be a prerequisite for other types of training programs, but alone they serve little practical purpose because they do not really get the manager's feet wet. Other, more involved programs, some of which are increasingly available on the World Wide Web and on online distance learning courses, contribute the context in which cultural facts must be understood.

Cultural assimilators are programs that many consultants and companies have developed in which trainees must respond to scenarios of specific situations in a particular country. A panel of experienced judges evaluates the trainee's assimilator performance and draws conclusions about trainee adaptability to a specific market. This type of program has been used in particular in cases of transfers abroad on short notice.

Sensitivity training enhances a manager's flexibility in situations that differ from those at home. For instance, when time is available, managers can be trained extensively in language, particularly if an exotic tongue is involved. Sensitivity training assumes that understanding and accepting oneself is critical to understanding a person from another culture.

Field experience exposes a manager to a different cultural environment for a limited amount of time. It is expensive, however, so field experience is rarely used as a training tool. One field experience technique that has been suggested when the training process needs to be rigorous is the host-family surrogate. This technique places a trainee and possibly his or her family in a domestically located family of the nationality to which they are assigned.[19]

Remember, however, that regardless of the degree of training, preparation, and positive personal characteristics, a foreign manager will always remain foreign. A manager should never rely on his or her own judgment when local managers can be consulted. In many instances, a manager should have an interpreter present at negotiations, especially if the manager is not completely bilingual. Overconfidence in one's language capabilities can create problems.

FUTURITIES

In recent years, governments, nongovernmental organizations, supranational authorities, and private sector global traders have wrestled with an unprecedented world trade problem: helping failed centrally planned economies transform into industrial market economies and strong democratic societies. In addition, the dawn of the new century brought an even greater cultural problem to the doorstep of the world trade community. Terrorism, environmental concerns, and a greater social sensitivity in the industrial countries encouraged, and at times forced, new attention to the needs of forgotten less developed countries, if not exploited for mineral resources and inexpensive labor.

Even the "developing countries" whose futures looked so rosy during the 1990s economic boom—Latin American nations prominent among them—have proven to be vulnerable to world recession. But at least international marketers know these cultures, by and large. Much needs to be learned about working with and marketing to the citizens and institutions within the LDCs, particularly those in Muslim societies so widely suspicious of Western intentions.

Emerging LDC Consumers

The distinction between developed and less-developed countries, particularly LDCs in Africa, is unlikely to change. Ongoing disparity between developed and developing nations is likely to be based, in part, on continuing debt burdens and problems with satisfying basic needs. Despite a new recognition of the LDCs' plight, political paralysis and diverted industrialized world attention could even increase polarization between the haves and the have-nots.

The population discrepancy between LDCs and the industrialized countries will continue to increase. In the developing world, the management and reduction of population growth will continue to be one of the major challenges of governmental policy, with significant impact on local lifestyles. If not solved, continued rapid increases in population will make it more difficult to ensure that the pace of economic development exceeds population growth. This task becomes even more complex considering that within countries with large population increases, heavy migration flows from rural to urban areas. The increasing number of mega-cities of more than 8 million inhabitants illustrates the change. In 1950, only London and New York, were that size. In 1975, there were 11 mega-cities, including six in the industrialized countries. In 1995, there were 23, with 17 of them in developing countries. In 2015, the projected number is 36, with 30 of them in the developing world, most within Asia (22). Urbanization is likely to place significant stress on economic activity and the provision of services but will also make it easier for marketers to direct their activities toward customers.

Another problem of many LDCs is the persistence of unfulfilled expectations, which fosters discontent. These countries must close the gap, either by improving economic reality—i.e., offering more goods at lower prices and increasing the general standard of living— or by reducing expectations. Unfortunately, not all political powers running the LDCs will recognize the need to align economic aspirations with reality. Some have and will continue to use vague promises of incipient wealth to solidify their power, using economics as a pretext to attack enemies allegedly standing in the way of the people's riches.

But global marketers should not simply stand back and passively await developing markets to mature. One can argue that the emergence of the 4 billion people (6 billion by 2040) who make up the bottom of the income pyramid (less than $1,500 income per year) presents a great opportunity for international marketers, particularly large multinationals. Products and services offered to developed or even emerging markets are not appropriate for LDCs, the reasoning goes, but large corporations have the technological, financial, and managerial resources to take fundamentally different approaches to profit from the LDC opportunity. Among the thoughts proposed are "microlending" that provides consumer buying power in manageable chunks, improved communications that promote practical and inexpensive aspirations, and harnessing advanced technologies for novel consumer solutions.[20]

Special Muslim Needs

Rather than continue to take the Middle East for granted as a usually pliant source of inexpensive petroleum, events at the turn of the century have forced a fresh look at Western policies toward those impoverished and politically polarized societies. Looking in a Mideastern mirror has not returned a pretty picture to Western eyes.

Economically, the developed world's approach to the Middle East, excluding Israel, has been one of benign neglect. What local regimes do with their oil revenues has been considered their business unless, like Iraq, they destabilize trade or threaten terrorism and catastrophic destruction. That has hardly been a policy aimed at improving the lives of consumers in those lands.

Culturally, ignorance has been the greatest common denominator in Western understanding of the region. Knowledge of Muslim thought and tradition, recognition of the average citizens' lives and aspirations, and understanding what will govern the growth of consumer societies in the Middle East has been lacking in the West, save for what oil and industrial traders have learned.

That must change. Perhaps the first step for global marketers is recognizing the region's strengths including its existing business culture. A large number of local business people do an outstanding job in Muslim countries.[21] It also means that the negative impression of the U.S. by many in the region must be changed. In March 2001, Charlotte Beers, former CEO of advertising agency Ogilvy & Mather, became U.S. Undersecretary of Public Diplomacy with the task of "branding foreign policy and marketing American values."

Search for the "Good Life"

Marketing has contributed as a change agent in former Warsaw Pact countries by educating consumers and helping them develop and practice patterns of thinking and behavior based on the rules of the market economy. But transition is a learning process that takes time. Highly prized fundamentals of the market economy—reliance on competition; support of the profit motive; willingness to live with corporate and personal risk—have not been easy for people in these markets to accept. Longstanding dependence on entrenched bureaucracies suspicious of any change has constrained the ability of governments to successfully shape the competitive environments of their nations.

Although Russia and Central Europe possessed about 35 to 40 percent of all the researchers and engineers working in the world, they suffer from a shortage of management skills suited to a market economy. In the past, management mainly consisted of skillful maneuvering within the allocation process. Central planning, for example, required firms to request tools seven years in advance; material requirements needed to be submitted two years in advance. Ordering was done haphazardly, since requested quantities were always reduced, and surplus allocations could always be traded with other firms. The driving mechanism for management was not responsiveness to existing needs but rather plan fulfillment through a finely honed allocation mentality.

The emerging regions are struggling to instill manager and worker commitments to hard work and acceptance of market economy uncertainties such as layoffs and bankruptcies, where once jobs and healthcare were guaranteed. Women have often been the ones feeling the worst effects of transition. Under previous regimes, women were expected to work full time, but the state provided daycare and healthcare. Women are no longer seen as having a social duty to work, but reform has also brought a dramatic decline in affordable childcare facilities and a deterioration in healthcare systems. In addition, economic hardship and uncertainty during transition has made it more difficult to feed and clothe one's family—responsibilities that have always fallen predominantly to women in these countries.

The new environment also complicates managerial decision making. Even simple reforms require an almost unimaginable array of decisions about business licenses, the setting of optimal tax rates, rules of business operation, definitions of business expense for taxation purposes, safety standards and rules concerning nondiscrimination, and consumer protection. Conditioned by the old ways of beating the old system, more than a few managers attempt to beat the new one through corruption and tax evasion.

Multinational firms expanding in the emerging democracies have been learning about their management training needs, unique in that simply applying established Western guidelines to such training is inappropriate. Business learning in transition economies must continue to focus on core business issues such as marketing, strategic planning, international business, and financial analysis. And it must emphasize both knowledge and behavioral change.

Marketing in Emerging Democracies

The speed and outcome of economic transformation has varied by country, based on each nation's popular aspirations, leadership, and endowments, and on its relationships with the global market. With marketing's ability to adapt to its environment, existing social structures and expectations in former centrally planned economies may create new marketing concepts or new marketing applications that blend the old with the new. For example, the spirit of collectivism may give unexpected rise to a new blend of individual social responsibility.

A continuing challenge for the expansion of international marketing is overcoming the lack of information about end users. Marketing research and data collection will continue to mature, but at their own pace. There has been a temptation to simply transplant what works in the West and dump it in the emerging democracies markets. But western nations have traditionally placed the individual consumer on a pedestal, which contrasts markedly with socialist economies, where the group and society were of key concern among people.

Finally, the new trade globalist should ask if the West in general and the United States in particular should transfer traditional western capitalistic methods and cultures anywhere anymore without mitigating their worst abuses of excessive consumption, environmental disregard, wealth-based social Darwinism, and the like. Today, even as newly emerging democracies are bringing freedom to and displaying more concern about the individual, the traditional industrialized nations are discovering the pressing importance of issues such as global warming and pollution and are urging more attention to societal priorities.

Rather than encouraging a simple replication of a consumption society anywhere in the world, it may be wiser to concentrate on improved standards of living while also passing on Western lessons about consumption-driven policies learned the hard way. The marketer can, for example, explore ways to reduce packaging and increase the environmental friendliness of products without waiting for emerging societies to grow concerned about such issues.

NOTES

1. Robert L. Kohls, *Survival Kit for Overseas Living* (Chicago: Intercultural Press, 1979), 3.
2. For the "global customer" thinking of two leading strategists see, Ernest Dichter, "The World Consumer," *Harvard Business Review* 40 (July–August 1962): 113–122; and Kenichi Ohmae, *Triad Power—The Coming Shape of Global Competition* (New York: The Free Press, 1985), 22–27.
3. James H. Sood and Patrick Adams, "Model of Management Learning Styles as a Predictor of Export Behavior and Performance," *Journal of Business Research* 12 (June 1984): 169–182.
4. Jagdish N. Sheth and S. Prakash Sethi, "A Theory of Cross-Cultural Buying Behavior," in *Consumer and Industrial Buying Behavior*, eds. Arch G. Woodside, Jagdish N. Sheth, and Peter D. Bennett (New York: Elsevier North-Holland, 1977), 369–386.

5. Geert Hofstede, Culture's Consequences: International Differences in Work-Related Values (Beverly Hills, CA: Sage Publications, 1984).
6. Geert Hofstede and Michael H. Bond, "The Confucius Connection: From Cultural Roots to Economic Growth," *Organizational Dynamics* 16 (Spring 1988): 4–21.
7. Sudhir H. Kale, "Grouping Euroconsumers: A Culture-Based Clustering Approach," *Journal of International Marketing* 3 (no. 3, 1995): 35–48.
8. Jan-Benedict Steenkamp and Frenkel ter Hofstede, "A Cross-National Investigation into the Individual and National Cultural Antecedents of Consumer Innovativeness," *Journal of Marketing* 63 (April 1999): 55–69.
9. Sudhir H. Kale, "Culture-Specific Marketing Communications: An Analytical Approach," *International Marketing Review* 8, no. 2 (1991): 18–30.
10. Hong Cheng and John C. Schweitzer, "Cultural Values Reflected in Chinese and U.S. Television Commercials," *Journal of Advertising Research* 36 (May/June 1996): 27–45.
11. Sudhir H. Kale, "Distribution Channel Relationships in Diverse Cultures," *International Marketing Review* 8, no. 3 (1991): 31–45.
12. "Exploring Differences in Japan, U.S. Culture," *Advertising Age International,* September 18, 1995, I-8.
13. James A. Lee, "Cultural Analysis in Overseas Operations," *Harvard Business Review* 44 (March–April 1966): 106–114.
14. Peter D. Fitzpatrick and Alan S. Zimmerman, *Essentials of Export Marketing* (New York: American Management Organization, 1985), 16.
15. "Expansion Abroad: The New Direction for European Firms," *International Management* 41 (November 1986): 20–26.
16. W. Chan Kim and R. A. Mauborgne, "Cross-Cultural Strategies," *Journal of Business Strategy* 7 (Spring 1987): 28–37.
17. "The Loneliness of the Hyundai Manager," *Business Week,* August 19, 1996, 12E4–6.
18. "Special Interest Group Operations," available at www.samsung.com; "Sensitivity Kick," *The Wall Street Journal,* December 30, 1996, 1, 4.
19. Simcha Ronen, "Training the International Assignee," in *Training and Career Development,* ed. I. Goldstein (San Francisco: Jossey-Bass, 1989), 426–440.
20. C.K. Prahalad and Stuart L. Hart, "The Fortune at the Bottom of the Pyramid," *Strategy and Business,* First Quarter 2002, 35–47.
21. John A. Quelch, "Does Globalization Have Staying Power?" *Marketing Management* 11 (March/April 2002), 18–23.

5

Trade, Politics, and Law

On the international front, success is often a matter of balanced interests.

The international trade environment is changing rapidly with, among other events, market consolidations in Europe, growing supranational agencies such as the WTO, and new information media such as the Internet. There is also the disproportionate influence of the United States, the sole superpower, on economics, diplomacy, and military might. It shouldn't be surprising that international trade law and regulation—the product of narrowly constructed court rulings, political backroom deals, diplomatic wrangling, zealous bureaucratic enforcement, and vocal public opinion in scores of sovereign jurisdictions—can at times bewilder even the seasoned trade globalist. Just look inside the food pantry.

To declare most products' countries of origin, importers in the United States must evaluate their products under two rulings. First, imports must adhere to the Gibson-Thomson ruling of 1940, which states that a product must be marked as originating in the country in which it has undergone a "substantial transformation." Thus, the labeling will communicate to consumers where the product was finished rather than where its materials originated. However, companies must also consider rules of the North American Free Trade Agreement (NAFTA) of 1992, which require that a product be marked as originating from the country in which it was converted from one product classification to another. Thus, U.S. marketers must mark products coming from NAFTA and non-NAFTA countries differently.

While the "substantial transformation" ruling seems to make logical sense, it may yield misleading labeling. A "substantial transformation" may be different depending on who is making the judgment; that is, various members of the supply chain may disagree regarding the place of the product's transformation. For example, Florida orange juice, if blended with 1 percent Brazilian orange juice, must be labeled "Made in Brazil." Similarly, the U.S. company Bestfoods had to label its Skippy brand peanut butter "Made in Canada," even though it was made in Arkansas with ingredients that were 90 percent from the United States. In an appeal to the U.S. Court of International Trade, Bestfoods successfully argued that since no more than 7 percent of the value of the product depended on Canadian ingredients, Skippy warranted a "Made in the U.S.A." label. Yet the rules remain open to exploitation. Mexican wine blended with a small percentage of wine from France could be marketed as French wine.[1]

TRADE INSTITUTIONS

It all began simply enough. Foreign trade and the marketing that inevitably is part of it are as old as civilization itself. The Etruscans, Phoenicians, Egyptians, Chinese, Spaniards, English, and Portuguese—to name but a few—harnessed trade as an instrument of wealth creation, social stability, and economic hegemony. In the time of the Roman Empire, the *Pax Romana,* the Roman Peace, brought law, common coinage, infrastructure, and relative security to the world of commerce. As a result, economic well-being within the empire rose sharply compared to the outside and other societies sought to share the benefits of belonging. To join, they agreed to pay tribute and taxes. Traders, more than marching Roman legions, expanded the Roman Empire. But when Rome's social decay weakened its ability to maintain the benefits of empire affiliation, former allies no longer saw any advantage in associating with Rome. They willingly cooperated with the tribal raiders at the Roman gates.

In medieval Europe, trade security needs prompted peasants to band together and seek protection guaranteed by feudal lords. But in time, foreign trade led by Italy, the German Hanse cities, and the Low Countries fostered marketplaces where merchants could trade goods freely rather than collectively. Capitalism, hand in hand with the Enlightenment and the ennoblement of the individual citizen, forever changed human existence. Today, world trade, once reserved for the conversations of business leaders, trade lawyers, academics, and politicians, has become a topic of debate for the general public. Corporations yearn for opportunities to expand into foreign markets and developing nations see trade as a way out of poverty. But workers in industrial nations fear international labor competition and social activists abhor environmentally unfriendly practices and questionable labor conditions.

The WTO

The World Trade Organization (WTO), formed in 1995, succeeded the General Agreement on Tariffs and Trade (GATT), which began as a set of rules for nondiscrimination, transparent procedures, and settlement of international trade disputes. One of the most important tools is the "most-favored nation" (MFN) clause, which calls for each member country to grant every other member country the most favorable treatment it accords to any other country with respect to imports and exports. In effect, MFN is the equal opportunity clause of international trade.

The WTO has greatly broadened the scope of international trade agreements. International rules now address some services and agricultural trade issues and world trade authorities have streamlined regulatory decision-making processes. However, nations have dramatically increased their use of so-called "safeguard" provisions that allow countries to retaliate immediately against sudden import surges without having to wait for lengthy WTO dispute resolutions.[2] In the spring of 2002, for example, both the United States and the European Union cited safeguards as justification for steel tariffs and threatened counter-tariffs. Overall, it bears remembering that while the WTO is not a forum for any individual firm, it sets the framework within which companies have to operate.

International Monetary Fund

The International Monetary Fund (IMF) was designed to provide stability for the international monetary framework. The result of using the U.S. dollar as the main IMF currency was a glut of dollar supplies during the 1960s, forcing floating exchange rates in 1971. However, even though this changed IMF's mission, the organization has clearly continued to help provide international liquidity to facilitate international trade. Substantial debts by less-developed countries (LDCs) and formerly socialist nations struggling to reform their economies have put the IMF under severe pressure in recent years. In addition, major currency fluctuations among old customers have stretched the resources of the IMF. The conditions under which the IMF provides its financing are often seen as brash and disruptive but are typical for economists who want to have a nation's economy perform according to theory. Practical constraints may well force the IMF to change its approach to lending.

World Bank

The World Bank was initially formed to aid countries suffering from the destruction of war. After completing this process most successfully, the bank has made major efforts to assist fledgling economies to participate in a modern economic trade framework. The bank works closely with the IMF to help resolve the debt problems of the developing world and former members of the Eastern bloc. A major debate, however, surrounds the effectiveness of the bank's expenditures. It appears that corrupt regimes squandered many of the funds and that many large projects turned into white elephants producing little economic progress. In Haiti, for example, 41 World Bank projects in the last half century involved more than $1 billion in loans. But more than 80 percent of Haiti's population still lives in poverty, up from 65 percent in 1987. Government corruption and leadership chaos contributed much to that failure, but World Bank/IMF prescriptions such as cutting tariffs and growing export crops such as coffee have allowed imports to displace food crops like sugar cane and rice,[3] helping to accelerate economic deterioration.

The World Bank is now trying to reorient its outlook, focusing more on institution building, the elimination of corruption, and the development of human capital through investments in education and health. A clearer differentiation of its role as an organization working on the micro level of specific projects within an economy— as opposed to the macro level of the IMF—is also likely to redirect the work of the bank. It has become clear that there is no single solution for bringing countries out of poverty.

Regional Institutions

The European Union provides completely free movement of capital, services, and people across national borders. Other regions have formed similar market agreements: the North American Free Trade Agreement (NAFTA), ASEAN in Asia, the Mercosur in Latin America, and the Gulf Cooperation Council (GCC). As noted in Chapter 2, countries formed these unions for different reasons.

Simultaneously, the private sector has begun to develop international trade institutions of its own. Particularly when governments are not quick enough to address major issues of concern to global marketers, business has taken the lead by providing a forum for the discussion of such issues. One example is the Transatlantic Business Dialogue, which is a nongovernmental organization (NGO) composed of business leaders from Europe and the United States. Recognizing the inefficiency of competing and often contradictory standards and lengthy testing procedures, this group is working to simplify global marketing through mutual agreements on an industry basis. Another is Transparency International, a nonprofit organization ranking countries based on their internal degree of corruption and bribery.

Nations have come to recognize that trade activities are of substantial importance to their economic well-being. Over the long term of maintaining a sustainable economic balance, the successful export activities of a nation are the key to affording imports that improve citizen well being. Today, virtually all nations wish to take part in international trade and make efforts to participate in it as much as possible.

TRADE AND THE UNITED STATES

Over the years, the U.S. share of international trade has eroded substantially. Not that U.S. exports have actually dropped. Over time, other trade partners entered the picture and aggressively obtained a larger world market share. U.S. exports have not kept pace with total world export growth, however, nor with the growth in U.S. imports. U.S. trade deficits—the value of imports less exports—grew from $29.5 billion in 1991 to an estimated $458 billion in 2002. That is the largest trade deficit in U.S. history.[4]

The United States economy is not as internationally oriented as are those of other nations, however, explaining one cause of huge trade deficits. U.S. exports as a share of the GDP are about 11 percent, a fraction of the international trade performance of many other nations such as Germany (20%) or the Netherlands (more than 50%). U.S. per capita exports are just a third of Germany's, for example, and less than one-fifth of the Netherlands'. Interpret those numbers with caution, however. They do not reflect the large size of the U.S. internal market.

America's international trade inexperience can be costly, as illustrated by classic blunders such as U.S.-Japanese trade negotiations in the wood products industry. The United States had negotiated with the Japanese government for more than a decade to allow more U.S. solid wood products to enter the Japanese market, particularly in the construction field. High-level meetings, ongoing negotiations, government financial support, and industry demonstration projects eventually achieved that goal. The Japanese changed building codes that had prohibited construction of multistory wooden buildings and made product certification less costly and complicated. Certification authority, previously the exclusive purview of the Ministry of Con-struction, was delegated to foreign testing organizations such as the American Plywood Association. Japan reduced its tariffs on processed solid wood products, and the U.S. Foreign Agricultural Service spent close to $18 million to promote U.S. wood product sales in Japan.

But Canada walked off with Japanese wood product market leader-ship. Its marketers were much quicker than U.S. companies to take advantage of the changes, obtain certification, and market aggres-sively. They proved that they understood the different specifications and grades of wood products used in Japan, they paid attention to product quality and appearance, and they demonstrated more com-mitment to market and after-sales service requirements. For instance, the Canadians published service manuals in Japanese. U.S. firms meanwhile provided information largely in English, tended to be less reliable as long-range suppliers, showed little interest in after-sales service, and did not meet Japanese quality and appearance standards.

U.S. job growth attributable to the wood product trade negotia-tions was marginal. American companies disregarded Japanese con-struction needs and instead tried to sell what they produced for the U.S. market. Relatively few Japanese buildings used construction and dimensions similar to American designs, meaning that U.S. compa-nies focused all of their energies on increasing their penetration of the smallest part of the market, and did so with only limited success. Even U.S. firms that did attempt to adjust their products to Japanese market requirements encountered major problems providing the longer equipment financing terms and product quality that Japan-ese buyers expected.

Conditions are changing. Managers' commitment to interna-tional trade have grown more intense. Many newly founded firms are global from the very beginning, giving rise to the term "born global." Electronic commerce has made it more feasible to reach to the global business community. The U.S. Department of State offers training in business-government relations to new ambassadors and now instructs them to pay close attention to the needs of the U.S. businesses operating overseas. In effect, recognition of international markets as a source of profit and growth for both customers and sup-pliers is increasing rapidly. The need for international marketing ex-pertise can be expected to continue to rise substantially in the early twenty-first century.

Policy Responses

In light of persistent trade deficits, growing foreign direct in-vestment, and the tendency by some firms and industries to seek legislative redress for failures in the marketplace, the U.S. Congress in the past two decades has been quite willing to provide the president with more powers to *restrict* trade. Many resolutions have also been passed and legislation enacted asking the president to pay closer attention to trade, but for reasons of protection rather than export encouragement.

Restricting Imports. The United States is still one of the strongest advocates of free trade. This advocacy is shared, at least officially, by nations around the world, yet national authorities including the U.S. government have become very creative in designing and implementing trade barriers. Examples are:

- Import policies such as tariffs and other import charges, quantitative restrictions, import licensing, quota systems, and customs barriers. Antidumping laws, for example, prohibit below-cost sales of imported products.
- Standards, testing, labeling, and certification.
- Government procurement rules such as "buy national" policies and closed bidding.
- Export subsidies such as export financing on preferential terms and agricultural export subsidies that displace exports in third-country markets.
- Lack of intellectual property protection: for example, inadequate patent, copyright, and trademark regimes.
- Services barriers such as limits on the range of financial services offered by foreign financial institutions, regulation of international data flows.
- Investment barriers including limitations on foreign equity participation and on access to foreign government-funded research and development programs; local content and export performance requirements, and restrictions on transferring earnings and capital.
- Anticompetitive practices with trade effects, such as anticompetitive activities of both state-owned and private firms that apply to services or to goods.
- Trade restrictions affecting electronic commerce such as burdensome and discriminatory regulations and standards and discriminatory taxation.[5]

One major method of restricting trade is promulgating nontariff barriers. Typically, these obstacles are much subtler than tariffs. Compared with tariffs or even subsidies—which are visible and at least force products to compete for market acceptance on dimensions other than price—some nontariff barriers are much more difficult to detect, prove, and quantify. Most famous in this regard are probably the measures implemented by France. To stop or at least reduce the importation of foreign video recorders, France ruled in the 1980s that all of them had to be sent through the customs station at Poitiers. This customs-house is located in the middle of the country, was woefully understaffed, and was open only a few days each week. In addition, the few customs agents at Poitiers insisted on opening each package separately in order to inspect the merchandise. Within a few weeks, imports of video recorders in France came to a halt. The French government, however, was able to point to the fact that officially all measures were in full compliance with international agreements.

The primary results of trade restrictions are actions that are contrary to the interests of the world and its citizens. Restrictions preserve industries healthy or otherwise, sometimes at great peril to the world trade framework and at substantial cost to consumers. But because the direct costs of these actions are mostly hidden, they do not provoke much public complaint when spread out over a multitude of individuals.

A widely quoted estimate contends that each year the total cost of U.S.-imposed import restraints to U.S. consumers alone is $70 billion. For example, abolishing import barriers in the apparel industry would let U.S. consumers save more than $21 billion. Consumer gains would be $3.2 billion for textiles, $1.3 billion for sugar, $1.2 billion for dairy products, and $54 million for peanuts.[6] And, said the U.S. Treasury Department, cutting global trade barriers by one-third would be equivalent to a tax cut of $2,500 per year for the typical U.S. family.[7] In Europe, barriers that save a single job increase costs by about 220,000 per year, 10 times the average European worker's wage.[8]

Promoting Exports. Many countries provide export assistance to their domestic companies to earn foreign currency, encourage domestic employment, and increase domestic economic activity. Government support typically subsidizes profit or reduces risk. There are instances where such intervention may be justified. Government support can be appropriate if it annuls unfair foreign practices, increases market transparency and therefore contributes to the better functioning of markets, or helps overcome—in the interest of long-term national competitiveness—the short-term orientation of corporate managers.

In the United States, a variety of agencies have formed the Trade Promotion Coordination Committee (TPCC) in order to continue to improve services to U.S. exporters. A listing of these agencies together with their Web sites appears in Exhibit 5.1 so that readers can

Exhibit 5.1: Members of the U.S. Trade Promotion Coordination Committee (TPCC)

Information on both individual TPCC agency programs and the National Export Strategy is available on the Internet. Information about individual TPCC agency programs can be obtained by using the following Internet addresses:

- National Trade Data Bank **(http://www.stat-usa.gov)**
- Agency for International Development **(http://www.usaid.gov)**
- Council of Economic Advisers **(http://www.whitehouse.gov)**
- Department of Agriculture **(http://www.fas.usda.gov)**
- Department of Commerce **(http://www.ita.doc.gov)**
- Department of Defense **(http://www.dtic.dla.mil)**
- Department of Energy **(http://www.osti.gov)**
- Department of Interior **(http://www.doi.gov)**
- Department of Labor **(http://www.dol.gov)**
- Department of State **(http://www.state.gov)**
- Department of Transportation **(http://www.dot.gov)**
- Department of the Treasury **(http://www.ustreas.gov)**
- Environmental Protection Agency **(http://www.epa.gov)**
- Export-Import Bank of the United States **(http://www.exim.gov)**
- National Economic Council **(http://www.whitehouse.gov)**
- Office of the U.S. Trade Representative **(http://www.ustr.gov)**
- Office of Management and Budget
  (http://www.whitehouse.gov/omb/circulars)
- Overseas Private Investment Corporation **(http://www.opic.gov)**
- Small Business Administration **(http://www.sba.gov)**
- U.S. Trade and Development Agency **(http://www.tda.gov)**

SOURCES: *Offices of the U.S. Government Trade Promotion Coordination Committee*, International Trade Center, at www.itcdc.com.

obtain the most up-to-date information about trade policy changes and export assistance.

The U.S. government provides an impressive array of data on foreign trade and marketing developments, as detailed in Chapter 6. (Other U.S. government trade assistance programs related to specific marketing tactics are cited in the various chapters of Part Three of this book.)

State and local government assistance can be extremely useful. For example, two California trade promotion organizations, the Bay

Area Economic Forum and the Los Angeles Area Chamber of Commerce, manage the www.tradeport.com Web site. TradePort is designed to be an easy-to-use tool offering one place to go for comprehensive trade information, trade leads, and company databases. The site includes a very useful set of guidelines for the beginning exporter, the Export Readiness Assessment (www.tradeport.org/ts/trade_expert/getting/assess/index.html), which we discuss in Chapter 6.

U.S. export support activities still lag far behind the private-sector supports provided by other major industrial nations, however. More important, the largest portion of total U.S. export promotion expenditures—almost 50 percent—continues to go to agriculture. Relatively few funds support export counseling, market research, and customer relations management technology.

TRADE, INVESTMENT, AND POLITICS

No manager can afford to ignore the policies and regulations of the country from which he or she conducts international marketing transactions. Government policies and legal systems will affect a company's international operations. Even though many laws and regulations may not be designed specifically to address international marketing issues, they can have a major impact on a firm's opportunities abroad. Minimum wage legislation, for example, affects the international competitiveness of a firm using labor-intensive production processes. The cost of domestic safety and environmental regulations may significantly affect the pricing policies of firms in their international marketing efforts.

Other legal and regulatory measures, however, are clearly aimed at international marketing activities. Some may be designed to help firms in their international efforts, such as by regulating gray market goods (see Chapter 12). The lack of enforcement of others may hurt the international marketer. For example, many firms are quite concerned about the lack of safeguards for intellectual property rights in China. Not only may product counterfeiting result in inferior goods and damage to the reputation of a company, it also reduces the chances that an innovative firm can recoup its investment in research and development and create new products.

Powerful Tools

Apart from regulatory involvement, the political environment in most countries tends to provide general support for the international marketing efforts of the country's firms. For example, a government may work to reduce trade barriers or to increase trade opportunities through bilateral and multilateral negotiations. Often, however, politics must balance trade considerations with competing interests such as foreign policy and national security. Then nations employ four primary tools to control trade: embargoes or trade sanctions, import controls, export controls, and regulation of their constituent firms' international marketing behavior.

Embargoes and Sanctions. Trade sanctions and embargoes tend to be politically rather than economically driven and are used frequently and successfully in times of war or to address specific grievances. The international marketing manager is often caught in this political web and loses business as a result. Frequently, firms try to anticipate sanctions based on their evaluations of the international political climate. Nevertheless, even when substantial precautions are taken, firms may still suffer substantial losses due to contract cancellations.

One key concern with sanctions, however, is that governments often think they are cost-free because they do not affect government budgets. But sanctions often impose significant loss of business to the private sector. One estimate claims that the economic sanctions held in place by the United States annually costs the country some $20 billion in lost exports.[9]

Import Controls. Import restrictions such as those discussed earlier in this chapter appear worldwide. Imports of particular products can be controlled through mechanisms such as tariffs, voluntary restraint agreements, or quota systems that result in quantitative import restraints. On occasion, countries cut off imports of certain products entirely in order to stimulate the development of a domestic industry.

For the marketer with international operations, such restrictions may mean that the most efficient sources of supply are not available because government regulations restrict importation from those sources. The result is either second-best products or higher costs for restricted supplies. This in turn means that the customer receives inferior service and often has to pay significantly higher prices and that the firm is less competitive when trying to market its products internationally.

Export Controls. Many nations have export control systems designed to deny or at least delay the sale of strategically important goods to adversaries or areas of conflict. Most nations make export controls the exception, rather than the rule, with exports considered to be independent of foreign policy. The United States, however, differs substantially from this perspective in that exports are considered to be a privilege rather than a right, and exporting is seen as a tool of foreign policy.

U.S. laws control all exports of goods, services, and ideas. It is important to note here that an export of goods occurs whenever goods are physically transferred from the United States. Services and ideas, however, are deemed exported whenever transferred to a foreign national, regardless of location. Permitting a foreign national from a controlled country to have access to a highly sensitive computer program in the United States is considered an export.

In order for any export from the United States to take place, the exporter needs to obtain an export license. The administering government agencies, in consultation with other government departments, have drawn up a list of commodities whose export is considered particularly sensitive. In addition, a list of countries differentiates nations according to their political relationship with the United States. Finally, a list of individual firms that are considered to be unreliable trading partners because of past trade-diversion activities exists for each country.

The process may sound overly cumbersome, but it does not apply in equal measure to all exports. Most international business activities can be carried out under NLR conditions, which stands for "no license required." NLR provides blanket permission to export. Products can be freely shipped to most trading partners provided that neither the end user nor the end use involved are considered sensitive. If exports incorporate high-level technologies sold to countries not friendly to the United States, the exporter must then obtain an export license, which consists of written authorization to send a product abroad.

Even though many commentators heralded the end of the Cold War as an opportunity for U.S. policymakers to elevate economic competitiveness to the top of their priority list, the State Department, Congress, and the Pentagon often remained preoccupied with fears of China, rogue states, and other threats of nuclear proliferation. Now that international terrorism has become a realized threat on American shores, regulations are not likely to ease soon. Security threats might even be worse, many say, because the world is no longer neatly divided into two powerful political camps keeping their regional clients more or less in check. The end of the Cold War also weakened the mutual bonds among allies. No longer compelled to jointly oppose the Soviets, democracies are free to pursue their own strategic interests.

Additionally, the increased foreign availability of high-technology products renders unilateral export controls less effective. If a nation does restrict the exports of widely available products, it imposes a major competitive burden on its firms. But how much of what technology does a foreign buyer need to become "dangerous" to the exporting nation? Answers are not clear. For example, nuclear weapons and sophisticated delivery systems were developed by the United States and the Soviet Union long before supercomputers became available, so rogue states might not need such machines to develop weapons of mass destruction. The high-pitched debate over military application of commercial technology exports continues, and the U.S. government continues to grapple with the conflict between its economic and security interests.

Regulated Marketing Behavior. Using the fourth tool of trade control, countries may implement special laws and regulations to ensure that the international business behavior of their exporting and multinational firms is conducted within the legal, moral, and ethical boundaries considered appropriate. The definition of appropriateness may vary from country to country and from government to government.

Marketing regulations include boycotts, antitrust measures, and anticorruption laws. Implementing them can be messy, however. For example, Arab nations or customers often require their suppliers not to deal with Israel. The U.S. government in turn adopted laws to prevent U.S. firms from complying with the Arab boycott. These laws include a provision to deny foreign income tax benefits to companies that comply with the boycott and also require notification of the U.S. government in case any boycott requests are received. U.S. firms that comply with the boycott are subject to heavy fines and curtailed export privileges. Boycotts put firms in a difficult position. Caught in a web of governmental activity, they may be forced to lose business, pay fines, or perhaps abandon operations in a country altogether.

Antitrust laws can apply to the international operations of firms as well as to domestic business. In the European Union, for example, the European Commission watches closely when any firm buys an overseas company, engages in a joint venture with a foreign firm, or makes an agreement with a competing firm. In a 2001 high-profile dustup, EU commissioners denied American-based General Electric permission to acquire American-based Honeywell—a deal already okayed by U.S. regulators—because of its potential impact on European customers and competition.

Given the increased globalization of national economies, it is time to rethink current approaches and ask whether any country can still afford to define the competition only in a domestic sense or whether competition has to be seen on a worldwide scale. Similarly, one can wonder whether countries will accept the infringement on their sovereignty that results from the extraterritorial application of any nation's law abroad.

Anticorruption regulation, in which the United States has taken a lead, outlaws the bribes that are standard procedure for dealing with government officials in some countries. Exercising what it deemed ethical and moral leadership, the U.S. Congress passed the Foreign Corrupt Practices Act in 1977, making it a crime for U.S. firms to bribe a foreign official for business purposes.

International marketers encounter the problem of ethics versus practical needs, leavened by the amounts of value exchanged. For example, it may be difficult to draw the line between providing a generous tip and paying a bribe in order to speed up a business transaction. On the other hand, bribes may open the way for shoddy performance and loose moral standards among managers and employees and may result in a spreading of generally unethical business practices. Unrestricted bribery could result in managers worrying more about how best to bribe rather than how best to produce and market products.

Key distinctions are important to the international manager, who must recognize reasonable ways of doing business internationally, including the difference between compliance with foreign expectations and outright bribery and corruption. The 1988 Trade Act clarifies the applicability of the Foreign Corrupt Practices legislation. It explains when a manager is expected to know about violations of the act and draws a distinction between facilitating routine governmental actions and influencing governmental policy decisions. Routine actions concern issues such as obtaining permits and licenses, processing governmental papers such as visas and work orders, providing mail and phone service, and loading and unloading cargo. Policy decisions refer mainly to situations in which obtaining or retaining contracts is at stake. The Trade Act does not prohibit facilitating routine actions, but illegally influencing policy decisions can result in severe fines and other penalties.

General standards of behavior are a critical issue as well for international marketers. Public concerns such as global warming, pollution, labor conditions and wages, political influence, and illegal and immoral executive acts differ in importance and details country by country. What might be frowned on or even illegal in one nation may be customary or at least acceptable in others.

For example, cutting down the Brazilian rain forest may be acceptable to the government of Brazil, but scientists, concerned consumers, and environmentalists may object vehemently because of the effect of global warming and other climatic changes. Mexico may permit the use of low safety standards for workers, but the buyers of Mexican products may object to the resulting dangers. In the area of moral behavior, firms are increasingly not just subject to government rules, but are also held accountable by the public at large. The resulting public scorn, consumer boycotts, and investor scrutiny might be more costly than correcting or avoiding the problems in the first place.

The leaders of international firms should assert leadership in implementing change. Not everything that is legally possible should be exploited. Although companies need to return a profit on their investments, these issues must be seen in the context of time. By acting on existing, leading-edge knowledge and standards, firms will be able to benefit in the long term by earning consumer goodwill and avoiding later recriminations.

Political Risk

One always hopes that host countries have stable and friendly governments, but those are not always easy to find. Managers must therefore continually monitor conditions abroad to determine the potential for political change that could adversely affect corporate operations.

Every nation creates some degree of political risk, but the range of risks varies widely from country to country. In general, political risk is lowest in countries that have a history of stability and consistency. In a number of countries, however, apparent consistency and stability on the surface have been quickly swept away by major popular movements that drew on the frustrations of the population.

Three major types of political risk can be encountered:

- Ownership risk, which exposes property and life;
- Operating risk, which refers to interference with the ongoing operations of a firm; and
- Transfer risk, which is mainly encountered when attempts are made to shift funds between countries.

Political risk can be the result of government action, but it can also be outside the control of government. The type of actions and their effects are classified in Exhibit 5.2.

Exhibit 5.2: Exposure to Political Risk

Loss May Be the Result of:

Contingencies May Include:	The actions of legitimate government authorities	Events caused by factors outside the control of government
The involuntary loss of control over specific assets without adequate compensation	• Total or partial expropriation • Forced divestiture • Confiscation • Cancellation or unfair calling of performance bonds	• War • Revolution • Terrorism • Strikes • Extortion
A reduction in the value of a stream of benefits expected from the foreign-controlled affiliate	• Nonapplicability of "national treatment" • Restriction in access to financial, labor, or material markets • Controls on prices, outputs, or activities • Currency and remittance restrictions • Value-added and export performance requirements	• Nationalistic buyers or suppliers • Threats and disruption to operations by hostile groups • Externally induced financial constraints • Externally imposed limits on imports or exports

SOURCE: José de la Torre and David H. Neckar, "Forecasting Political Risks for International Operations," in H. Vernon-Wortzel and L. Wortzel, *Global Strategic Management: The Essentials.* 2nd ed. (New York: John Wiley and Sons, 1990), 195. Copyright © 1990 John Wiley and Sons. Reprinted by permission of John Wiley and Sons, Inc.

Risks of Violence. A major political risk in many countries involves conflict and violent change. If conflict breaks out, violence directed toward the firm's property and employees is a strong possibility. Guerrilla warfare, civil disturbances, and terrorism often take an anti-industry bent, making companies' property and their employees potential targets. International terrorists have frequently targeted U.S. corporate facilities, operations, personnel abroad, and even locally owned franchises of multinational firms. Terrorists design their acts to be rich in symbolism, hence the September 11, 2001 attacks on the Pentagon and that monument to globalism, the World Trade Center. Overseas, multinational corporation offices are prominent symbols of U.S. power without the elaborate security and restricted access of U.S. diplomatic offices and military bases. As a result, U.S. businesses are the primary target of terrorists worldwide and remain the most vulnerable targets in the future.[10]

Revolutions and Coups. Coups d'état can result in drastic changes in government. The new government may attack foreign multinational corporations as remnants of the Western-dominated colonial past, as has happened in Cuba, Nicaragua, and Iran. Even if such changes do not represent an immediate physical threat to firms and their employees, they can have drastic effects. The past few decades have seen such coups around the globe seriously impede the conduct of international marketing.

Government Policy Changes. Less dramatic but still worrisome are changes in government policies caused not by changes in the government itself but by pressure from nationalist or religious factions or widespread anti-foreign feeling. Policy changes rooted in nationalist and anti-foreign sentiment can lead to asset confiscation and expropriation. Some industries are more vulnerable than others to such drastic policies because of their importance to the host country economy and their inability to shift operations elsewhere. For these reasons, sectors such as mining, energy, public utilities, and banking have been particular targets of such government actions.

Expropriation is the seizure of assets by a government with payment of compensation to the owners. Expropriation has appealed to some countries because it demonstrates nationalism and immediately transfers a certain amount of wealth and resources from foreign companies to the government. It does exact costs from the country, however, to the extent that it makes other firms hesitant to invest future funds.

Expropriation does provide compensation to the former owners. However, compensation negotiations are often protracted and result in settlements that are frequently unsatisfactory to the owners. For example, governments may offer compensation in the form of local, nontransferable currency or may base the compensation on the book value of the firm. Even though firms that lost assets to expropriation may deplore the low levels of payment obtained, they frequently accept them in the absence of better alternatives. Fortunately, expropriation as a policy tool has sharply decreased over time. Apparently, governments have recognized that the self-inflicted damage caused by expropriation exceeds the benefits.

Confiscation is similar to expropriation in that it results in a transfer of ownership from the foreign firm to the host country, but without compensation.

Domestication is another kind of government action that is subtler but nearly as damaging a political risk as confiscation and expropriation. The goal is the same, to gain control over foreign investment, but the method is different. Through domestication, the government demands partial transfer of ownership and management responsibility and imposes regulations to ensure that a large share of the product is locally produced and a larger share of the profit is retained in the country.

Domestication can have profound effects on the international marketer for a number of reasons. First, if a firm is forced to hire nationals as managers, poor cooperation and communication can result. If the domestication is imposed within a very short time span, corporate operations overseas may have to be headed by poorly trained and inexperienced local managers.

Second, domestic content requirements may force a firm to purchase supplies and parts locally, which can result in increased costs, inefficiency, and lower-quality products, thus further damaging a firm's interest.

Third, export requirements imposed on companies may also create havoc for the international distribution plan of a corporation and force it to change or even shut down operations in other countries.

Fourth, domestication will usually shield the industry within a country from foreign competition. As a result, inefficiencies will be allowed to grow due to a lack of market discipline. In the long run, this will affect the international competitiveness of an operation abroad, and it may become a major problem when, years later, the government considers ending domestication requirements.

Most businesses operating abroad face a number of other risks that are less dangerous, but probably more common, than the drastic ones already described. Governments that face a shortage of foreign currency sometimes will impose *exchange controls* on the movement of capital in and out of the country. Such controls may make it difficult for a firm to remove its profits or investments from the country. Sometimes, exchange controls are also levied selectively against certain products or companies in an effort to reduce the importation of goods that are considered to be a luxury or unnecessary. Prolonged negotiations with government officials may be necessary in order to reach a compromise on what constitutes a "valid" expenditure of foreign currency resources. Because the goals of government officials and corporate managers may often be quite different, such compromises, even when they can be reached, may result in substantial damage to the international marketing operations of a firm.

Countries may also raise the rates of *taxation* applied to foreign investors in an effort to control firms and their capital. They might on occasion apply different or stricter tax rules to foreign investments. The rationale often is the seeming underpayment of taxes by such investors, comparing their payments to those of long-established domestic competitors. Overlooked is the fact that new investors in foreign lands tend to "overinvest" by initially buying more land, space, and equipment than is needed immediately and by spending heavily so that facilities are state-of-the-art. This desire to accommodate future growth and to be highly competitive in the early investment stages will, in turn, produce lower profits and lower tax payments. Yet over time, these investment activities should be very successful, competitive, and job-creating. Selective tax increases for foreign investors may result in much-needed revenue for the coffers of the country, but they can severely damage the operations of the foreign investors. This damage, in turn, may result in decreased income for the country in the long run.

In many countries, domestic political pressures can force governments to impose controls on imported products or services, particularly in sectors considered highly sensitive from a political perspective, such as food or healthcare. If a foreign firm is involved in these areas, it is a vulnerable target of price controls because the government can play on its people's nationalistic tendencies to enforce the controls. Particularly in countries that suffer from high inflation and frequent devaluations, the international marketer may then be forced to choose between shutting down the operation or continuing production at a loss in the hope of recouping that loss once the government chooses to loosen or remove its price restrictions. How a firm can adjust to price controls is discussed in greater detail in Chapter 11.

Managing Political Risk. Managers face political risk whenever they conduct business overseas, but there may be ways to reduce it. Obviously, if a new government dedicated to removing all foreign influences comes into power, a firm can do little. In less extreme cases, however, managers can take actions to reduce risk if they understand the root causes of the host country policies.

Most important is the ability to *blend in* through the accumulation and appreciation of factual information about a country's history, political background, and culture before making a long-term investment decision. Also, a high degree of sensitivity by a firm and its employees to country-specific approaches and concerns are important dimensions that help a firm to blend into the local landscape rather than standing out as a foreign object. Corporations can also protect against political risk by closely monitoring political developments. Increasingly, private-sector firms offer assistance in such monitoring activities, permitting the overseas corporation to discover potential trouble spots as early as possible and react quickly to prevent major losses.

Adverse governmental actions are usually the result of a country's nationalism, a local desire for independence, and opposition to colonial remnants. If a country's citizens feel exploited by foreign firms, government officials are more likely to take action. To reduce the risk of government intervention, a firm needs to demonstrate that it is concerned with the country's society and that it considers itself an integral part of the country rather than simply an exploitative foreign corporation. Ways to do this include intensive local hiring and training practices, good pay, more charity, and more socially useful investment. In addition, a company can form joint ventures with local partners to demonstrate a willingness to share its benefits with nationals. Although such actions will not guarantee freedom from risk, they will certainly lessen the exposure.

Firms can also take out *insurance* to cover losses due to political risk. Most industrialized countries offer insurance programs for their firms doing business abroad, as discussed in Chapter 3.

Many governments encourage foreign investments, especially if they believe that the investment will produce economic and political benefits domestically. Some governments have opened up their economy to foreign investors, placing only minimal constraints on them, in the hope that such policies will lead to rapid economic development. Others have provided for substantial subsidization of new investment activities in the hope that investments will generate additional employment. The international marketer should pay close attention to the extent and forms of the *incentives* available from foreign governments. Although market forces must drive international marketing decisions, incentives can make the difference in an otherwise close call.

LEGAL CLIMATES

So far we have discussed laws reflecting changes in a country's political environment. Of course, every nation has a broader body of law affecting marketing, which the international manager must understand.

Cultural Contrasts

Laws reflect a society's ways of organizing its affairs, prescribing behavior, and sanctioning those who break the rules. Cultural fundamentals heavily influence how a society enacts laws and applies them in day-to-day life. Naturally, countries with different cultures tend to have different legal environments. Japan and the United States, for example, have substantially different cultural traditions. Differences in their approaches to law epitomize the divergent legal practices one can find around the globe. The United States has developed into an increasingly litigious society, in which institutions and individuals are quick to take a case to court. As a result, court battles are often protracted and costly, and simply the threat of a court case can reduce marketing opportunities. In contrast, Japan's legal tradition tends to minimize the role of the law and of lawyers. Some possible reasons include the relatively small number of courts and attorneys, the delays, the costs and the uncertainties associated with litigation, the limited doctrines of plaintiffs' standing and rights to bring class action suits, the tendency of judges to encourage out-of-court settlements, and the easy availability of arbitration and mediation for dispute resolution.

Some estimates suggest that the number of lawyers in the United States is as much as 48 times higher than in Japan, based on the fact that Japan has only about 12,500 fully licensed lawyers. However, comparisons can be misleading because officially registered lawyers in Japan perform a small fraction of the duties performed by American lawyers. After accounting for the additional roles of American lawyers, the number of "lawyers" in Japan appears to be approximately one-fifth that of the United States.[11]

But reasons for the differences run deeper. Social traditions play a major role in the American-Japanese contrast. How businesses in each culture handled similar disasters illustrates the point. When two jumbo jets crashed ten days apart in Dallas and in the mountains near Tokyo, Americans and Japanese shared a common bond of shock and grief. Soon, however, all parties in Japan—from the airline to the employers of victims—moved to put the tragedy behind them. In the United States, legal tremors were felt for years.

Lawyers hustled to the scene of the Delta Air Lines accident at the Dallas–Fort Worth airport and set up shop at an airport hotel. Proclaimed San Francisco attorney Melvin Belli, "I'm not an ambulance chaser—I get there before the ambulance." Within 72 hours, the first suit against Delta was filed. Insurance adjusters working for Delta quickly went to work as well.

Seven thousand miles away, Japan Air Lines president Yasumoto Takagi humbly bowed to families of the 520 victims and apologized "from the bottom of our hearts." He vowed to resign once the investigation was complete. JAL offered families about $2,000 each in condolence payments, then negotiated settlements reported to be worth between $166,000 and $450,000, depending on the age and earning power of each victim. Only one family sued.

Behind these differences lie standards of behavior and corporate responsibility that are worlds apart. "There is a general Japanese inclination to try to settle any disputes through negotiations between the parties before going to court," said Koichiro Fujikura, a Tokyo University law professor. Added Carl Green, a Washington, D.C., attorney and specialist on Japanese law: "There is an assumption of responsibility. In our American adversarial society, we don't admit responsibility. It would be admitting liability."

Japanese legal experts expected settlements to be as high as 500 million yen—about $2.1 million—apiece. Negotiations were prolonged. But with families believing that JAL was sincerely sorry, "their feelings were soothed," according to attorney Takeshi Odagi. For the family that did file a lawsuit, it took fifteen years for the appellate court to rule that the two children of a Japanese businessman on board the plane were entitled to claim compensation.

Japan's legal system encourages these traditions. "Lawyers don't descend in droves on accident scenes because they barely have enough time to handle the suits they have," explained John Haley, a law professor at the University of Washington who has studied and worked in Japan. "There are fewer judges per capita than there were in 1890," Haley added. Only 500 lawyers are admitted to the bar each year.[12]

Common versus Code Law

From an international business perspective the two major legal systems worldwide can be categorized into common law and code law. Common law is based on tradition and depends relatively less on written statutes and codes and more on precedent and custom than does code law. Common law originated in England and is the system of law found today in the United States.

Code law emphasizes written statutes. Countries with code law try to spell out all possible legal rules explicitly. Code law is found in the majority of the nations of the world. In general, countries with the code law system have much more rigid law than those with the common law system. In the latter, courts adopt precedents and customs to fit the cases, allowing the marketer a better idea of the basic judgment likely to be rendered in new situations.

Although wide in theory, the differences between code law and common law and their impact on the international marketer are not always as broad in practice. For example, many common law countries, including the United States, have adopted commercial codes to govern the conduct of business. Host countries may adopt a number of laws that affect a company's ability to market, such as the laws discussed in this chapter affecting the entry of goods, antidumping/below-cost sales of products, and licensing.

In addition, many countries have health and safety standards that may, by design or by accident, restrict the entry of foreign goods. Japan, for example, has particularly strict health standards that affect the import of pharmaceuticals. Rather than accepting test results from other nations, the Japanese government insists on conducting its own tests, which are time consuming and costly. It claims that these tests are necessary to take into account Japanese peculiarities. Yet some importers and their governments see these practices as thinly veiled protectionist barriers.

Very specific legislation may also exist to regulate specific types of marketing activity, such as advertising. For instance, many countries prohibit specific claims by marketers comparing their product to that of the competition and restrict the use of promotional devices. Some countries regulate the names of companies or the foreign language content of a product's label. Even when no laws exist, the marketer may be hampered by regulations. For example, in many countries, governments require a firm to join the local chamber of commerce or become a member of the national trade association. These institutions in turn may have internal regulations that set standards for the conduct of business and may seem quite confining to the international marketer.

Finally, the enforcement of laws may have a different effect on domestic and on foreign marketers. For example, the simple requirement that an executive has to stay in a country until a business conflict is resolved may prove to be quite onerous.

Managing Legal and Political Issues

The effect of politics on international marketing is determined by the bilateral political relations between home and host countries and by the multilateral agreements governing relations among groups of countries.

The government-to-government relationship can have a profound effect, particularly if it becomes hostile. Numerous examples exist of the linkage between international politics and international marketing. A premier example is U.S.-Iranian relations following the 1979 Iranian revolution. Although the internal political and legal changes in the aftermath of that revolution would certainly have affected international marketing in Iran, the deterioration in U.S.-Iranian political relations had a significant impact. Clashes between the two governments completely destroyed any business relationships, regardless of corporate feelings or agreements on either side. It took more than twenty years to reopen governmental dialogue between the two countries.

The Helms-Burton Act (cumbersomely named the "Cuban Liberty and Democratic Solidarity Act") of 1996 provided a more recent example of government-to-government disputes. Passed in response to the Cuban Air Force shooting down two unarmed small planes, the law granted individuals the right to sue, in U.S. courts, subsidiaries of those foreign firms that had invested in properties confiscated by the Cuban government in the 1960s. In addition, managers of these firms were to be denied entry into the United States. Many U.S. trading partners strongly disagreed with this legislation. In response, Canada proposed suing U.S. firms that had invested in properties taken from royalists in 1776, and the European Union threatened to permit European firms to countersue subsidiaries of U.S. firms in Europe and to deny entry permits to U.S. executives.

International political relations do not always have harmful effects on international marketers. If bilateral political relations between countries improve, business can benefit. The savvy international marketer will anticipate changes in the international political environment, good or bad, and plan and act accordingly. Sometimes, however, management can only wait until the emotional fervor of conflict has subsided and hope that rational governmental negotiations will let cooler heads prevail. Although a full understanding of another country's legal and political system will rarely be possible, the good manager will be aware of the importance of this system and will get a good lawyer, working with people who do understand how to operate within the system.

Many areas of politics and law are hardly immutable. Viewpoints can be modified or even reversed, and new laws can supersede old ones; the international marketer has various options when dealing with a country's internal politics. One high-risk approach is to simply ignore prevailing rules and hope to get away with it. A second, traditional option is to provide input to trade negotiators and expect any problem areas to be resolved in multilateral negotiations. The drawback to this option is, of course, the quite time-consuming process involved.

A third option involves supporting coalitions or constituencies that can motivate legislators and politicians to consider and ultimately implement change. This is the classic lobbying function, which can be pursued in various ways. One is the recasting or redefinition of issues. Terminology can have a powerful effect on perception. For example, changing the name of the trading status long called "most favored nation" (MFN)—a GATT term that does not designate favoritism—to the legally equivalent "normal trade relations" (NTR) diffused domestic American debate over trade relations with China.

Beyond terminology, marketers can promote benefits to legislators and politicians. For example, the manager can explain how a change in regulation or law will improve employment and the economy. Ask suppliers, customers, and distributors to add their voices lobbying for change.

Developing such coalitions is not an easy task, however. Companies often seek assistance from well-connected individuals and firms that can provide access to policymakers and legislators. In other words, they hire lobbyists to help them. Such assistance usually is particularly beneficial when narrow economic objectives or single-issue campaigns are needed. Many countries and companies have lobbied effectively in the United States. Estimates of the number of U.S. lobbyists representing foreign entities range into the thousands. A key factor in successful lobbying in a host country is showing support from local citizens and companies.

U.S. firms have usually been less adept at developing proper representation abroad than in the domestic arena. For example, our survey of U.S. international marketing executives found that knowledge and information about trade and government officials was ranked lowest among critical international business information needs. This low ranking implies that many U.S. firms are far less successful lobbying governments abroad than are foreign entities petitioning U.S. lawmakers.

Although representation of the firm's interests to government decision makers and legislators is entirely appropriate, the international marketer must also consider any potential side-effects. Major questions can be raised if such representation becomes too persistent, appears disingenuous, or otherwise incurs unfavorable scrutiny from politicians and publics. In such instances, short-term gains may be far outweighed by long-term negative repercussions if the international marketer is perceived as exerting too much political influence.

International Law

In addition to the politics and laws of specific countries, the trade globalist must consider the overall international political and legal environment. Although no enforceable body of international law exists, certain international forums, treaties, and agreements respected by a number of countries profoundly influence international business operations. The World Trade Organization (WTO), for example, defines internationally acceptable economic practices for its member nations. Although it does not directly affect individual firms, it does influence them indirectly by providing a more stable and predictable international market environment.

International trade negotiators have made a number of efforts to simplify the legal aspects of international business procedures. For example, firms patenting their products once had to register them separately in each country to ensure protection. In response to the chaos and expense of such procedures, several multilateral simplification efforts have been undertaken, as noted in Chapter 10. Similar multilateral agreements have been applied to trademarks.

The international legal environment also affects the marketer embroiled in jurisdictional disputes. Because no enforceable body of international law exists, firms usually are restricted by both home and host country laws. If a conflict occurs between contracting parties in two different countries, a question arises concerning which country's laws will be followed. Sometimes the contract will contain a jurisdictional clause, which settles the matter. If not, the parties to the dispute can follow either the laws of the country in which the agreement was made or those of the country in which the contract will have to be fulfilled. Deciding on the laws to be followed and the location to settle the dispute are two different decisions. As a result, a dispute between a U.S. exporter and a French importer could be resolved in Paris with the resolution based on New York State law.

The parties to a business transaction can also choose either arbitration or litigation. Managers usually avoid litigation because it often involves extensive delays and is very costly. In addition, firms may fear discrimination in foreign countries. Companies therefore tend to prefer conciliation and arbitration because these processes result in much quicker decisions. Arbitration procedures are often spelled out in the original contract and usually provide for an intermediary who is judged to be impartial by both parties.

FUTURITIES

The U.S. national economy has become too intertwined with world trade to be considered independent from it. It will be critical for the U. S. to develop a positive, not reactive, trade policy. The future belongs to free and open trade rather than protectionism and unfair trade practices that invite retaliation.

A New Collaboration and Issues of Control

The new century may also witness a new perspective on government-business relations. Whatever the specifics of the U.S. policy response, a marketing-orientation in critical. Key considerations include:

- A focus on market opportunities that make a difference;
- Identifying the needs and desires of foreign customers;
- An industry commitment to government market-opening approaches; and
- A link between trade policy and domestic assistance to firms.

Who's in Control? Very important as well is the locus of control of trade policy. By shifting the power of setting trade policy from the administration to agencies or even to states, the term *new federalism* could be given a quite unexpected meaning and might cause progress at the international negotiation level to grind to a halt. No U.S. negotiator can expect to retain the goodwill of foreign counterparts if he or she cannot place on the table issues that can be negotiated without constantly having to check back with different authorities. However, after winning the hard-fought battle for the restoration of "trade promotion authority" (once known as "fast track" approval) in August 2002, the White House can now negotiate trade treaties that Congress can approve or discard but cannot amend.

Who Should Control? With the Soviet Union gone and Russia in disarray, the United States, it's often said, is now the "world's sole remaining superpower." But it is difficult to reach consensus about how to use global influence and what the outcome will be. Those embracing the notion of "empire," a *Pax Americana* of U.S.-enforced—and presumably U.S.-defined—peace and prosperity, point to the power vacuum the U.S. has already had to fill by default. But those of less imperial mien warn against a world backlash that would greet hegemonic behavior on America's part. In trade issues, at least, the adverse reaction might have already begun with the European Union's vigorous protests aimed at U.S. steel tariffs and export subsidies. The exercise of leadership need not become the sovereignty power trip that anti-imperial critics fear. The real issue is *how* the United States behaves on the world stage and what the outcome of current policies will be. World leadership is a treasure Americans can grasp and nurture and use to improve lives and wealth on a global level.

Let's not forget how the United States won its leadership: through unprecedented generosity to others that began with the Marshall

Plan, astute policy making more often than not, and good fortune. And most of the time, American allies in the industrialized world cheered the United States on, welcoming American military protection, lessons of social justice, and cultural icons. Americans cannot, however, take leadership for granted. No empire has lived as long as its beneficiaries expected. Americans should take this period of leadership as the opportunity to build world prosperity. Americans need to remember that no one nation can go it alone for long, in trade or any other dimension of global interaction. Leadership requires willing followers—or "associates" or "colleagues"—their trust inspired by word but only truly earned by deed. Leaders will be questioned and challenged to prove that they still deserve the support of the led. The United States and its trade globalists should expect that and welcome the chance to show how they are leading the world to a commonly accepted state of affairs.

There will be mistakes on occasion, and at times unpopular stances will need to be defended. Whether the criticism is justified must always be a matter of open debate, openly welcomed. As issues such as the political decisions in the 2002 steel tariff debate have indicated our trading partners aren't going to be shy. But the steel debate has given the United States an excellent chance to enunciate its strategic view at a time when it has everyone's attention. There is a political price tag associated with strong U.S. support for free trade. The limited protection of a domestic industry may be such a price.

Finally, America shouldn't arrogantly forget that it is not the sole superpower in economic terms. The European Union's increasing cohesion and growth makes the bloc a major economic player. Its trade and business regulations increasingly determine how business operates worldwide, even in the U.S. as General Electric learned when the antitrust authority in Brussels turned down its merger plans. In addition, given the size of their populations, China and India may be waiting in the wings, ready to take on the mantle of regional leadership and global partnership.

What Is Control? Then again, "empire" isn't what it used to be. Neither the United States nor any other nation will have the unfettered imperial powers of old. The United Nations, compacts such as the Kyoto Treaty on the environment, the International Criminal Court, and the WTO, for example, exert supranational influence that is likely to grow stronger as the world gets smaller. Some problems such as global warming obviously require supranational solutions.

Creativity and a growing willingness to recognize common problems will encourage nations to support cooperative solutions. In the trade arena, for instance, consultants at McKinsey & Co. have proposed an ambitious solution to the world's steel capacity glut lurking behind international steel trade wars. By jointly funding an international consortium buying and destroying excess capacity, producing nations saddled with inefficient steel plants can cut those industrial albatrosses gracefully. Governments and major steelmakers would "share the pain," as McKinsey put it, including covering the huge labor and pension liabilities that have prevented legacy U.S. and European plants from closing.[13] It will take such big-picture thinking to solve otherwise intractable global trade problems.

Contemporary U.S. politics, or politics in any democracy, are ever changing. So as you read this book and contemplate your international marketing ventures, keep in mind how events, especially since the September 11, 2001 World Trade Center and Pentagon attacks, can alter policy and the structure of government radically. Will the Bush administration and those to follow take a more multilateral approach to world diplomacy and trade negotiation? What of similar political change in Europe, the future of zigzagging policies in Russia and Latin America, the flexing of trade muscles in China and the rest of Asia, and the long overdue internationalist awakening of Africa? As technologies bring nations' communications, transportation, and military threats ever closer, multilateralism certainly appears to be the best course for all involved.

Some will insist, however, that bilateral approaches to trade are best, even if only because they can resolve narrow problems relatively quickly. Growth in bilateral legislation and the increasingly country-specific orientation of trade negotiators bear witness to the appeal. However, every time bilateral negotiations take place, their very nature excludes a multitude of other interested parties. To be successful, negotiations must produce outcomes acceptable to many and sustainable for prolonged periods. Otherwise, there will certainly be resentful losers and winners of perhaps Pyrrhic victories.

NOTES

1. Jack Lucentini, "A Sticky Case," July 17, 2000, *The Journal of Commerce;* Neville, Peterson, Williams, "Country-of-Origin Rules Are Tangled," *The Journal of Commerce,* November 17, 1999, 10; Cam Simpson, "Made in Korea Fraud Snares Area Firm," *The Chicago Sun-Times,* October 30, 1999, NWS 1.
2. Elizabeth Olson, "WTO Loophole Allows a Surge in Protectionism," *The New York Times,* June 13, 2002.
3. Daniel Altman, "As Global Lenders Refocus, a Needy World Waits," *The New York Times,* March 17, 2002.

4. Bureau of Economic Affairs, www.bea.gov, accessed Nov. 15, 2002.

5. Office of the United States Trade Representative, *2000 National Trade Estimate Report on Foreign Trade Barriers,* Washington, D.C., March 27, 2000.

6. G. C. Hufbauer and K. A. Elliott, *Measuring the Costs of Protection in the United States* (Washington, D.C.: Institute for International Economics, 1994).

7. "Fact of the Day," *The Globalist,* May 1, 2002, www.theglobalist.com.

8. Gary Clyde Hufbauer, "The Cost of Protection in the European Community," in Patrick A. Messerlin (ed.), *Measuring the Cost of Protection in Europe: European Commercial Policy in the 2000s* (Washington, D.C.: Institute for International Economics, 2001).

9. Gary Clyde Hufbauer, Jeffrey J. Schott, and Kimberly Elliott, *Economic Sanctions Reconsidered: History and Current Policy,* 3rd ed. (Washington, D.C.: Institute for International Economics, 2002).

10. Michael G. Harvey, "A Survey of Corporate Programs for Managing Terrorist Threats," *Journal of International Business Studies* (Third Quarter 1993): 465–478.

11. Stuart M. Chemtob, Glen S. Fukushima, and Richard H. Wohl, *Practice by Foreign Lawyers in Japan* (Chicago: American Bar Association, 1989), 9.

12. Clemens P. Work, Sarah Peterson, and Hidehiro Tanakadate, "Two Air Disasters, Two Cultures, Two Remedies," *U.S. News and World Report,* August 26, 1985, 25–26; "2 British Teenage Girls Declared Children of JAL Crash Victim," Kyodo News Service, March 13, 2000.

13. Etienne Denoël, Sigurd I. Mareels, and Simon Winter, "Saving Steel," *The McKinsey Quarterly* 2, (2002).

PART 2

INTERNATIONAL MARKETING STRATEGIES

Part Two describes the strategies of international marketing available to companies—from exporting to direct investment, joint venturing, and other significant foreign commitments—which range from simple to complex. To begin choosing which are best for a given firm at a specific time for a specific set of market conditions, consider the patterns of international expansion typical of American firms. They move from responding to the requests of a few friendly resellers in foreign markets or participating in online marketplaces and getting enough extra revenue at low risk—nothing more. Then they move to aggressively increase their export volume, and then take the next step: moving to the "multidomestic" strategy of maintaining separate country-by-country operations sales and even assembly and manufacturing facilities. Ultimately, the company treats the world as one market and one logistics arena. Geography becomes just another way to segment markets.

Chapter 6, "Exporting and International Market Entry," focuses on a firm's initial approach to global markets, where different laws, regulations, and distribution channels make marketing activity a big step beyond the familiar procedures at home.

Chapter 7, "Multinational and Global Marketing," deals with advanced international marketing activities and the global marketing concerns of the integrated multinational firm.

Chapter 8, "Taking Services Global," recognizes that when services form the key component of an offering, marketing them globally can differ from the approaches supporting product-dominated offerings.

6

Exporting and International Market Entry

There are many ways to take an offering to the world.

Maynard Sauder, president and CEO of ready-to-assemble furniture maker Sauder Woodworking Company of Archbold, Ohio, thought for the longest while that exporting was not for him. Supplying national general merchandisers such as Wal-Mart, Kmart, Sears, and JCPenney with products in the $19 to $399 range, annual sales growth was humming at 12 to 15 percent—all of it in the domestic market. Exports were negligible and occurred almost by accident. For instance, the firm started to sell products in the Caribbean because a salesman vacationed there.

But Sauder became serious about exporting when he hired a large corporation's former export manager who had caught his eye. "I wasn't sure we could make it on price, and then I wondered if customers outside the U.S. would accept our designs," Sauder recalls. However, the company's proximity to particleboard suppliers in central Ohio helped keep prices competitive worldwide. As for design, "Our styles and colors have proved very acceptable, especially in France, where our penetration has been remarkable. We're doing very well in Turkey, too," Sauder proudly states.

Today, Sauder Woodworking does business in more than 70 countries, shipping more than $525 million in goods annually. Domestic volume has gone flat, while international accounts have posted an average annual increase of 30 percent. "It took us three to four years to reach a critical mass in exporting, but I knew after a year or so that we were going to give our program full support, and that we were in it for the long pull, not casually, and not lukewarm," he explains. "We proved in a very short time that we can compete anywhere in the world."[1]

EXPORT READINESS

Sauder Woodworking epitomizes the success a manufacturer can achieve in entering world markets when—just like at home—it can provide high-quality products at competitive prices. But exporting is more than just doing the same thing "over there" that you've been doing in your home markets. Of course, your products have to meet the same marketing standards in any market: fulfilling a need, promoting the product as serving that need, making it available for purchase, and pricing it attractively. But different laws, regulations and paperwork, new types of distribution channels, plus the uniqueness and cultural milieu of individual markets make the exporting experience a big step beyond the familiar procedures of marketing at home.

Few companies in the United States are born to be global at the outset, thanks to the vastness of the American domestic marketplace. But the increasingly global nature of competition and the growing ease of reaching foreign markets make exporting an option for all but the smallest manufacturers and service providers to consider. And with e-business having eliminated geographic marketing barriers, pondering the export option becomes unavoidable. Simply posting a Web site will draw international search engine traffic and buying inquiries, if not actual orders, whether a firm seeks them or not. (Successfully fulfilling those orders and actively pursuing such foreign buying interest does, however, require explicit attention to export marketing principles.)

Most firms start their international involvement with exporting, and most exporters are small and medium-sized firms that are to ready "go international." Two notable lessons about export readiness stand out from the Sauder story. First, Sauder had market advantages to exploit. Second, top management commitment and the influence of a new, export-savvy executive provided the "change agents" that propelled Sauder Woodworking toward export markets and sustained that vision during those four years needed to reach a "critical mass," as Maynard Sauder put it.

Product Readiness

Naturally enough, export readiness centers on one's product or service. If it succeeds in the domestic market, it might well have appeal elsewhere when it satisfies the needs and fits the culture of consumers. Even better is the product with unique capabilities that competitors do not provide and might be hard to manufacture locally. A new technology or a unique capability backing a service can be unbeatable in the right markets. Sometimes, national origin itself can be a competitive advantage: for example, just being "from America" implies an important degree of technical superiority, or being "made in Italy" gives a product a fashionable or trendy cachet.

It could be that changes to the product—enhancements, or stripping a product of frills to emphasize its basic features—might increase its appeal outside its traditional domestic markets. Recognize, too, that products with flagging health domestically might still have appeal elsewhere, particularly in less-developed countries where consumer preferences and disposable income favor consumer and industrial basics. Additionally, selling your product in a new market could uncover new product ideas and enhancements—originating from new customers, new competitors, or your own engineers studying local-use conditions—that you can bring back to the domestic market.

Additionally, ask the deceptively easy questions: *What* is my product? *Why* do people buy it? Actually, many companies do not take adequate time to ask those questions, much less answer them even in domestic markets, instead assuming that an engineer's concept of superior features or a salesperson's enthusiasm for competitively superior bells and whistles are all that are needed to carry the day. But as the apt saying goes: People do not buy electric drills, they buy holes. Whether your offering is a tangible good, a purely intangible service, or (as many products are) a combination, the "what" and the "why" of your offering are determined by customers seeking solutions to their actual problems, not by what your engineers and salespeople think those problems are. If the reason people buy includes a significant service and support component or service complement, can your company or its agents and distributors provide those features abroad adequately?

Assessing a product's potential and appeal in foreign markets can and should be a seriously thorough investigation. Chapter 4 reviews the cultural environments that play a large role in determining whether products and services, particularly those aimed at consumers, will succeed in a market. Chapter 9 discusses the market research tools marketers can employ for the task of probing everything from climatic through environmental, to economic, and cultural factors that determine a product's export success. Though the targets of market research might differ, the basic research approach to a market is similar whether the product is aimed at consumers or business buyers. Start with the less expensive secondary research of market statistics and existing reports before considering the costly custom studies of primary research.

Company Readiness

As experienced marketers know, having the right product, cost structure, and infrastructure is just the beginning of a successful venture. A company's management and available resources must be ready, able, and willing to build and support the venture.

Change Agents. Internally, enlightened management that discovers and understands the value of international markets is the key change agent. Education, international experience and expertise, an interest in foreign cultures and a commitment to growth within the context of a "shrinking world"—all should influence top management thinking. Of course, it takes adept operations management to make top management's vision workable. Whether it is a new employee or a resourceful and committed manager already at the firm, the new export thrust requires someone—typically a marketing manager with adequate staff—responsible for the success of the export program.

A significant internal event can be another major change agent. Developing a new product or identifying an existing one as ripe for selling abroad can be such an event. For example, a manufacturer of hospital beds learned that beds it was selling domestically for $600 each were being resold in a foreign country for $1,300.

Externally, foreign demand for the product or service is the most powerful outside influence on a firm's decision to export. Sometimes inquiries from abroad and unsolicited orders make that demand obvious. But research finds that the most successful exporters generally start on their own initiative rather than wait for something to happen.[2]

Domestic competitors can also trigger change. Their involvement captures top management attention, legitimizes the notion of exporting, and can raise fears of competitive strength and eventual encroachment even on one's domestic markets. As always, time spent on competitive intelligence and maintaining industry contacts at conferences and trade shows is good business.

Domestic distribution channels might encourage an export program. Often, a company's dealers, manufacturers' reps, resellers, and other distributors are engaged in some degree of international marketing. To increase their international distribution volume, they encourage purely domestic firms also to participate in the international market.

Banks and professional service firms such as accountants or advertising agencies can be major change agents by alerting domestic clients to international opportunities. Although such service providers historically follow their major multinational clients abroad, increasingly they are establishing a foreign presence on their own. They hope to service foreign clients and help their domestic clients expand their international reach. Export agents—one type of professional service firm geared specifically to international growth—actively seek new international business activity from domestic companies.

Chambers of commerce and other business associations can pique an interest in exporting. And governments at the national or local level can also be major change agents by providing information, active advice, actual financial incentives, and timely political support.

Company Capabilities. Having the right product or service offering, top management vision, and middle management skills, plus the external influences encouraging a firm to export, what else does the company need to get started? The organization's strategic focus and commitment are essential. Does the possibly expensive and often frustrating pursuit of export sales actually fit the firm's strategy and goals? Does the company have solid reasons for exporting, or is its export interest based on little more than managers' desires to travel at the company's expense?

Furthermore, is the export thrust a long-term growth strategy, or do senior managers consider it just a quick fix or a showy diversion during tough times? Will management stay the course if, as often happens, the export program operates at a loss during its early years? Will the venture enhance corporate competitiveness and financial strength, as measured by return on investment, payback periods, and other specific metrics? What is the company's criterion for export "success"?

Will the export program win active and enthusiastic support from company rank-and-file employees? Will you be able to train or hire customer support people to handle problems in foreign markets, and converse with customers in their native languages? And can the company's production, supply, and management capacities handle new foreign customers as well as regular growth in its domestic markets?

In addition, does the company have the financial resources to adequately mount an export venture and stick with it through the investment periods required early in process? Will exporting drain funds needed for other important company ventures, such as new product development, a sales force expansion, or an e-business start-up?

In addition to the traditional capabilities and opportunities of exporting, the World Wide Web puts virtually every company with a Web site into global markets. Even if choosing to not promote its products or its site to foreign buyers, a company will find itself identified by Web search engines, right alongside its competitors. Foreign customers will come knocking, like it or not. But if it chooses to make the right system investments, even a small company can compete with industrial giants in cyberspace.

Formally assessing your company's export readiness is worth the effort. Two California trade promotion organizations, the Bay Area Economic Forum and the Los Angeles Area Chamber of Commerce, provide a very useful set of Export Readiness Assessment guidelines at their www.TradePort.com Web site. Numerous government sources, including the Trade Information Center of the U.S. Department of Commerce (www.trade.gov/td/tic/) and the U. S. Commercial Service's Export Counseling office (www.usatrade.gov) can assist with export readiness information and advice.

GROWING THROUGH EXPORTING STAGES

As American companies increased their exporting activity in the latter decades of the twentieth century, certain patterns of export involvement emerged. Firms tend to more or less advance along stages of exporting until they reach a level of stability that is right for their capabilities and products or until they abandon their exporting aspirations. Quickly reviewing those patterns can help a company's management plan its own export involvement, know what is and isn't realistic to expect, and prepare for prudent growth as foreign selling opportunities appear. The patterns are dynamic; the population of exporting firms within various stages does not remain stable. Overall, researchers of U.S. firms have found that, in any given year, 15 percent of exporters will stop exporting by the next year, while 10 percent of nonexporters will enter the foreign market. The most critical junctures for the firm are the points at which it begins or ceases exporting.[3]

Traditionally in the United States, the vast majority of firms have not been at all interested in the international marketplace, though e-business and global competition are rapidly undermining that apathy. Typically, the uninterested company will not even fill an unsolicited export order, but a company might become partially interested if such orders keep arriving and if it has already become emboldened by ongoing success in expanding its domestic markets.[4]

Uninterested firms might be suffering from uninformed management. To bring senior executives up to the point of seeing the possibilities, the export-minded marketer could tap trade associations and conferences for information communicating the tangible benefits of exporting. Look for testimonials from successful small exporters, case studies, and data showing export activity by industry, export profitability statistics, and reports about the impact of specific export activities on the balance of trade.

Export Awareness

With a few completed foreign orders on its books, a firm enters the *export awareness* stage. It gradually begins to explore international markets, and management is willing to consider the feasibility of exporting. At this stage the firm becomes an experimental exporter, usually to psychologically close countries. However, management is still far from being committed to international marketing activities. Executives worry about financing, export practices, communication, technical advice, and securing adequate sales effort.

Senior managers—typically the company's chief executive and chief marketing officer—need to be aware of export services that can address those concerns and should seek small-volume export financing by banks and government agencies. Employees should become familiar with routine export documentation, handling problems, and facilitation of the international funds transfers. As the firm's experience begins to build, its managers should expose themselves to foreign exhibitions, trade fairs, and business contacts.

Four approaches to export markets[5] can be taken by the firm at this delicate stage of exporting education:

- *Passively filling orders* from domestic buyers who then export the product provides export sales for which another firm takes the risk, handles the paperwork, and wins the profit. However, having one's brand appear in a foreign market and sold successfully can set the stage for direct export involvement later.
- *Selling to domestic agents for foreign buyers* also shifts the exporting risk to another firm.
- *Exporting indirectly through intermediaries,* such as export management companies, trading companies, or international trade consultants—channels discussed later in this chapter—provides access to established experts and contacts while maintaining some degree of control over the sale. Selling through such channels

often becomes the stable business model for small- to medium-size exporters.

- *Exporting directly* requires the firm to handle all aspects of the sale and customer service itself. Though it likely is not a way to first test the foreign appeal of one's product, direct exporting is often the logical eventual outcome for firms whose export presence grows to major strategic importance but stops short of investment in foreign market subsidiaries.

According to the U.S. Department of Commerce, selling to domestic buyers or agents constitutes perhaps 30 percent of U.S. exports.[6] Firms can mix and match their approaches. Selling through intermediaries to some markets, but experimenting with direct sales in physically or psychologically close markets is one way of building export volume, for example, and preparing for more venturesome direct selling down the road.

Export Adaptation

At the next stage of export development, the firm evaluates the impact that exporting has had on its general activities. Here, of course, the possibility exists that a firm will be disappointed with its international market performance and will withdraw from these activities. On the other hand, it frequently will continue to operate as an experienced small exporter, finding its strategic comfort level at that stage of growth.

The final stage of this process is *export adaptation*. Typically, firms reach this stage when export transactions comprise 15 percent of sales volume and company planning begins to depend on that revenue. At that point, exporting is more than just ancillary business to the firm. The company has become a strategic participant in the international market and adjusts its activities to changing exchange rates, tariffs, and other variables. Management, seeing exporting in a favorable light, is ready to explore the feasibility of exporting to additional countries that are psychologically farther away. Financing long-term export growth becomes a key concern, particularly for smaller firms.

Each stage of export involvement makes unique demands on top and middle management attention. Firms at an export awareness stage—partially interested in the international market—are primarily concerned with operational matters such as information flow and the mechanics of carrying out international business transactions. Its managers understand that they need totally new bodies of knowledge and expertise. As their exposure to international markets grows, managers begin to think about tactical marketing issues, such as communication and sales effort.

Finally, firms that have reached the export adaptation phase are mainly strategy- and service-oriented. They worry about longer-range issues such as service delivery and regulatory changes. Utilizing the traditional marketing concept, they recognize that increased sophistication in international markets translates into increased application of marketing knowledge. The more they become active in international markets, the more those firms understand that an international marketing orientation—manifest in capabilities such as trained foreign service personnel—is just as essential as it is in the domestic market.

Balance Risk and Reward

As a firm progresses through internationalization stages, unusual things can happen to both risk and profit. Paradoxically for the nascent exporter, as the management team's expertise and familiarity with exporting grows, so do concerns over the firm's risk exposure. Learning as they go, managers confront new and unfamiliar risk factors, particularly as net export profits are weak or nonexistent during the early months or years of the export program. International earnings during initial investment stages probably cannot at all match those of established domestic operations. The shortfall tempts many executives to stop exporting.

Understanding the internationalization stages and the behavior of risk and profitability associated with each can help management overcome the temptation to cut and run and instead recognize that negative developments likely are only short term. Yet, export success does require the firm to be a risk taker, investing in competitive strength and market share, building efficiency and effectiveness, and learning from experience. Fortunately, as the next section explains, exporters can find partners willing to share the risk and help with the tasks.

GETTING HELP FROM EXPORT INTERMEDIARIES

When an export-minded company lacks sufficient capital, personnel, commitment, or other resources to sell directly to international markets, it can get help from *export intermediaries:* channel partners such as export management companies and export trading companies. Another option is selling to OEMs (original equipment manufacturers) or other domestic manufacturers that will include a company's product as a component or ingredient in other products or product lines destined for export.

Market intermediaries who specialize in bringing firms or their goods and services to the global market can be crucial to export success because their special expertise can help overcome a company's knowledge and performance gaps. Often, they have detailed information about the competitive conditions in certain markets, or they have personal contacts with potential buyers abroad. Operating much like distributors and resellers in domestic markets, export intermediaries can also assist by evaluating credit risk, calling on customers abroad in person, and handling the physical delivery of the product to the buyer.

Export Management Companies

Export management companies (EMCs) are domestic firms that specialize in performing international marketing services as commission representatives or as distributors for several other firms. Most EMCs are quite small, having been formed typically by one or two principals with experience in international marketing or in a particular geographic area. Their expertise enables them to offer specialized services to domestic corporations.

EMCs have two primary forms of operation. They either take title to goods and operate internationally as distributors on their own account, or they perform services as agents.

EMCs as Distributors. As a distributor taking title to goods, the EMC offers a conventional export channel. It does not have any form of geographic exclusivity, and it tends to negotiate price with suppliers on every transaction. By assuming the trading risk and operating in its own name, such a distributor EMC reaps more profit than an EMC acting as an agent. The domestic manufacturer selling to the distributor EMC is in the comfortable position of having sold its merchandise and received its money without having to deal with the complexities of the international market. On the other hand, the manufacturer is unlikely to gather much international marketing expertise and therefore continues to operate as a purely domestic firm.

EMCs as Agents. As an agent, an EMC is likely to have either an informal or formal contractual relationship, which specifies exclusivity agreements and, often, sales quotas, price arrangements, and promotional support payments. Because EMCs often serve a variety of clients, their mode of operation may vary from client to client and from transaction to transaction, operating, for instance, as an agent for one client and a distributor for another. Either way, from a selling viewpoint the agent EMC is primarily in charge of developing foreign marketing and sales strategies and establishing contacts abroad.

Because the agent EMC does not share in the profits from a sale, it depends heavily on commissions from a high sales volume. It might therefore be tempted to take on as many products and as many clients as possible, potentially spreading itself too thin. This risk is particularly great for small EMCs. The agent EMC must also concentrate a substantial amount of effort on the development of domestic clients, often the firms that are unwilling to commit major resources to international marketing efforts. They must be convinced that it is worthwhile to consider international marketing, and that task takes time that the agent EMC could have spent selling goods to foreign customers.

EMCs with specific expertise in selecting markets because of language capabilities, previous exposure, or specialized contacts appear to be the ones that are most successful and useful to their clients. By sticking to their expertise and representing only a limited number of clients, such agent services can be quite valuable.

EMC Compensation and Relationships. Whether compensated primarily by reseller's profit margins or agents commissions, EMCs will expect extra compensation for international marketing efforts: the market development, promotion, research, and other direct expenses associated with foreign market penetration. The EMC might charge a fee to the manufacturer or request a discounted product price. One way or the other, the domestic manufacturer will pay. EMCs cannot offer a free ride. Otherwise, despite promises, the EMC may simply add the manufacturer and product to its product offering in name only and do nothing to achieve international market penetration.

The EMC in turn faces the continuous problem of retaining a client once it achieves foreign market entry. Many firms use EMCs mainly to test international markets, expecting to become a direct exporter once they've established successful operations. As a result there is a conflict between the EMC and its clients, with one side wanting to retain market power by not sharing too much international market information and the other side wanting to obtain that power. That often results in short-term relationships and a lack of cooperation—a serious problem because successful international market development is based on long-term efforts.

For the EMC concept to work, both parties must fully recognize the delegation of responsibilities; the costs associated with these activities; and the need for information sharing, cooperation, and mutual reliance. Manufacturers should treat EMC relationships as they would a domestic channel commitment. This requires a thorough investigation of the intermediary and the advisability of relying on its efforts, a willingness to cooperate on a prolonged basis, and a willingness to reward it properly for these efforts. The EMC in turn must adopt a flexible approach to managing the export relationship. As access to the Internet makes customers increasingly sophisticated, EMCs must ensure that they continue to deliver true value to their clients by acquiring, developing, and deploying resources such as new knowledge about foreign markets or about export processes.

Internet Collaborations

Even though the bursting of the "dot-com" speculative bubble tarnished the image of e-business strategies with many a manager, doing business online is proving to be a prudent, and even competitively necessary, strategy for companies that take the time to provide genuine customer value, domestically and internationally. But the power of e-business goes well beyond what a single firm can do with its own site on the Web. A firm can buy a presence on an electronic marketplace or "portal," participate in reverse auctions (where the buyer chooses the lowest-priced credible bidder), and use the promotion power and reach of popular online trading networks to efficiently expand its worldwide marketing presence.

The well-conceived e-business site is much more than just a promotional and order-taking vehicle; at their best, individual company Web sites provide networks linking suppliers and customers, exchanging manufacturing, marketing, logistical, and financial information instantly, anywhere in the world. A number of firms sell e-commerce networking applications. One of the leaders, whose capabilities epitomize what's available to online exporters, is the Unify Suite software that Unibex, Inc. (www.unibex.com) promotes for what it calls "collaborative commerce."

Unibex ("the Universal Business Exchange"), launched by a group including AT&T, Dun & Bradstreet, General Electric, Microsoft, and the U.S. Chamber of Commerce, enables small and medium-sized businesses to sell their products and source components anywhere in the world with just a few personal computer keystrokes. The Unibex software allows companies to anonymously sign on and submit requests for goods or services using an array of categories, including location, product type, payment, and shipping terms. Customers then receive bids from businesses hoping to land contracts. Once a buyer chooses bids and learns the bidders' identities, negotiations can begin. Unibex allows users to attach documents, such as confidentiality agreements, contracts, and purchase orders. The participation of Dun & Bradstreet permits users to check each other's company profiles by tapping into D&B's vast international database of company information and references. Designed for companies in the "middle market" of $2 million to $2 billion sales, Unibex partners with specialist providers of online tools, such as supply-management catalog creation, and language translation. Unibex allows users to locate freight forwarders, bankers, accountants, or customs brokers once they close a deal. The system has several thousand users in more than 25 countries and expects to accumulate 1.5 million users within five years.

Trading Companies

Another major facilitating intermediary is the trading company. Europeans originated the concept when monarchs chartered traders that enjoyed exclusive trading rights and government protection. Some trading companies are legendary, such as the Netherlands' East India Company. Some are household names today: Sumitomo, Mitsubishi, Mitsui, and C. Itoh among them. General trading companies play a unique role in world commerce by importing, exporting, countertrading, investing, and manufacturing. Because of their vast size, they can benefit from economies of scale and perform their operations at very slim profit margins.

For example, Japanese trading companies, the *sogoshosha*, have been successful for four reasons:

- By concentrating on market information and information systems, these firms have superior ability to gather, evaluate, and translate data into business opportunities.
- Economies of scale and vast transaction volume allow them to negotiate preferential treatment in transportation rates and routes.
- Sogoshosha serve large markets in Japan and around the world and can benefit from opportunities for barter trade.
- Sogoshosha have access to vast quantities of capital, both within Japan and in the international capital markets. They can therefore carry out many transactions that are larger and riskier than is palatable or feasible for other firms.[7]

Trading companies were considered a mainly Japanese phenomenon for many decades, cultural factors being the reason. But with help from their governments, successful trading companies have operated in Korea, Brazil, and Turkey. Meanwhile, as more Japanese firms have set up their own global networks, the sogoshosha share of Japan's trade activities has diminished.

U.S. Middlemen. In the United States, the Export Trading Company (ETC) Act has been designed to improve the export performance of small and medium-sized firms. Export trading companies can avoid antitrust obstacles when they seek Department of Commerce precertification for planned joint activities. The law permits bank participation to improve ETC access to capital.

ETCs allow small- and medium-sized exporters to share foreign marketing costs. For example, one manufacturer alone would not have to bear the cost of a foreign warehouse on its own. A consortium of firms can jointly rent a foreign warehouse. Similarly, individual firms need not each station a service technician abroad at substantial cost. Joint funding of a service center by several firms makes the cost less prohibitive for each. The trading company concept also offers a one-stop shopping center for both the exporter and its foreign customers. The trading company ensures that all international functions will be performed efficiently, and the foreign customer can deal with fewer individual firms.

The Export Trading Company Act permits a wide variety of possible structures for an ETC. Product-oriented trading companies concentrate on a limited number of products and offer their market penetration services only for these products. Trading companies may also be geographically oriented, targeting one particular foreign region, or can be focused on certain types of projects, such as turnkey operations and joint ventures with foreign investors. Finally, trading companies may develop an industry-oriented focus, handling only goods of specific industry groups, such as metals, chemicals, or pharmaceuticals.

ETC Operations. Independent of its form of operation, an ETC can deliver a wide variety of services. It can be active chiefly as an agent, or it can purchase products or act as a distributor abroad. It can provide information on distribution costs and even handle domestic and international distribution and transportation. This can range from identifying distribution costs to booking space on ocean or air carriers and handling shipping contracts.

Although ETCs seem to offer major benefits to many U.S. companies wishing to penetrate international markets, exporters have not used them extensively. By 2002, the U.S. Department of Commerce had certified only 186 individual ETCs. Yet these certificates covered more than 5,000 firms, mainly because various trade associations had applied for certification for all of their members according to the Department of Commerce.

Manufacturers participating in trading companies sponsored by groups should know the importance of being market driven. Some companies might simply use the trading company to dispose of otherwise unsalable merchandise. International sales, however, depend primarily on the demand and the market. An ETC must balance the demands of the market and the supply produced by its members in order to be successful.

LICENSING AND FRANCHISING

Licensing and franchising are alternatives open to and used by all types of firms, large and small. Rather than exporting products, licensors and franchisers sell limited rights to foreign firms to use their intellectual property. Licensing and franchising offer flexibility in one's approach to international markets, reflecting the needs of the firm and the circumstances in the market. Licensing and franchising are especially important because they provide additional opportunities for market expansion. For example, a small firm may choose to use licensing to benefit from a foreign business concept or to expand without much capital investment. A multinational corporation might use the same strategy to rapidly enter foreign markets in order to take advantage of new conditions and foreclose some opportunities to its competition. These options can be used both in place of and in addition to other exporting strategies.

Licensing Strategies

Under a licensing agreement, one firm, the licensor, permits another to use its intellectual property in exchange for compensation designated as a royalty. The property might include patents, trademarks, copyrights, technology, technical know-how, or specific marketing skills. For example, a firm that has developed new packaging for liquids can permit other firms in foreign markets to use the same process. Licensing therefore amounts to exporting and importing intangibles.

Considerable Pros. Licensing has intuitive appeal to many potential international marketers. As an entry strategy, it may require neither capital investment nor knowledge and marketing strength in foreign markets. By earning royalty income, it provides an opportunity to obtain an additional return on research and development investments already incurred. After initial costs, the licensor can reap benefits until the end of the contract period. Licensing reduces risk of exposure to government intervention because the licensee is typically a local company with leverage against government action. Licensing will help to avoid host country regulations that are focused on equity ventures.

Licensing gives the licensor the chance to test foreign markets without major investments of capital or management time. And a licensor can enter selected single or multiple markets quickly, jumping ahead of competitors with a technology, trademark, or patentable skill. Licensing is growing more popular as the World Trade Organization and governments in general increase the protections afforded intellectual property. In instances of high levels of piracy, a licensing agreement with a strong foreign partner may also add value because the partner becomes a local force with a distinct interest in rooting out unlicensed activities.

Licensing offers a foreign licensee the opportunity for immediate market entry with a proven concept. It therefore reduces the risk of R&D failures, the cost of designing around the licensor's patents, or the fear of patent infringement litigation. Furthermore, most licensing agreements provide for ongoing cooperation and support, thus enabling the licensee to benefit from new developments.

Brands and trademarks have become particularly important in world commerce as communications and entertainment markets consolidate. The internationally recognized names or logos of designers, literary characters, sports teams, and movie stars are particularly potent, giving a licensee's locally produced product instant market appeal. As names appear on clothing, games, foods and beverages, gifts and novelties, toys, and home furnishings—sometimes on products unrelated to the original brand—licensors often succeed in making millions with little effort. British designer Laura Ashley started the first major furniture program, licensing her name to Henredon Furniture Industries. Coca-Cola licensed its name to Murjani for use on blue jeans, sweatshirts, and windbreakers. Licensing costs in such instances are typically an average fee of 5 percent of the wholesale price.

Licensors and licensees alike must avoid using a trademark on a product too far removed from its origins or on products that will tarnish the licensor's reputation. You must research consumer preferences and perceptions carefully to avoid market positioning blunders. For example, when Germany's Löwenbräu was exported to the United States, it was the number-one imported beer sold in the market. But when Miller Brewing Company licensed the name for a domestically brewed product, consumer perceptions of the brand changed drastically for the worse.

Finally, licensing may enable you to enter a foreign market that is closed to either imports or direct foreign investments. In addition, licensing arrangements may include other contractual benefits to licensors, such as agreements to buy materials and components only from the licensor.

Inevitable Cons. Licensing has some disadvantages. Agreements are likely to leave the international marketing functions to the licensee. As a result, the licensor may not gain sufficient international marketing expertise to ready itself for subsequent world market penetration. Moreover, the initial toehold in the foreign market may not be a foot in the door. Depending on the licensing arrangement, quite the opposite may take place. In exchange for the royalty, the licensor may create its own competitor not only in the markets for which the agreement was made but also in third markets.

Therefore, some companies hesitate to enter many licensing agreements. For example, Japanese firms are delighted to sell goods to China but are unwilling to license the Chinese to produce the goods themselves. They fear that because of the low wage structure in China, such licenses could create a powerful future competitor in markets presently held by Japan.

Licensing agreements typically have time limits, which some foreign governments might not allow to be extended. If the licensee ties in with the licensor's global marketing network and the license lapses, quality control in terms of both production and marketing effort can become a concern.

And licensing does have its political critics. The United Nations Conference on Trade and Development (UNCTAD), for instance, complains that licensing older technologies unfairly withholds new capabilities from less-developed countries that need them.

Key Licensing Negotiation Issues. The key issues in negotiating licensing agreements include the scope of the rights conveyed, compensation, licensee compliance, dispute resolution, and the term and termination of the agreement. The more clearly these are spelled out, the more trouble-free the licensing deal.

Defining rights conveyed involves specifying the technology, know-how, or show-how to be included, their format, and associated guarantees. An example of format specification is an agreement on whether manuals will be translated into the licensee's language.

Compensation issues may be heavily disputed and argued. The licensor typically wants a share of the profits from the license to cover:

- Transfer costs, which are all variable costs incurred in transferring technology to a licensee and all ongoing costs of maintaining the agreement;

- R&D costs incurred in researching and developing the licensed technology; and
- Opportunity costs incurred by the foreclosure of other sources of profit, such as exports or direct investment. To cover these costs, the licensor wants a share of the profits generated from the use of the license.

In theory, royalties can be considered profit sharing. In practice, licensees usually do not want to include allowances for opportunity costs, and they often argue that R&D costs have already been covered by the licensor through the profit from previous sales. Regardless of what they're called, however, compensation amounts range between the licensor's minimum necessary return and the cost of the licensee's next-best alternative. Compounding the negotiation, those price points keep changing as technologies and other intellectual properties mature, lose their competitive uniqueness, and suffer flagging profit-making potency. Growing sophistication among licensees, and greater involvement by governments in licensing arrangements also change the negotiation balance as time goes on.

Compensation methods can take the form of running royalties, such as 5 percent of the licensee sales, with or without up-front payments, service fees, and disclosure fees for proprietary data. Sometimes, government regulations restrict the collection of royalties or know-how payments. In such instances, the knowledge transferred can be capitalized as part of a cooperative venture, with a specific value placed on the information. The licensor then receives payments as profits or dividends.

Licensee compliance on a number of dimensions must be stipulated in the agreement:

- Export control regulations;
- Confidentiality of the intellectual property and technology provided; and
- Record keeping and provisions for periodic licensor audits, which are usually conducted at least once a year.

Dispute resolution discussions center on the choice of law for contract interpretation and the choice of forum. Typically, the parties involved choose a third country's law to govern the agreement. Obviously, choose that third country carefully. For example, Swedish law, which is often used, stipulates that the law of the licensee's country governs on certain issues.

When the negotiating parties cannot agree on an applicable legal system, they can adopt an arbitration clause spelling out the procedure. For instance, the model clause of the International Chamber of

Commerce states, "All disputes arising in connection with the present contract shall be finally settled under the Rules of Conciliation and Arbitration of the International Chamber of Commerce by one or more arbitrators appointed in accordance with the said rules." Also needed is a statement regarding the arbitrators' authority.

The term, termination, and survival of rights must be specified. The licensor must study government regulations in the licensee's market. If the conditions are not favorable—such as the maximum duration of an agreement—the negotiating parties should apply for a waiver.

Franchising Strategies

Franchising is a form of licensing whereby a parent company, the franchiser, grants an independent entity, the franchisee, the right to do business in a prescribed manner. This right can take the form of selling the franchiser's products or using its name, production, and marketing techniques, or general business approach. The major forms of franchising are manufacturer-retailer systems (such as car dealerships), manufacturer-wholesaler systems (such as soft drink companies), and service firm–retailer systems (such as lodging services and fast-food outlets). One can differentiate between product/trade franchising, where the major emphasis rests on the product or commodity to be sold, and business format franchising, where the focus is on ways of doing business.

Franchising is often thought of as a strategy to be used for foreign-market entry only by large consumer-oriented firms, yet it can be useful for any business with international appeal. Of the nearly 2,900 franchise systems in the United States, more than 20 percent have units in other countries.[8] Franchising is also a viable alternative for small business marketers offering a specialized business concept. Automation Papers Company, a New Jersey–based supplier of high-technology paper products, is an example. Franchisees receive rights to the Automation Papers trademarks, intensive training for local staff members, and the benefit of the franchiser's credit lines and advertising budget.

Pros and Cons. The typical reasons for international franchise expansion are market potential, financial gain, and saturated domestic markets. The franchise benefits the franchisee because it reduces risk by implementing a proven concept. In Malaysia, for example, the success rate for franchises is 90 percent, compared to the 20 percent success rate of all new businesses.[9] Franchising agreements are usually also beneficial from a governmental perspective. For the source–country, franchising does not replace exports or jobs. For the recipient/ country, it takes little outflow of currency, and the bulk of the profit generated remains within the country.

Despite the benefits, there are some problems. Would-be franchisers must know that their special capabilities that are worth franchising. Also, those capabilities, such as trademarks and business processes must be standardized so they are transferable and reproducible by those who've paid to learn them. Selection and training of franchisees is critical. Many franchise systems have run into difficulty by expanding too quickly and granting franchises to unqualified entities.

On the other hand, standardization does not mean 100 percent uniformity. Adjustments might be necessary to meet local market conditions. Key to success is developing a program that maintains a high degree of recognition and efficiency while being responsive to local cultural preferences. Although the local franchisee knows the market best, the franchiser still needs to understand the market for product adaptation purposes and operational details. The franchiser should be the conductor of a coordinated effort by the individual franchisees—sharing ideas and engaging in joint efforts.

Another key issue is sustainability and the barriers to competitive entry the franchised business system can maintain. Can the product or service and the general style of operation be readily copied? Government intervention can also raise major problems. For example, government restrictions on the type of services to be offered or on royalty remissions can prevent franchising arrangements or lead to a separation between a company and its franchisees. What can go wrong? Researchers find a laundry list of franchising items that can go awry and impede an international franchising strategy:[10]

- Locating good and reliable franchisees overseas.
- Knowing how to franchise overseas.
- Protection of industrial property and trademarks in foreign countries.
- Obtaining information on market prospects overseas.
- Familiarity with business practices overseas.
- Foreign government regulations on business operations.
- Foreign regulations or limitations on royalty fees.
- Negotiation with foreign franchisees.
- Foreign regulations or limitations on entry of franchise business.
- Collection and transfer of franchise fee.
- Quality or quantity of product or service.
- Providing technical support overseas.
- Pricing franchise for a foreign market.

- Advertising franchise overseas.
- Sourcing and availability of raw materials, equipment, and other products.
- Shipping and distribution of raw materials required to operate a foreign franchise.
- Financing franchise operations overseas.
- Shipping and handling of equipment needed to operate a foreign franchise.

Master franchising is an option many international franchisers use to encourage better-organized and more successful growth. They select foreign partners and award them the rights to a large territory that they can subfranchise. As a result, the franchiser gains market expertise and an effective screening mechanism for new franchises without incurring costly mistakes. However, in order to preserve control, many companies also prefer to own their outlets abroad.[11]

FUTURITIES[12]

The United States is increasingly vulnerable in its international trade position. Although U.S. exports of goods and services were almost $1 trillion in 2002, the trade deficit was more than $435 billion. Deficits of this magnitude are unsustainable in the long run. An export performance by U.S. firms that matches or even exceeds our imports will increasingly be crucial for the nation and should be achievable since U.S. firms clearly underexport when compared to other nations.

Exports are also an important contributor to national employment. We estimate that $1 billion of exports supports the creation, on average, of about 11,500 jobs. Still, U.S. merchandise exports comprise only 11 percent of GDP, compared to 28.3 percent for Germany and 25.4 percent for the United Kingdom. Many small and medium-sized U.S. exporters are too complacent to globalize since they are content with a vast domestic market.

On the positive side, U.S. exporters have the benefit of well working government programs—such as the working capital guarantee program by the Export-Import Bank of the United States—which provide financing assistance. On the regulatory side, a stable international trade environment is, in itself, an important support for smaller-sized firms. Trade disputes, particularly between large regions or countries, may remind small and mid-sized exporters of the proverb "when elephants stomp, the grass gets crushed." They are the ones least able to circumvent trade sanctions or to quickly shift to new markets. A specific review focus on smaller firms would be helpful when it comes to government policies such as export administration regulations.

Finally, companies themselves need to make major commitments to international operations by devoting financial and managerial resources to the tasks. But they need more help in a very dynamic environment. In our interconnected world, the likelihood of continued and closer global linkages and interdependence is high.

NOTES

1. Daniel McConville, "An Accidental Exporter Turns Serious," *World Trade,* March 1996, 28; Sauder Company Web site, www.sauder.com, accessed April 16, 2001.
2. Anthony C. Koh and Robert A. Robicheaux, "Variation in Export Performance Due to Differences in Export Marketing Strategy: Implications for Industrial Marketers," *Journal of Business Research* 17 (November 1988): 249–258.
3. Andrew B. Bernard and J. Bradford Jensen, *Exceptional Exporter Performance: Cause Effect or Both,* Census Research Data Center, Pittsburgh, Carnegie Mellon University, 1997.
4. Yoo S. Yang, Robert P. Leone, and Dana L. Alden, "A Market Expansion Ability Approach to Identify Potential Exporters," *Journal of Marketing* 56 (January 1992): 84–96.
5. See *Approaches to Exporting,* National Trade Data Bank, U.S. Department of Commerce, accessible at its www.stat-usa.gov site.
6. See *Approaches to Exporting,* National Trade Data Bank, U.S. Department of Commerce, accessible at its www.stat-usa.gov site.
7. Yoshi Tsurumi, *Sogoshosha: Engines of Export-Based Growth* (Montreal, Quebec: Institute for Research on Public Policy, 1980).
8. Leonard N. Swartz, "International Trends in Retailing: Franchising Successfully Circles the Globe," Arthur Consulting, December 1999, http://www.accenture.com.
9. Ibid.
10. Ben L. Kedia, David J. Ackerman, and Robert T. Justis, "Changing Barriers to the Internationalization of Franchising Operations: Perceptions of Domestic and International Franchisors," *The International Executive,* 37 (Number 4, July/August 1995): 329–348.
11. Faye S. McIntyre and Sandra M. Huszagh, "Internationalization of Franchise Systems," *Journal of International Marketing* 3 (Number 4, 1995): 39–56.
12. Material in this section is excerpted from testimony of author Michael R. Czinkota delivered to the U.S. House of Representatives Committee on Small Business April 24, 2002.

7

Multinational and Global Marketing

How to deploy company operations worldwide.

Harnessing advanced international marketing strategies to build and manage operations in more than one national market requires skills and resources beyond those employed by exporters. Multinational firms supervising a group of subsidiaries and other investments in foreign lands face issues such as local versus headquarters control and product/service standardization versus offerings tailored to individual markets. Then, at the highest level of international marketing involvement, genuine global marketers—pioneers in the twentieth century and now the acknowledged models for worldwide commerce—integrate their foreign and domestic operations into relatively seamless enterprises for which a portfolio of nations becomes "the market" for unified strategies.

This chapter focuses on the global marketer's concerns, the factors that drive strategy, and the options available to achieve a global marketing vision. Marketing managers begin by aligning their firms' capabilities and the realities of their investment markets. They turn to global account management for their major accounts that are themselves international players. They assess competition in terms of globalized market segments to be served. And while they use global task forces to consolidate and distribute their knowledge, they implement marketing programs so that the old adage "think globally, act locally" becomes their mantra guiding customer value creation and business policies in foreign locales.

Typically, companies first experiment with exporting before choosing markets for direct investment. Market factors, barriers to trade, cost factors, and investment climate are the major motivations for foreign direct investment, with market factors usually playing the major role. Global firm investments can range across different levels of commitment and control, from wholly-owned subsidiaries to joint ventures. Although many firms prefer full ownership in order to retain full control, such a posture is often not possible because of governmental regulations. It might not even be desirable. Depending on the global organization and the strategic needs of the firm, joint ventures with only partial ownership may be profitable alternatives.

Strategic alliances, or partnerships, represent yet another option as companies seek complementary technologies and skills around the world. Given the complexities and cost of technological progress, the number of these alliances, sometimes encouraged through government assistance, is rapidly growing. In addition, as countries increasingly develop service-based economies, contractual arrangements in lieu of equity investments become a useful market expansion option.

THE GLOBAL IMPERATIVE

Whatever solutions they offer to customers, multinational marketers share common challenges. Technological advances and competitive pressures make new product life cycles shorter than ever—as product development costs skyrocket and large market segments find it hard to digest the advances—even in the most industrialized societies. Available investment capital isn't limitless, but the political aspirations of emerging and even developed markets sometimes seems so.

Determined Global Marketers

The $11 billion home appliance industry is a good example of manufacturers embracing globalization. Many U.S.-based manufacturers face increased competition domestically from foreign companies, and while U.S. market growth appeared sluggish, markets abroad have beckoned with opportunities. The European market, for example, is growing quite rapidly, the breakdown of barriers within the European Union has made establishing business there even more attractive, and household appliance penetration is much less than in the saturated American market.

To take advantage of the opportunity, appliance giants like General Electric, Whirlpool, Electrolux, and Bosch-Siemens have acquired regional manufacturers or formed strategic alliances with them. Whirlpool also bought the entire appliance business of Dutch electronics giant N.V. Philips, giving it 10 European plants, some popular regional brands, and a third-ranked market share on the continent behind Electrolux and Bosch-Siemens. Complemented by growth in the awakening Asian market and a solid footing in Latin America, Whirlpool growth in those markets, plus Central Europe and South Africa, extended the firm's worldwide reach to 170 countries.

Regional product differences illustrate the complexities of implementing a global strategy. The British favor front-loading washing machines, while the French swear by top-loaders. The French prefer to cook their food at high temperatures, causing grease to splatter onto oven walls, which calls for self-cleaning ovens. This feature is in less demand in Germany, where lower temperatures are traditionally used. Manufacturers are hoping that European integration will bring about cost savings and product standardization. The danger to avoid is developing compromise products that in the end appeal to no one.

Although opportunities do exist, competition is keen. Margins have suffered as manufacturers—more than 300 in Europe alone—scrape for business. The major players have decided to compete in all the major markets of the world. "Becoming a global appliance player is clearly the best use of our management expertise and well-established brand line-up," Whirlpool executives have said. Whirlpool's long-term goal is to leverage its global manufacturing and brand assets strategically across the world.

Meanwhile, joint ventures present their share of challenges to the global marketers. For example, in Whirlpool's Shanghai facility, teams of American, Italian, and Chinese technicians have had to work through three interpreters to set up production. Not everyone has succeeded with such a strategy. Some have stumbled by betting on the wrong partners. And for those who go it alone when expanding to new markets, the biggest challenge is to establish their brand names as household words and to penetrate mass merchandising channels.[1]

Irresistible Pressures

Many marketing managers have to face increasing globalization of markets and competition similar to the challenges in the home appliance market. Even the biggest companies in the biggest home markets cannot survive on domestic sales alone if they are in globalizing industries. They have to be in all major markets to survive the shakeouts expected to leave three to five players per industry at the beginning of the twenty-first century, or be satisfied to be only niche market specialists.

Globalization reflects a business orientation based on the belief that the world is becoming more homogeneous and that distinctions between national markets are not only fading but, for some products, will eventually disappear. The inefficiencies of duplicating product development and manufacturing in each country become more apparent, and the pressure to leverage resources and coordinate activities across borders gains urgency.

Globalization Drivers. Four factors—market, cost, environment, and competition—drive the process.[2]

Consumers in the industrialized world are becoming more similar in education, income, lifestyles, aspirations and use of leisure time. High purchasing power and well-developed infrastructures create attractive markets in which new products find ready buyers. Distribution channels are becoming more global, and some retailers have established powerful global brands, such as Benetton, McDonald's, and Starbucks. Cross-border channel consolidation increases the pressure on manufacturers to rationalize international marketing programs.

Cost avoidance is a powerful globalization motivation. Single-nation markets may not be large enough for a company's country subsidiaries to achieve all possible economies of scale and scope, especially given the dramatic changes in the marketplace. Take, for example, the heavily contested consumer goods sectors, where launching a new brand may cost $100 million or more. Companies such as Unilever and Procter & Gamble probably are not going to spend precious resources on one-country projects. And in many cases, expanded market participation and activity concentration can accelerate the accumulation of learning and experience.

Market environments have been favorable to globalization. Government barriers have fallen dramatically in recent years. Increasing consumer wealth and mobility, rapid information transfer across borders, and publicity about the benefits of globalization all accelerate the process, along with technological evolution. Newly emerging markets will benefit from advanced communications by leapfrogging stages of economic development.

To remain competitive, global rivals have to intensify their marketing everywhere by attempting to sustain advantages that, if weakened, could leave them vulnerable to market share erosion worldwide. For example, companies introduce, upgrade, and distribute new products faster than ever before. Without keeping a program in fighting trim in all key regions, a marketer risks seeing carefully researched ideas picked off by other global players.

Leading companies by their very actions drive the globalization process. There is no structural reason why soft drinks should be at a more advanced stage of globalization than beer and spirits, which remain more local, except for the opportunistic behavior of Coca-Cola. Similarly, Nike and Reebok have driven their businesses in a global direction by creating global brands, a global customer segment, and a global supply chain.

Nonetheless, the four globalization drivers have affected countries and industrial sectors differently. While some industries, such as paper and soft drinks, are truly globally contested, some others, such as government procurement, are still quite closed and will open up only during a decades-long evolution. Commodities and manufactured goods are already in a globalized state, while many consumer goods are accelerating toward more globalization. Similarly, the leading trading nations of the world display far more openness than low-income countries, thus advancing the state of globalization in general.

Mininationals. A new group of global players is taking advantage of today's more open trading regions and newer technologies. "Mininationals,"[3] or newer companies with sales between $200 million and $1 billion, are able to serve the world from a handful of manufacturing bases, compared with having to build a plant in every country as the established multinational corporations once had to do. Their smaller bureaucracies have also allowed them to move swiftly to seize new markets and develop new products with greater flexibility.

For example, Cochlear, an Australian company specializing in the production of implants for the profoundly deaf, finds exports account for 95 percent of its $40 million sales, the result of a real annual compounded growth rate of 25 percent throughout the 1990s. Cochlear maintains a global technology lead through its strong links with hospitals and research units around the world and through its collaborative research with a global network of institutions.

In many cases, mininationals have developed new markets themselves. For example, Symbol Technologies, Inc. of Bohemia, New York, invented the field of handheld laser scanners and now dominates the business. In a field that did not even exist in 1988, Cisco Systems, Inc., of Menlo Park, California, grew from a mininational to an entity that has over 14,500 employees in more than 200 offices in 55 countries. Other mininationals continue to focus on their core products and services, growing and excelling at what they do best.

Mininationals have proven the wisdom in some enduring global marketing truths:

- Keep focused and concentrate on being number one or number two in a technology niche.
- Stay lean by having a small headquarters to save on costs and to accelerate decision making.

- Take ideas and technologies to and from wherever they can be found.
- Welcome employee expertise regardless of nationality to globalize thinking.
- Solve customers' problems by involving them rather than pushing standardized solutions at them.

PLANNING GLOBAL STRATEGY

Global marketing planning starts with a clear definition of the business of the firm or, as in large companies, the strategic business unit (SBU), organized around similar customers, similar products, or similar buyer needs served. Planning must be multifunctional with participation from marketing, production, finance, distribution, and procurement managers. Geographic representation is critical. The executive with highest-level experience in regional or global markets should head the effort.

Realistic Analyses

Start planning by understanding the underlying success factors common to the firm's markets. Planning global strategy on a country-by-country basis can result in spotty worldwide market performance. Portfolio-based planning processes that focus simultaneously across a broad range of markets help to balance risks, resource requirements, competitive economies of scale, and profitability to gain stronger long-term positions.[4] Analyze the common features of customer requirements and choice factors and the structure of the global industry in order to identify the profitability and competitive drivers.

For example, Ford Motor Company strategy begins not with individual national markets, but with understanding trends and sources of profit in the global automobile market. What are the trends in world demand? What are the underlying trends in lifestyles and transportation patterns that will shape customer expectations and preferences with respect to safety, economy, design, and performance? What is the emerging structure of the industry, especially with regard to consolidation among both automakers and their suppliers? What will determine the intensity of competition between the different automakers? The level of excess capacity in the worldwide auto industry is likely to be a key influence.[5] If competition is likely to intensify, which companies will emerge as winners? An understanding of scale economies, the state of technology, and the other factors that determine cost efficiency is likely to be critically important.

Organizational resource limitations provide the planner's reality check. Industrial giants with deep pockets may be able to establish a presence in any market they wish, while more thinly capitalized companies may have to move cautiously. Human resources may also present a challenge for market expansion. A survey of multinational corporations revealed that good marketing managers, skilled technicians, and production managers were especially difficult to find. The shortage is even worse when searching for people with cross-cultural experience to run future regional operations.

Critical Choices

A realistic, objective assessment is likely to lead to tough decisions to focus on certain markets, customer segments, and product positionings while bypassing others. In pursuing price leadership, for example, the global marketer offers an identical product or service at a lower cost than the competition. This often means investment in scale economies and strict control of costs, such as overhead, research and development, and logistics. The alternative strategy, differentiation industrywide or within a single segment, takes advantage of the marketer's real or perceived superiorities on customer value elements, such as design or after-sales service.

Cost leadership and differentiation are not mutually exclusive within a global plan and should be balanced appropriately. For instance, product components manufactured to one worldwide standard on one production line can be assembled into differing final products backed by unique positioning and brand differentiation to meet local customer tastes. And the "mass customization" product design movement that emerged in the 1990s permits low-cost tailoring of manufactured goods to individual customer specifications. Similarly, marketers who opt for high differentiation cannot forget to monitor costs because customer value perceptions rely at least in part on price for the quality obtained. Therefore, most global marketers combine high differentiation with cost containment, their global activities further contributing to scale economies in production and marketing.

Market Choices. A global strategy does not imply that a company should serve the entire globe. Critical choices include where to spend resources and where to hang back. The usual approach to market choice is to start by picking regions and then countries within them. Regional groupings might follow the organizational structure of existing multinational management or export offices, such as splitting Europe into northern, central, and southern regions that display similarities in demographic and behavioral traits. An important consideration is that data may be more readily available if the marketer groups markets according to existing structures and frameworks.

Portfolio models have been popular with marketers for this analysis. Some models, such as those used by General Electric, McKinsey & Co., and A.D. Little, have achieved something of a branded status of their own in management circles, adapted as necessary to meet a particular planner's unique needs. Such models generally use two dimensions to describe the relative characteristics of a product, a company, a market, or other entity. The relative position on the dimensions of the entity compared to others suggests certain strategies, such as whether to invest more, divest, or hold steady. Such a matrix approach has become classic shorthand for strategic choices.

Global marketing portfolio models typically involve two measures:

- The business unit's strengths as measured by relative market share, product fit, contribution margin, market presence, or other metrics.
- Market attractiveness according to metrics such as size, growth rate, number and type of competitors, governmental regulation, or economic and political stability.

A strategic business unit (SBU) position in a relatively attractive market (often called a "star") appears as a candidate for growth and further investment in the typical model. A company in a weak position in an unattractive market (a "dog") should consider abandoning that position, the model suggests. But those are the easy choices. The strategist earns his or her pay with decisions in more ambiguous territory: whether to invest and challenge better-established players in attractive markets, or whether to harvest profits in relatively unattractive markets where the SBU is strong ("cash cows"). Of course, assessing competitors and anticipating competitive reactions are implicit in working the model.

Diversity versus concentration questions inevitably arise as a business unit allocates finite resources among various markets. The basic alternatives are concentration on a small number of markets and diversification, which is characterized by growth in a relatively large number of markets. Expansion strategy is determined by market-, mix-, and company-related factors, such as:

- *Market factors* determine market attractiveness of the market in the first place. With high and stable growth rates only in certain markets, the SBU will likely opt for a concentration strategy, which is often the case for innovative products early in their life cycle. If demand is strong worldwide, as the case may be for consumer goods, diversification may be attractive.
- *Concentration* will occur with markets responding to marketing efforts at marginally increasing rates. But when the cost of acquiring additional market share points becomes too high, marketers tend to begin looking for diversification opportunities.
- *Product uniqueness* might create a significant lead time over competition, making diversity a less urgent option. Very few products, however, enjoy such a luxury for long.
- In many product categories, marketers will be affected by *marketing mix and distribution spillover effects.* Consider, for example, the impact of satellite channels on advertising in Europe, where ads for a product now reach most West European markets simultaneously. The greater the degree to which the SBU can standardize its marketing mix elements, the more likely it will follow a diversification approach and achieve economies of scale in marketing.
- The *objectives and policies* of the company itself will influence the expansion decision. It most likely will concentrate its market approach when it must maintain extensive interaction with intermediaries and clients.

The conventional wisdom of globalization requires a presence in all of the major triad markets (North America, Europe, and the Far East) of the world. In some cases, markets may not be attractive in their own right but may have some other significance, such as being the home market of the most demanding customers, thereby aiding in product development, or being the home market of a significant competitor. Therefore, three factors should determine country selection for global marketers: the stand-alone attractiveness of a market (e.g., China in consumer products due to its size); global strategic importance (e.g., Finland in shipbuilding due to its technological lead in vessel design); and possible synergies (e.g., entry into Latvia and Lithuania after success in the Estonian market given the market similarities).

Segment Choices. Groups of similar customers within markets might differ sufficiently from other groups to warrant individual marketing mixes. By tailoring the marketing approach to each attractive group, or segment, the marketer can portray a standardized product as meeting whatever unique needs each group has. Political boundaries might not matter as the astute marketer searches for intermarket segments grouping similar customers in more than one market.

Such market-spanning segments already exist for many marketers. The teenage segment, an obvious example, centers on common tastes in sports and music fueled by their computer literacy, travels abroad, and, in many countries, financial independence.[6] A media revolution creates a common fabric of teenage attitudes and tastes as satellite TV and global networks such as MTV are both helping create this segment and providing global marketers access to the teen audience worldwide. Given that teenagers around the world are concerned with social issues, particularly environmentalism, socially involved themes have been particularly successful image-positioning devices. Despite intrasegment similarities, marketing mix adjustments might be needed to best appeal to subsegments. Though Levi's jeans achieved global teenage acceptance, for example, European teens reacted negatively to the urban realism of Levi's U.S. ads, prompting the manufacturer to portray a mythicized America in its European advertising.[7]

Similarly, two other distinct segments ready for a panregional approach have appeared, especially in Europe. These include trendsetters who are wealthier and better educated, who tend to value independence, refuse consumer stereotypes, and appreciate exclusive products. The second market-spanning segment encompasses Europe's affluent businesspeople, who regularly travel abroad and have a taste for luxury goods.[8]

Choosing appropriate *segmentation bases* is the greatest challenge for the global marketer. The objective is identifying groups that are substantial enough to merit individual attention and can also be reached efficiently by marketing tools. Some 230 million teenagers in the Americas, Europe, and the Asia-Pacific (with the teens of the Americas spending nearly $60 billion of their own money yearly) are a big enough group and as a group are easily reachable through their own electronic and print media favorites.

However, creativity rooted in solid understanding of markets and product benefits should guide the selection and testing of candidate segment bases. Obvious bases might not discriminate efficiently enough among different customers. Using household income alone may be quite a poor gauge of class and behavior, for example. Chinese consumers spend less than 5 percent of their total outlays on rent, transportation, and health, while a typical U.S. household spends 45 to 50 percent. Additionally, income distinctions do not reflect education or values—two increasingly important barometers of middle-class status and buying behavior.

Global marketers have traditionally used environmental bases for segmentation. Yet, using geographic proximity, political system characteristics, economic standing, or cultural traits as stand-alone bases may not provide relevant data for decision making. A combination of them might produce more meaningful results.

Attitudes and lifestyles can provide robust segmentations differentiating purchase behavior. For instance, the middle-class family is one of the segments pursued by global marketers around the world. But defining the composition of this global middle class is tricky, given the varying levels of development among nations in Latin America and Asia. Some researchers, particularly in the affluent and extensive American market, have developed comprehensive models categorizing individuals by deep-seated interests and attitudes.

One such model on the international scale, the Roper Reports Worldwide Global Consumer Survey, interviewed 1,000 people in 35 countries who ranked 56 values by the importance they hold as guiding principles in their lives. Analysis boiled the results into a six-segment model.[9] "Strivers," the largest group, are slightly more likely to be men than women, and they place more emphasis on material and professional goals than do other groups. One-third of people in developing Asia are Strivers, as is about one-fourth of the population in Russia and developed Asia, Roper declared. The researcher dubbed other groups with similarly descriptive titles: "Devouts," "Altruists," "Intimates," "Fun Seekers," and "Creatives." A country-by-country analysis contended that Great Britain led the world in wanting to protect the family, Brazil had the most Fun Seekers, Saudi Arabia ranked first in faith, the Netherlands had the highest percentage worldwide in esteeming honesty, and Korea was the front-runner in valuing health and fitness.

While such models have important implications for product appeals and advertising creative strategies, lifestyle and attitude segments can easily become meaningless for practical decisions elsewhere in the marketing mix. Do Strivers prefer Brand A more than Intimates do? Which advertising media, for instance, efficiently single out Fun Seekers without spilling inappropriate messages into the Devout segment? Expensive and complicated research might shed some light on those questions, but is it worth the effort and are there enough Intimates or Fun Seekers in a market to justify treating them as separate segments in the first place?

Because environmental and statistically homogenous segments might not be separately reachable with tailored marketing mix elements, some analysts use mix elements themselves as *marketing management segmentation bases*, grouping segments with high mix-variable homogeneity, each reachable with its own standardized marketing strategy.[10] Whether the marketer uses segmentation bases related to product, promotion, pricing, or distribution, their influence should be related to environmentally based variables.

Product-related bases include the degree to which products are culture oriented, which stage of the product life cycle they occupy, consumption patterns, attitudes toward product attributes (such as country of origin), as well as consumption infrastructure (for example, telephone lines for modems). The growth of microwave oven sales, for example, has been surprising in low-income countries; however, microwaves have become status symbols and buying them more of an emotional issue. Many consumers in these markets also want to make sure they get the same product as available in developed markets, thereby eliminating the need in many cases to develop market-specific products. Adjustments will have to be made, however. Noticing that for reasons of status and space, many Asian consumers put their refrigerators in their living rooms, Whirlpool makes refrigerators available in striking colors such as red and blue.

Promotional bases might require local solutions rather than regional approaches. Similar influences may be exerted by the availability, or lack, of media vehicles or government regulations affecting promotional campaigns.

Pricing bases such as price sensitivity may lead the marketer to go after segments that insist on high quality despite high price in markets where overall purchasing power may be low, just to ensure global or regional uniformity in the marketing approach. Affordability is a major issue for customers whose buying power may fall short for at least the time being. Offering only one option may exclude potential customers of the future who are not yet part of a targeted segment. Some companies offer an array of products at different price points to attract such customers and to keep them as they move up the income scale.

Distribution bases become more important as distribution systems converge and global retailers proliferate. For example, toy manufacturers may look at markets not only for numbers of children but also by how effectively and efficiently they can be reached by global chains, such as Toys 'R' Us versus purely local outlets.

PUTTING GLOBAL STRATEGY TO WORK

Companies that exploit the efficiencies from similarities in product development, engineering, purchasing, manufacturing, marketing and sales, distribution, and other areas—while identifying and respecting genuine national and regional differences—will outperform others in terms of market share, cost, quality, productivity, innovation, and return to shareholders. In truly global companies, very little decision making occurs that does not support the goal of treating the world as a single market. Planning for and execution of programs take place on a worldwide basis.

With the global strategy selected and with target markets and segments identified, the global marketer must make and implement decisions in four areas:

- The degree of standardization in the product offering.
- The marketing program beyond the product variable.
- Location and extent of value-adding activities.
- Competitive scenarios.

Tuning the Program

Product. Globalization is not equal to standardization except for the core product or the technology used to produce it. The components used in a personal computer may to a large extent be standard, with the localization needed only in terms of the peripherals; for example, IBM produces 20 different keyboards for Europe alone. Product standardization may result in significant cost savings upstream. For example, Stanley Works' compromise between French preferences for handsaws with plastic handles and "soft teeth" and British preferences for wooden handles and "hard teeth"—to produce a plastic-handled saw with "hard teeth"—allowed consolidation for production and results in substantial economies of scale. At Whirlpool, using common platforms allows European and American appliances to share technology and suppliers to reduce costs and to streamline production. Many of the same components are used for products that eventually are marketed to segments looking for top-of-the-line or no-frills versions.[11]

In determining the optimal combination of products and product lines to be marketed, a firm should consider choices for individual markets as well as transferring products and brands from one region or market to another. Companies such as Procter & Gamble, 3M, and Henkel create strategic-planning units to work on products with global potential. These units, such as 3M's EMATs (European Marketing Action Teams), consist of members from the country organizations that market the products, managers from both global and regional headquarters, and technical specialists.

Insufficient research and a tendency to overstandardize can scuttle effective product strategies. If a product is launched on a broader scale without formal research of regional or local differences, the result may be failure. An example is Lego A/S, the Danish toy manufacturer, which decided to transfer sales promotion tactics successful in the U.S. market unaltered to other markets, such as Japan. This promotion included approaches such as "bonus packs" and gift promotions. However, Japanese consumers considered these promotions wasteful, expensive, and not very appealing.[12] Similarly, AT&T has had its problems abroad selling largely reworked U.S. models. Even after spending $100 million in adapting its most powerful switch for European markets, its success was limited because phone companies there prefer smaller switches.[13] Often, the necessary research is conducted only after a product or a program has failed.

Marketing. Nowhere is the need for the local touch as critical as in the execution of the marketing program. The marketer seeks uniformity in elements of global strategy (e.g., positioning) while localizing tactical elements (e.g., distribution). This approach has been called "glocalization." For example, Unilever achieved great success with a fabric softener that used a common positioning, advertising theme, and symbol (a teddy bear) but different brand names (e.g., Snuggle, Cajoline, Kuschelweich, Mimosin, and Yumos) and bottle sizes. Even Coca-Cola, one of the world's most global marketers, practices some local market adaptation.

But sometimes the amount of localization required is minimal. Gillette Co. scored a huge success with its Mach 3 shaver when it was rolled out in the United States, Europe, and Japan with a common approach based on the premise that men everywhere want the same thing in a shave. Although the language of its TV commercials varied, the theme ("The best a man can get") and most of the film footage were the same.

Value-added Activities. Globalization strives to reduce costs by pooling production or other activities or exploiting factor costs or capabilities within a system. Rather than duplicating activities in multiple, or even all, country organizations, a firm concentrates its activities. For example, Texas Instruments has designated a single design center and manufacturing organization for each type of memory chip. To reduce high costs and to be close to markets, it placed two of its four new memory chip plants in Taiwan and Japan. To reduce high R&D costs, it entered a strategic alliance with Hitachi. Many global marketers have established R&D centers next to key production facilities so that concurrent engineering can take place every day on the factory floor. To enhance the global exchange of ideas, the centers have joint projects and are in real-time contact with each other.

The quest for cost savings and improved transportation methods has allowed some marketers to concentrate customer service activities rather than having them present in all country markets. For example, Sony used to have repair centers in all the Scandinavian countries and Finland; today, all service and maintenance activities are actually performed in a regional center in Stockholm, Sweden.

Competitiveness. A company with regional or global presence will not have to respond to competitive moves only in the market where it is being attacked. A competitor may be attacked in its profit sanctuary to drain its resources, or its position in its home market may be challenged.[14] When Fuji began cutting into Kodak's market share in the United States, Kodak responded by drastically increasing its advertising in Japan and created a new subsidiary to deal strictly with that market.

The ability to cross-subsidize competitive battles with resources from other markets gives global players a competitive advantage over more localized rivals.[15] In fighting globalized competitors, one major market lost may mean losses in others, resulting in a domino effect, so jockeying for overall global leadership may result in competitive action in any part of the world. Thus "wars" have erupted between major global players in industries such as soft drinks, automobile tires, computers, and cellular phones.

Opening new markets often triggers new competitive battles, as happened in the 1990s in Russia, in Mexico after the signing of the North American Free Trade Agreement, and in Vietnam after the normalization of relations with the United States. Given their multiple bases of operation, global marketers may defend against a competitive attack in one country by countering in another country or, if the competitors operate in multiple businesses, countering in a different product category altogether. In the cellular phone category, the winners in the future will be those who can better attack less mature markets with cheaper phones while providing Internet-based devices elsewhere.[16]

Tuning the Organization

The successful global marketers of the future will be those who can achieve a balance between local and regional/global concerns. Marketers who have tried the global concept have often run into problems with local differences. Especially early on, global marketing was seen as a standardized marketing effort dictated to country organizations by headquarters. For example, when Coca-Cola re-entered the Indian market in 1993, it invested most heavily in its Coke brand, using its typical global positioning, and saw its market leadership slip to Pepsi. Recognizing the mistake, Coke re-emphasized a popular local cola brand (Thums Up) and refocused Coke brand advertising to be more relevant to the Indian consumer.[17]

Globalization calls for the centralization of decision-making authority far beyond that of the multidomestic approach of relatively autonomous country subsidiaries. But inflexible planning and implementation can doom a global thrust. Neither headquarters nor independent country managers alone can call the shots. Rather, companies need to gather the good ideas that come from different parts of the company and feed them into global planning. Once a strategy has been jointly developed, headquarters may want to permit local managers to develop their own programs within specified parameters rather than force them to adhere strictly to a rigid formula. For example, Colgate-Palmolive allows local units to use their own advertisements, but only if they can prove the local ads outperform the global benchmark version.

As we note in Chapter 14 discussing how to organize global marketing operations, a key requirement is personal interchange. Many companies encourage or even require mid-level managers to gain experience abroad during the early or middle stages of their careers. The more experience people have in working with others of different nationalities—getting to know other markets and surroundings—the better a company's global philosophy, strategy, and actions will be integrated locally. Periodic meetings of marketing managers and worldwide conferences allow employees to discuss their issues and local approaches to solving them. IBM, for example, has a Worldwide Opportunity Council, which sponsors fellowships for employees who study business cases from around the world and develop global solutions. IBM has found that some country organizations find it easier to accept input from other country organizations than from headquarters.

In another example, Levi Strauss & Co. convenes managers from its worldwide operations for a meeting of the minds twice a year. Levi's success turns on its ability to fashion a global strategy that gives foreign managers the freedom to adjust their tactics to meet the changing tastes of their home markets. Headquarters managers exercise control where necessary. Organizing foreign operations as subsidiaries rather than relying on a patchwork of licensees protects Levi's cherished brand identity and image of quality. The company also keeps ahead of its competition by exporting its pioneering use of computers to track sales and manufacturing.

Overall, the best approach to motivate local manager enthusiasm for global strategies includes policies such as:

- Ensuring that local managers participate in global brand strategy development.
- Encouraging local managers to generate ideas for possible regional or global use. Acknowledging local potential, global marketers can pick up successful brands in one country and make them cross-border stars.
- Maintaining a product portfolio that includes local as well as regional and global brands.
- Allowing local managers control over their marketing budgets so that they can respond to local customer needs rather than deplete budgets with forced participation only in uniform campaigns.[18]

In addition, companies that best motivate local managers foster a global identity that favors no specific country, especially a "home" country. Their management teams feature several nationalities and country organization representatives. The management development system is transparent, allowing executives of all nationalities an equal chance for the fast track to top management.

INVESTING DIRECTLY ABROAD

The actual mechanics of global expansion require some degree of direct investment, which can be literal in terms of acquiring foreign assets, or figurative in terms of gaining access to assets through contracts. Each approach has its advantages and drawbacks. Contractual arrangements are a useful alternative or complement to other international options and can also be an acceptable response to government ownership restrictions.

The international marketer invests directly via full ownership, strategic alliances, or joint ventures (a special type of strategic alliance) to create or expand a permanent interest in an enterprise. Investment implies a degree of control over the enterprise. Since foreign direct investment often requires substantial capital and a firm's ability to absorb risk, the most visible players in the area are large multinational corporations. These firms invest to enter markets or to ensure reliable sources of supply. Let's look closer at direct investment issues and, later in the chapter, contractual arrangements.

Foreign direct investment has grown tremendously. The annual volume of such investments—which the United Nations defines as "enterprises which own or control production or service facilities outside the country in which they are based"—exceeded $1 trillion in 2000, up from $865 billion the year earlier.[19] Among global investors, U.S. firms are major players due to significant investments in the developed world and in some developing countries. Companies from other countries have also engaged in major foreign direct investment activity, much of it in the United States. Foreign direct investment is a major avenue for foreign market entry and expansion.

The top multinational companies come from a wide variety of countries and depend heavily on their international sales. Some have revenues larger than many countries' domestic output, although multinational firms in general seem to have an optimal size that increases the costs of operations when exceeded.[20] Many of the large multinationals operate in well over 100 countries. For some, their original home market accounts for only a fraction of their sales. And in some firms, even the terms *domestic* and *foreign* are no longer used as they strive to consider issues only from a global perspective. Through their investment, multinational corporations bring economic vitality and jobs to their host countries and often pay higher wages than the average domestically owned firms. At the same time, however, trade follows investment and foreign direct investors often bring with them imports that could weaken a nation's international trade balance.

Why Direct Investment?

Direct investment can capture all the benefits of international marketing, most notably growth, more revenue, and greater profit. Acquiring foreign firms, for example, is the fastest way to grow internationally. And through such expansion, the corporation also gains the ownership advantages of political know-how and expertise, better intelligence about political actors and opportunities, and readier access and skill dealing with political and business leaders.

Another incentive is that foreign direct investment permits corporations to circumvent current barriers to trade and operate abroad as a domestic firm, unaffected by duties, tariffs, or other import restrictions. In addition to government barriers, customers might impose restrictions by insisting on domestic goods and services, and local buyers may wish to buy from sources that they perceive to be reliable, which means buying from local producers. For some products, country-of-origin effects may force a firm to establish a plant in a country that has a built-in positive stereotype for production location and product quality.

Still other direct investment incentives are access to low-cost resources, reliable supply, and market stability with strong growth potential.

Corporate investors have been categorized as either resource seekers, market seekers, or efficiency seekers:

- *Resource seekers* search for either natural resources (e.g., mineral, agricultural, or oceanographic) or human resources (low-cost or highly skilled labor). Over time, their investment location might change with trends in labor advantages and availability of the natural resources sought.
- *Market seekers* are companies searching for better opportunities and expansion options.
- *Efficiency seekers* attempt to obtain the most economic sources of production. They frequently have affiliates in multiple markets with highly specialized product lines or components and exchange their production in order to maximize the benefits to the corporation.

As large multinationals expand, their suppliers often follow, asked to service the resulting foreign derived demand. For example, many Japanese automakers have urged their home country suppliers to begin production in the United States. Advertising agencies often move abroad to service foreign affiliates of their domestic clients. Similarly, engineering firms, insurance companies, and law firms are often invited to provide their services abroad. Sometimes, the supplier, fearing the expanding client will take its business elsewhere, will invest abroad on its own to forestall such a potentially dangerous development.

Government incentives often spur foreign direct investment, as host countries seek jobs for their citizens and income for their economies. They provide fiscal incentives largely through tax allowances; financial incentives through advantageous funding and loan guarantees; and nonfinancial incentives such as guaranteed purchases, infrastructure investments, or special protection from competition through tariffs, import quotas, and local content requirements. However, incentives by themselves are unlikely to spur investment decisions if proper market conditions do not exist. Consequently, when individual states or regions within a country offer special incentives to foreign direct investors, they may be competing against each other for slices of a limited pie rather than increasing the size of the pie. Further, some observers question whether foreign investment actually creates many new jobs as newcomers import equipment, parts, and even personnel. An additional problem is the new investor's effect on established domestic firms, which do not benefit from incentives designed to attract new investment.

Controversial Ventures

All foreign direct investors, and particularly multinational corporations, are viewed with a mixture of awe and dismay. Governments and individuals praise them for bringing capital, economic activity, and employment, and investors are considered key transferers of technology and managerial skills. But others decry any nation's dependence on multinational corporations, which can withhold benefits as well as bring them to a market.

Critics, such as the globalization protesters making headlines at international economic conferences in recent years, accuse international direct investors of de facto re-colonization: actually draining resources from their host countries, stealing away skilled labor and exploiting the unskilled, pillaging the environment, and subverting legitimate political forces. By raising money locally, multinationals are blamed for starving smaller capital markets. By importing foreign technology, critics contend, the multinationals either discourage local technology development or only transfer outmoded knowledge. By increasing competition, they are declared the enemy of domestic firms. There are concerns about foreign investors' economic and political loyalty toward their host government and a fear that such investors will always protect only their own interests and those of their home governments. And, of course, their sheer size, which sometimes exceeds the financial assets that the government controls, makes foreign investors suspect. Note that Americans at times hurl similar accusations at foreign firms investing in the United States.

Clearly, a love-hate relationship frequently exists between governments and the foreign direct investor. As the firm's size and investment volume grow, the benefits it brings to the economy increase. At the same time, the dependence of the economy on the firm increases as well. Given the many highly specialized activities of international companies, their experts are often more knowledgeable than government employees and are therefore suspected of being able to circumvent government rules. Particularly in developing countries, the knowledge advantage of foreign investors may offer opportunities for exploitation.

In light of the desire for foreign investment and the accompanying fear of it, some organizations such as the United Nations, the Organization for Economic Cooperation and Development, and the International Labor Organization have proposed investment guidelines. Typically, these recommendations address the behavior of foreign investors in areas such as employment practices, consumer and environmental protection, political activity, and human rights. Corporations may not be legally bound by the guidelines, but they should consider their implications for corporate activities. The multinational firm can and should be a leader in improving economic and business practices and standards of living around the world. The true leaders will do so. Firms that do not accept national sovereignty or do not respect individuals will encounter growing hostility, resistance to their operations, and declining international success.

Ownership Options

Direct foreign investors have a wide variety of ownership choices, ranging from 100 percent ownership to a minority interest. Each level results in varying degrees of flexibility for the corporation, ability to control business plans, and degrees of risk assumed. In some instances, firms tend to keep using the same ownership model. However, it may be better to make the ownership decision flexibly, on each occasion making the choice a function of corporate needs, market environments, and government regulation.

Full Ownership. For many firms, the foreign direct investment decision is, initially at least, considered in the context of 100 percent ownership. Sometimes, this is the result of ethnocentric considerations, based on the belief that no outside entity should have an impact on corporation management. At other times, the issue is one of principle.

To make a rational decision about the extent of ownership, management must determine how much control it really needs to be successful. Often full ownership may be desirable but not essential. At other times, it may be necessary, particularly when strong linkages exist within the corporation. Interdependencies between and among local operations and headquarters may be so strong that anything short of total coordination will not be acceptable, such as if the company needs centrally controlled product design, pricing, or advertising to maintain consistency across markets. But that determination must be made carefully, to be sure that other ownership arrangements would not suffice.

Increasingly, the international environment is growing hostile to full ownership by multinational firms. Host governments might exert political pressure to obtain national control of foreign operations, or they might limit ownership options through legal restrictions such as caps on profit repatriation. In addition to government concerns, general market instability can deter full ownership of foreign direct investment. Instability may arise in political upheavals or changes in regimes, but more often the political risk comes from threats of political action, complex and drawn-out bureaucratic procedures, and the prospect of arbitrary and unpredictable alterations in regulations after the investment decision has been made.

Strategic Alliances. Strategic alliances, or strategic partnerships, are formal or informal arrangements between two or more companies with a common business objective—even if they are fierce rivals in other markets outside the scope of their alliance. Strategic alliances consist of informal cooperation (e.g., research/data exchange); contractual agreements (e.g., licensing, contract manufacturing, management contracts); or joint ventures involving equity exchanges. (If there are more than two partners, they are consortia.) Strategic alliances are more than the traditional customer-vendor relationship but less than an outright acquisition. Designed to pool partners' complementary strengths, the great advantage of such alliances is their ongoing flexibility. Partners can adjust agreements easily as market conditions change.

There are many reasons for the growth of strategic alliances: growing global competition, rapid increases in the investment required for technological progress, and a growing risk of failure. Market development is one common focus for partnerships, as penetrating foreign markets is a primary objective of many companies. Some alliances are designed to defend home markets. Others intend to spread the cost and risk of production and development efforts. Even though major corporations form many of the strategic alliances to compete for very large projects, such alliances are by no means confined to giant multinational firms. U.S. firms, mostly high-tech start-ups, have sought partnerships with Japanese companies to secure new markets, profits, and applications without a loss of equity and the risk of investment. Their alliances can include nonexclusive distribution or licensing deals.

Of course, look closely before entering an alliance. Depending on the objectives of the other partners, companies may wind up having their strategy partially driven by their competitors. Competitors may also gain strength through coalitions, unplanned transfers of technology might take place, and unexpected competitors might appear as a result. The most successful alliances are those that match the complementary strengths of partners to satisfy a joint objective. Often the partners have different product, geographic, or functional strengths, which the alliance can build on. Considering growing international competition and the rising cost of innovation in technology, strategic alliances are likely to continue their growth in the future.

Joint Ventures. Joint ventures are strategic alliances of two or more organizations for more than a transitory period, in which participating partners share assets, risks, and profits. Equality of partners is not necessary. In some joint ventures, each partner holds an equal share; in others, one partner has the majority of shares. The partners' contributions to the joint venture can also vary widely. Contributions may consist of funds, technology, know-how, sales organizations, or plant and equipment.

Joint ventures provide governmental and commercial benefits. They can help overcome existing market access restrictions and open up or maintain market opportunities that otherwise would not be available. Host governments often pressure firms either to form or accept joint ventures to reduce the control foreigners can exercise over local operations. Government-related reasons are the major rationale for joint ventures in developing countries (four times more frequent than in industrialized nations).[21]

From a commercial perspective, if a corporation can identify a partner with a common goal and if the two firms' international activities are sufficiently independent from each other, joint ventures may represent the best vehicle for international expansion. JVs allow a mutually advantageous pooling of resources, particularly when each partner has a specialized advantage in areas that benefit the joint venture: superiorities in technologies, distribution, customer access, or local supply, for example. Joint ventures also permit better relationships with local organizations such as labor unions.

The most important attributes of the local partner are its reputation in the local market and its financial standing.[22] If the local partner can bring political influence to the undertaking, the new venture may be eligible for tax incentives, grants, and government support and may be less vulnerable to political risk. Negotiations for certifications or licenses may be easier because authorities may not treat the venture as a foreign firm. Relationships between the local partner and the local financial establishment may enable the joint venture to tap local capital markets. The greater experience—and therefore greater familiarity—with the culture and environment of the local partner may enable the joint venture to be more aware of cultural sensitivities and to benefit from greater insights into changing market conditions and needs.

A final major commercial reason to participate in joint ventures is the desire to minimize the risk of exposing long-term investment capital while at the same time maximizing the returns from capital already invested.[23] As corporations shorten their investment planning time frame, this financial reasoning assumes growing importance.

As in all partnerships there are problems. With joint ventures troublesome areas involve implementing the concept and maintaining the relationship. Many governments that require a joint venture formation are inexperienced in foreign direct investment; their joint venture legislation and regulations are often subject to substantial interpretation and arbitrariness. Frequently, different levels of control are permitted depending on the type of product and the shipment destination. In some instances, only portions of joint venture legislation are made public. Other internal regulations are communicated only when necessary. Such situations create uncertainty, which increases the risk for the participants.

Major problems can also arise in maintaining the joint venture relationship. As one widely quoted statistic states, 7 out of 10 joint ventures fall short of expectations or are disbanded.[24] The reasons include conflicts of interest, problems with disclosure of sensitive information, disagreements over sharing profits, and a general lack of communication before, during, and after the venture's formation. In some cases, managers are interested in launching the venture but are too unconcerned about actually running the enterprise. In other instances, managers dispatched to the joint venture by the partners may feel differing degrees of loyalty to the venture and its partners. Reconciling such conflicts of loyalty is one of the greatest human resource challenges for joint ventures.[25]

Many of the problems encountered by joint ventures stem from a lack of careful, advance consideration of how to manage the new endeavor. A partnership works on the basis of trust and commitment, or not at all.   Areas of possible disagreement include the whole range of business decisions covering strategy, management style, accounting and control, marketing policies and practices, production, research and development, and personnel. The joint venture may, for example, identify a particular market as a profitable target, yet the headquarters of one of the partners may already have plans for serving this market that would require competing against its own joint venture.

Similarly, the issue of profit accumulation and distribution may cause discontent. If one partner supplies the joint venture with a product, that partner will prefer that any profits accumulate at headquarters and accrue 100 percent to one firm rather than at the joint venture, where profits are partitioned according to equity participation. The other partner might not be enthusiastic about that arrangement. Profit distribution can lead to disputes when one partner wants to distribute profit as dividends and the other partner wants profits reinvested.

The first requirement when forming a joint venture is finding the right partner. Partners should have common objectives yet should bring different, needed skills to the relationship. A JV makes little sense if both partners have the same strengths.

Negotiating the JV agreement is a critical step in which partners should make extensive provisions for contingencies. Questions such as profit accumulation and distribution, and market orientation must be addressed in the initial agreement; otherwise, they may surface as points of contention over time. And because JVs operate in dynamic business environments, they must be adaptable to changing market conditions. The initial partnership agreement should provide for changes in the original concept so that the venture can grow and flourish.

At the same time, a joint venture agreement should include an exit plan for dissolution if business conditions and priorities change significantly. Agreements should cover issues such as conditions of termination, disposition of assets and liabilities, protection of proprietary information and property, rights over sales territories, and obligations to customers. In addition, it is important to plan for the continued employment or termination of the people working in a dissolved joint venture.

Another specialized form of joint venture is the *government consortium* in which government support, perhaps with subsidies, participates. Usually, such consortia are designed to cope with escalating costs in a sector where a government seeks to build or maintain global leadership. To combat the high costs and risks of research and development in advanced technologies, research consortia have emerged in the United States, Japan, and Europe.

Since the passage of the Joint Research and Development Act of 1984 (which allows both domestic and foreign firms to participate in joint basic research efforts without the fear of antitrust action), well over 100 consortia have been registered in the United States. These U.S.-based consortia pool their resources for research into technologies ranging from artificial intelligence and electric car batteries to those needed to overtake the Japanese lead in semiconductor manufacturing. The Europeans have several mega-projects to develop new technologies, and Japanese consortia have worked on producing the world's highest-capacity memory chip and advanced computer technologies. On the manufacturing side, commercial jet maker Airbus Industries is a consortium backed by France's Aerospatiale, Germany's DASA, Britain's British Aerospace, and Spain's Construciones Aeronauticas.

INTERNATIONAL MARKETING BY CONTRACT

Contracts can be used to put corporate resources to work abroad without a significant investment and can also be an acceptable response to host government ownership restrictions. For example, contracts might focus on cross-marketing—e.g., outsourced services or contract manufacturing—where the contracting parties conduct complementary activities not within the firm's core competencies.

In a management contract, the supplier provides an integrated service without incurring either the risk or the benefit of owning the skills involved. The activity is quite different from other contractual arrangements because the client's people directly implement the relevant skills and knowledge at the foreign location. The international marketer can use management contracts in various ways. When equity participation (either full ownership or a joint venture), is not possible or must be relinquished, a contract can maintain one's participation in a venture. Depending on the terms, a company might even be able to exert some degree of control. For example, a corporation might have to relinquish manufacturing to foreign firms, yet a management contract could allow it to retain control over distribution.

Yet management contracts should not be seen only as a last line of defense. Management contracts can be a most useful tool for overcoming lack of expertise. Any business model can rely on an outside party with specialized knowledge, irrespective of the area. Some companies in the service sector have independent units that specialize in delivering management services. For example, the German airline Lufthansa manages the "back room" operations of various airlines. A management contract can be the critical element in the success of a project. The turnkey operation is a specialized form of management contract that permits a client to acquire a complete operational system with the skills required to keep it running. It eliminates the related problems of finding and dealing with individual contractors and subcontractors. Responsibilities for the turnkey package are clear, and the negotiation and supervision of the operation are straightforward.

Management contracts provide benefits to both parties. For the client they provide ready access to organizational skills, expertise, support services that would be difficult and costly to replicate locally. Plus, the project will be totally owned, controlled, and operated by the customer unless otherwise stipulated. As a result, many host government consider management contracts to be useful alternatives to foreign direct investment and control. Suppliers enjoy

similar advantages. Their risk of participating is substantially lowered, yet they operate as insiders, influencing strategic activities,
such as design specifications or sourcing. In addition, providing outsourced services allows a firm to commercialize its experience.

Of course, there can be problems. For the client there are the risks
of overdependence and loss of control if, for example, the management contractor maintains all international relationships. On the contractor's side, the major risks are the loss or termination of a contract
and the resulting personnel problems and unpredictable expenses.

FUTURITIES

Global marketing will continue to expand as the most potent competitive reaction a firm can mount against rivals who are themselves
building global brands and worldwide networks. Such expansion
strengthens the competition marketers confront as they promote the
use of market forces and the expression of market signals—via pricing, for example—in decision making. Two additional lessons will
enhance global marketers' successes in the 2000s: greater integration of far-flung operations by leading multinationals and greater
use of community relations to strengthen their positions in local
markets.

Metanational Strategy

We've seen in this chapter how so-called "mininationals"(companies
smaller than typical "multinationals") are able to nimbly move
around the globe with product and pricing flexibility. And with the
new century comes a new label for the most flexible of global marketers: "metanationals."

Conceptually, becoming a global company has meant marketing
to nations worldwide. But with the advent of the knowledge economy, companies must innovate based on information they *acquire*
worldwide—to innovate by learning from the world.

After studying 36 multinational corporations over five years, a trio
of European researchers[26] found a few, based in the U.S., Asia, and
Europe, that had successfully tapped innovation, technology, and
marketing knowledge resources in markets around the world and integrated them into "centerless" global enterprises.

For example, ST Microelectronics NV of Geneva, the 1987 merger
of two semiconductor companies, one French, one Italian, is now
the world's third largest semiconductor producer. Its 13 strategic al-

liances produced 45 percent of its $6.36 billion revenue in 2001. Keeping overhead low and the organization flat, the company gathers worldwide expertise, shares it internally, and pushes decision making as far out to its subsidiaries as it can. "The way we think about globalization is strategic, to have an integrated presence in all the major markets: R&D, sales and marketing, manufacturing," said an ST executive. "Technology R&D is centralized in Crolles (France) and Agrate (Italy); product development is dispersed. Because product design must be close to the customer, we have dispersed it all around the world" using virtual teams linked electronically. Ironically, one of the researchers explained, ST benefited from "being born in the wrong place." It had to look beyond Italy and France to get the expertise it needed to flourish.[27]

Community Strategies

Flourishing in the twenty-first century meeting governmental and public opinion demands for corporate social responsibility. This will be essential, not discretionary. Global marketers will be expected to serve all customers equally and nondiscriminately, lest public outrage depress sales or block operations. They will be expected to put their skills and experience to work increasing the quality of life in the markets where they operate. The result will be new opportunities for both customers and firms. Governments in Europe, for example, are welcoming private-sector programs to provide job training for inner-city youth, meet the needs of immigrants, and solve massive pollution problems. And in Eastern and Central Europe, where the lines between the private and public sectors are still being drawn, firms have a unique opportunity to take a leadership role in shaping new societies.

There's growing evidence that global marketers are responding to the call of "community relations" strategies. Such programs win good employees as well as praise from local opinion leaders. For example:

- British Petroleum invests in community activities in Casanare, Colombia, where it is developing oil interests. Committing millions to the region's development, BP set up a loan fund for entrepreneurs, technical schools, a center for pregnant women and nursing mothers, reforestation programs, local infrastructure construction, and jobs outside the oil industry.
- Gap Inc. changed the name of its program from Gap Foundation to Gap Community Relations. It links company brands to local service projects, such as providing its free Old Navy School Bus Service for student field trips. In addition, Gap's sourcing pilot

program will work with manufacturers to design projects in education, health, and childcare in Bangladesh, India, and Indonesia.

- Merck donated the drug Mectizan to 18 million people suffering from river blindness in less- developed countries and cut the price of an anti-AIDS drug to beat the competition and enlarge public access to the medicine.[28]

Surveying 200 corporate community relations managers recently, the Center for Corporate Community Relations at Boston College found 40 percent of them reporting more top management support, with 36 percent of them citing a larger budget and 23 percent reporting more staffing for community-oriented programs. About 87 percent of respondents said their companies encourage local managers to be involved in local communities; 31 percent of companies incentivize involvement with bonuses.[29]

Noting that 84 percent of employees feel that a company's community image is important, according to his surveys, Bradley K. Googins, director of the Center reasons, "In an era when finding and retaining quality people is getting increasingly difficult, perhaps the time has come for chief executives to give their employees both financial and spiritual reasons to stay on board."[30]

NOTES

1. "Whirlpool in the Wringer," *Business Week*, December 14, 1998, 83–84; "Did Whirlpool Spin Too Far Too Fast?," *Business Week*, June 24, 1996, 134–136; Regina Fazio Maruca, "The Right Way to Go Global: An Interview with Whirlpool CEO David Whitwam," *Harvard Business Review* 72 (March–April 1994): 134–145; "Whirlpool Hangs Its Rivals out to Dry," *USA Today*, December 10, 1993, 3B; "GE's Brave New World," *Business Week*, November 8, 1993, 64–69.
2. George S. Yip, "Global Strategy . . . In a World of Nations?" *Sloan Management Review* 31 (Fall 1989): 29–41; Susan P. Douglas and C. Samuel Craig, "Evolution of Global Marketing Strategy: Scale, Scope, and Synergy," *Columbia Journal of World Business* 24 (Fall 1989): 47–58.
3. "Turning Small into an Advantage," *Business Week*, July 13, 1998, 42–44; Michael W. Rennie, "Born Global," *The McKinsey Quarterly* (Number 4, 1993): 45–52; and Mininationals Are Making Maximum Impact," *Business Week*, September 1993, 66–69.
4. G. D. Harrell and R. O. Kiefer, "Multinational Market Portfolios in Global Strategy Development," *International Marketing Review* 10 (Number 1, 1993): 60–72.
5. "Europe's Car Makers Expect Tidy Profits," *The Wall Street Journal*, January 27, 2000, A16.
6. Shawn Tully, "Teens: The Most Global Market of All," *Fortune*, May 16, 1994, 90–97.

7. "The Euroteens (and How Not to Sell to Them)," *Business Week*, April 11, 1994, 84.
8. S. Vandermerwe and M. L'Huillier, "Euro-Consumers in 1992," Business Horizons 32 (January–February 1989): 34–40.
9. Tom Miller, "Global Segments from 'Strivers' to 'Creatives,'" *Marketing News*, July 20, 1998, 11; and www.roper.com.
10. I. B. Baalbaki and N. K. Malhotra, "Marketing Management Bases for International Market Segmentation: An Alternate Look at the Standardization/Customization Debate," *International Marketing Review* 10 (No. 1, 1993): 19–44.
11. "Call It Worldpool," *Business Week*, November 28, 1994, 98–99.
12. Kamran Kashani, "Beware the Pitfalls of Global Marketing," *Harvard Business Review* 67 (September–October 1989): 91–98.
13. "AT&T Slowly Gets Its Global Wires Uncrossed," *Business Week*, February 11, 1991, 82–83.
14. W. Chan Kim and R. A. Mauborgne, "Becoming an Effective Global Competitor," *Journal of Business Strategy* 8 (January–February 1988): 33–37.
15. Gary Hamel and C. K. Prahalad, "Do You Really Have a Global Strategy?" *Harvard Business Review* 63 (July–August 1985): 75–82.
16. "Nokia Widens Lead in Wireless Market While Motorola, Ericsson Fall Back," *The Wall Street Journal*, February 8, 2000, B8.
17. James A. Gingrich, "Five Rules for Winning Emerging Market Consumers," *Strategy and Business* (Second Quarter 1999): 19–33.
18. John A. Quelch and Edward J. Hoff, "Customizing Global Marketing," *Harvard Business Review*, May–June 1986.
19. United Nations, *World Investment Report 2000*, (New York: United Nations, 2000); www.un.org.
20. Lenn Gomes and Kannan Ramaswamy, "An Empirical Examination of the Form of the Relationship between Multinationality and Performance," *Journal of International Business Studies* 30 (Number 1, 1999): 173–188.
21. Paul W. Beamish, "The Characteristics of Joint Ventures in Developed and Developing Countries," *Columbia Journal of World Business* 20 (Fall 1985): 13–19.
22. Ali K. Al-Khalifa and S. Eggert Peterson, "The Partner Selection Process in International Joint Ventures," *European Journal of Marketing* 33 (No. 11/12, 1999).
23. Charles Oman, *New Forms of International Investment in Developing Countries* (Paris: Organization for Economic Cooperation and Development, 1984), 79.
24. Yankelovich, Skelly and White, Inc., *Collaborative Ventures: A Pragmatic Approach to Business Expansion in the Eighties* (New York: Coopers and Lybrand, 1984), 10.
25. Oded Shenkar and Shmuel Ellis, "Death of the 'Organization Man': Temporal Relations in Strategic Alliances," *The International Executive* 37 (Number 6, November/December 1995): 537–553.
26. Yves L. Doz, J. Santos, P. Williamson, *Global to Metanational: How Companies Win in the Knowledge Economy*, (Boston: Harvard Business School Press, 2001).
27. Lawrence M.Fisher, "STMicroelectronics: The Metaphysics of a Metanational Pioneer," *Strategy+Business* 28 (2002, Booz Allen Hamilton at www.bah.com).
28. Bradley K. Googins, "Why Community Relations is a Strategic Imperative," *Strategy+Business* 28 (2002, Booz Allen Hamilton at www.bah.com).
29. Ibid.
30. Ibid.

8

Taking Services Global

How to deliver a good service internationally in an acceptable way.

International services marketing is a major and growing component of world business and the fastest growing segment of world trade. Services often accompany goods, but they are also, by themselves, an increasingly important part of any economy. Services and goods are closely related, of course. People and businesses buy both to solve problems and exploit opportunities, whether it is a design engineer in Singapore seeking a faster signal processing chip or a teenager in Berlin dreaming of being more attractive to her friends. In both cases, those people buy a product so they can use it themselves to solve their problem. People buy services, however, to have the problem solved for them. Or, as services marketing expert Leonard Berry has put it, "A good is an object, a device, a thing. A service is a deed, a performance, an effort."[1]

Services tend to be more intangible, personalized, and custommade than goods and are usually marketed differently. While goods are shipped and distributed to physical locations circumscribed by national borders, services are not tied to geography. They can be transferred across borders or originated abroad, and the service provider can be transferred to the customer or the customer can be transferred to the service territory. Services also take a different approach to providing customer satisfaction. Rather than delivering a preproduced solution, as does a product that is quality checked before leaving the factory shipping dock, the service is "manufactured," so to speak, at the point and time of delivery. The customer does not buy a tangible thing that can be probed and poked. The customer buys a performance promise. The burden of delivering on that promise falls not on a factory assembly line, but on the company front-line personnel actually performing the service: the accountant at a client office, the cleaning service people, the consulting engineers, the data entry keypunchers. Managing that process domestically, with clients a short hop away, is challenging enough. Managing successful service delivery on a global scale grows geometrically in complexity as more new markets are served.

SERVICE CHARACTERISTICS

Services may complement goods; at other times, goods may complement services. But not always. Increasingly, they compete against goods and become an alternative offering. For example, rather than buying a car (a good), one can lease it (a service). Similarly, stand-alone services can compete against each other.

Customers won't respond to offers unless they are assured that the critical product and service components will perform as promised. Capital goods sales contracts, therefore, often include a service dimension. In the aircraft industry, for example, the buyer often contracts not only for the physical item, the plane, but also for training of personnel, maintenance service, and the promise of continuous technological updates. Similarly, computer hardware sales are linked to the availability of proper servicing and software. Companies increasingly ask consulting firms to not only recommend but also to implement IT strategies.

Linking goods and services can make international marketing efforts quite difficult. The foreign aircraft buyer might want service support for 10 years. If the seller is a U.S. firm, the original sale and all subsequent service transactions will require a new export license application. That can breed uncertainty if political environments seem volatile. As a result, sales may be lost to firms in countries that can unconditionally guarantee the long-term supply of support services.

Services cannot be stored in inventory. They must be produced on the spot as needed. That's clearly a complication for delivering the service globally when and where the customer wants it. Therefore, they often require entirely new forms of distribution. Traditional channels are often multitiered and long and therefore slow. They often cannot be used because of the perishability of services. A weather news service, for example, either reaches its audience quickly or rapidly loses its value. As a result, direct delivery and shorter distribution channels are often required when comparing goods and services. To operate on a global scale, service providers need to be distribution innovators.

CUSTOMER PERCEPTIONS

Different customer segments frequently will view service characteristics differently. Their perceptions, their needs in terms of use conditions, and other factors influence their choices. For example, the intangible dimension of "on-time arrival" by airlines may be valued differently by college students than by business executives. Similarly, a 20-minute delay will be judged differently by a passenger arriving at her final destination than by one who has just missed an overseas connection. And, as we noted in Chapter 4, being "on time" has different meanings in different cultures.

Internationally, the different experiences and cultural forces that shape perceptions can vary widely market-to-market, particularly for services, which usually are custom-made, highly personalized, and thus subject to strong cultural influences and maybe even hostility. For example, some critics deride the international distribution of U.S. films and television programming as an imposition of U.S. culture. Services are subject to many political vagaries occurring almost daily; their high visibility makes them convenient targets for blame no matter how undeserved. In short, even a good service is doomed to failure if it is delivered in a culturally unacceptable fashion.

Because sensitivity to culture, beliefs, and preferences is imperative in the services industry, marketers frequently develop independent service systems in individual countries or homogenous regions. Each system might borrow from a global template of attributes, but it is tailored to local customer preferences in the way it is marketed and delivered. On the other hand, customization contravenes the efficiencies of offering a standardized solution worldwide, which improves service consistency, a key characteristic if a service provider is to repeatedly live up to its promises made to customers.

Buyers have more problems evaluating services than goods. The service is an intangible promise, and it might involve expertise beyond the buyer's knowledge (e.g., brain surgery) or have outcomes the buyer cannot easily discern (e.g., the long-term value of an executive refresher course). Even when service providers are willing and able to provide more transparency and the details of the service are clear, equivalent, and available to all interested parties, the buyer's problem is complicated: Customers receiving the same service may use it differently and service quality may vary for each delivery. As a result, service offerings are not directly comparable, which makes quality measurements quite challenging. Therefore, the reputation of the service provider plays an overwhelming role in the customer choice process.

GROWTH DRIVERS

In the past few decades, the U.S. economy has increasingly become a service economy. The service sector now produces 78 percent of the

U.S. gross domestic product (GDP) and employs 80 percent of the private sector workforce, according to the Coalition of Service Industries, a trade group. U.S. services exports totaled $280 billion in 2002, about 29 percent of all exports. All that activity enriched many firms and industries, such as consulting firms, advertising agencies, engineering firms, and construction companies. Competition in international services is rising rapidly at all levels, contributing an average 60-plus percent to the gross domestic product of industrial nations. Even in the least developed countries, services typically contribute at least 45 percent of GDP.

Major shifts in the business environment and technology innovations have been driving the rapid growth of international services marketing, along with a reduction of governmental regulation of services in the United States and other nations. The primary deregulated industries in the United States have been transportation, banking, and telecommunications. Regulatory policy might change, however, given the corporate accounting scandals of 2002.

Although the effects of U.S. deregulation might seem to be just domestic, experience has shown that they spread rapidly worldwide. For example, U.S. telecommunications deregulation following the 1984 breakup of AT&T spawned new competition not only in the United States: Japan deregulated its telecommunications monopoly, NT&T, shortly afterward, and European deregulation followed in the mid-1990s. In the airline industry, deregulation in the United States forced price and service competition worldwide among carriers competing with U.S. airlines for lucrative U.S. international traffic. However, regulators themselves often aren't as enthusiastic about unleashing competition, despite the possible efficiencies. Trade negotiations under GATT auspices still wrestle with the $1 trillion in telecommunications savings ($500 billion in the developing world alone) that could be achieved worldwide through 2010 if national telecommunications monopolies play along. Many have dragged their feet, so far.

Deregulation within industries also drives service growth. Traditional professional association strictures against advertising, for example, have helped to make many service fields more competitive. International markets are one frequently untapped possibility for market expansion and have therefore become a prime target for such service firms. Just imagine the fertile field new democracies can offer political consultants!

Technological advancement is another major factor in increasing service trade by creating new ways of doing business and expanding. For example, Ford Motor Company uses one major computer system to carry out its new car designs in both the United States and Europe. This practice not only reduces expenditures on hardware but also permits better utilization of existing equipment and international design collaboration by allowing design groups in different time zones to use the equipment around the clock. Also, banks can offer their services worldwide through automatic teller machines or telephone banking. Consultants can advise via videoconferences, and teachers can teach the world through "e-learning" and multimedia classrooms. And new robotics technology allows surgeons to perform operations on patients half a world away. Distance and geographic boundaries are becoming at best minor obstacles to service growth.

Information technology allows data-intensive firms based anywhere to employ relatively low-cost labor anywhere in the world, "delocalizing" the service. For example, India increasingly provides international data services to markets worldwide. Skilled labor working at lower wages manually processes data transmitted to India in raw form and then returns it to its markets of origin. India was expected to reach $10 billion in data services exports by the year 2002.[2] However, other countries are beginning to offer competitive services as they too increase the value of their service exports. Working with a Delaware-based company, data entry personnel in Accra, Ghana, process New York City parking tickets, for example.

SERVICES' GLOBAL TRADE PROBLEMS

With its growing importance in world trade, new problems have beset the service sector. Even though many concern governmental issues, they are important enough to merit a brief review.

Data Collection

Service transactions are often invisible statistically as well as physically. The fact that governments have precise data on the number of trucks exported, down to the last bolt, but little information on reinsurance reflects past governmental inattention to services.

Only recently have governments recognized that the income and jobs created by service exports are just as important as those from products sold abroad. Insufficient knowledge and information had made it difficult for governments to gauge the effect of service transactions internationally or to influence service trade. Consequently, international service negotiations have progressed only slowly, and governmental regulations are often put into place without precise information on their impact on actual trade performance.

Fortunately, many governments are beginning to improve services sector measurements.

Regulation

Typical regulatory obstacles to services trade create two major problems: barriers to entry and interference in service performance. Governments often justify barriers to entry by citing national security and economic security. For example, regulators claim that only nationals should conduct banking or that it should be operated entirely under government control. Sometimes, the issue is protecting service users, particularly bank depositors and insurance policyholders. Some countries claim that competition in socially important services is unnecessary and wasteful and should be avoided. Another justification for barriers is the frequently-used infant industry rationale: "With sufficient time to develop on our own, we can compete in world markets." Often, however, this argument is used simply to prolong the ample licensing profits generated by restricted entry.

Impediments to services typically consist of nontariff barriers such as local sourcing laws, employment restrictions, direct government competition, or limits on service size or volume. Yet, defining a barrier to service marketing is not always easy. For example, Taiwan gives an extensive written examination to prospective accountants (as do most countries) to ensure that licensed accountants are qualified to practice. Naturally, the examination is given in Chinese. The fact that few German accountants read and write Chinese, and hence are unable to pass the examination, does not necessarily constitute a barrier to trade in accountancy services.

Even when barriers to entry do not exist or can be overcome, service companies have difficulty performing effectively abroad once they achieve access to the local market. One reason is that rules and regulations based on tradition may inhibit innovation. A more important reason is that governments aim to pursue social or cultural objectives through national regulations. Of primary importance here is the distinction between discriminatory and nondiscriminatory regulations. Regulations that impose larger operating costs on foreign service providers than on the local competitors, that provide subsidies to local firms only, or that deny competitive opportunities to foreign suppliers are a proper cause for international concern. The discrimination problem becomes even more acute when foreign firms face competition from government-owned or government-controlled enterprises. On the other hand, nondiscriminatory regulations may be inconvenient and may hamper business operations, but they offer less opportunity for international criticism.

For example, government regulations at state and federal levels are the main barriers to service marketers entering the U.S. market, such as banking, insurance, and accounting. The chief complaint of foreign countries is not that the United States discriminates against foreign service providers but rather that the United States places more severe restrictions on them than do other countries. In addition, the various regulatory processes give little weight to international policy issues and often operate in isolation from executive branch direction. A coherent approach toward international commerce in services is hardly likely to emerge from the disparate decisions of agencies, such as the Interstate Commerce Commission (ICC), the Federal Communications Commission (FCC), the Securities and Exchange Commission (SEC), and the many licensing agencies at the state level.

Since 1997, a General Agreement on Trade in Services (GATS) has been part of the World Trade Organization. GATS is the first multilateral, legally enforceable agreement covering trade and investment in the services sector. Similar to earlier agreements in the product sector, GATS applies most-favored-nation treatment, national treatment, transparency in rule making, and the free flow of payments and transfers to service trade. Market-access provisions restrict the ability of governments to limit competition and new-market entry. In addition, negotiators made sector agreements for the movement of personnel, telecommunications, and aviation. However, GATS agreements did not extend to several important sectors, such as financial services and entertainment. In addition, many provisions, being new, are very narrow and might be expanded during the Doha Round of trade negotiations.

MARKETING SERVICES GLOBALLY

To be successful, the international services marketer must first determine the nature and the aim of the service offering market by market: What solution does it provide to the buyer? What problem does it solve? What opportunity does it exploit? Then as with products, the marketer must design and implement country-appropriate marketing plans as we discuss in Chapters 10 through 13.

Tactical Requirements

However, marketing and communicating service benefits differs significantly from product marketing in some important ways. For instance, accurately measuring service performance—often an intangible benefit—can be tricky. And while demonstrations might be possible, offering actual samples isn't possible, particularly for complex services. The specific solution the customer is buying—a consultant's business recommendation, for example, or the waste treatment facility constructed by an engineering firm—doesn't exist until the service is rendered.

The role of personnel deserves special consideration in the international marketing of services. Because the customer interface is intense, companies must train foreign market personnel carefully. Because the service person is both the producer as well as the marketer of the service, recruitment and training techniques must focus on customer relationship management and image projection as well as competence in the design and delivery of the service. Appearance is of critical importance; most of the time the person delivering the service—rather than the service itself—will communicate the spirit, value, and attitudes of the service vendor. This close interaction with the consumer will also have organizational implications. While tight control over personnel may be desirable, international service delivery standards require some flexibility for local conditions.

Delivering services with adequate consistency requires trust for delegating large amounts of responsibility to individuals and service subsidiaries. Sole ownership helps strengthen this trust. Research has shown that service firms expanding abroad tend to prefer establishing full-control ventures. Only when costs escalate and the company-specific advantage diminishes will service firms seek out shared-control ventures.[3]

Pricing and financing require special attention. Because services cannot be stored, service delivery systems must be able to respond to demand fluctuations and provide pricing flexibility in a manner that maintains the ongoing supplier-customer relationship. Again, technology comes to the rescue. By constantly monitoring future flight ticket sales, airline computers adjust prices to distribute demand across available airline seats, for example. And computerized databases allow "reverse auctions" in which suppliers compete on a real-time basis to reduce bid prices to win orders from buyers. The Priceline.com service for travel services is one prominent example.

The intangibility of services also makes financing more difficult than for product marketing, even for financial institutions with large amounts of international experience. The value of services is more difficult to assess, service performance is more difficult to monitor, and services are difficult to repossess.

Finally, marketers must consider distribution implications of international services. Usually, short and direct channels are required to be close to customers, understand what they really want, and then give it to them tailor-made.

International Opportunities

Although many firms are already active in the international service arena, others often do not perceive their existing competitive advantage. Numerous services have great potential for internationalization.

Financial institutions can offer some functions very competitively in the international field of banking services, thanks to e-commerce extending their direct reach to customers. Construction, design, and engineering services are another sector ripe for global marketing by firms exploiting economies of scale in expertise and the ability to specify other suppliers at the project planning stage. Technology extends the reach of legal and accounting services: There's no reason why transcripts need to be processed in an antechamber on Park Avenue; Dublin will do just fine. Professional service firms can also aid foreign firms and countries to improve business and governmental operations.

In computer and data services, international potential is rapidly growing because many small and medium-sized firms worldwide still need substantial assistance. Teaching services in both academic and business environments have a substantial international growth opportunity, particularly through technology-enabled "e-learning." Removing the confinement of the classroom may well trigger the largest surge in learning that humankind has ever known. Management consulting services can work with institutions and corporations around the globe. Yet consulting services are particularly sensitive to the cultural environment, and their use varies significantly by country and field of expertise.

All domestic service expenditures funded from abroad by foreign citizens also represent a service export. This makes tourism an increasingly important area of services trade. For example, every foreign visitor who spends foreign currency in the United States generates export volume in the U.S. current account. The natural resources and beauty offered by so many countries have already made tourism one of the most important services trade components, to the extent it can weather growing fears of terrorism.

Partnering with foreign firms represents a powerful opportunity for service companies. For example, information technology expertise from one country could be combined with financial resources from another. Combining international advantages in services may ultimately result in organizations with even greater competitive muscle.

Getting Started

Services that are delivered mainly in support of goods most likely should follow the path of the product. Or service firms can follow their customers' and clients' international expansion, a growth model that accounting, advertising, and banking firms have used extensively.

Absent complementary products or existing clients to follow internationally, a service provider should search for market situations abroad that are similar to the domestic market, concentrating in its area of expertise. For example, a design firm learning about construction projects abroad can investigate the possibility of rendering its design services. Similarly, a management consultant learning about the plans of a foreign country or firm to computerize operations can explore the possibility of overseeing a smooth transition from manual to computerized activities.

Another opportunity consists of identifying and anticipating change abroad. A country introducing new transportation services, for example, becomes a market for related distribution and consulting services. Marketers should stay informed about international projects sponsored by domestic organizations such as the U.S. Agency for International Development, as well as international organizations such as the United Nations, the International Finance Corporation, or the World Bank.

FUTURITIES

The global services economy will be knowledge-based, its most precious resource being information and ideas. Unlike the classical factors of production—land, labor, and capital—information and knowledge are not bound to any region or country but are almost infinitely mobile and infinitely capable of expansion.

Changes in technology also make available vast amounts of data worldwide. Therefore, the management of information becomes as important as the information itself. The premium will be on the organization, maintenance, and use of huge, current, and accurate databases covering customers, vendors, regulations, and standards. Knowledge distribution experts will form an entire new profession with two distinct specializations: *Knowledge Focusers* will be in charge of ensuring that the right kind of information is provided. *Knowledge Erasers* will concentrate on weeding out old or outdated data, in order to limit capacity constraints of information storage and to delete corporate information that may lead to future interpretation problems. Due to rising public concerns about the dissemination of information, the role of privacy experts will also be on the increase.

Electronic commerce will mitigate and in some cases eliminate geographic boundaries such as those that traditionally hampered global retail growth. Any retailer will be just a mouse click away. Unlike e-commerce sites that succumbed to the dot-com crash of 2000-2001, retailers with sensible business models that have recognized their global logistics needs are already harvesting the early promises of borderless online business. Little-known companies can gain visibility and credibility on the Web, saving on travel costs in the bargain. Even a small firm can develop a polished and sophisticated Web presence and promotion strategy. Customers are less concerned about geographic location if they feel the firm is electronically accessible. Nonetheless, global service marketers must be patient in waiting for online access to become available in less- developed markets, and they must recognize how language and cultural differences will require Web site tailoring to individual markets.

NOTES

1. Leonard L. Berry, "Services Marketing Is Different," in *Services Marketing,* ed. Christopher H. Lovelock (Englewood Cliffs, NJ: Prentice-Hall, 1984), 30.
2. "Software Industry in India," *India Times,* www.india-times.com, March 14, 1999.
3. M. Krishna Erramilli and C. P. Rao, "Service Firms' International Entry-Mode Choice: A Modified Transaction–Cost Analysis Approach," *Journal of Marketing* 57 (July 1993): 19–38.

PART 3

MANAGING GLOBAL MARKETING

Part Three examines the marketing elements that implement global marketing strategies. Our approach assumes solid domestic marketing knowledge, describing and citing the similarities and differences marketers will encounter when taking export, investment, and strategic alliance strategies to foreign shores. In manipulating and implementing the marketing mix for maximum effect, the old adage "think globally, act locally" becomes a critical guiding principle.

Chapter 9, "International Market Research," examines the process and information sources for reducing the uncertainty in strategic and tactical global marketing decisions.

Chapter 10, "Global Product and Brand Management," emphasizes product development and adaptation, branding, and portfolio management concepts in the international setting.

Chapter 11, "Pricing in Global Markets," examines the complexities, often unforeseen, in pricing and price perceptions in world markets.

Chapter 12, "Global Distribution and Logistics," discusses the critical distribution, logistics, and supply chain management issues.

Chapter 13, "International Negotiation and Communication," emphasizes local adaptation of communications vehicles.

Chapter 14, "Organizing for Global Marketing," examines the appropriate management structures.

Chapter 15, "Twenty-First Century Trade Globalists," cites a vision for world trade as a tool for world prosperity if marketers make the right choices.

9

International Market Research

Where to go when you need to know.

Insufficient preparation and information is the single most important cause of failure in the international marketplace. Major mistakes often occur because the firm and its managers do not have an adequate understanding of the business environment. Many firms either do not believe that international market research is worthwhile, or they face human and financial resource bottlenecks impeding it. Yet building a good knowledge base is a key condition for subsequent marketing implementation, particularly as competitors improve their own research capabilities.

Market research takes two forms: secondary, less expensive information using data already collected by others; and primary, in which the firm collects data itself. This chapter discusses secondary data first, focusing primarily on ways you can obtain basic information quickly and efficiently from governments, international organizations, directories, trade associations, or online databases and ensure that it is reasonably accurate. Once you complete secondary research, you might need primary research for investigating critical issues in detail. Your sensitivity to different international environments and cultures will guide your choice of primary research methods be they interviews, focus groups, observation, surveys, or experimentation.

OPPORTUNITY ANALYSIS

Any business research project should start with a basic question that, oddly enough, managers frequently forget to address explicitly, either domestically or internationally: Does the research value outweigh its cost? Assessing the value of research requires setting objectives for research, which will vary from business to business and will depend on target market opportunities, a firm's global marketing expertise and other strengths, plus the competition it faces. The opportunity is the paramount concern, making the foreign market opportunity analysis a prime research objective for most companies.

Three-stage Foreign Opportunity Analysis

Conducting the foreign market opportunity analysis is done best by a three-step approach:

1. Preliminary screening for attractive markets. Key question: *Which foreign markets warrant detailed investigation?*

Initially, the analyst should not conduct a painstaking and detailed analysis of the world on a market-by-market basis. Instead, take a broad-brush approach to narrow down the possibilities for international marketing activities. Begin with a cursory analysis of general market variables such as per capita GDP, mortality rates, and population figures. These factors will not provide detailed market information, but they will enable the researcher to determine whether the corporation's objectives might be met in those markets. For example, expensive labor-saving consumer products might not be successful in the People's Republic of China because their price may be a significant proportion of the prospect's annual salary, and the perceived benefit to the customer may be only minimal. Such cursory evaluation will help reduce the number of markets to be considered to a more manageable number: from 200 to 25, for example.

2. Assessment of industry market potential. Key question: *What is the aggregate demand in each of the selected markets?*

Next, the researcher will require information about each individual market for a preliminary evaluation. This information typically identifies the fastest-growing markets, the largest markets for a particular product, market trends, and market restrictions. Although precise and detailed information for each product probably cannot be obtained, it probably is available for general product categories. Governmental restrictions on markets must be considered as well. As an example, we can determine that certain developing nations represent fast-growing markets for computer hardware and software. But export licensing regulations may prohibit such trade. Again, this overview will be cursory but will serve to evaluate markets quickly and reduce the number of markets subject to closer investigation.

3. Company sales potential analysis. Key question: *How attractive is the potential demand for company products and services?*[1]

At this stage, the researcher must select appropriate markets and shift the focus to market opportunities for a specific product or brand, including existing, latent, and incipient markets. General product category information is not sufficient for such company-specific decisions. The researcher needs a competitive assessment that matches markets with corporate strengths and the market potential for specific products. In addition, the research should identify demand-and-supply patterns and evaluate any regulations and standards. Research objectives may include obtaining detailed information for penetrating a market, for designing and fine-tuning the marketing mix, or for monitoring the political climate of a country so that the firm can expand its operation successfully.

SECONDARY RESEARCH ABROAD

Knowing the research objective, the analyst can determine the type of information needed. It is likely that management will need both macro and micro secondary and primary data. Our survey of U.S. business executives found that the international information they consider most critical are:

Government Data

- Tariff information
- U.S. export/import data
- Nontariff measures
- Foreign export/import data
- Data on government trade policy

Corporate Data

- Local laws and regulations
- Size of market
- Local standards and specifications
- Distribution system
- Competitive activity

Data Sources

A wide variety of sources provides secondary data for international marketing research purposes. We review major sources briefly here and, in Appendix A at the end of this chapter, list more than 100 key private sector and government publications and organizations that monitor international issues.

Governments. Governments, typically the sources of the widest and most varied data, usually address macro and micro issues and provide specific data services. Macro information includes population trends, general trade flows between countries, and world agricultural production. Micro information includes materials on specific industries in a country, their growth prospects, and their foreign trade activities. Specific data services might provide custom-tailored information responding to the detailed needs of a firm. Alternatively, some data services may concentrate on a specific geographic region.

Most countries offer a wide array of national and international trade data. Closer collaboration between governmental statistical agencies also makes those data more accurate because it is now much easier to compare data, such as bilateral exports and imports, to each other. Government information is usually available from commercial counselors or commercial attachés at embassies and consulates.

Governments increasingly provide up-to-date information online. Growing centralization of trade data is an important development. For example, online information about the European Union in 11 languages is available at www.europa.eu.int.

U.S.-based marketers investigating any country should not overlook the information available from the Department of Commerce's Trade Information Center, at www.export.gov. The Center is operated by the DOC's International Trade Administration for the 20 federal agencies comprising the Trade Promotion Coordinating Committee (TPCC), which are responsible for managing the U.S. Government's export promotion programs and activities.

International Organizations. International organizations often provide useful data for the researcher. The *Statistical Yearbook* of the United Nations contains international trade data on products and export and import data by country. The *World Atlas* published by the World Bank provides useful general data on population, growth trends, and GDP figures. The World Trade Organization (WTO) and the Organization for Economic Cooperation and Development (OECD) also publish quarterly and annual trade data on their member countries. Finally, organizations such as the International Monetary Fund (IMF) and the World Bank publish occasional staff papers that evaluate region- or country-specific issues in depth.

Service Organizations. A wide variety of service organizations that provide international information include banks, accounting firms, freight forwarders, airlines, and international trade consultants. Although some of this information is available without charge, it is often of a very general nature, provided as an "appetizer" for the sale of specific market data for a fee.

Trade Associations. Associations such as world trade clubs and domestic and international chambers of commerce (for example, the American Chambers of Commerce Abroad at www.uschamber.org/

international/) can provide valuable information about local markets, trade issues, and trends affecting international marketers.

Industry trade associations also offer useful data collected from their members and published in aggregate form. Though often quite general in nature because of the wide variety of clientele served, industry trade association data provide valuable first looks into a market. They also permit performance comparisons of a company to its industry averages.

Directories and Newsletters. Many industry directories are available on local, national, and international levels, identifying individual firms in a market. Some are quite detailed in the information provided.

Many newsletters cover specific international issues such as trade finance, contracting, bartering, countertrade, international payment flows, and customs news. Published by banks or accounting firms for clients and prospects, such newsletters usually cater to narrow audiences but can provide important information to the marketer interested in a specific area.

Electronic Information Services. Electronic information services can provide search results within minutes, sparing the researcher hours of sorting through diverse sources. International online computer database services provide market reports and news in return for user fees. A large number of databases, publications, and search engines available on the Internet provide information about products and markets, trade statistics, technical standards, and trade regulations on specific products. Many online publications and data services offer late-breaking information available at all hours.

Governments often prepare information guides for specific countries that provide an overview of the political environment, geography, and holidays. More important to the international marketer, these guides also contain information about market opportunities, regulations, and key contacts. In preparation for an initial market evaluation or entry, using these guides can be quite beneficial, particularly since they are usually free or very low priced. For an example of country and industry reports prepared by the U.S. government, go to www.export.gov.

Electronic information services often are well worth the cost. But despite their ease of access, services cover only a portion of international publications. Also, they are heavily biased toward English-language publications. As a result, relying solely on electronic information might mean overlooking some valuable input. Treat electronic sources as an important but not exclusive dimension for international market research.

Are the Data Right for You?

Evaluate secondary data for their appropriateness to the task at hand before investing time or money in acquiring them. First, consider the quality of the data source, focusing on the purpose and method of the original data collection. Next, assess the quality of the information itself: Is it reliable, accurate, and recent? Then determine the compatibility and comparability of the data. Because someone collected them with another purpose in mind, decide if the data meet your needs and examine if market data from different sources can be compared. For example, the term *middle class* is likely to have very different implications for income and consumption patterns in different parts of the world.

Creativity might lead to using proxy data for otherwise unknown quantities. For example, the market penetration of television sets could be used as a proxy variable for video recorder market potential. Or plans for new port facilities can suggest the future containerization needs of shippers. A society's level of computerization may indicate its future software need. But creativity incurs risk. Always cross-check results and conclusions with other sources of information or with experts.

Data Privacy

Be alert to individual societies' attitudes about secondary and primary data privacy. Many societies are increasingly sensitive, a concern that has grown exponentially because of e-business and access to databases that are valuable to marketers but might be considered privileged by information providers.

In 2002, the European Union passed a directive on privacy and electronic communications. Extending earlier legislation, it maintains high standards of data privacy to ensure the free flow of data throughout the EU's 15 member states. The new directive requires member states to block transmission of data to non-EU countries if those countries do not have domestic legislation that provides for a level of protection judged as adequate by the EU. The EU has a strict interpretation of its citizens' rights to privacy. There is an opt-in approach for unsolicited email: Online marketing firms and other Internet operators can send commercial email only after the customer has specifically asked them to do so. Placing invisible data-tracking devices, such as "cookies" on a computer, is prohibited until after a user has been provided with adequate information about their purpose.

The directive also reflects an EU compromise in light of the September 11 attacks and the growing frequency of cybercrime. Due to requests by key e-commerce partners such as the United States, the EU revised its policy to accommodate criminal investigations. Under the new directive, companies in the EU will still have to erase information immediately after the one- to two-month period needed for billing purposes. However, governments can now require operators to store data for longer periods of time, if deemed necessary for security reasons.[2]

Divergent government policies increasingly require international marketers to adopt global privacy rules for managing online information and earning certification from privacy-minded watchdog groups. In a word, privacy has become yet another of the legal and cultural issues to which global business strategies must adapt.

PRIMARY RESEARCH ABROAD

Marketers use primary research to fill essential information gaps that secondary research does not address or does not examine with sufficient detail to aid a specific business decision. Different environments, attitudes, and market conditions—the very factors that make research necessary—also complicate international primary research far more than domestic research projects.

Primary research is essential for strategic international marketing, particularly market segmentation. Competitiveness requires a firm to segment markets beyond the traditional macro variables of income or consumer spending, to account for target consumer lifestyles and attitudes, factors that influence buying behavior in a single culture, and might also identify consumer similarities across borders. In marketing to women, for example, demographics probably do not tell the important parts of the story in non-Western cultures, where local social norms and economic conditions might well differ widely country to country. On the other hand, an attractive market segment could consist of educationally elite readers who read *Scientific American, Time, Newsweek, The Financial Times,* and *The Economist.* Members in this group are likely to have more in common with each other than with their fellow citizens.

Meeting Your Requirements

Determine your information requirements as precisely as possible *before* designing a primary research project. Using expensive survey, focus group, and other primary research methods for fishing expeditions will only waste money you should have devoted to more secondary investigations. For instance, secondary research can address a question such as the market potential for "furniture" in Indonesia, but primary research might be needed to hone in on your particular product such as modular assembly case goods (chests, cabinets, tables, etc.). Also, primary research might be the only way to probe the current attitudes of consumers and business buyers—viewpoints that will predict the future of a marketing campaign, for questions such as: What effect will a new type of packaging have on our "green" consumers in Germany, France, and England?

How Much Central Control? Should you use a centralized, coordinated, or decentralized research approach? The organization of your company and the importance of the decisions determine the level of control that worldwide headquarters should have over international marketing research activities.

Centralized research gives control to headquarters, which sets all project specifications that local country operations implement. Headquarters analyzes the findings. Such an approach can be valuable when probing corporate policies and strategies, ensuring that all international studies are comparable. On the other hand, headquarters staff might not be sufficiently familiar with local market situations to design research appropriately. Headquarters' cultural biases might influence research activities. And headquarters' staffs might be too small or inexperienced to run a complex international inquiry.

Coordinated research uses an intermediary such as an outside research agency to bring headquarters and country operations together, permitting more local-global interaction and strategic responsiveness to local conditions.

Decentralized research requires corporate headquarters to establish the broad thrust of projects, then delegate design details, supervision, implementation, and analysis to local country operations. This approach works well when international markets differ significantly because it permits significant adaptation to local circumstances. However, implementing research activities on a country-by-country basis may cause unnecessary duplication, a breakdown in knowledge sharing, and incompatible results.

To avoid having local country operations unnecessarily duplicating work already done elsewhere, maintain an intracorporate flow of market information at all times, so local managers stay abreast of information produced by their counterparts. A local unit might also develop its own research initiatives—a creative way to overcome culturally induced response problems, for example—which a researcher elsewhere could adapt to his or her market.

Decentralized research doesn't mean headquarters can avoid a role in global inquiries. Without some degree of overall global strategy, local researchers left to their own devices will develop different ways of collecting and tabulating data. Their respective findings will not be compatible, and the company will lose potentially valuable information about major changes and trends.

In-house or Outsourced Service? One major factor in deciding whether to use outside research services is the size of your international operations and globally savvy internal staff. But no matter how large it is, a company is unlikely to possess specialized research expertise for every single market it currently serves or plans to serve. A firm might decide to delegate the research task to outside groups, particularly when corporate headquarters staffers have little or no familiarity with a local research environment. An outside researcher with global expertise can coordinate a large-scale project when you require specialized research skills. Many leading marketing research agencies operate worldwide in order to accommodate the research needs of their multinational clients. The New York Chapter of the American Marketing Association maintains a searchable online database of research firms worldwide, at http://www.greenbook.org/.

When selecting outside research providers, look first at the quality of information rather than the cost. Low price is no substitute for lack in data pertinence or accuracy. Carefully evaluate the capabilities of an outside organization and compare them with the capabilities available in-house and from competing firms. Although general technical capabilities are important, the prime selection criterion should be previous research experience in a particular country and a particular industry. Some experience is transferable from one industry or country to another; however, the more the corporation's research needs overlap an agency's past research accomplishments, the more likely it is that the research task will be conducted satisfactorily.

Which Tools to Use? Selecting primary research techniques depends on a variety of factors. First, how much objectivity is necessary? Standardized techniques are more useful for collecting objective data than subjective information. Gathering unstructured data will require more open-ended questions and more time than structured data. Because the willingness and ability of respondents to spend the time and provide a free-form response are heavily influenced by factors such as culture and education, the prevailing conditions in the country and segments to be studied need to be understood in making these decisions.

Among other technique selection questions, Are data to be collected in the real world or in a controlled environment? Must the research capture historical facts or gather information about future developments and subsequent purchase intentions? Cultural and individual preferences, which vary significantly among nations, play a major role in those decisions and in determining the most appropriate research techniques. U.S. managers frequently prefer to gather large quantities of data through surveys, which provide numbers that can be manipulated statistically and directly compared to other sets of data. Managers in some other countries apparently prefer the "soft" approach, however. For example, much of Japanese-style market research relies heavily on two kinds of information: soft data, obtained from visits to dealers and other channel members, and hard data about shipments, inventory levels, and retail sales.

Once you determine the structure and type of data you need, choose among several types of research instruments, each providing unique strengths and weaknesses and different depths of information.

Interviews with knowledgeable people can be of great value, particularly when seeking specific answers to narrow questions. Interviewees have their biases, so look to them for in-depth expertise and opinions rather than information projectable to wide audiences.

Focus groups tap the interaction of a small group of knowledgeable people gathered to discuss a particular topic for a limited period of time: two to four hours. Usually, the ideal focus group size is 7 to 10 participants. Their interaction might reveal hidden issues that would not have been addressed in an individual interview. The skill of the group leader in stimulating discussion is crucial to the success of a focus group. Discussions are often recorded on tape and subsequently analyzed in detail.

Focus groups, like in-depth interviews, do not provide statistically projectable information, but they can provide information about perceptions, emotions, and other underlying attitudes. In addition, once individuals gather, focus groups are highly efficient in terms of rapidly accumulating a substantial amount of information. Technology allows focus groups to convene via video or the Internet, generating interaction from all corners of the globe.

When conducting international research via focus groups, be aware of the role of culture in the discussion. Not all societies encourage frank and open exchange and disagreement among individuals. Status consciousness may lead to all participants agreeing with one group member. Disagreements may be considered impolite, or certain topics may be taboo.

Observation techniques require the researcher to play the role of a nonparticipating observer of activity and behavior. Observation can be personal or impersonal. It can be obtrusive or unobtrusive, depending on whether the subject is aware or unaware of being observed. In international marketing research, observation can be extremely useful in shedding light on practices not previously encountered or understood. This aspect is particularly valuable for the researcher who is totally unfamiliar with a market or market situation and can be quickly apprised through, for example, participation in a trade mission.

Observation can also help in understanding phenomena that are hard to assess with other techniques. For example, Toyota engineers and designers unobtrusively observed how Southern California women with long fingernails have trouble opening doors and operating various knobs on car dashboards, leading Toyota to redraw some of its automobile features.

Observations have their pitfalls, however. For example, people may react differently when they discover that someone has been watching. The degree to which the observer has to be familiarized or introduced to other participants may vary. The complexity of the task may depend on language obstacles. In Europe, for example, researchers schedule in-store research photography and interviews well in advance, preceded by a full round of introductions to store management and personnel. In some countries, such as Belgium, a researcher must remember that people speak four different languages, which might change from store to store.

Surveys are the tool for collecting quantitative data from defined audiences. Unlike the techniques previously discussed, which are designed to collect qualitative information about attitudes and behavior, surveys attempt to describe conditions among large groups. If structured properly, the data might be statistically projectable beyond the respondent base. Often, researchers will conduct qualitative studies to define issues and suggest the population characteristics to investigate statistically, and then design and run a survey.

Researchers usually administer survey questions via mailed questionnaires or through interviews by phone or in person. Surveys assume that the population under study can understand and respond to the questions posed and, in the case of mail and telephone surveys, that postal systems are reliable, address information is available, and that target audiences possess listed telephones.

Shortcomings, such as social and cultural constraints can hamper surveys. Some people may be reluctant to respond in writing. In some nations, entire population segments—women, for example—may be totally inaccessible to interviewers. Surveys are often considered inappropriate for examining new product features under development because of consumer biases and their inability to understand features with which they have no experience.

Despite such shortcomings, surveys are useful for rapidly accumulating data amenable to statistical analysis. On a global scale, even though quite difficult, comparative research has been carried out very successfully across nations, particularly when the environments studied are similar enough to limit the influence of uncontrollable variables. Some researchers have, however, successfully conducted comparative surveys even in quite dissimilar environments.[3] With constantly expanding technological capabilities, international marketers will be able to use the survey technique more frequently in the future.

Questionnaires require careful attention to content, format, and wording—constituting a research science and art beyond the scope of this book but well worth studying by any marketer with international aspirations. Even if you hire a research specialist to do the work, you should be familiar with the questionnaire process to ensure a project proceeds as intended. A number of good sources for questionnaire and survey design are available.[4]

International research poses important and unique challenges to questionnaire design that normally are not encountered in domestic studies. The differences start with language and culture, which determine how to word questions to minimize misunderstanding. One of this book's authors, for example, used the term *group discussion* in a questionnaire for Russian executives, only to learn that the translated meaning was *political indoctrination session.*

The key consideration is fastidious attention to guidelines that make sense in any survey venue: keep questions clear; use simple rather than complex words; avoid ambiguous words and questions; omit leading questions; ask questions in specific terms; and avoid generalizations and estimates. When working internationally, translation adds a significant additional burden. Using the translation-retranslation approach helps to detect inadvertent blunders: One translator adapts a question to the language of the market under study; a second translator returns the foreign wording to the researcher's native language. An additional safeguard is the use of alternative wording: The researcher asks the same question with different wording at various points in the questionnaire in order to check for consistent interpretation by respondents.

Among other special questionnaire considerations internationally:

- Open-ended questions capture more in-depth information, but they also increase the potential for interviewer bias. Even so, open-ended questions help respondents answer questions in their own frames of reference, making them very helpful in cross-cultural research, experts say.[5]

- Another cross-cultural question format decision is the choice between direct and indirect questions and which are culturally acceptable. In some cultures, you can ask respondents directly about employees, performance, standards, and financing, for instance. In others, particularly in Asia or the Middle East, such questions are thought to be rude and insulting.[6]

- The researcher must also be sure to adapt the complexity of the question to the level of understanding of the respondent. For example, a multipoint scaling method, which may be effectively used in a developed country to discover the attitudes and attributes of company executives, may be a very poor instrument if used among poorly educated rural entrepreneurs where demonstration aids are useful.[7]

- The question format should also ensure data equivalence, particularly for questions that attempt to collect attitudinal, psychographic, or lifestyle data. In a developed country, for example, a white-collar worker may be part of the middle class, while in a less-developed country the same person would be part of the upper class. Or a survey concerning grocery shopping habits might require data from housewives in one country but from housemaids in another.[8]

- Be sure respondents are able and willing to answer certain questions, given their education, societal restrictions, and motivations. For example, in countries where tax evasion is routine, answers to income questions will be misleading. In Brazil, individuals will rarely admit to owning an imported car, even though many imports appear on the streets of Rio de Janeiro.

Finally, be sure to pretest questionnaires—again a good idea in any venue, domestic or foreign. Ideally, pretest with a subset of actual respondents, but at least pretest with knowledgeable experts. Even though a pretest may mean time delays and additional cost, the risks of poor research are simply too great for this step to be omitted.

Pick Appropriate Samples. Many methods that have been developed in industrialized countries for compiling survey samples are useless abroad. Address directories might not be available, for instance. Multiple families may live in one dwelling. Differences between population groups living in highlands and lowlands may require differentiating those segments.

A dearth of basic demographic information may prevent the design of a sampling frame. Often, innovative sampling methods need to be devised in order to ensure representative responses. For example, an American entrepreneur hoping to distribute American companies' catalogs to affluent residents of Mexico City couldn't find market demographics and associated mailing lists in the conventional sense. So he asked his company's local investors for membership lists of the city's exclusive golf clubs, and he obtained directories of the parents of students at some of the city's exclusive private schools.[9]

Monitor Progress. The international marketing researcher must check the quality of the data collection process. In some cultures, locals consider questionnaires useless, administered primarily to humor the researcher. When such interviewer cheating might be frequent, spot-checks on the process are vital to ensure reasonable data quality. And apply realism checks to data. For example, if marketing research in Italy reports that people consume very little spaghetti, the researcher should consider whether individuals responded to their use of purchased spaghetti rather than homemade spaghetti. Also, compare collected data to secondary information and to analogous data from a similar market to get a preliminary feel for data quality.

Handling Collected Primary Data

The researcher should, of course, use the best tools available and appropriate for analyzing research findings, even when they originate in less-developed markets. But don't fool yourself by using overly sophisticated tools to examine unsophisticated data; even the best tools will not improve data quality. Again, this is a subject whose details are best left to other books and research specialists.[10]

Reporting results to others, communicate at all levels: headquarters management to local operations managers. Otherwise, the multinational synergistic benefits of research will be lost. Sharing results multinationally, perhaps through a company printed or online newsletter, also demonstrates how managers in other markets can adapt successful research projects to their own businesses. Then the entire organization benefits by improving its international marketing research capabilities.

Finally, research findings must be applied to decisions, and managers must follow up to ensure that happens. Will the product development engineers actually add features to a new product that consumers in a target market consider important? Without such follow-up, research tends to become a mere "staff" function, increasingly isolated from corporate "line" activity. If that happens, global marketers are at risk by flying blind.

CREATING AN INTERNATIONAL
INFORMATION SYSTEM

Multinational marketers usually need information that's broader and more contemporary than a simple compilation of individual international research projects. An information system must integrate relevant and timely inputs from many sources into a flexible format easily accessed by managers.

Such a system faces special challenges, such as making diverse markets' data compatible and comparable. To enrich the basic knowledge that companies collect from the marketplace and from their internal transaction records, companies increasingly use tools such as environmental scanning, Delphi studies, and scenario building.

Environmental Scanning

Environmental scanning continuously tracks political, social, commercial, and economic conditions in target markets, regions of opportunity, and worldwide institutions. The precision required varies with a company's needs, which must be fully understood before the international information system framework is designed. More immediate needs tend to require detail, while long-term strategic decision-making needs big-picture thinking, lest managers get bogged down in minutiae.

You can scan the environment in various ways. One method consists of obtaining factual input regarding many variables from many sources. For example, the U.S. Census Bureau collects, evaluates, and adjusts a wide variety of demographic, social, and economic characteristics of foreign countries. Similar information can be obtained from international organizations such as the World Bank or the United Nations.

But that might not be enough. Multinational marketers often need other inputs, particularly when forecasting developments. Content analysis of communications within markets—literally counting the number of times preselected words, themes, symbols, or pictures appear in a given medium—is one method of spotting trend-setting events and inferring changes ahead.

Ensure that you balance breadth with depth when scanning the environment, lest global information become too generalized to make a difference to decision makers. And keep in mind that internationally there may be a fine line between tracking and obtaining information, and misappropriating corporate secrets. With growing frequency, governments and firms claim that their trade secrets are being obtained and abused by foreign competitors. The perceived threat from economic espionage has led to legislation[11] and accusations of government spying networks trying to undermine the commercial interests of companies.[12]

Delphi Studies

Delphi studies are a method for creative and highly qualitative knowledge-gathering from experts polled on a subject because they cannot meet physically. Delphi studies collect judgments from those who know instead of seeking the average responses of many possessing only limited knowledge. Typically, Delphi studies are carried out with groups of about 30 well-chosen participants who possess in-depth expertise in an area of concern, such as future developments in the international trade environment. These participants are asked via mail, email, or fax to identify and rank the major issues in the area of concern and explain their thinking. Next, all participants review the aggregated viewpoints of all group members, expressing their agreement or disagreement with the issues, the rankings, and the comments. After several rounds of such challenge and response, a reasonably coherent consensus emerges.

The Delphi technique is particularly useful because panelists can respond on their own schedules. Delphi bridges large distances and therefore makes individuals quite accessible at a reasonable cost. It builds respondent interaction, but it might take months to run through the rounds of challenge and response. An important consideration is the careful selection and motivation of panelists so they don't ignore the process. And do not let communication technology drive the study, lest it exclude key participants able to use only less sophisticated methods.

Scenario Building

Some companies use scenario analysis to examine different configurations of key variables. For example, they vary predictions about economic growth rates, import penetration, population growth, and political stability to envision new environmental conditions that will affect corporate strategy. The trick is to identify the crucial variables and their best-case, worst-case, and likely changes in the near and long term.

Scenario builders need to recognize the nonlinearity of factors. To simply extrapolate from currently existing situations is insufficient. Frequently, extraneous factors may enter the picture with a significant impact. Finally, in scenario building recognize the possibility of joint occurrences because changes may not occur in isolation internationally. For example, political instability might compound the problems caused by a developing nation's insolvency. Technology advances accelerate the growth of emerging direct and substitute competition and reduce international buyers' search costs.

Of course, for scenarios to be useful, management must respond to them by formulating contingency plans for unexpected situations. The difficulty is devising scenarios that are unusual enough to trigger new thinking yet sufficiently realistic to be taken seriously by management.[13]

FUTURITIES

Advances in technology have spawned new research approaches that improve consumers' ability to be heard and marketers' ability to listen. In particular, Web-based research and email surveys make it easier to extend information gathering globally, with accuracy and at lower cost. Manufacturers and dealers can portray product details and shopping environments visually and aurally, adding realism to the research experience. And the technology can track and interpret consumers' interest and how they gather information.

Researchers can administer surveys via email or on a Web site. Posted on a site, certain questions or an entire questionnaire can appear or not depending on the site visitor's characteristics (collected in a registration process) or interests (pages visited). Email questionnaires, as with regular mail surveys, work best when sent to recipients with known characteristics. And because email eliminates the cost of questionnaire printing and mailing, the researcher can survey more diverse audiences economically. Experience indicates that such electronic inquiries speed response and increase response rates compared to mail surveys. And researchers can plug electronic responses directly into databases and analytical software without additional data entry costs or errors.[14]

It would be too simplistic, however, to assume that survey content digitization is all it takes to research globally on the Web. The researcher must account for cultural differences and design a survey compatible with respondents' values, rituals, and symbols. Use culture-specific heroes to deliver encouragement and testimonials, for example. A Web site could offer product users in high-context cultures, such as Korea, the opportunity to "join a community" of respondents. In contrast, visitors from low-context cultures such as the United States can be asked about product features immediately.[15]

In addition, such electronic research suffers from a lack of confidentiality because email discloses the sender's identity. That might trigger privacy issues that could limit the use of such tools in some nations or regions. Also, an overused tool could lose its novelty with respondents and high response rates might decline over time.

Nonetheless, new technologies offer the new trade globalist an array of new opportunities that will grow increasingly varied. In the future, a leading marketing research expert has predicted, Web-based surveys will become the norm, not the exception.[16]

Appendix

Market Information Sources

European Union

EUROPA
The umbrella server for all institutions
www.europa.eu.int

I'M-EUROPE
Information on telematics,
   telecommunications, copyright, IMPACT
   program for the information market
http://www.2.echo.lu/ OR:
http://www.igd.fhg.de/archive/1995_www95
   /proc

CORDIS
Information on EU research programs
www.cordis.lu

EUROPARL
Information on the European Parliament's
   activities
www.europarl.eu.int

EuroStat
europa.eu.int/comm./eurostat

Delegation of the European Commission to
   the US Press releases, EURECOM:
   Economic and Financial News, EU-US
   relations, information on EU policies and
   delegation programs
www.eurunion.org

Citizens Europe
Covers rights of citizens of EU member states
citizens.eu.int

EUR-LEX
Portal to European Law
europa.eu.int/eur-lex

Euro
The Single Currency
euro.eu.int

European Agency for the Evaluation of
   Medicinal Products
Information on drug approval procedures
   and documents of the Committee for
   Proprietary Medicinal Products and the
   Committee for Veterinary Medicinal
   Products
www. emea.eu.int

European Centre for the Development of
   Vocational Training
Under construction with information on the
   Centre and contact information
www.cedefop.gr

European Environment Agency
Information on the mission, products and
   services, and organizations and staff of the
   EEA
www.eea.eu.int

NOTE: Physical locations have been given only in the absence of URLs.

European Investment Bank
Press releases and information on borrowing
   and loan operations, staff, and publications
www.eib.org

European Monetary Institute
Related Treaty provisions setting up the
   Institute, rules of procedure, function and
   staff, list of publications
www.ecb.int

European Training Foundation
Information on vocational education and
   training programs in Central and Eastern
   Europe and Central Asia
www.etf.eu.int

Office for Harmonization in the Internal
   Market
Guidelines, application forms, and other
   information for registering an EU
   trademark
www.oami.eu.int/en/default.htm

Council of the European Union
Information and news from the Council with
   sections covering Common Foreign and
   Security Policy (CFSP) and Justice and
   Home Affairs Under Construction
ue.eu.int/

Court of Justice
Overview, press releases, publications, and
   full-text proceedings of the court
europa.eu.int/cj/en/index.htm

Court of Auditors
Information notes, annual reports, and
   other publications
www.eca.eu.int

European Community Information Service
www.eurunion.org

European Bank for Reconstruction and
   Development
www.ebrd.com

European Union
www.eurunion.org

United Nations

www.un.org

Conference of Trade and Development
www.unctad.org

Department of Economic and Social Affairs
www.un.org/ecosocdev/

Industrial Development Organization
www.unido.org

International Trade Centre
UNCTAD/WTO
www.intracen.org

UN Publications
www.un.org/pubs/sales.htm

United Nations Educational, Scientific and
   Cultural Organization (UNESCO)
www.unesco.org

United Nations Social Indicators
www.un.org/depts/unsd/social/main2.htm

U.S. Government

Agency for International Development
www.usaid.gov

Customs Service
www.customs.ustreas.gov

Department of Agriculture
www.usda.gov

Department of Commerce
www.commerce.gov

Department of State
www.state.gov

Department of the Treasury
www.ustreas.gov

Federal Trade Commission
www.ftc.gov

FedStats
www.fedstats.gov

Global Trends 2015
www.cia.gov/cia/publications/
   globaltrends2015

United States Census Bureau
www.census.gov

U.S. Commercial Service
http://usatrade.gov

United States House of Representatives
   Law Library
lectlaw.com/inll/1.htm

World Fact Book
www.odci.gov/cia/publications/factbook/
   index.html

International Trade Commission

500 E Street NW
Washington, D.C. 20436
www.usitc.gov

Small Business Administration
www.sbaonline.sba.gov

U.S. Trade and Development Agency
www.tda.gov

World Trade Centers Association
www.wtca.org

Council of Economic Advisers—
   www.whitehouse.gov/cea
Department of Defense—**www.dod.gov**
Department of Energy— **www.energy.gov**
Department of Interior—**www.doi.gov**
Department of Labor—**www.dol.gov**
Department of Transportation—
   www.dot.gov
Environmental Protection Agency—
   www.epa.gov
National Trade Data Bank—**www.stat-usa.gov**
National Economic Council—
   www.whitehouse.gov/nec
Office of the U.S. Trade Representative—
   www.ustr.gov
Office of Management and Budget—
   www.whitehouse.gov/omb
Overseas Private Investment Corporation—
   www.opic.gov

Selected Organizations

American Bankers Association
www.aba.com

American Bar Association
Section of International Law and Practice
www.abanet.org/intlaw/home.html

American Management Association
www.amanet.org

American Marketing Association
www.ama.org

American Petroleum Institute
www.api.org

Asia-Pacific Economic Cooperation Secretariat
www.apecsec.org.sg

Asian Development Bank
www.adb.org

Association of South East Asian Nations
   (ASEAN)
Publication Office
www.asean.or.id

Better Business Bureau
www.bbb.org

Canadian Market Data
www.strategis.ic.gc.ca

Chamber of Commerce of the United States
www.uschamber.org

Commission of the European Communities
   to the United States
www.eurunion.org

Conference Board
www.conference-board.org

Deutsche Bundesbank
www.bundesbank.de

Electronic Industries Association
www.eia.org

Export-Import Bank of the United States
www.exim.gov

Federal Reserve Bank of New York
www.ny.frb.org

Gallup
www.gallup.com

Greenpeace
www.greenpeace.org

Iconoculture
iconoculture.com

IRSS (Institute for Research in Social
Science)
www.irss.unc.edu/data_archive/home.asp

Imagitrends
pages.prodigy.net/imagiweb/index.htm

Inter-American Development Bank
www.iadb.org

International Bank for Reconstruction and
Development (World Bank)
www.worldbank.org

International Monetary Fund
www.imf.org

International Telecommunication Union
www.itu.int

LANIC (Latin American Network
Information Center)
www.lanic.utexas.edu

Michigan State University
Center for International Business Education
and Research
globaledge.msu.edu/ibrd/ibrd.asp

Marketing Research Society
111 E. Wacker Drive, Suite 600
Chicago, IL 60601

National Association of Manufacturers
www.nam.org

National Federation of Independent Business
www.nfib.org

NNSP (National Network of State Polls)
www.unc.edu/depts/nnsp/archives.htm

Organization for Economic Cooperation
and Development
www.oecd.org

Organization of American States
www.oas.org

The Roper Center for Public Opinion
Research
www.ropercenter.uconn.edu

Roper Starch Worldwide
www.roper.com

Society for International Development
www.sidint.org

Transparency International
www.transparency.org

Indexes to Literature

Business Periodical Index
H.W. Wilson Co.
950 University Avenue
Bronx, NY 10452

New York Times Index
www.nytimes.com

Public Affairs Information
Service Bulletin
11 W. 40th Street
New York, NY 10018

Reader's Guide to Periodical Literature
www.tulane.edu/~horn/rdg.html

Wall Street Journal Index
www.wsj.com

Directories

American Register of Exporters and Importers
38 Park Row, New York, NY 10038

Arabian Year Book
Dar Al-Seuassam Est. Box 42480
Shuwahk, Kuwait

Directories of American Firms Operating in
Foreign Countries
World Trade Academy Press
Uniworld Business Publications Inc.
50 E. 42nd Street
New York, NY 10017

The Directory of International Sources of
Business Information
Pitman
128 Long Acre, London WC2E 9AN, England

Encyclopedia of Associations
Gale Research Co.
Book Tower, Detroit, MI 48226

Polk's World Bank Directory
R.C. Polk & Co.
2001 Elm Hill Pike
P.O. Box 1340, Nashville, TN 37202

Verified Directory of Manufacturer's
Representatives
MacRae's Blue Book Inc.
817 Broadway, New York, NY 10003

World Guide to Trade Associations
K.G. Saur & Co.
175 Fifth Avenue, New York, NY 10010

Price Information

ARI Network/CNS
Chemical Business Newsbase
COLEACP
Commodity Options
Commodities 2000
Market News Service of ITC
Nikkei Shimbun News Database
Reuters Monitor
UPI
US Wholesale Prices

Company Registers

ABC Europe Production Europe
Biocommerce Abstracts & Directory
CD-Export (CD-ROM only)
Company Intelligence
D&B Duns Market Identifiers (U.S.A.)

D&B European Marketing File
D&B Eastern Europe
Dun's Electronic Business Directory
Firmexport/Firmimport
Hoppenstedt Austria
Hoppenstedt Germany
Hoppenstedt Benelux
Huco-Hungarian Companies
ICC Directory of Companies
Kompass Asia/Pacific
Kompass Europe (EKOD)
Mexican Exporters/Importers
Piers Imports
Polu-Polish Companies
SDOE
Thomas Register
TRAINS(CD-ROM being developed)
UK Importers
UK Importers (DECTA)
US Directory of Importers
US I/E Maritime Bills of Lading
World Trade Center Network

Tariffs and Trade Regulations

Celex
ECLAS
Justis Eastern Europe (CD-ROM only)
Scad
Spearhead
Spicer's Centre for Europe
TRAINS(CD-ROM being developed)
US Code of Federal Regulations
US Federal Register
US Harmonized Tariff Schedule

Standards

BSI Standardline
Noriane/Perinorm
NTIS Bibliographic Data Base
Standards Infodisk ILI (CD-ROM only)

Shipping Information

Piers Imports
Tradstat World Trade Statistics
US I/E Maritime Bills of Lading

NOTES

1. S. Tamer Cavusgil, "Guidelines for Export Market Research," *Business Horizons* 28 (November–December 1985): 29. Copyright 1985 by the Foundation for the School of Business at Indiana University.
2. "EU Vote Relaxes E-Privacy Rules," *Reuters.com*, May 31, 2002.
3. For an excellent example, see Alan Dubinsky, Marvin Jolson, Masaaki Kotabe, and Chae Lim, "A Cross-National Investigation of Industrial Salespeople's Ethical Perceptions," *Journal of International Business Studies* 22 (1991): 651–670.
4. An excellent reference is C. Samuel Craig and Susan P. Douglas, *International Marketing Research* 2nd ed. (New York: John Wiley & Sons, 2000).
5. Sydney Verba, "Cross-National Survey Research: The Problem of Credibility," in *Comparative Methods in Sociology: Essays on Trends and Applications,* ed. I. Vallier (Berkeley: University of California Press, 1971), 322–323.
6. Camille P. Schuster and Michael J. Copeland, "Global Business Exchanges: Similarities and Differences around the World," *Journal of International Marketing* (Number 2, 1999): 63–80.
7. Kavil Ramachandran, "Data Collection for Management Research in Developing Countries," in *The Management Research Handbook,* eds. N. Craig Smith and Paul Dainty (London: Routledge, 1991), 304.
8. C. Samuel Craig and Susan P. Douglas, *International Marketing Research,* 2nd ed. (Chichester: John Wiley & Sons, 2000).
9. Dianna Soils, "Grass-Roots Marketing Yields Clients in Mexico City," *The Wall Street Journal,* October 24, 1991, B2.
10. An excellent guide to this subject is Gilbert Churchill and Dawn Iacobucci, *Marketing Research* (Cincinnati: South-Western, 2002).
11. B. R. Shapiro, "Economic Espionage," *Marketing Management* (Spring 1998): 56–58.
12. Peter Clarke, "The Echelon Questions," *Electronic Engineering Times* (March 6, 2000): 36.
13. David Rutenberg, "Playful Plans," Queen's University working paper, 1991.
14. J. Ilieva, S. Baron, and N. M. Healey, "Online surveys in Marketing Research: Pros and Cons," *International Journal of Marketing Research,* 44:3 (2002) 361–376.
15. D. Luna, L. A. Peracchio, and M. D. de Juan, "Cross-Cultural and Cognitive Aspects of Web Site Navigation," *Journal of the Academy of Marketing Science,* 30:4 (2002) 397–410.
16. William D. Neal, "Still Got It; Shortcomings Plague the Industry," *Marketing News* (Sept. 16, 2002), 37.

10

Global Product and Brand Management

Products and brands must "speak" your customers' "language."

By the end of the 1980s, with disposable razors taking up 50 percent of the market, executives at Gillette, the $9.3 billion Boston-based consumer product marketer, decided to jettison what they saw as a dead-end strategy. The disposable razor had become a commodity. Consumers bought them solely on the basis of price and convenience. Gillette needed a differentiator, a high-value branded product that could earn substantially more market share. Rather than stick with their old strategy, Gillette managers decided to create a new category, the shaving system, and take control of it.

In 1990, after 10 years of research and development, Gillette introduced its Sensor twin-bladed shaving system, which produced a markedly better shave and also returned Gillette to an indisputable leadership position. The next step was to see whether three blades could do a better job than two. In order to ensure that consumers did not simply scoff at three blades as a marketing gimmick, the product—and communication about it—had to be demonstrably better. After five more years of R&D, ceaseless product improvement, and constant product testing around the world, Gillette launched the Mach 3 razor. The company concentrated as much on developing a great new brand as well as a great new product, backing it with new value propositions and a one-market worldwide strategy based on several premises:

- Because product sales would probably take off immediately, manufacturing had to ensure that it had enough capacity to avoid shortages at the outset.
- To facilitate smooth global introduction, all packaging, point-of-sale, and other promotional material had to be the same—translated into thirty languages. The company purposefully keeps the number of words on the front of the package to a minimum to avoid the need for design alterations.
- All advertising was based on a single campaign that was released in

every market with minor local adjustments and translations. Gillette delayed the European introduction by two months to accommodate Europeans' traditional summer holiday.

- Pricing needed built-in elasticity, but by carefully testing the concept with consumers, Gillette fixed a profitable price point based on the expected number of blades per user per year.

By 2000, Mach 3 had become the success its developers and marketers had hoped. It had captured more than 20 percent of the global blade and razor market, with individual country market shares ranging from 13 to 16 percent. Copycats quickly followed with lower-priced razors, validating the product's appeal and the wisdom of Gillette's aggressive global product introduction strategy.[1]

Gillette's Mach 3 saga shows that developing and managing a product portfolio in the global marketplace is a great challenge in pursuit of an attractive opportunity. But having a single brand and a standardized product that plays well around the world is a luxury only a very few marketers can enjoy. Local product and marketing mix adaptation to one degree or another is likely for most global marketers. Even Coca-Cola, one of the world's most global marketers, practices some local market adaptation. The main goal of the product development process, therefore, is not to develop a standard product or product line but to build adaptability into products and product lines to achieve worldwide appeal. Marketers need to be alert for best-practice product and marketing characteristics emerging locally that will travel well across borders.

This chapter discusses the processes marketers should employ to achieve global uniformity without compromising the needs of local markets. Then we examine the product and brand portfolio strategies that reify the "think globally, act locally" axiom. Finally, we review the special challenges of when and how to adapt existing domestic products for foreign markets.

BALANCED GLOBAL PRODUCT DEVELOPMENT

Product development is the heart of the global marketing process. New products should be developed, or old ones modified, to cater to new or changing customer needs on a global or regional basis while at the same time satisfying corporate technical and financial objectives. With competition increasingly able to react quickly to new product introductions, a firm that adopts a worldwide approach is better able to develop products quickly with specifications compatible on a worldwide scale. A firm that leaves product development to independent units will incur greater difficulties transferring its experience and technology.

But worldwide products should be adaptable. Many multinational corporations develop each product for potential worldwide usage, but adjust features to unique market requirements whenever technically feasible. Some design their products to meet major market regulations and other key requirements and then, if necessary, make adjustments for smaller markets on a country-by-country basis. For example, Nissan developed lead-country models that can, with minor changes, be made suitable for local sales in the majority of markets. It provides a range of additional models that can be adapted to the needs of local segments. Using this approach, Nissan has been able to reduce the number of basic models from 48 to 18.[2] This approach also permits a concurrent new product introduction in all the firm's markets. Companies like 3M and Xerox have developed most of their products with this objective in mind.

Some markets may require unique approaches. Some manufacturers enter developing markets, such as Eastern Europe and China, with older, cheaper products before selling them up-to-date versions.[3] In a world economy where most of the growth is occurring in developing markets, the traditional approach of introducing a global product may keep new products out of the hands of consumers because of their premium prices. As a result, Procter & Gamble figures out what consumers in various countries can pay and then develops products they can afford. For example, in Brazil, the company introduced a diaper called Pampers Uni, a less-expensive version of its mainstream product. The strategy was to create price tiers, hooking customers early and then encouraging them to trade up as their incomes and desire for better products grow.

New Global Product Processes

New product ideas can and do come from just about everywhere: inside the company, or outside from customers, distributors, or the citizen on the street. Internationally, external sources close to the cultural and economic needs of local markets play a very important new product ideation role. Competitors are a major outside source of ideas as well.

Customers can be the best sources for product ideas, particularly in business and industrial sectors. Lead users—companies, organizations, or individuals who are ahead of trends or have needs that go beyond what is available at present—have been the source of many commercially important products in a variety of industries, more so than company R&D labs. For example, a car company seeking a new braking system may look at racing teams or even the aerospace industry for new ideas. Those businesses have a strong incentive to stop speeding vehicles before they run out of runway.[4] Of the 30 products with the highest world sales in the 1990s, 70 percent trace their origins to manufacturing and marketing rather than laboratories, thanks to customer input.[5]

Many companies work with complementary-goods producers to devise new solutions; Whirlpool and Procter & Gamble jointly developed new solutions for cleaning clothes, for example. Individual customers can join the process through the Internet, a survey and chat room medium some foresighted manufacturers have used to solicit customer comment about features and benefits long before prototype development. For example, Sony set up a Web site to support hackers who are interested in exploring and developing new types of games that could be played on the Sony PlayStation.

Global companies already have an advantage in being able to utilize a broad range of resources from around the world and apply them as needed anywhere else on the planet. For example, when a major U.S. photocopier manufacturer faced an eroding small-copier market share in Europe because of Japanese incursions, it asked its Japanese subsidiary to develop an addition to the company's product line. The company has since sold the product in the United States as well.

Screening and Adapting. Most companies screen new product ideas on market, technical, and financial criteria. But too often, companies focus on understanding only current market demand rather than underlying market need. Repositioning a concept might overcome an initially negative customer. For example, cereal marketers present their products as snacks in countries with no significant breakfast habit. Procter & Gamble created the perception that dandruff—traditionally a nonissue for the Chinese—is a social stigma. It offered a product (Head & Shoulders antidandruff shampoo) to solve the problem and it captured more than half the Chinese shampoo market.[6]

A product idea that at some stage fails to earn a go-ahead is not necessarily scrapped. Most progressive companies maintain data banks of "miscellaneous opportunities," which can be a fruitful source of product ideas adaptable to markets other than the original customers its designers had in mind.

The product development process can be initiated by any unit of the organization, in the parent country or abroad. If the initiating entity is a subsidiary that lacks technical and financial resources for implementation, another entity of the firm is assigned the responsibility, usually the parent and its central R&D department. Experts increasingly recommend, however, that companies use foreign-based resources to improve their international contacts and R&D inputs. Many multinationals find their R&D should be located close to their markets to satisfy local styles, needs, and possibly regulations. Pharmaceutical industry regulations often require U.S. companies to have European formulation laboratories, for example.

The activities of a typical global program start with the managing unit's responsibility for accomplishing:

- Single-point worldwide technical development and design of a new product that conforms to the global design standard and global manufacturing and procurement standards.
- Transmitting the completed design to each affected unit.
- All other activities necessary to plan, develop, manufacture, introduce, and support the product in the managing unit as well as direction and support to affected units to ensure that concurrent introductions are achieved.
- Integration and coordination of all global program activities.

The affected units, on the other hand, have prime responsibility for:

- Identifying unique requirements to be incorporated in the product goals and specifications as well as in the managing unit's technical effort.
- All other activities necessary to plan, manufacture, introduce, and support products in affected units.
- Identifying any nonconcurrence with the managing unit's plans and activities.

During the early stages of the product development process, management should concentrate on identifying and evaluating the requirements of both the managing unit and the affected units and incorporating them into the plan. During the later stages, the emphasis is on the efficient development and design of a global product with a minimum of configuration differences and on the development of supporting systems capabilities in each of the participating units. This approach effectively cuts through the standardized-versus-localized debate and offers a clear-cut way of determining and implementing effective programs in several markets simultaneously. It offers headquarters the opportunity to standardize certain aspects of the product while permitting maximum flexibility, whenever technically feasible, to differing market conditions.

To cut down on development time, companies like NEC and

Canon use multidisciplinary teams that stay with the project from start to finish, using a parallel approach toward product launch. Designers start to work before feasibility testing is over, and manufacturing and marketing begin gearing up well before the design is finished. Such teams depend on computer systems for designing, simulating, and analyzing products. Toyota Motor Company estimates that it will, sometime in the future, develop a new automobile in one year (its RAV4 mini-sport-utility vehicle was brought to market in 24 months), while some of its competitors may spend as much as 5 years on the process.[7] However, with new and discontinuous technologies for which market response is not clear, longer development cycles are still common and advisable.

R&D Follows Brainpower

Companies make R&D investments abroad for four general reasons:

- To aid technology transfer from parent to subsidiary.
- To develop new and improved products expressly for foreign markets.
- To develop new products and processes for simultaneous application in world markets of the firm.
- To generate new technology of a long-term exploratory nature.[8]

In truly global companies, the location of R&D is determined by the location of specific skills, resulting in greater roles for local R&D centers that collectively scan the world for ideas that will cross borders. Placing research operations abroad may also ensure access to foreign scientific and technical personnel and information, either in industry or at leading universities. The unique features of the market may also drive the location decision. For example, most of the major car makers have design centers in California to allow for the monitoring of technical, social, and aesthetic values of the fifth-largest car market in the world. Furthermore, the many technological innovations and design trends that have originated there give it a trendsetting image.

Given the increasing importance of emerging markets, many marketers believe that an intimate understanding of these new consumers can be achieved only through proximity. Consequently, Unilever has installed a network of innovation centers in 19 countries, many of which are emerging markets such as Brazil, China, and Thailand.[9]

Many companies regionalize their R&D efforts; for example, U.S.-based multinational corporations often base their European R&D facilities in Belgium because of its central location and desirable market characteristics, which include serving as headquarters for the European Union and providing well-trained personnel. Regional centers may also be needed to adequately monitor customer trends around the world. Sharp, one of Japan's leading electronics companies, set up centers in Hamburg, Germany, and Mahwah, New Jersey, in addition to its two centers at home.[10]

Centers of Excellence. The consensus among marketers is that many more countries are now capable of developing products and product solutions that can be applied on a worldwide basis. This realization has led to networks of "centers of excellence" such as those Colgate-Palmolive set up around the world, clustering countries with geographic, linguistic, or cultural similarities to exploit the same marketing plans. Unilever extended the innovation centers it opened for personal care products to its food businesses, starting with ice cream.

Countries have an edge if there is strong local development in a particular product category—such as hair care in France and Thailand—creating an abundance of research and development talent. Local management or existing products with a history of sensitivity to corporate core competency also helps win a worldwide role for a country unit. For example, ABB Strömberg in Finland was designated a worldwide center of excellence for electric drives, a category for which it is a recognized world leader. Centers of excellence do not necessarily have to be focused on products or technologies. Some excel at critical management functions, such as sales and marketing. Whatever the format, the most important tasks of centers of excellence are to leverage the company's leading-edge capabilities and to continually enhance them so the firm remains at the forefront of its industry.[11]

Friendly Hosts. Governments like R&D center investments, sometimes providing incentives to investors, but sometimes demanding R&D facilities as a condition for making other investments. On occasion, global investors shy away, seeing no need for the additional expense. However, local R&D efforts can provide positive publicity for the company involved. Internally, having local R&D may boost morale and elevate a subsidiary above the status of a manufacturing operation. Japan, India, Brazil, and France are all examples of countries that have tried to influence multinational corporations. So is China, whose government has maintained a preference for foreign investors who have promised a commitment to technology transfer, especially in the form of R&D centers. Volkswagen's ability to develop its business in China is largely due to its willingness to do so.

In many multinational corporations that still employ multidomestic (autonomous country subsidiary) strategies, product development efforts amount to product modifications: making sure that a product satisfies local regulations, for example. Local content requirements might require major development input from the affected markets. In these cases, local technical people identify alternate, domestically available ingredients and prepare initial tests. More involved testing usually takes place at a regional laboratory or at headquarters.

Teamwork and Testing

International, multifunction teams should be in charge of global product development activity. They give concepts tough scrutiny at specified stages of the development cycle, prune weaker ideas, and streamline decision making. At the least, an international team member should be assigned a permanent role in each product development team. In addition, some global corporations hold periodic meetings of purely international teams.

A typical international team may consist of five members, most of whom have a product and a geographic responsibility. Others may be from central R&D and domestic marketing planning. The function of international teams is to support subsidiaries and ensure international input, particularly from customers. Teams might also include personnel from strategic alliance partners. R&D capability may in fact be the prime reason for an alliance in the first place.

The final stages of the product development process will involve testing the product, which can be expensive: $1 to $1.5 million per global market. Domestically, more than two-thirds of new products fail, according to at least one survey.[12] But internationally, many companies test concepts and products even less than they do in domestic markets, relying instead on instinct and hunch. That leaves them vulnerable to the most serious international new product blunder: assuming that other markets have the same priorities and lifestyles as the domestic market.

Test markets provide one antidote, such as introducing the product in one country—for instance, Belgium or Ireland—and basing the go/no go decision for the rest of Europe on the performance of the product in that test market. Some countries are emerging as popular test markets for global products. Brazil is a test market used by Procter & Gamble and Colgate before rollout into the Latin American market. Unilever uses Thailand for a test market for the Asian market.

Test marketing allows a complete test of the marketing mix: formulation, packaging, advertising, and pricing. Test marketing is indispensable because prelaunch surveys only tell researchers what people *say* they will do, not what they *actually* do. And test markets might reveal how competitors would react to a full product rollout. It might be difficult to limit the scope of a test, however, particularly if local media are not available to confine promotion and distribution to a cost-efficient area. Localized media might be lacking even in developed markets, prompting test marketers to use surrogate test methods, such as laboratory test markets, microtest markets, and forced distribution tests.

The Global Launch

The impact of an effective global product launch can be great, but so can the cost of one that is poorly executed. High development costs as well as competitive pressures are forcing companies to rush products into as many markets as possible. But at the same time, a company can ill afford new products that are not effectively introduced, marketed, and supported in each market the company competes in.

A global product launch means introducing a product into countries in three or more regions within a narrow time frame. To achieve this, a company must undertake a number of measures. The country managers should be involved in the first stage of product strategy formulation to ensure that local and regional considerations are part of overall corporate and product messages. A product launch team (consisting of product, marketing, manufacturing, sales, service, engineering, and communication representatives) can also approach problems from an industry standpoint, as opposed to a home-country perspective, enhancing product competitiveness in all markets.

Adequate consideration should be given to localization and translation requirements before the launch. This means that the right messages are formulated and transmitted to key internal and external audiences. Support materials have to take into account both cultural and technical differences. The advantage of a simultaneous launch is that it boosts the overall momentum and attractiveness of the product by making it immediately available in key geographic markets. Global product launches typically require more education and support for sales channels than do domestic efforts or sequential regional efforts because of the diversity of distribution channels.

A successfully executed global launch offers several benefits. First, it permits the company to showcase its technology in all major markets at the same time. Setting a single date for the launch functions as a strict discipline to force the entire organization to gear up quickly for a successful worldwide effort. A simultaneous worldwide introduction also solves the "lame duck" dilemma of having old models available in some markets while customers know of the existence of the new product. If margins are most lucrative at the early stages of the new product's life cycle, they should be exploited by getting the product to as many markets as possible from the outset. An additional benefit of a worldwide launch may be added publicity opportunities as happened with the introductions worldwide of Microsoft's Windows 95, 98, and 2000 versions.

MANAGING GLOBAL PORTFOLIOS

Most marketers have a considerable number of individual items in their product portfolios. They can expand existing product lines to new markets or new segments or add new products to existing market operations. Adding new markets or market segments, for example, could involve expanding to geographically similar markets or markets with similar customer and competitive characteristics. The manager would look for markets with similarities to present-day operations in terms of product lines, brands, and brand positionings.

Corporate objectives determine the approach to portfolio analysis. One option begins with a strategic mapping of existing, contemplated, and competitive products, product lines, or business units in terms of their relative market share and their market growth. Mapping yields an easily communicated overview of product problems and opportunities, clearly distinguishing among "cash cows" (high share in slow-growth markets), "stars" (high share in rapid-growth markets) and "problem child" situations of low share in growing markets. In expanding markets, any company not growing rapidly risks falling behind for good.

Portfolios should also be used to assess market, product, and business links.[13] This effort will allow the exploitation of market similarities through actions such as creating new business units and standardizing product lines, products, and marketing programs. Look for opportunities to serve similar markets, leverage research and development objectives, use similar technologies, and share similar marketing experiences.

Exhibit 10.1 shows a market-product-business portfolio for a food company, such as Nestlé or Unilever. The interconnections are formed by common target markets served, R&D sharing, common technologies, and the benefits that can be drawn from sharing com-

Exhibit 10.1: Example of Market-Product-Business Portfolio

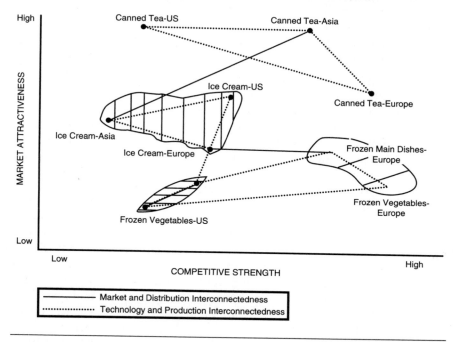

SOURCE: Adapted from Susan P. Douglas and C. Samuel Craig, "Global Portfolio Planning and Market Interconnectedness," *Journal of International Marketing* 4 (Number 1, 1996): 93–110.

mon marketing experience. The example indicates possibilities within regions and between regions: frozen foods both in Europe and the United States and ice cream throughout the three mega-markets.

Advantages

The major advantages provided by the product portfolio approach are:

1. A global view of the competitive landscape, especially when longer-term considerations are included.
2. A guide for the formulation of a global marketing strategy based on the suggested allocation of finite resources among product lines.
3. A guide for setting marketing objectives for specific markets

based on the role of each product line in each of the markets served—to generate cash or to block the expansion of competition, for example.

4. A convenient visual communication tool integrating a substantial amount of information in an appealingly simple format tracing links among units and products.

Before making strategic choices based on such an analysis, the global marketer should consider the risks related to variables such as entry mode, exchange rates, costs, and management tactical preferences—elements that might not appear in the formal portfolio assessment. For example, the cost of entry into one market may be lower because the company already has a presence there and the possibility exists that distribution networks may be shared.

The portfolio assessment also needs to be put into a larger context. For example, the Korean market and Korean automakers may not independently warrant urgent action on the part of the leading companies. However, as part of the global strategic setting in the auto industry, both the market and its companies become critically important. Asia is expected to account for 70 percent of the growth in the world auto market between 2000 and 2004. Korea, along with China and Japan, is one of the three most important vehicle markets in Asia and can be considered an ideal platform for exporting to other parts of the world. Consequently, European, American, and Japanese automakers have scouted Korea for technology and marketing synergies beyond the immediate benefits of simply selling to Korean customers.

Disadvantages

Applying the product portfolio approach has some limitations. International competitive behavior does not always follow the same rules as the firm's domestic market. For example, the major local competitor may be a government-owned firm whose main objective is to maintain employment. Or a new market entrant's activity could spur unforeseen competitive reactions and more aggressive strategies, rendering earlier portfolio analyses obsolete. Government regulations—minimum local content rules, for instance—can skew local market dynamics, as can market tastes.

The fact that multinational firms produce the same products in different locations may have an impact on consumer perceptions of product risk and quality. If the product is produced in a developing country, for example, the marketer has to determine whether a well-known brand name can compensate for the concern a customer might feel. The situation may be more complicated for retailers importing from independent producers in developing nations under the retailer's private labels. In general, country-of-origin effects on product perceptions are more difficult to determine since the introduction of hybrid products.

Global Brand Portfolios

Branding is one of the major beneficiaries of a well-conducted portfolio analysis. Brands are important because they shape customer decisions and, ultimately, create economic value. Research repeatedly shows that brand is a key factor behind the decision to purchase in both consumer and business-to-business situations. In addition, strong brands are usually able to charge a price premium. Research into the connection of brand strength and corporate performance at 130 multinational companies revealed that strong brands generate total returns to shareholders that are 1.9 percent above the industry average, while weaker brands lag behind the average by 3.1 percent.[14]

Brands are a major benefit to the customer as well. They simplify everyday choices, reduce the risk of complicated buying decisions, provide emotional benefits, and offer a sense of community. In technology (e.g., computer chips), where products change at an ever-increasing pace, branding is critical—far more so than in packaged goods, where a product may be more understandable because it stays the same or very similar over time.

A strong brand name accelerates a product's acceptance in new markets and product categories. In a global marketplace, customers often are aware of brands even though the products themselves may not be available. This was the case, for example, in many of the former Soviet republics before their markets opened up. Such market power is usually in the hands of brand-name companies, which must determine the most effective use of this asset across markets. The value of brand assets can be seen in acquisitions where prices have been many times over the book value of the company purchased. Many of the world's leading brands command high brand equity values compared to the average brand.[15]

Portfolio Decisions. Global marketers have three choices of branding within the global, regional, and local dimensions: Brands can feature the corporate name, family brands can cover a wide range of products or product variations, or individual brands can be promoted for each item in the product line. With the increase in strategic alliances, co-branding, in which two or more well-known brands are combined in an offer, has also become popular.

Because branding is an integral part of overall corporate identity, global marketers centralize management of the brand asset, charging strategic business unit management, global teams, or global managers with maintaining guidelines without simultaneously hampering local initiative.[16] For example, Black & Decker's experience positioning a new brand of power tools worldwide required consistent positioning to overcome the company's brand image problems with a key market segment, as reported in the article, "Development and Management of a Global Brand," in Exhibit 10.2.

In addition to the use of a global brand name from the very beginning, many marketers are consolidating their previously different individual market brand names, often for the same or similar products, with global or regional brand names. That can achieve marketing economies and greater product acceptance by consumers and intermediaries. The drawback is the loss of local flavor.

Nestlé's global branding program illustrates how a portfolio accommodates a worldwide mix of local and global identities:

- SBU and general management take responsibility for worldwide corporate brands and SBU-specific worldwide strategic brands. They set policies for each brand's positioning, labeling standards, packaging features, and other related marketing-mix issues, such as communications platforms. About 40 percent of the company's sales come from products covered by the corporate brand name.
- SBU and regional managers take the same responsibility for regional strategic brands.
- Local brands fall within the purview of local marketing organizations.
- Local strategic brands are monitored by the SBUs for positioning and labeling standards.[17]

The brand portfolio needs to be reviewed periodically. A number of global marketers are focusing their attention on A-level brands with the greatest growth potential while dropping noncore brands to reduce production, marketing, storage, and distribution costs. It is increasingly difficult for the global company to manage purely local brands. The surge of private label products has also put additional pressure on B-level brands. However, before discarding a brand, managers need to evaluate its current sales, customer loyalty, potential, and trends. For example, eliminating a local brand that may have a strong following, has been created by local management, and shows potential to be extended to nearby markets is not necessarily in the best interests of the company.

Exhibit 10.2: Development and Management of a Global Brand

In 1992, Black & Decker launched a new range of professional portable power tools under the DeWalt brand, in response to a global competitive threat from the Japanese Makita brand that had increased its market share in the fast-growing professional tool market. The company had determined that the quality of Black & Decker professional tools was not what was causing them to lose share to Makita. Instead, the reason was the brand-name perception of Black & Decker among professional contractors. Contractors did not believe in the performance of tools made by the same company that made toaster ovens, popcorn makers, and consumer-grade power tools.

After the successful launch of DeWalt in the United States, the same approach has been used in Australia, Canada, Europe, Latin America, and Asia. A set of guidelines govern the marketing of the brand, which is approaching $1 billion in worldwide sales. Some of the areas covered in the guidelines include the brand's position, logo/color, industrial design, brand extensions, and packaging and catalog numbering. In addition to ensuring consistencies, these guidelines also enable country managers to share their best-practice ideals with others in the system. A global team has been set up to monitor these policies as well as to ensure exchange of ideas on the brand.

The DeWalt brand is positioned as the premier brand of tools and accessories for people who make their living using professional grade power tools. This adroit positioning allows efficient target marketing. Although do-it-yourselfers are not part of the targeted effort, they very often choose products used by professionals, thereby broadening the market. As part of this positioning, DeWalt is never combined with Black & Decker products in marketing communication programs. All of this allows DeWalt to charge a premium price for their products.

The visual identity program for DeWalt is used to project clearly the image the company wants to project worldwide. The DeWalt logo uses bold, capital letters and a solid color (yellow) to project strength. The purpose of this guideline is not only to ensure consistency but also to ensure appropriate legal protection for the brand.

Part of the consistency dimension relates to controlling the industrial design of the tools. The four design centers located in Singapore, Frankfurt, Civate (Italy), and Towson, Maryland, have to adhere to agreed-upon rules with any deviation requiring approval from the global team. Similarly, extending the brand to new products or categories needs approval to avoid dilution of the brand.

As both customers (such as large contractors) and intermediaries (such as Home Depot or Hagebau) are becoming more global, packaging standards will have to change. This means one global packaging execution per tool using icon packaging with a country-specific sticker attached. DeWalt is also using one catalog number for each product for all geographic regions.

SOURCE: Courtesy of David Klatt, Black & Decker, March 2000.

Private Brand Competitors. There has been a significant shift in the relationship between retailers and consumers. Before 2000, the consumer's prime loyalty was to the manufacturer's brand, with retailers being just the intermediary. Now, consumers see themselves as a Safeway or Tesco person, not as a Heinz or BirdsEye person. Emerging strong intermediaries have fueled the increase in private brand goods, also called "private labels" or "store brands." Private brands can cover many products with, for example, the retailer's own brand name, or they can cover only individual products or product lines. The overall penetration of private brand goods in the United Kingdom is 30 percent, in Germany 23 percent, in Switzerland 23 percent, and in France 20 percent. Over the past 20 years, private brand sales in the United States have averaged 14 percent of supermarket sales. As both the trade and consumers become more sophisticated, private brands' market share is expected to reach U.K. levels in many parts of Europe and the world. The level of private brand share will vary by country and by product category reflecting variations in customer perceptions, intermediary strength, and behavior of leading branders.[18]

While private brand success depends heavily on economic conditions and the self-interest of retailers, new factors are adding to private brand strength. Improved quality and brand segmentation and repositioning are having an effect internationally. While most consumers still state that they prefer the comfort, security, and value of a manufacturer's brand over a private brand, many of them do not hesitate to try a private brand, researchers find.[19] Encouraged by this, private brands have been expanding. In Canada, for example, Loblaw's President's Choice brand and its regular private brand line squeeze national brands in between the two. Some U.S. chains have also started carrying this line of premium products.

With increasing opportunities to manufacture products for their distributors' private brands, international marketers will have to chose from among several possible strategic responses.

- If the marketer operates in an environment where consumers have an absolute preference for manufacturers' brands and where product innovation is a critical factor of success, the marketer can refuse to participate. Brand leaders can attack private brands and thereby direct their ambitions on smaller competitors, which often may be local-only players.
- The argument for strategic participation is that since the private brand phenomenon cannot be eliminated, it is best to be involved. Reasons include capacity filling, economies of scale, improved relationships with the trade, and valuable information

about consumer behavior and costs. However, the notion that profits from private brand manufacture can be used for promotion of the manufacturer's own brands may be eliminated by the relatively thin margins and the costs of having to set up a separate private brand manufacturing and marketing organization. And participation in the private brand category may be inconsistent with the marketer's global brand and product strategy by raising questions about quality standards, by diluting management attention, and by affecting consumers' perception of the main branded business.

- Many marketers pursue a mixture of these strategies as a function of marketing and market conditions. Wilkinson Sword, for example, produces private brand disposable razors for the most dominant chain in Finland, the K-Group, thereby enabling it to compete on price against other branded products (especially the French Bic) and increasing its share of shelf space. While H.J. Heinz produces insignificant amounts for private brand distributors in the United States, most of its U.K. production is for private brand.

ADAPTING EXISTING PRODUCTS

Murray, Inc. has had to change the way it has made lawn mowers for decades. Its riding and walking models are now quieter because of new noise standards imposed by the European Union. "We had to slow down the fan blade to cut noise," says Ray Elmy, vice president for design engineering. "However, it will not exhaust and bag grass as well, and our costs have increased." Despite increased production costs, the company made the changes because a significant portion of its $1 billion in sales comes from European customers. Murray's changes are not unique. Regulated products in the European Union must meet certain standards.

However, marketers should not consider product adaptation only in the context of one market. Ask how changes can contribute to operations elsewhere. A new feature for a product or a new line item may have appeal on a broader scale. Take the Boeing 737, for example. Due to saturated markets and competitive pressures, Boeing started to look for new markets in the Middle East, Africa, and Latin America for the 737 rather than kill the program altogether. To adjust to the idiosyncrasies of these markets, such as softer and shorter runways, the company redesigned the wings to allow for shorter landings and added thrust to the engines for quicker takeoffs. To make sure that the planes would not bounce even if piloted by less experienced captains, Boeing redesigned the landing gear and installed low-pressure tires to ensure that the plane would stick to the ground after initial touchdown. In addition to becoming a success in the intended markets, the new product features met with approval around the world and made the Boeing 737 the best-selling commercial jet in history.[20]

Adaptation Variables

To the buyer, a "product" is really a mix of tangible (e.g., performance, price, product characteristics, and features) and intangible (e.g., brand image, service reputation, country of origin, and styling) attributes, many of which are outstanding candidates for adapting an offering to foreign markets. But which should be adapted and which should remain standardized? For which markets? Increasingly, companies are attempting to develop global products by incorporating differences regionally or worldwide into one basic design. This is not pure standardization, however. To develop a standard in the United States, for example, and use it as a model for other markets is dramatically different from obtaining inputs from the intended markets and using the data to create a standard. What is important is that adaptability is built into the product around a standardized core.

The benefits of standardization—that is, selling the same product worldwide—are cost savings in production and marketing. And having to face the same competitors in the major markets of the world will add to the pressure of having a worldwide approach to international marketing. But in most cases, demand and usage conditions vary sufficiently across the globe to require some local adaptations in most product categories. The argument that the world is becoming more homogenous may actually be true for only a limited number of consumer products that have universal brand recognition and minimal product knowledge requirements for use. Industrial products, such as steel, chemicals, and agricultural equipment, tend to be less culturally grounded and warrant less adjustment than consumer goods. Similarly, marketers in technology-intensive industries, such as scientific instruments or medical equipment, find universal acceptability for their products.

When to Adapt. Adaptation needs in the industrial sector may exist even though they may not be overt. As an example, rating product performance capacities differs around the world. Typically, the performance specifications of a German product are quite precise. If a

German product is said to have a lifting capacity of 1,000 kilograms, it will perform precisely up to that level. The U.S. counterpart, however, is likely to have an actual capacity 50 or even 100 percent better than the rated capacity, as a safety measure. Buyers of Japanese machine tools have also found that those will perform at the specified level but not beyond them, as would their U.S.-made counterparts.

Consumer goods generally require product adaptation because of heavy cultural influence on their use. Economic conditions also matter; low incomes might require marketers to simplify products to make them more affordable. A detailed examination of 174 consumer-packaged goods destined for the developing countries has shown that, on average, 4.1 changes per product were made in terms of brand name, packaging, measurement units, labeling, constituents, product features, and usage instructions.[21] Only 1 of 10 products was transferred without modification.

The factors that determine the need for either mandatory or discretionary product adaptation include those related to market characteristics, product dimensions, as well as company considerations.[22]

Market Environment. As noted in Chapter 5, host country *government regulations* often present the most stringent market requirements. Government regulations are probably the single most important factor contributing to product adaptation and, because of bureaucratic red tape, often the most cumbersome and frustrating factor to deal with. Sometimes the requirements may serve no purpose other than political (such as protection of domestic industry or response to political pressures). Because of the sovereignty of nations, individual firms need to comply but can influence the situation by lobbying, directly or through their industry associations, for the issue to be raised during trade negotiations. Government regulations may be spelled out, but firms need to be ever vigilant in terms of changes and exceptions.

Nontariff barriers include product standards, testing or approval procedures, subsidies for local products, and bureaucratic red tape. The nontariff barriers requiring product adjustments usually concern elements outside the core product. Because nontariff barriers are usually in place to keep foreign products out and/or to protect domestic producers, getting around them may be the toughest single problem for the international marketer. With a substantial decrease in tariff barriers, nontariff forms of protectionism have increased. On volume alone, agricultural product certification dominates the list.

The cost of compliance with government regulations is high. The U.S. Department of Commerce estimated that a typical machine manufacturer can expect to spend between $50,000 and $100,000 a year on complying with foreign standards. For certain exports to the European Union, that figure can reach as high as $200,000.[23] Small companies with limited resources may simply give up in the face of seemingly arbitrary harassment. For example, product testing and certification requirements have made the entry of many foreign companies into Japanese markets quite difficult, if not impossible.[24] Japan requires testing of all pharmaceutical products in Japanese laboratories, maintaining that these tests are needed because the Japanese may be physiologically different from Americans or Swiss. Similarly, foreign ski products were kept out because Japanese snow was somehow unique. Many exporters, rather than try to move mountains of red tape, have found ways to accommodate Japanese regulations. U.S. cookie marketers, for example, create separate product batches to meet Japanese requirements and avoid problems with the Japanese Health and Welfare Agency.

Another way to keep a particular product or producer out of a market is to insist on particular standards. For instance, since the European Union chose ISO 9000—quality standards created by the International Organization for Standardization—as a basis to harmonize varying technical norms of its member states, some of its trading partners have accused it of erecting a new trade barrier against outsiders.

Customer characteristics are as important as governmental influences on the product adaptation decision. Even when the benefits sought are quite similar, the product characteristics customers demand may dictate product adaptation. Quaker Oats' extension of the Snapple soft drink product to Japan suffered from lack of fit on three dimensions: the glass bottles the drink comes in are almost twice the size that Japanese customers are used to; the product itself was too sweet for the palate; and the Japanese did not feel comfortable with the sediment that characteristically collects at the bottom of the bottle.[25]

GE Medical Systems designed a product specifically for Japan in addition to computerized tomography scanners produced for the U.S. market. The unit is smaller because Japanese hospitals are smaller than most U.S. facilities and also because of the smaller size of Japanese patients.[26]

Three factors determine cultural and psychological acceptability for products and services: consumption patterns, psychosocial characteristics, and general cultural criteria. Ask questions such as these for every product under consideration:[27]

I.   Consumption Patterns
   A. Pattern of Purchase
     1. Is the product or service purchased by relatively the same consumer income group from one country to another?
     2. Do the same family members motivate the purchase in all target countries?
     3. Do the same family members dictate brand choice in all target countries?
     4. Do most consumers expect a product to have the same appearance?
     5. Is the purchase rate the same regardless of the country?
     6. Are most of the purchases made at the same kind of retail outlet?
     7. Do most consumers spend the same amount of time making the purchase?
   B. Pattern of Usage
     1. Do most consumers use the product or service for the same purpose or purposes?
     2. Is the product or service used in different amounts from one target area or country to another?
     3. Is the method of preparation the same in all target countries?
     4. Is the product or service used along with other products or services?
II. Psychosocial Characteristics
   A. Attitudes Toward the Product or Service
     1. Are the basic psychological, social, and economic factors motivating the purchase and use of the product the same for all target countries?
     2. Are the advantages and disadvantages of the product or service in the minds of consumers basically the same from one country to another?
     3. Does the symbolic content of the product or service differ from one country to another?
     4. Is the psychic cost of purchasing or using the product or service the same, whatever the country?
     5. Does the appeal of the product or service for a cosmopolitan market differ from one market to another?
   B. Attitudes Toward the Brand
     1. Is the brand name equally known and accepted in all target countries?
     2. Are customer attitudes toward the package basically the same?
     3. Are customer attitudes toward pricing basically the same?
     4. Is brand loyalty the same throughout target countries for the product or service under consideration?

III. Cultural Criteria
1. Does society restrict the purchase and/or use of the product or service to a particular group?
2. Is there a stigma attached to the product or service?
3. Does the usage of the product or service interfere with tradition in one or more of the targeted markets?

Often, the manufacturer need not make physical product changes, only a change in the product's positioning. Health and beauty-care products often rely on careful positioning to attain a competitive advantage. And the selling of "lifestyle" brands is common for consumer goods for which differentiation may be more difficult. Lifestyle imagery may be more difficult for competitors to copy, but it is also more susceptible to changes in fashion.

The present stage of economic development of the overseas market should influence management's product adaptation decisions. As a country's economy advances, buyers are in a better position to buy and to demand more sophisticated products and product versions. Conversely, economic decline calls for managing the affordability of products.

Economic conditions will affect packaging in terms of size and units sold in a package. In developing markets, products such as cigarettes and razor blades are often sold by the piece so that consumers with limited incomes can afford them. Soft drink companies have introduced four-can packs in Europe, where cans are sold singly even in large stores. On the other hand, products oriented to families, such as food products, appear in larger sizes in developing markets. Pillsbury packages its products in six- and eight-serving sizes for developing countries, whereas the most popular size in the North American market is for two.

Competition must be monitored closely. Analysis might reveal holes in the market or suggest avoiding certain market segments. Even when an international marketer is competing with local manufacturers and must overcome traditional purchasing relationships, concentrating on one segment alone and targeting carefully can allow a firm to stay ahead of competition.

Climate and geography will usually have an effect on the total product offering. Some products are vulnerable to the elements. The marketer must consider two sometimes-contradictory aspects of packaging for the international market. On the one hand, the product itself has to be protected against longer transit times and possibly for longer shelf life. Then again, the firm must be sure not to use prohibited preservatives.

Product Characteristics. Product characteristics both actual and perceived are the core of the product offering, making some items good candidates for standardization, others not.

Product ingredients must conform to local market legal, social, and religious requirements. As an example, DEP Corporation, a Los Angeles manufacturer of hair and skin products, takes particular pains to make sure that no Japan-bound products contain formaldehyde—an ingredient commonly used in the United States but illegal in Japan. To ensure the purity of the Japanese batches, the company repeatedly cleans and sterilizes its chemical vats, checks all ingredients for traces of formaldehyde, and checks the finished product before shipment.

When religion or custom determines consumption, ingredients may have to be replaced in order for the product to be acceptable. In Islamic countries, for example, animal fats have to be replaced by ingredients such as vegetable shortening. In deference to Hindu and Muslim beliefs, McDonald's makes its "Maharaja Mac" with mutton in India.

Branding considerations offer the international marketer a number of options, although standardization in branding is strongest in culturally similar markets. Standardization of product and brand do not necessarily move hand in hand; a regional brand may well have local features, or a highly standardized product may have local brand names. Standardizing names to reap promotional benefits can be difficult, however, because a particular name may already be established in each market and the action raises objections from local managers. In some markets, host governments require brand name changes, at times in an effort to control the marketing power of foreign companies.

Additionally, brand names often do not travel well. Semantic variations can hinder product acceptance overseas. Even the company name or the trade name should be checked. NameLab, a California-based laboratory for name development and testing, suggests these approaches:

1. Translation: Little Pen Inc. would become La Petite Plume, S.A., for example.
2. Transliteration: This requires the testing of an existing brand name for connotative meaning in the language of the intended market. Flic Pen Corporation, for example, would be perceived in France as a manufacturer of writing instruments for the police because the slang term *flic* connotes something between "cop" and "pig." In other instances, marketers seek positive connotations for brand names, such as in China where Coca-Cola managed to invest its otherwise neutral name with a definition of "tasty and happy."

3. Transparency: This can be used to develop a new, essentially meaningless brand name to minimize trademark complexities, transliteration problems, and translation complexities. Sony is an example.
4. Transculture: This means using a foreign-language name for a brand. Vodkas, regardless of where they originate, typically have Russian-sounding names or at least Russian lettering. Perfume names frequently sound French.

Packaging serves three major functions: protection, promotion, and user convenience, which influence product adaptation. Packaging will vary as a function of transportation mode, transit conditions, and length of time in transit. An exporter should anticipate inadequate, careless, or primitive loading methods. The labels and loading instructions should be not only in English but also in the market's language as well as in symbols. Pilferage is a problem in a number of markets and has forced companies to use only shipping codes on outside packaging.

The promotional aspect of packaging relates mostly to labeling. The major adjustments concern regulations for bilingual labeling and adequate product and content descriptions. If in doubt, a company should study foreign competitors' labels. Also, package aesthetics must be a consideration in terms of the promotional role of packaging. This mainly involves the prudent choice of colors and package shapes.

As for convenience, package size varies according to purchasing patterns and market conditions, such as a general lack of household refrigeration and therefore the purchase of smaller quantities. Marketers are wise to monitor packaging technology developments in the world marketplace. For example, aseptic containers for fruit drinks and milk originated in Sweden. Also, demand for more environmentally friendly packaging affects international marketers, particularly when exporting to environmentally sensitive populations such as Western Europe.

Appearance considerations influence adaptations in product styling, color, size, and other visual attributes. Colors play an important role, for example, because they communicate in a subtle way in developed societies but have direct meanings in more traditional societies. For instance, in the late 1950s, when Pepsi-Cola changed the color of its coolers and vending machines from deep regal blue to light ice blue, the result was catastrophic in Southeast Asia. Pepsi had a dominant market share, which it lost to Coca-Cola because light blue is associated with death and mourning in that part of the world. The only way companies can protect themselves against incidents of this kind is through thorough on-site testing.

Product operation might require adaptation; the product as it is offered in the domestic market may not be operable in the foreign market. For example, one of the major differences appliance manufacturers confront is electrical power systems, which might even vary within a single country. Exporters should determine for themselves the needed adjustments by observing competitive products or having their product tested by a local service. Although many complicating factors may be eliminated in the future through standardization efforts by international organizations, today's most blatant blunders in international marketing are usually the result of exporters' failure to adjust their products to local systems.

An exporter may also have to adapt the product to different usage contingencies. Ticket vending machines for the French subway need to be waterproof, since they are hosed down. Similarly, for the Australian market, video poker screens are built to take a beating because gamblers there take losing more personally than anywhere else.[28] In general, the international marketer should be open to ideas for new uses for the product being offered.

Quality counts because products generally do not compete on price alone, and maintaining a perceived quality advantage might require product or promotional adaptation. Marketers should resist the temptation to overlook the importance of quality perceptions, even when entering developing markets. An important aspect of improving quality is an emphasis on design. Some countries, such as Singapore and Taiwan, provide financial assistance to help companies improve product design. Cash grants help defer design costs, and publicity-oriented programs increase overall design consciousness.[29]

Service availability is critical in foreign markets, distant from a company's regular service and repair facilities. In some cases, products abroad may not even be used for their intended purpose and may thus require modifications not only in product configuration but also in service frequency. For instance, snowplows exported from the United States are used to remove sand from driveways in Saudi Arabia. Closely related to servicing is the issue of product warranties, which are effective promotional tools in many foreign markets. Warranties can be uniform only if the use conditions do not vary drastically and if the company is able to deliver equally on its promise anywhere it has a presence.

Country of origin of a product has a considerable influence on the quality perceptions of a product. Country-of-origin effects lessen as customers become more informed. Also, as more countries develop manufacturing capacity, the origin of products becomes less important. This can already be seen with so-called hybrid products: a U.S. multinational company manufacturing the product in Malaysia, for example.

Company Characteristics. The issue of product adaptation most often climaxes in the question, "Is it worth it?" The answer depends on the firm's ability to control costs, correctly estimate market potential, and, finally, secure profitability, especially in the long term. However, the question that used to be posed as "Can we afford to do it?" should now be "Can we afford not to do it?" Thorough research is essential, as is a willingness to forego short-term profit in the early years of investing in an international marketing program.

A critical element of the adaptation decision has to be human resources, that is, individuals to make the appropriate decisions. Individuals are needed who are willing to make risky decisions and who know about existing market conditions. A characteristic of the U.S. export boom in the late 1980s was that foreigners and recent immigrants were often the first to see overseas opportunities. Foreign-born managers may look for goods that many U.S. executives overlook or consider too difficult for the international marketplace.

Coping with Counterfeiting

Counterfeit goods are any goods bearing an unauthorized representation of a trademark, patented invention, or copyrighted work that is legally protected in the country where it is marketed. The issue of intellectual property protection will become increasingly more important for the United States and the European Union in the coming years. Hardest hit by counterfeiting are the most innovative, fastest-growing industries, such as computer software, pharmaceuticals, and entertainment. The practice has spread from the traditionally counterfeited products: high-visibility, strong brand name consumer goods. In addition, previously the only concern was whether a company's product was being counterfeited; now, companies have to worry about whether the raw materials and components they themselves purchase for production are real.

The European Union estimates that trade in counterfeit goods now accounts for 2 percent of total world trade. The International Chamber of Commerce estimates the figure at close to 5 percent. In general, countries with lower per capita incomes, higher levels of corruption in government, and lower levels of involvement in the international trade community tend to have higher levels of intellectual property violation.

Counterfeiting problems occur in three ways and, depending on the origin of the products and where they are marketed, require different courses of action. Approximately 75 percent of counterfeit goods are estimated to be manufactured outside the United States; 25 percent are either made in the United States or imported and then labeled there. U.S. companies can sue over problems originating in the United States. Counterfeit products that originate overseas and that are marketed in the United States should be stopped by the customs barrier. When an infringement occurs overseas, action can be brought under the laws of the country in which it occurs.

Legal Remedies. The first task in fighting intellectual property violation is to apply for patents, register trademarks, and make copyright ownership clear at the first time of publication or creation of the protected work and every time thereafter. The rights granted by a patent, trademark, or copyright in the United States do not confer protection in a foreign country. There is no such thing as an international patent, trademark, or copyright.

Although there is no shortcut to worldwide protection, some advantages exist under treaties or other international agreements. These treaties, under the World Intellectual Property Organization (WIPO), include the Paris Convention for the Protection of Industrial Property, the Patent Cooperation Treaty, the Madrid Arrangement for International Registration of Trademarks, the Berne Convention for the Protection of Literary and Artistic Works, and the Universal Copyright Convention, as well as regional patent and trademark offices such as the European Patent Office. Applicants are typically granted international protection throughout the member countries of these organizations.[30]

After securing intellectual property rights, the international marketer must act to enforce these rights. Four types of action against counterfeiting are legislative action, bilateral and multilateral negotiations, joint private sector action, and measures taken by individual companies.

In the U.S. *legislative* arena, the Omnibus Tariff and Trade Act of 1984 amended Section 301 of the Trade Act of 1974 to clarify that the violation of intellectual property rights is an unreasonable practice within the statute. The act also introduced a major carrot-and-stick policy: The adequacy of protection of intellectual property rights of U.S. manufacturers is a factor that will be considered in the designation of Generalized System of Preferences (GSP) benefits to countries. The United States has denied selected countries duty-free treatment on goods because of lax enforcement of intellectual property laws.

The Trademark Counterfeiting Act of 1984 made trading in

goods and services using a counterfeit trademark a criminal rather than a civil offense, establishing stiff penalties for the practice. The Semiconductor Chip Protection Act of 1984 clarified the status and protection afforded to semiconductor masks and the chip circuitry designs. Protection will be available to foreign-designed masks in the United States only if the home country of the manufacturer also maintains a viable system of mask protection. The Intellectual Property Rights Improvement Act requires the U.S. Trade Representative to set country-specific negotiating objectives for reciprocity and consideration of retaliatory options to ensure intellectual property protection. The United States imposed punitive tariffs on $39 million of Brazilian imports to retaliate against Brazil's refusal to protect U.S. pharmaceutical patents. In 1997, the Digital Millennium Copyright Act (DMCA) brought U.S. law into compliance with the electronic property copyright protections of the World Intellectual Property Organization (WIPO) Copyright Treaty.

The U.S. government is seeking to limit counterfeiting practices through bilateral and multilateral *negotiations* as well as education. A joint International Trade Administration and Patent and Trademark Office action seeks to assess the adequacy of foreign countries' intellectual property laws and practices, to offer educational programs and technical assistance to countries wishing to establish adequate systems of intellectual property protection, to offer educational services to the industry, and to review the adequacy of U.S. legislation in the area.

Major legislative changes abroad have occurred in the past few years in, for example, Taiwan and Singapore, where penalties for violations have been toughened. The WTO agreement includes new rules on intellectual property protection under the Trade-Related Aspects of Intellectual Property Rights (TRIPS) agreement. Under them, trade-related intellectual property will enjoy 20 years of protection. More than 100 countries have indicated they will amend their laws and improve enforcement. Violators of intellectual property will face retaliation not only in this sector, but in others as well. Similarly, the NAFTA agreement provides extensive patent and copyright protection. European countries have also been at the forefront of such efforts with the European Patent Convention and the Community Patent Convention.

A number of *industry/private-sector joint efforts* have emerged in the battle against counterfeit goods. In 1978, the International Anti-Counterfeiting Coalition was founded to lobby for stronger legal sanctions worldwide. The coalition consists of 375 members. The International Chamber of Commerce established the Counterfeit Intelligence and Investigating Bureau in London, which acts as a clearinghouse capable of synthesizing global data on counterfeiting.

In today's environment, *companies* are taking more aggressive steps to protect themselves against knockoffs of trademarked goods. For example, new labeling materials are extremely difficult to duplicate. Copy protection schemes for digital recordings are proving to be an active battleground as new protection methods beget new code-cracking techniques requiring more advanced protections, etc. Some companies, such as Disney, have tried to legitimize offenders by converting them into authorized licensees, which become part of the fight against counterfeiters because their profits are affected by fakes.

Many companies maintain close contact with the various agencies charged with helping them. Computer makers, for example, loan testing equipment to customs officers at all major U.S. ports, and company attorneys conduct seminars on detecting pirated software and hardware. Other companies retain outside detectives to watch the market and help law enforcement officers conduct raids.

FUTURITIES

Environmental issues loom large for twenty-first century marketers, providing new opportunities and obstacles. For example, manufacturers will increasingly be expected to take responsibility for their products from cradle to grave and beyond, including product disposal, recycling, and even legal liability for once accepted products, such as asbestos.

Although some consumers show more interest in truly "natural" products even if they are less convenient, in most industrialized nations they will require products that are environmentally friendly but with similar performance and value. Many a corporate management is likely to resist the additional business cost and taxes required for environmental protection, but delaying will simply leave a firm more vulnerable to competitors.

Meanwhile, new products will "go global" at an accelerated pace, with some products' life cycles shortening to months, if not weeks, before rivals can copy them. Product introduction will grow more complex, expensive, and risky, yet rewards will have to be accumulated more quickly.

Global issues addressed early in the new product process do not, however, point to more product standardization. Companies will have to be ready to deliver more mass customization. Customers in the twenty-first century are no longer satisfied with just a product: They want it to precisely meet their needs and preferences.

Emerging economies with low production costs will be able to replicate products more quickly and cheaply. Countries such as China, India, and the Philippines offer large pools of skilled people at labor rates much lower than in Europe, Japan, or the United States. All this talent also results in a much wider dissemination of technological creativity, a factor that will affect the innovative capability of firms. For example, the data indicate that foreign know-how comprised half of all U.S. patent applications in 2001. This indicates that firms need to make such foreign knowledge part of their production strategies, or to develop consistent comparative advantages in production technology in order to stay ahead of the game. Similarly, workers engaged in the production process must attempt, through training and skill enhancement, to stay ahead of foreign workers who are willing to charge less for their time.

Finally, as competition intensifies on a global scale, companies will increasingly turn to strategic alliances and partnering to benefit from resources they need and to spread risks they cannot assume alone. Partners will not need to be large in order to make a major contribution. Depending on the type of product, very small firms can serve as coordinating subcontractors and collaborate in product and service development, production, and distribution.

NOTES

1. Glenn Rifkin, "Mach 3: Anatomy of Gillette's Latest Global Launch," *Strategy & Business* (Number 2, 1999): 34–41; "Gillette Flays Asda over 'Inferior' Tri-Flex Razor," *Marketing Week,* June 10, 1999, 9; and Hamantha S. B. Herath and Chan S. Park, "Economic Analysis of R&D Projects: An Options Approach," *The Engineering Economist* 44 (number 1, 1999): 1–35.
2. Kenichi Ohmae, "Managing in a Borderless World," *Harvard Business Review* 67 (May–June 1989): 152–161.
3. "Blade-runner," *The Economist,* April 10, 1993, 68.
4. Eric von Hippel, Stefan Thomke, and Mary Sonnack, "Creating Breakthroughs at 3M," *Harvard Business Review* 77 (September–October 1999): 47–57.
5. "Could America Afford the Transistor Today?" Business Week, March 7, 1994, 80–84.
6. Laurel Wentz, "World Brands," *Advertising Age International,* September 1996, i–21.
7. Durward K. Sobek, Jeffrey K. Liker, and Allen C. Ward, "Another Look at How Toyota Integrates Product Development," *Harvard Business Review* 76 (July–August 1998): 36–49; "Advantage for Toyota," *The Wall Street Journal,* August 5, 1989, 35.
8. Robert Ronstadt, "International R&D: The Establishment and Evolution of Research and Development Abroad by U.S. Multinationals," *Journal of International Business Studies* 9 (Spring–Summer 1978): 7–24.

9. James A. Gingrich, "Five Rules for Winning Emerging Market Consumers," *Strategy & Business* (Second Quarter 1999): 68–76.

10. "Sharp Puts the Consumer on Its New-Product Team," *Business International,* December 14, 1992, 401–402.

11. Karl Moore and Julian Birkinshaw, "Managing Knowledge in Global Service Firms: Centers of Excellence," *Academy of Management Executive* 12 (November 1998): 81–92; Laurel Wentz, "World Brands," *Advertising Age International,* September 1996, i–21.

12. David S. Hopkins, "Survey Finds 67% of New Products Fail," *Marketing News,* February 8, 1986, 1.

13. Susan P. Douglas and C. Samuel Craig, "Global Portfolio Planning and Market Interconnectedness," *Journal of International Marketing* 4 (Number 1, 1996): 93–110.

14. David C. Court, Mark G. Leiter, and Mark A. Loch, "Brand Leverage," *The McKinsey Quarterly* 35 (Number 2, 1999): 100–110.

15. David A. Aaker, *Managing Brand Equity: Capitalizing on the Value of a Brand Name* (New York: Free Press, 1995), 21–33.

16. David Aaker and Erich Joachimsthaler, "The Lure of Global Branding," *Harvard Business Review* 77 (November/December 1999): 137–144.

17. Andrew J. Parsons, "Nestlé: The Visions of Local Managers," The McKinsey Quarterly 36 (Number 2, 1996): 5–29.

18. David Dunne and Chakravarthi Narasimhan, "The New Appeal of Private Labels," *Harvard Business Review* 77 (May–June 1999): 41–52; John A. Quelch and David Harding, "Brands Versus Private Labels," *Harvard Business Review* 74 (January–February 1996): 99–109.

19. François Glémet and Rafael Mira, "The Brand Leader's Dilemma," The McKinsey Quarterly 33 (Number 2, 1993): 3–15.

20. Andrew Kupfer, "How to Be a Global Manager," *Fortune,* March 14, 1988, 24–27.

21. John S. Hill and Richard R. Still, "Adapting Products to LDC Tastes," *Harvard Business Review* 62 (March–April 1984): 92–101.

22. Adapted from V. Yorio, *Adapting Products for Export* (New York: Conference Board, 1983), 7. Reprinted with permission.

23. Erika Morphy, "Cutting the Cost of Compliance," *Export Today* 12 (January 1996): 14–18.

24. Vernon R. Alden, "Who Says You Can't Crack Japanese Markets?" *Harvard Business Review* 64 (January–February 1986): 52–56.

25. Kirk Loncar, "Look Before You Leap," *World Trade,* June 1997, 92–93.

26. Kate Betrand, "Marketing to the Land of the Rising Yen," *Business Marketing* 12 (October 1986): 77–86.

27. Adapted from Steuart Henderson Britt, "Standardizing Marketing for the International Market," *Columbia Journal of World Business* 9 (Winter 1974): 32–40. Copyright © 1974 Columbia Journal of World Business. Reprinted with permission.

28. Carla Kruytbosch, "The Minds behind the Winners," *International Business,* January 1994, 56–70.

29. John S. Blyth, "Other Countries Lead U.S. in Supporting Design Efforts," Marketing News, February 13, 1989, 14–15.

30. An Introductory Guide for U.S. Businesses on Protecting Intellectual Property Abroad," *Business America,* July 1, 1991, 2–7.

11

Pricing in Global Markets

The international price that's right
is a complex question.

Price is the one element of the marketing mix that most managers understand least. In it is a complex of commercial concerns leavened by politics, government regulation in both destination and origin markets, social forces, cultural perceptions, geographic distances, currency fluctuations, and unfamiliar distribution channel demands. Yet the marketer's objective remains the same: creating profitable demand for an offering. Price is best understood within the context of the entire offer, especially the quality of the product and related services. Exporters can emphasize how the quality and reliability of delivery meet a buyer's needs, for example, to minimize pressure to reduce prices.

In this chapter, we will review pricing fundamentals influencing international transactions. Then we examine the mechanisms of pricing for export sales, pricing foreign subsidiaries' goods, and pricing goods exchanged among units of the same corporation. Along the way, we look at exporters' countertrade and leasing options, and review the "dumping" issues that often take center stage during international trade disputes and domestic politics.

SETTING EXPORT PRICES AND TERMS

Price is an active instrument of customer value and competitive advantage that cannot be developed without considering the elements of marketing strategy. Price, for example, is a powerful positioning tool. Pricing challenges—e.g., pricing a new market entry, changing price to attack or react to rivals, and multiple-product price coordination—are technically the same as problems in domestic markets. External and internal forces create opportunities and constraints.

"Skimming," "parity," or "penetration" strategies launch new products or respond to competitive thrusts and target market trends. The key is flexibility and coordination with the rest of the marketing program. Rising raw materials costs might force finished goods prices up, so extra promotional spending might improve brand image, combat customer price sensitivity, and counter the attractiveness of substitute goods. The target market establishes the basic premise behind a price. Effective pricing addresses market requirements (e.g., willingness and ability to pay) within the context of the company's business objectives, whether they are designed to maximize profit, market share, return on investment, barriers to competitive entry, customer switching costs, or some other performance goal.

Export Pricing and Costs

Three price-setting strategies for international marketing are:

1. Standard worldwide pricing, regardless of the buyer, (if foreign product or foreign marketing costs are negligible).
2. Dual pricing differentiates between domestic and export prices.
3. Market-differentiated pricing.[1]

Pricing Strategies. The first two methods are cost-oriented, relatively simple to establish, and easy to understand. A standard price might be based on average unit costs of fixed, variable, and export-related costs. Dual pricing sets different domestic and export prices, the latter determined by cost-plus or by marginal cost methods.

Cost-plus adds a target profit margin to the actual domestic and foreign costs allocated to the product, which ensures a profit but creates higher prices. A rigid cost-plus strategy covering all costs including exporting expenses can result in export prices higher than a standard worldwide price. While many, especially new, exporters use this method to avoid the uncertainties of international business, market forces and internal goals might force them to reconsider. Some exporters therefore adopt *flexible cost-plus pricing*, which allows for variations in special circumstances.[2] The marketer might give discounts depending on the customer, the size of the order, or the intensity of competition, or change prices to counter exchange rate fluctuations. Nevertheless, profit is still a driving motive, and pricing is more static as an element of the marketing mix.

The *marginal cost method* considers only the direct costs of producing and selling products for export as the floor for prices. Fixed costs for plants, R&D, and domestic overhead as well as domestic marketing costs are disregarded. An exporter can thus lower export prices to be competitive otherwise unreachable markets. If the exporter is large, this might lead to dumping accusations claiming the product is priced below average cost—generally higher than marginal cost.

Market-differentiated pricing is based on actual demand and marketplace conditions, though not too low to return a profit. In this approach, marginal costs determine a pricing base around which prices might change frequently. Adequate and timely market information is critical to this dynamic price management method.

Escalating Exporting Costs. In preparing a quotation, the exporter must be careful to include unique export-related costs as well as normal costs shared with the domestic side of the business, such as:

1. The cost of modifying the product for foreign markets.
2. Operational costs of the export operation: personnel, market research, additional shipping and insurance costs, communications costs with foreign customers, and overseas promotional costs.
3. Foreign market entry costs: tariffs and taxes; commercial credit and political risks associated with a buyer in a different market; and foreign exchange risks.

The combined effect of clear-cut and hidden costs causes export prices to domestic prices. Exhibit 11.1 illustrates four exporting scenarios compared with a typical domestic situation. The first case is relatively simple, adding only the CIF (cost, insurance, freight) and tariff charges. The second adds a foreign importer and thus lengthens the foreign part of the distribution channel. In the third, a value-added tax (VAT) is imposed on the full export selling price, which represents the "value added" to or introduced into the country from abroad. The fourth case simulates a situation typically found in less-developed countries where distribution channels are longer and can easily double the landed (CIF) price.

Price escalation can result in different-sized price increases across markets. Customers who shop around for lower prices or distributors unhappy about their margins in certain markets might force a marketer to abandon a market altogether. Exporters can combat price escalation through accurate information and creative strategies such as the following methods, which emphasize cutting costs:

- *Reorganize the channel of distribution:* Eliminate some distribution levels. But, shortening the value chain might incur other new costs such as new intermediaries' demands for better discounts.
- *Adapt the product:* Use less expensive ingredients or unbundle costly features. Remaining features, such as packaging, can also be cheapened. If price escalation causes differentials between markets that customers might discover, alter the product by changing styling and packaging, for example.
- *Reclassify the product's tax or tariff status:* Products may qualify for entry under different categories and import levies. The marketer

Exhibit 11.1: Export Price Escalation

International Marketing Channel Elements and Cost Factors	Domestic wholesale-retail channel	Export Market Cases			
		Case 1 Same as domestic with direct wholesale import cif/tariff	Case 2 Same as 1 with foreign importer added to channel	Case 3 Same as 2 with vat added	Case 4 Same as 3 with local foreign jobber added to channel
Manufacturer's net price	6.00	6.00%	6.00%	6.00%	6.00%
+ Insurance and shipping cost (CIF)	—	2.50%	2.50%	2.50%	2.50%
= Landed cost (CIF value)	—	8.50%	8.50%	8.50%	8.50%
+ Tariff (20% on CIF value)	—	1.70%	1.70%	1.70%	1.70%
= Importer's cost (CIF value + tariff)	—	10.20%	10.20%	10.20%	10.20%
+ Importer's margin (25% on cost)	—	—	2.55%	2.55%	2.55%
+ VAT (16% on full cost plus margin)	—	—	—	2.04%	2.04%
= Wholesaler's cost (= importer's price)	6.00	10.20%	12.75%	14.79%	14.79%
+ Wholesaler's margin (33 1/3% on cost)	2.00	3.40%	4.25%	4.93%	4.93%
+ VAT (16% on margin)	—	—	—	.79%	.79%
= Local foreign jobber's cost (= wholesale price)	—	—	—	—	20.51%
+ Jobber's margin (33 1/3% on cost)	—	—	—	—	6.84%
+ VAT (16% on margin)	—	—	—	—	1.09%
= Retailer's cost (= wholesale or jobber price)	8.00	13.60%	17.00%	20.51%	28.44%
+ Retailer's margin (50% on cost)	4.00	6.80%	8.50%	10.26%	14.22%
+ VAT (16% on margin)	—	—	—	1.64%	2.28%
= Retail price (what consumer pays)	12.00	20.40%	25.50%	32.41%	44.94%
Percentage price escalation over domestic		70%	113%	170%	275%
Percentage price escalation over Case 1			25%	59%	120%
Percentage price escalation over Case 2				27%	76%
Percentage price escalation over Case 3					39%

SOURCE: Helmut Becker, "Pricing: An International Marketing Challenge," in *International Marketing Strategy*, eds. Hans Thorelli and Helmut Becker (New York: Pergamon Press, 1980), 215. Reprinted with permission.

may have to lobby hard for changes, but the results may be considerable savings. For example, when the U.S. Customs Service ruled that multipurpose vehicles were light trucks and, therefore, subject to 25 percent tariffs (and not the 2.5 percent levied on passenger cars), Britain's Land Rover had to argue that its $56,000 luxury vehicle, the Range Rover, was not a truck. When the United States introduced a luxury tax (10 percent of the part of a car's price that exceeded $33,000), Land Rover worked closely with the U.S. Internal Revenue Service to establish that its vehicles were trucks (since trucks were free of such tax). However, it had to make slight adjustments in the vehicle, since the IRS defines a minimum weight for trucks at 6,000 lbs. Land Rover's following year model weighed in at 6,019 lbs.[3]

- *Assemble or produce the product overseas*: Through foreign sourcing, the exporter may receive an additional benefit to lower cost: duty drawbacks. A U.S. exporter may be refunded up to 99 percent of duties paid on imported goods when they are exported or incorporated into articles that are subsequently exported within five years of the importation. Levi-Strauss, for example, imports zippers from China that are sewn into the company's jackets and jeans in the U. S. The amount that Levi's reclaims can be significant: The duty on zippers can climb to 30 percent of the product's value.
- *Emphasize nonprice benefits*: Quality, after-sales service, warranties, etc. (not necessarily price concessions), can add to the value the customer receives, or at least perceives, from your offer.

Of course, appropriate export pricing requires proper accounting procedures. Otherwise, hidden costs will bring unpleasant surprises. For example, negotiations in Middle Eastern countries or Russia may last three times longer than the average domestic negotiations, dramatically increasing the costs of doing business.

Negotiating Prices. In-person or electronic negotiations give the exporter another opportunity to combat price escalation. During the actual negotiations, pricing should be postponed until all other substantive issues have been agreed upon. Since quality and reliability of delivery are the critical dimensions of supplier choice, the exporter may want to reduce pressure on price by emphasizing these two areas and how they fit with the buyer's needs.

An importer may reject an exporter's price at the outset in the hopes of obtaining concessions, such as discounts, an improved product, better terms of sales/payment, and other costly demands. Prepare for this by getting relevant information on the target market by developing counterproposals for possible objections. For example, if the importer states that better offers are available, ask for more details and show how the total package is better. In the rare case that the importer accepts the initial bid without comment, the exporter should make sure the extended bid is correct. Furthermore, competitive prices should be reviewed periodically to ensure that the price reflects changing market conditions accurately.

Export Pricing Terminology

Terms should indicate price and when ownership of goods passes from seller to buyer. *Incoterms* are the internationally accepted standard definitions for terms of sale set by the International Chamber of Commerce (ICC, at www.iccwbo.org) since 1936. Incoterms 2000 went into effect on January 1, 2000, with significant revisions to better reflect changing transportation and communication technologies.

Incoterms Alphabetics. Incoterms have four categories:

- "E" terms refer to the seller making goods available to the buyer only at the seller's own premises.
  - **EXW.** Prices quoted "ex-works" apply only at the point of origin, and the seller agrees to place the goods at the disposal of the buyer at the specified place on the date or within the fixed period. All other charges are for the account of the buyer.
- "F" terms, call upon the seller to deliver the goods to a carrier appointed by the buyer.
  - **FCA.** One of the new Incoterms is "free carrier," which replaced a variety of **FOB** terms for all modes of transportation except vessel. FCA (named inland point) applies only at a designated inland shipping point. The seller is responsible for loading goods into the means of transportation; the buyer is responsible for all subsequent expenses. If a port of exportation is named, the costs of transporting the goods to the named port are included in the price.
  - **FAS.** "Free alongside ship" at a named U.S. port of export means that the exporter quotes a price for the goods including charges for delivery of the goods alongside a vessel at the port. The seller handles the cost of unloading and wharfage. Loading, ocean transportation, and insurance are left to the buyer.
  - **FOB.** "Free on board" applies only to vessel shipments. The seller quotes a price covering all expenses up to, and including, delivery of goods on an overseas vessel provided by or for the buyer.
- "C" terms require the seller to contract for carriage but without

assuming the risk of loss or damage to the goods or additional costs after the dispatch.

- **CFR.** Under "cost and freight" to a named overseas port of import, the seller quotes a price for the goods including the cost of transportation to the named port of debarkation from the vessel. The cost of insurance and the choice of insurer are left to the buyer.
- **CIF.** With "cost, insurance, and freight" to a named overseas port of import, the seller quotes a price including insurance, all transportation, and miscellaneous charges to the point of debarkation from the vessel. If other than waterway transport is used, the terms are **CPT** ("carriage paid to") or **CIP** ("carriage and insurance paid to").
- "D" terms require the seller to bear all costs and risks to bring the goods to the destination determined by the buyer.
- **DDP.** With "delivered duty paid," the seller delivers the goods, with import duties paid, including inland transportation from import point to the buyer's premises. With **DDU** ("delivered duty unpaid"), only the destination customs duty and taxes are paid by the consignee.

Ex-works signifies the maximum obligation for the buyer; delivered duty paid puts the maximum burden on the seller. Careful determination and clear understanding of terms used, and their acceptance by the parties involved, are vital if subsequent misunderstandings and disputes are to be avoided.

Competitive Tools. Increasingly, exporters quote more inclusive terms. The benefits of taking charge of the transportation on either a CIF or DDP basis include the following:

- Exporters can offer foreign buyers an easy-to-understand "delivered cost" for the deal.
- By getting discounts on volume purchases for transportation services, exporters cut shipping costs and can offer lower overall prices to prospective buyers.
- Control of product quality and service is extended to transport, enabling the exporter to ensure that goods arrive to the buyer in good condition.
- Administrative procedures are cut for both the exporter and the buyer.[4]

When taking control of transportation costs, however, the exporter must know the impact of additional costs on the bottom line. Implemented incorrectly, the approach can create volatile shipping rates, unexpected import duties, and restive customers. Most exporters do not want to go beyond the CIF quotation because of uncontrollables and unknowns in the destination country. Whatever terms are chosen, the program should be agreed to by the exporter and the buyer(s) rather than imposed solely by the exporter.

Freight forwarders are useful in determining and reducing costs, preparing quotations, and other management tasks. Freight forwarders with large volume purchases get lower freight and insurance charges. Some freight forwarders can also provide additional value-added services, such as handling the marketer's duty-drawback receivables.

Export Terms of Payment

The exporter negotiates export credit and terms with an eye on the amount of payment, competitive terms and practices, ability to finance, and relative strength of the parties involved.[5] A well-established exporter with a unique product and accompanying service has greater leverage than a newcomer to the market.

Negotiated Risks. Basic methods of payment vary from cash in advance to open account or consignment selling, neither of which is feasible for longer-term relationships. But they are useful in limited situations. A marketer may use multiple methods of payment with the same buyer. For example, a distributor may purchase samples on open account, but pay for orders with a letter of credit.

Cash in advance (most favorable to the exporter) removes all risk and provides immediate cash. It is not widely used, however, except for smaller, first-time transactions or where there is reason to doubt about the importer's ability to pay. These terms are also used for custom-made products because of the increased risk to the exporter. In some instances, however, the importer may not be able to buy on a cash-in-advance basis because of government restrictions.

Letters of credit issued by a bank at the request of a buyer promise that the bank will pay a specified amount of money on presentation of documents stipulated in the letter of credit, usually the bill of lading, consular invoice, and a description of the goods.[6] Often used in international transactions, they can be classified along three dimensions: irrevocable versus revocable; confirmed versus unconfirmed; and revolving versus nonrevolving. A letter of credit substitutes the bank's credit for the buyer's credit and is as good as the issuing bank's access to dollars. In custom-made orders, an irrevocable letter of credit may help the exporter secure pre-export financing. The importer will not need to pay until the documents have been accepted by the bank, thus giving an additional float. The major caveat is that the exporter must comply with all the terms detailed in the letter of credit.

Drafts, similar to personal checks, are the actual means of payment. Most drafts are documentary; i.e., the buyer must get possession of various shipping documents before getting possession of the goods in the transaction. Clean drafts—orders to pay without any other documents—are mainly used by multinationals dealing with their own subsidiaries and in well-established relationships.

Consignment selling, the most favorable term to the importer, allows the importer to defer payment until the goods are actually sold. This approach, not widely used, puts the total burden on the exporter, and its use should be carefully weighed against the purposes of the transaction. Consignment selling may be the only way a new exporter can gain acceptance from intermediaries, for example.

Managing Currency Fluctuation

Another important export pricing and payment issue is the currency in which to invoice. Exchange rate movements can harm one of the parties. If the price is quoted in the exporter's currency, the exporter will get exactly the price it wants but may lose some sales. If the exporter needs the sale, it may accept the currency risk and invoice in the importer's currency.

When invoicing in foreign currencies, an exporter can at least know how much it will eventually receive by using the mechanism of the *forward exchange market,* as explained in Chapter 3.

Weak Currency. When the exporter's domestic currency is weak, the exporter should consider strategies such as:

1. Stress price benefits.
2. Expand product line.
3. Shift sourcing to domestic market.
4. Exploit all possible export opportunities.
5. Cash-for-goods trade.
6. Full-costing.
7. Speed repatriation.
8. Minimize expenditure in local currency.

Strong Currency. When the exporter's domestic currency is strong, the exporter should consider strategies such as:

1. Nonprice competition.
2. Improve productivity/cost reduction.

3. Sourcing overseas.
4. Prioritize exports.
5. Countertrade with weak currency countries.
6. Marginal-cost pricing.
7. Slow collections.
8. Buy needed services abroad.[7]

Additional responses to strong country of origin currencies include:

- *Market re-focus.* If lower values of the target market currencies make exporting more difficult by, for example, making collections times longer, marketers may start looking at other markets for growth. In some cases, the emphasis may switch to the domestic market, where market share gain at the expense of imports may be the most efficient way to grow.
- *Streamlined operations.* The marketer may start using more aggressive methods of collection, insisting on letters of credit and insurance to guarantee payments, or tightening control of distribution networks.
- *Shift in production.* Especially when currency shifts are seen as long-term, marketers will increase direct investment.

The Leasing Option

About 8 out of 10 U.S. companies lease equipment, making equipment leasing a $244 billion industry in 2002, the Equipment Leasing Association estimates. Organizational customers frequently prefer to lease major equipment rather than buy. It is a major force in the United States, Japan, and Germany and has grown significantly elsewhere, for example, in Russia. Trade liberalization around the world will benefit lessors as governments drop regulations limiting outside lessors.

For the firm selling products such as printing presses, computers, forklift trucks, and machine tools, leasing may allow penetration of markets in which an outright sale is impossible. Leasing often sidesteps trade balance restrictions even as lessors service their own equipment, an important consideration in countries where trained personnel are in short supply. The main benefit for the lessor is that total net income, after charging off pertinent repair and maintenance expenses, is often higher than from a sale.

Many leasing companies have become more than a source of capital, developing new value-added services that have taken them from asset financiers to asset managers or forming relationships with others who can provide these services. In some cases, lessors have even evolved into partners in business activities.

A Word on Dumping

Inexpensive imports often trigger accusations of dumping—that is, selling goods overseas for less than in the exporter's home market or at a price below the cost of production, or both. Charges of dumping range from those of Florida tomato growers against Mexican vegetable growers to those of the Canadian Anti-Dumping Tribunal, which ruled that U.S. firms were dumping radioactive diagnostic reagents in Canada. Such disputes are quite common, especially in highly competitive industries, such as computer chips, and steel. Importers counter that domestic producers frequently invoke legislation to protect their markets from legitimate foreign competition.

Dumping can be predatory dumping or unintentional. Predatory dumping refers to a foreign firm intentionally selling at a loss in another country in order to increase its market share, amounting to an international price war. Unintentional dumping is the result of time lags between the dates of sales transaction, shipment, and arrival. Exchange rates can change so that the final sales price falls below the cost of production or below the price prevailing in the exporter's home market. It has been argued that current dumping laws, especially in the U.S., do not adequately account for such forces as floating exchange rates, which make dumping appear to be more widespread than it is.[8]

In the United States, domestic producers may petition the U.S. International Trade Administration within the Department of Commerce to determine that sales have been at less than fair market value. If the Commission finds that domestic industry is being, or is threatened with being, materially injured by the imports, the remedy is an antidumping duty equal to the dumping margin. International agreements and U.S. law also provide for duties designed to offset the advantages imports would otherwise receive from the foreign government subsidies. However, governmental action against dumping and subsidized exports violating WTO regulations may hurt the very industries seeking relief, as countries impose retaliatory duties against alleged violators.

To minimize the risk of being accused of dumping (as well to be protected from dumping), the marketer can focus on value-added products and increase differentiation by including services in the product offering. For example, if the company operates in a sensitive or economically vulnerable industry, it may seek to collaborate with local companies in gaining market access.[9]

PRICING BY FOREIGN OPERATIONS

Many global marketers, both U.S.- and foreign-based,[10] emphasize nonprice competition, yet they rank pricing high as a marketing tool overseas, even though their nondomestic pricing decisions are made at middle management levels in a majority of firms.

Tailoring Market Prices

Price setting within individual country markets is driven by the typical corporate issues and objectives. Also, the major problem areas in international pricing have been meeting competition, cost, lack of competitive information, distribution and channel factors, and government barriers, according to a survey of 42 U.S.-based multinational corporations.[11] But because these factors vary among countries, Companies' pricing policies move by country with these factors, even as market integration requires coordination of prices across markets.

Dynamic Global Objectives. Multinationals tend to make pricing decisions close to each market's prevailing conditions, but the relationship is symbiotic: Coordination and strategic direction come from headquarters, yet pricing decisions also influence corporate strategy. For example, many foreign-based companies produce in, rather than export to, the United States to remain competitive in the market by increasing the dollar component of their output. Many have had to cope with higher wages in their home markets, increasing shipping costs, and unfavorable exchange rates. They have been willing to sacrifice immediate earnings for market share gain or maintenance.

Pricing strategies will vary by market situation and product positioning decisions. The basics of first-time pricing, price adjustment (standard v. premium) and product line pricing (branded v. private label) apply. Timing of price changes will vary with the company's objectives, for example, underselling a major competitor versus meeting profit goals in the face of changing foreign exchange rates.

Cost Floors. Overseas operations provide numerous potential cost challenges: allocation of manufacturing and marketing costs in a pricing model and how much overhead, R&D, and other indirect costs to allocate to a product, a product line, and entire country operations, such as intermarket allocation of a regional advertising campaign in multimarket media.

Currency inflation impacts foreign operations pricing, especially because it is usually accompanied by host government controls. Inflationary environments call for constant price adjustments, for instance. In markets with hyperinflation, pricing may be in a stable currency with daily translation into the local currency. In such volatile environments, the marketer may want to shift supply arrangements, pursue rapid inventory turnover, shorten credit terms, and ensure that contracts have a choice of currency or an escalator clause.

In the opposite scenario—in deflationary times—strategies may include:

- Target pricing, in which efficiencies are sought in production and marketing to meet price-driven costing.
- Value pricing, to move away from coupons, discounts, and promotions to everyday low prices.
- Stripping down products, to offer quality without all the frills.
- Adding value by introducing innovative products sold at a modest premium, accompanied by strong merchandising and promotion so customers will perceive the additions to be worth it.
- Getting close to customers with new technologies (e.g., the Internet and EDI) to track their needs and your costs more closely.[12]

Demand Ceilings. Demand sets price ceilings in a given market. Price sensitivity—the degree of demand change as prices change—is a critical factor, especially if cost structures change. A status-conscious market that insists on products with established reputations will be inelastic, allowing for far more pricing freedom than a market where price consciousness drives demand. But with increased information, status consciousness has been mitigated by a more practical consumer sensibility: top quality at competitive prices.[13] Consumer perceptions will affect the marketer's freedom in making pricing decisions.

Intermediaries also affect the prices the company can charge. A successful strategy requires close channel coordination to ensure intermediaries' margins. At the same time, there is enormous pressure on manufacturers' margins from intermediaries who are growing in size and global presence and demanding low-cost, direct-supply contracts.[14]

Market Structure and Competition. Competition helps set the price within the parameters of cost and demand. A company may choose to compete directly on price or elect for nonprice measures.

- In a pricing response, bundled prices (e.g., value deals on a combination of products), loyalty programs, selective price cuts, or new products can be offered.
- On the nonprice front, value-added benefits and services, such as warranty repairs and liberal credit terms, or brand image activities can be added.

In some cases, market structure changes might force a strategic realignment such as product line alterations or new strategic alliances within a market. A local competitor with political clout could be especially troublesome by seeking host government protections aimed at foreign-owned subsidiaries, particularly if the sector is high profile or deemed critical to the host nation's strength.

Government Price Controls. Governments influence prices and pricing directly by tariffs, taxes, and price controls. Setting maximum prices has been defended primarily on political grounds: It stops inflation and an accelerating wage-price spiral, and consumers want it. Supporters also maintain that price controls raise the income of the poor. Operating in such circumstances is difficult. Achieving price changes can be frustrating; for example, a company may wait 30 to 45 days for an acknowledgment of a price-increase petition.

To fight price controls, multinationals can demonstrate that they are not getting an acceptable return on investment and that, without an acceptable profit opportunity, future investments will not be made and production perhaps will be stopped.[15] Cadbury Schweppes sold its plant in Kenya because price controls made operations unprofitable. At one time, Coca-Cola and PepsiCo withdrew their products from the shelves in Mexico until they received a price increase. Pakistani milk producers terminated their business when they could not raise prices.

Companies can cite these arguments against price controls:

- The maximum price often becomes the minimum price if a sector is allowed a price increase, because all businesses in the sector will take it regardless of cost justification.
- The wage-price spiral advances vigorously in anticipation of controls.
- Labor often turns against restrictions because they are usually accompanied by an income policy or wage restrictions.
- Noninflationary wage increases are forestalled.
- Government control not only creates a costly regulatory body but also is difficult to enforce.
- Authorities raise less in taxes because less money is made.

- A government may have to bail out many companies with cheap loans or make grants to prevent bankruptcies and unemployment.[16]
- The best way for multinationals to avoid price controls is to work with governments, especially in the developing countries.

Coordinating Multimarket Strategies

Many local market influences are the key drivers of country-subsidiary prices, but coordination is increasingly necessary as regional markets consolidate, most notably in Europe. Also, increasing numbers of global and regional brands require intermarket price coordination. Yet, local subsidiaries need latitude in pricing.

Studies have shown that foreign-based multinational corporations allow their U.S. subsidiaries considerable freedom in pricing due to the size and unique features of the market. Also, these subsidiaries often control the North American market—a Canadian customer cannot get a better deal in the United States, and vice versa—and that distances create a natural barrier against arbitrage practices that would be more likely to emerge in Europe.[17] However, recent experience has shown that pricing coordination has to be worldwide because parallel imports will surface in any markets in which price discrepancies exist.

Integration Threat. The advent of the euro illustrates how all firms will need to reexamine the positioning of their businesses. The potential advantages of a single-currency Europe are considerable, but the Euro also threatens businesses of all nationalities, sizes, and forms. More production and operating strategy decisions will be made on the basis of true cost differentials—proximity to specific inputs, materials, immobile skills, or niche customers, for example. Consolidation will be the norm for many country business units whose existence was in some way perpetuated by using different currencies.

Intracompany transaction pricing—prices among company business units and headquarters—becomes more troublesome with currency consolidation. Transparency allows tax authorities to easily enforce transfer price uniformity.

If discrepancies among markets are not justified by market differences such as consumption preferences, competition, or government interference, parallel importation may occur. Parallel imports into affluent markets will force prices to the lowest level as buyers simply go to the cheapest available source. For example, Portugal may influence prices in Germany through parallel imports and centralized buying power.

"Price Corridor" Solution. The recommended approach is a "pricing corridor"—a range within which national prices vary. The company sets the maximum and minimum prices that country organizations can charge—enough to allow flexibility as a result of differences in price elasticities, competition, and positioning but not enough to attract parallel imports that may start at price differences of 20 percent and higher.[18] The corridor would be much narrower for easily transportable items like photographic film than for immobile products such as industrial machinery. This approach moves pricing authority away from country managers to regional management and requires changes in management systems and incentive structures. In Europe, as in future regional currency consolidations, manufacturers will do well to compromise between individually market-optimized prices and a uniform regional price. Uniformity will occur over time as consumers and national economies slowly adjust.

PRICING INTRACOMPANY TRANSACTIONS

Transfer (intracorporate) pricing is the pricing of sales to members of the multinational corporate family. With rapid globalization and consolidation across borders, estimates have up to two-thirds of world trade taking place between related parties, including shipments and transfers from parent company to affiliates as well as trade between alliance partners.[19] Transfer pricing must be managed in a world of varying different tax rates, foreign exchange rates, governmental regulations, and other economic and social challenges. Allocating resources among multinational units requires central management to achieve these objectives:

(1) competitiveness in the international marketplace;
(2) reduction of taxes and tariffs;
(3) management of cash flows;
(4) minimization of foreign exchange risks;
(5) avoidance of conflicts with home and host governments; and
(6) internal concerns, such as goal congruence and motivation of subsidiary managers.[20]

Despite the financial importance of intracorporate sales, even among the largest companies, only 28 percent have made transfer pricing a part of their overall corporate policies, according to Ernst & Young. A full 30 percent still view transfer pricing only as a compliance matter.[21]

Setting Transfer Prices

Transfer prices can be based on costs or market prices. The *cost approach* uses an internally calculated cost with a percentage markup added. The *marketprice approach* is based on an established market selling price, with that price minus a discount used to allow the buying division a profit. In general, a cost-based price is easier to manipulate because the base itself may be full, variable, or marginal cost.

Critical Considerations. Factors with a major influence on intracompany prices include:

(1) market conditions in the foreign country;
(2) competition in the foreign country;
(3) reasonable profit for the foreign affiliate;
(4) U.S. federal income taxes;
(5) economic conditions in the foreign country;
(6) import restrictions;
(7) customs duties;
(8) price controls;
(9) taxation in the foreign country; and (10) exchange controls.[22]

More than 210 multinational corporation senior financial executives cited market conditions in general and those relating to competition situation in particular as key variables.[23] In some markets, especially in Asia, competition may prevent an international firm pricing at will because local competitors have lower labor costs. This practice may provide entry to the market and a reasonable profit to the affiliate, but in the long term, it may become a subsidy to an inefficient business. Further, tax and customs authorities may object because underpricing means that the seller earns less income and pays duties on a lower base price on entry to the destination country.

Economic conditions in a market, especially the imposition of controls on movements of funds, may require the use of transfer pricing to allow the company to repatriate revenues. For example, a U.S.-based multinational corporation with central procurement facilities required its subsidiaries to buy all raw materials from the parent; it began charging a standard 7 percent for its services, which include guaranteeing on-time delivery and proper quality. The company estimates that its revenue remittances from a single Latin American country, which restricted remittances from subsidiaries to parent companies, increased by $900,000 after the surcharge was put into effect.[24]

Corporate Objectives and Policies. Transfer pricing objectives may lead to conflicts, especially if influencing factors vary dramatically from market to market. For example, specific policies should motivate subsidiary managers to avoid decisions that conflict with overall corporate goals. If policies give a poorer picture of the subsidiary's performance, this should be taken into account in performance evaluations.

Three approaches to transfer pricing have emerged over time:

- *Cost-based* (direct cost or cost-plus). The rationale is that it increases the profits of affiliates and that their profitability will eventually benefit the entire corporation. Most often, firms use cost-plus pricing, requiring every affiliate to be a profit center.
- *Market-based* (discounted "dealer" price derived from end market prices). Deriving transfer prices from the market is the most marketing-oriented method; it takes local conditions into account.
- *Arm's-length* pricing—what unrelated parties would reach on the same transaction. Many trade constituents, such as governments, favor this approach, but it becomes difficult when there isn't a reference point in a product category. Also, it is often difficult to convince external authorities that true negotiation occurred.

Transfer pricing can mitigate environmental influences in overseas markets. High transfer prices on goods shipped to a subsidiary and low ones on goods imported from it will minimize the tax liability of a subsidiary operating in a country with a high income tax. On the other hand, a higher transfer price may increase the import duty, especially if it is assessed on an *ad valorem* basis. Exceeding a certain threshold may boost the duty substantially into a luxury category and have a negative impact on the subsidiary's competitive posture. Adjusting transfer prices for the opposite effects of taxes and duties is a delicate balancing act.

Transfer prices may also help to balance the effects of fluctuating currencies when one partner is operating in a low-inflation environment and the other in one of rampant inflation. Also, transfer pricing becomes an important tool for recouping expenses from joint ventures, especially if governments restrict profit repatriation. [25]

Furthermore, a firm can manipulate a subsidiary's financial and competitive position by reducing transfer prices. It can trim start-up costs, penetrate a market niche more quickly, and guarantee long-term survival.

The best time to address the entire transfer price and taxation question is when the company is considering a major expansion or restructuring of operations. Pieces of the puzzle are interdependent. For example, a portion of a unit's R&D and marketing activities can be funded in a relatively low tax jurisdiction.

Transfer Pricing Challenges

Transfer pricing management complexity grows geometrically as all of the subsidiaries with differing environmental concerns are added. Fluctuating exchange rates make planning even more challenging, but to prevent double taxation and meet other requirements, the firm's pricing practices must be uniform. Many have adopted a philosophy that honors an obligation to be a good fiscal citizen, avoiding artificial tax-avoidance schemes. They believe that the primary goal of transfer pricing is to support and develop commercial activities.[26]

Managements face two general types of transfer pricing challenges. The first, internal, concerns the motivation of those affected by the pricing policies of the corporation. The second, external, deals with relations between the corporation and all tax authorities.

Fair Performance Metrics. Manipulating intracorporate prices complicates internal control and actual performance measures. Judging a subsidiary's profit performance as unsatisfactory when it was expected to be a net source of funds creates morale problems. Cultural differences among subsidiary managements might complicate matters further, especially if the need to subsidize less-efficient members is not made clear. Adjusting control mechanisms such as through dual bookkeeping will help headquarters reduce intracorporate friction and give appropriate credit where due.

Jealous Jurisdictions. Transfer prices inevitably involve foreign and domestic tax and regulatory jurisdictions. Generally, tax authorities will honor agreements among companies if the agreements are commercially reasonable and the companies are consistent.[27] but that doesn't mean they are not looking closer nowadays. For example, the U.S. Internal Revenue Service has begun tighter scrutiny of transfer pricing and has filed claims against hundreds of companies in recent years. Experts calculate that foreign-based multinationals evade at least $20 billion in U.S. taxes. Japan has created specific transfer pricing legislation, and marketers for not providing information in time to meet deadlines set by the government. German tax authorities are carefully checking intracompany charges. Countries such as Argentina, Brazil, and Mexico—which are dismantling exchange controls, high import duties, and other non-tariff barriers—turn to transfer pricing rules to accomplish the same ends.

Some fear that imminent global tax wars will target specific, prosperous industries. To avoid warfare, the Organization for Economic Cooperation and Development (OECD) published its transfer-pricing guidelines in mid-1995, with periodic revisions since then. Experts also speculate that the European Court may move to standardize corporate tax rates within the European Union.

The entire tax equation has become more complicated because many countries zealously protect customs duties, particularly when they generate more revenue than local business income taxes. As global communications improve, governments will share more tax information. Multinational firms should move cautiously, recognizing that they won't be able to hide transfer pricing practices from local governments.

Taxing Issues

The Internal Revenue Code gives the Commissioner of the IRS vast authority to reallocate income between controlled foreign operations and U.S. parents, and between U.S. operations of foreign corporations. It also focuses on licensing and other transfer of intangibles such as patents and trademarks.

The IRS has adopted the arm's-length standard for transfer pricing. Since 1994, U.S. firms have had to disclose whether or not they that method.[28] OECD guidelines for transfer pricing are similar to those used by U.S. authorities. Some experts who argue that the arm's-length standard is only applicable for commodities businesses have proposed a simpler approach using formulas such as California's system that factors in percentages of world sales, assets, and other indicators. Even with e-business expanding through world commerce, the fundamental economic relationships underlying transfer pricing and taxation will remain the same. The arm's-length principle will probably be retained and adapted to address cross-border activities in a virtual economy.[29]

Arm's-length price determination, according to Section 482 of the Internal Revenue Code, can use four methods in this order:

(1) The comparable uncontrolled price method;
(2) The resale price method;
(3) The cost-plus method; and
(4) Any other reasonable method.

The comparable uncontrolled pricing method is the starting point for testing transfer prices. In some cases, marketers have created third-party transactions to create a benchmark for appropriate comparisons. Under the resale method—best applied to transfers to subsidiaries for ultimate reselling—the company subtracts the subsidiary's profit from an uncontrolled selling price. The amount is compared with a similar product marketed by the multinational. The cost-plus approach best applies to transfers of components or unfinished goods to overseas subsidiaries. The arm's-length approximation is achieved by adding an appropriate markup for profit to the seller's total cost of the product.[30] The key is to apply such markups consistently over time and across markets.

However, comparisons are impossible for unique products or for goods traded only with related parties. Adjusting price comparisons for differences in the product mix or for inherently different facts and circumstances is unreliable.

Therefore, the most accepted of the "other reasonable methods" is the functional analysis approach,[31] which measures the profits of each of the related companies and compares it with the proportionate contribution to total income of the corporate group. It addresses the question of what profit would have been reported if the intracorporate transactions had involved unrelated parties. Understanding the functional interrelationships of the various parties—that is, which entity does what—determines each entity's contribution to the total income.

Since 1991, the IRS has signed and negotiated more than 400 *advance pricing agreements* (APAs) with multinationals to stem the tide of unpaid U.S. income taxes. Since 1998, it opened that option to small and medium-sized companies. Advance agreements on transfer prices eliminate court challenges, costly audits, and potentially harsh penalties. In the U. S., a transfer pricing violation can mean a 40 percent penalty on the amount of underpayment; in Mexico it can reach 100 percent.

The main criticism of advance agreements is the exorbitant amounts of staff time that each agreement requires.[32] Some also argue that such agreements may produce worse transfer pricing systems as companies with otherwise effective intracompany processes replace them with poorly designed ones to satisfy the tax authorities.[33] And some companies are wary of sitting down with tax authorities for fear of other issues emerging. In some cases, companies can seek a bilateral APA that is negotiated simultaneously with the tax authorities of both countries. Basically, the company sits back and watches the tax people divvy up its earnings. But bilateral APAs are rare. Most multinationals debate the value of proactive tax negotiations and many countries, especially those with emerging economies, do not have bilateral tax agreements with the U. S. In such cases, a company can negotiate a unilateral APA with the IRS on its cross-border operations with that country.[34]

The most difficult transfer pricing negotiations concern *intangibles* because comparables are unavailable. The IRS requires the price or royalty rate to result in a fair distribution of income between the units. This requires marketers to analyze and attach a value to each business function (e.g., manufacturing, marketing, and distribution). Comparable transactions or, if absent, industry norms should be used to calculate the rates of return for each function.

COUNTERTRADE OPTIONS

General Motors exchanged automobiles for a trainload of strawberries. Ford traded cars for sheepskins from Uruguay and potatoes from Spain. Pepsi accepted, in exchange for soft drink concentrate, products ranging from sesame seeds to sisal for making rope. The government of India swapped palm oil from Sudan for the construction of a railroad link.[35] All those were countertrade transactions that represent a modern form of the ancient art of barter. Countertrade consists of transactions explicitly linking export and import sales to an exchange of goods, services, or ideas. Among the leading reasons for using countertrade causes are an absolute lack of money, a lack of money with value or acceptability, easier transactions using goods, shrinking established markets, and substantial product surpluses. Throughout the 1990s, countertrade use steadily increased. The American Countertrade Association estimates that 25 percent of world exports are now linked to countertrade transactions.

Upside

World debt crises and exchange rate volatility have made ordinary trade financing very risky, so many countries see great benefits in countertrade transactions. Heavily indebted nations, especially in the developing world, cannot obtain the trade credit or financial assistance necessary to afford imports. Faced with the possibility of not having imports at all, they resort to countertrade to maintain product inflow. However, countertrade does not reduce commercial risk.

Like other forms of barter, countertrade permits traders to cloak their prices or at least mitigate the effects of price and exchange controls. Particularly in commodity markets with operative cartel arrangements such as oil or agriculture, prices can be overstated to hide discounts that expand market share or mask dumping activities. Thus, it is an excellent tool for entering new markets. Many countries welcome the reciprocity countertrade creates among trading partners. It allows them to avoid competition from outside their bilateral sphere and makes them new distribution channels in new markets for an exporter.

Downside and Beyond

Despite the benefits of countertrade, there are strong economic arguments against it, mainly on efficiency grounds. Countertrade requires accounts to be settled on a country-by-country or even transaction-by-transaction basis. That could result in exchanging otherwise uncompetitive goods at the expense of economic efficiency and growth. Countertrade is a source of great controversy and confusion, with attitudes for and against it found around the world. Detractors claim that it creates economic distortions. Many companies cloak their countertrades with secrecy, apparently out of fear that acknowledging their dealings would imply problems with their products. The result, of course, is rumor and confused public opinions that make it difficult to cope with countertrade decisively.

Types of Countertrade

Traditional traders directly barter goods of approximately equal value. While anything is possible—e.g., mango juice in exchange for jet aircraft maintenance—simple barter transactions are used less often today. Increasingly, countertraders have used more sophisticated versions of exchanging goods, such as the *counterpurchase*, or parallel barter, agreement based on two separate contracts that use some amount of cash to balance discrepancies between the values of exchanged goods. It is now the most frequently used form of countertrade.

In the *buyback*, or compensation, arrangement, one party agrees to supply technology or equipment that enables the second party to produce goods with which it pays the first party. In the past decade, such buyback arrangements have extended to encompass many developing and newly industrialized nations.

A more refined form of barter, aimed at reducing the effect of the immediacy of the transaction, is called a *clearing arrangement*. Here, clearing accounts are established in which firms can deposit and withdraw the results of their countertrade activities. Although the account may be out of balance on a transaction-by-transaction basis, the agreement stipulates that over the long term, trading partners will restore balance to the account. Sometimes, additional flexibility is given to the clearing account by permitting *switch trading*, in which credits in the account can be sold or transferred to a third party.

Another form of barter enjoying growing popularity is called the *offset*. Governments, typically buying military goods, require the seller to engage in transactions that offset the military purchase's impact on a country's balance of payments. Offsets can include coproduction, licensed production, subcontractor production, technology transfer, or overseas investment, typically in nonrelated industries. The downside is that such deals might strengthen competitors, reward inefficient producers, and reduce innovation.

Debt swaps enable debtors, typically third-world governments and private companies, to exchange their debts for something else, such as loans owed to other creditors or equity in local enterprises.

Countertrade Readiness

Countertrade growth has spawned new specialists to handle such transactions. Firms can handle the trades in-house or seek outside intermediaries to facilitate them.

Traditional trading companies frequently act as third-party countertrade intermediaries relying on their extensive worldwide connections to move goods more easily than their manufacturing clients can, earning profits from steep fees as well as from the discounts and markups of transactions.

Another type of intermediary is the countertrade information service provider, which provides databases on products and regulations in various countries. These firms also provide computerized matchmaking services between debtors and creditors.

Smaller countertrade intermediaries successfully compete by pursuing a niche strategy based on specialized geographic or product knowledge and develops countertrade transactions that may be too small for a multinational firm to handle profitably. Overall, both in-house and out-of-house countertrade approaches have pros and cons (see Exhibit 11.2).

Preparing to Deal. To develop an in-house capability for handling countertrade, a company first needs to determine the import priorities of its products to the target country or firm. Are they highly desirable and/or necessary and less likely to be subject to countertrade requirements or are they luxury items?

Next, the company needs to identify which countertrade arrangements and regulations exist in the country to which it exports. Awareness of the alternatives available and of the percentages demanded will strengthen one's bargaining position at the precontract stage. It is also important to incorporate all costs into the pricing scheme Since it is quite difficult to increase the price of goods once a "cash-deal" price has been quoted.

Next, the company should identify the most "salable" countertrade: Is this the best deal possible? This exercise should not be limited just to countertraded products for internal use. One's

Exhibit 11.2: Organizing for Countertrade: In-house versus Third Parties

	Advantages	Disadvantages
In-house	• Lower costs • Customer contact • More control • More flexibility • More learning	• Less expertise • Reselling problems • Recruitment and training costs • Less objectivity • Problems coordinating inter-functional staff
Third Parties	• Export specialists • Customer contacts • Reselling contacts • Legal acumen • More objectivity	• May be costly • Distanced from customer • Less flexibility • Less confidentiality • Less learning

SOURCE: Charles W. Neale, David D. Shipley, and J. Colin Dodds, "The Countertrading Experience of British and Canadian Firms," *Management International Review* 31 (Number 1, 1991): 33.

distributors and suppliers might be able to buy countertraded goods. As a result, even companies that do not see themselves as international marketers may suddenly be confronted with countertrade demands.

At this point, the company should be able to decide whether to engage in countertrade. The use of an accounting or tax professional is essential to comply with difficult and obscure tax regulations in this area. All of the risks of a particular countertrade must be assessed—the quality of the goods to be obtained, delivery times, and supplier reliability.

It is also useful to explore the impact of countertrade on future prices, both for the price of the specific goods obtained and for the world market price of the category of goods. Shifts in world market prices may severely affect profitability over time. The effect of a countertrade transaction on the world market price should also be considered, especially for large-volume transactions.

Then, take the long view. How will the new countertrade relationship serve the company's future plans and goals, regardless of short-term economic effects? A countertrade transaction should remain a means for reaching long-term objectives and not become an end in itself.

FUTURITIES

As products enter the mature phase of their life cycles, they take on commodity characteristics, as semiconductors did in the 1980s. Therefore, small price differentials per unit become crucial. Even for consumer products, price competition will be substantial, especially because of the increased dissemination of technology. As a result, exchange rate movements may play more significant roles in maintaining the competitiveness of the international firm. Government management of trade will continue to influence international pricing in other ways. Through subsidization, targeting, and government contracts, nations will attempt to stimulate their international competitiveness.

Concurrently, however, international marketers will continue to differentiate themselves on a nonprice basis, appealing to markets via services, quality, or other attributes of the total offering. By accomplishing such an objective successfully, a firm can buy itself freedom from short-term fluctuations in its business relationships.

E-commerce promises to accelerate these trends by making complete market information available on a real-time basis to all buyers and sellers, whether they are exporting for money, countertrading, manufacturing and selling through global networks, or are individual consumers. Manufacturers will have less ability to put different prices on identical products in different markets. Thanks to the Internet, sustaining price premiums and even surviving in key markets will require extraordinary attention to product differentiation, market segmentation, and competitively superior offer value.

NOTES

1. D. V. Harper and J. L. Caldwell, "Pricing," in *Marketing Manager's Handbook*, eds. S. H. Britt and Norman Guess (Chicago: Dartnell, 1983), 723–736.
2. S. Tamer Cavusgil, "Unraveling the Mystique of Export Pricing," *Business Horizons* 31 (May–June 1988): 54–63.
3. "What's in a Name," *Economist*, February 2, 1991, 60.
4. "How Exporters Efficiently Penetrate Foreign Markets," *International Business*, December 1993, 48.
5. "Getting Paid: Or What's a Transaction For?" *World Trade*, September 1999, 42–52; and Chase Manhattan Bank, *Dynamics of Trade Finance* (New York: Chase Manhattan Bank, 1984): 10–11.
6. David K. Eiteman, Arthur I. Stonehill, and Michael H. Moffett, *Multinational Business Finance* (Reading, MA: Addison-Wesley, 1997), 480–508.

7. Source: Adapted from S. Tamer Cavusgil, "Unraveling the Mystique of Export Pricing," *Business Horizons* 31 (May–June 1988): 54–63.
8. Paul Magnusson, "Bring Anti-Dumping Laws Up to Date," *Business Week*, July 19, 1999, 45.
9. D. Nejdet, "An Ethical and Legal Synthesis of Dumping: Growing Concerns in International Marketing," *Journal of Business Ethics* 17 (Nov. 1998): 1747–1753.
10. J. J. Boddewyn, R. Soehl, and J. Picard, "Standardization in International Marketing: Is Ted Levitt in Fact Right?" *Business Horizons* 29 (Nov.–Dec. 1986): 69–75; Saeed Samiee, "Pricing in Marketing Strategies of U.S.- and Foreign-Based Companies," *Journal of Business Research* 15 (March 1987): 17–30.
11. J. C. Baker and J. K. Ryans, "Some Aspects of International Pricing: A Neglected Area of Management Policy," *Management Decisions* (Summer 1973): 177–182.
12. "Stuck!" *Business Week*, November 15, 1993, 146–155.
13. "The New Affluent Japanese Consumer: Affluent and Ready to Shop for the Right Products," *Business International*, Jan. 27, 1992, and M. Van Horn, "Consumer Revolution in the Japanese Market," *Export Today* 7 (May 1991): 54–56.
14. Alan D. Treadgold, "The Developing Internationalisation of Retailing," *International Journal of Retail and Distribution Management* 18 (1990): 4–11.
15. Victor H. Frank, "Living with Price Control Abroad," *Harvard Business Review* 63 (March–April 1984): 137–142.
16. Ibid.
17. Saeed Samiee, "Pricing in Marketing Strategies of U.S.- and Foreign-Based Companies," *Journal of Business Research* 15 (March 1987): 1.
18. Stephen A. Butscher, "Maximizing Profits in Euroland," *Journal of Commerce*, May 5, 1999, 5.
19. "Transfer Pricing Moves to the Forefront," *Journal of Commerce*, November 14, 1997, 3A.
20. W. M. Abdallah, "How to Motivate and Evaluate Managers with International Transfer Pricing Systems," *Management International Review* 29 (1989): 65–71.
21. Ernst & Young, *Strategic Transfer Pricing*, available at http://www.ey.com.
22. Jane O. Burns, "Transfer Pricing Decisions in U.S. Multinational Corporations," *Journal of International Business Studies* 11 (Fall 1980): 23–39.
23. Ibid.
24. "How to Free Blocked Funds via Supplier Surcharges," *Business International*, December 7, 1984, 387.
25. D. J. Fowler, "Transfer Prices and Profit Maximization in Multinational Enterprise Operations." *Journal of International Business Studies* (Winter 1975): 9–26.
26. Michael P. Casey, "International Transfer Pricing," *Management Accounting* 66 (October 1985): 31–35.
27. Erika Morphy, "Spend and Tax Politics," *Export Today*, April 1999, 50–56.
28. Weston Anson, "An Arm's Length View of Transfer Pricing," *International Tax Review* (December 1999): 7–9; "Pricing Foreign Transactions," *Small Business Reports* (April 1993): 65–66.
29. Brad Rolph and Jay Niederhoffer, "Transfer Pricing and E-Commerce," *International Tax Review* (September 1999): 34–39.
30. David P. Donnelly, "Eliminating Uncertainty in Dealing with Section 482," *International Tax Journal* 12 (Summer 1986): 213–227.

31. Gunther Schindler, "Income Allocation under Revenue Code Section 482," *Trade Trends* 2 (September 1984): 3.
32. Stephen Barlas, "Taxation of Foreign Companies," *Management Accounting* 74 (June 1993): 10.
33. "Pricing Yourself into a Market," *Business Asia,* December 21, 1992, 1.
34. "Knocking on the IRS's Door," *Export Today,* April 1999, 52–73.
35. Ismail Fauziah, "Countertrade Is A Viable Means to Boost Business," *New Straits Times Press* (Malaysia), October 28, 1999, 18.

12

Global Distribution and Logistics

Getting goods to market calls for international teamwork.

Channels of distribution and logistics systems—the network of intra- and extracompany entities, relationships, and functions broadly known as the supply chain or the value chain—provide the essential links connecting producers and customers. Channel relationships are the heart of the teamwork essential for international marketing success because the majority of international sales involve distributors. Their role hardly stops with the physical movement of goods. Channels also manage the flows of information, communication, and product ownership that accompany goods. And channel decisions are the most long-term of all marketing mix factors because the more the supply chain members operate as a team, rather than a collection of independent businesses, the more effective the overall international marketing effort will be.

International marketers generally use one or more of three basic approaches to their customers:

- Selling directly to customers through their own field sales forces or electronic commerce.
- Selling through independent intermediaries, usually at the local level.
- Relying on an outside distribution system that may have regional or global coverage.

Because most marketers cannot or do not want to control the distribution function completely, structuring the supply chain becomes a crucial task. An experienced exporter may decide that control is of utmost importance and choose to perform tasks itself and incur the information collection and adaptation costs. An infrequent exporter, on the other hand, may be quite dependent on experienced intermediaries to get its product to markets. Global marketers meanwhile work with distributors at the local and regional market level or might be forced to establish new supply chains on their own.

In this chapter, we'll examine the decisions involved in the structuring and management of foreign channels of distribution, the logistics processes that physically move goods worldwide, and the lessons e-business is teaching as it revolutionizes channels and logistics.

INTERNATIONAL DISTRIBUTION CHANNELS

Distribution channels can vary from direct, producer-to-consumer types to elaborate, multilevel channels employing many types of intermediaries, each serving a particular purpose. In worldwide marketing, channel configurations for the same product will vary within industries, even within the same firm, because national markets often have their unique features. This may mean dramatic departures from preferred policy for a company.

Domestically and internationally, the information that channels manage is usually multidirectional, both vertical and horizontal. For example, the manufacturer relies heavily on retailers for data on possible changes in demand. The three information flows through channels—physical, transactional, and informational—do not necessarily take place simultaneously or occur at every level of the supply chain. Agent intermediaries, for example, act only to facilitate the information flow; they do not take title and often do not physically handle the goods. Similarly, electronic intermediaries have to rely on facilitating agents to perform the logistics function of their operation.

Channel Design

Because companies sell only a few products directly to foreign users, an international marketer has to choose alternative ways to move products to chosen markets, using methods that might depart substantially from domestic practices. The marketer must make design decisions about channel length—the levels and types of intermediaries—and channel width, the number of institutions of each type in the channel roster. An industrial goods marketer might grant exclusive distribution rights to a foreign entity, whereas a consumer goods marketer might want to use as many intermediaries as possible to ensure intensive distribution.

Eleven factors—the "11 Cs"—determine channel design, some of them external to the firm but most dictated by internal strategies and company capabilities. These factors' individual influences will vary from one market to another, and seldom, if ever, can one factor

---

Exhibit 12.1: The 11Cs Checklist

External Factors

- ❏ 1. Customer characteristics
- ❏ 2. Distribution culture
- ❏ 3. Competition

Internal Factors

- ❏ 4. Company objectives
- ❏ 5. Character
- ❏ 6. Capital
- ❏ 7. Cost
- ❏ 8. Coverage
- ❏ 9. Control
- ❏ 10. Continuity
- ❏ 11. Communication

---

be considered without examining its interaction with the others. The marketer developing new marketing channels or modifying and managing existing channels should use the 11 Cs checklist shown in Exhibit 12.1 to determine the proper approach to target audiences before selecting channel members to fill the roles. The external factors are givens, since the firm must adjust to the existing structures. The marketer can exercise some degree of control over the 8 internal factors.

Adjusting to External Factors. Customers' key characteristics—their *demographics* and *psychographics*—form the basis for channel design decisions. Answering questions such as what customers need—as well as why, when, and how they buy—determine how to make products available to them in a competitively advantaged way.

In the early stages of product introduction, the international marketer may concentrate efforts on only the most attractive markets and later, having attained a foothold, expand distribution. Or the marketer might use more than one channel to reach the same type of customer. Industrial product manufacturers might use dealers to reach private sector buyers but sell direct to governments through special sales offices, a practice common in the United States. Marketers might also find that primary target audiences differ from one market to another. For example, in Japan, McDonald's did not follow the U.S. pattern of locating restaurants in the suburbs. The masses of young pedestrians that flood Japanese cities were more promising prospects than affluent but tradition-minded car owners in the suburbs.[1]

Entering a market, the manufacturer should examine the existing *distribution culture* and *channel structures* for its type of product. Not doing so could be costly. For example, the structure and underlying relationships of Japanese distribution channels are frequently cited as an important reason why many foreign firms cannot achieve major market penetration. In any case, and in every country, international marketers must study distribution systems in general and the types of linkages between channel members for their specific type of product. Usually, the international marketer has to adjust to existing structures to gain distribution. For example, in Finland, 92 percent of all distribution of nondurable consumer goods is through four wholesale chains. Without their support, significant penetration of the market is not possible.

Trying to change existing distribution systems, such as streamlining the supply chain by cutting out some middlemen, is likely to be quite difficult in many foreign markets. Even in the United States, controversy over direct sales via the Internet illustrates how touchy established channel members can get. Manufacturers often need to share direct-sale revenues with channel members that, arguably, developed local market demand in the first place.

The marketer's analysis should extend to the relationships among channel members. How interdependent are they? If vertically integrated, for what reasons—ownership, contract, or the use of expert or referent power by one of the channel members? The Japanese distribution system often financially links producers, importers, distributors, and retailers either directly or through a bank or a trading company. Interdependence in a number of southern European markets is forged through family relationships or is understood as an obligation.

Foreign legislation affecting distributors and agents is an essential part of the distribution culture of a market. For example, legislation may require that foreign companies be represented only by firms that are 100 percent locally owned. In China, for example, foreign companies were barred from importing, distributing, or providing after-sales service their own products. These functions were to be performed by Chinese companies or Sino-foreign joint ventures. Since China joined the WTO, however, these restrictions are being phased out.

Although distribution decisions have been mostly tactical on a market-by-market basis, marketing managers have to recognize increasing globalization in the distribution function as well. This is taking place in two significant ways. Distribution formats such as supermarkets are crossing borders, especially to newly emerging markets. And intermediaries themselves are going global on their own or through strategic alliances. Within the European Union, for instance, a growing number of EU-based retailers are merging and establishing a presence in other European Union markets, partly in response to American mass merchandiser incursions. Some intermediaries enter foreign markets by acquiring local entities or forming alliances. Nor is their expansion limited to physical facilities; intermediaries license their skills and trademarks across borders as well. Although intermediary consolidation potentially gives marketers access to wider markets, stronger channel members inevitably put pressure on manufacturers' margins. The appropriate response is building solid relationships with channel members that will resist competition. In many cases, marketers provide new technologies to intermediaries to strengthen relationships and raise channel members' costs of switching from manufacturer-specific systems.

Channels used by *competitors* may be the only product distribution system accepted by both the trade and consumers. In this case, the international marketer's task is to use the structure effectively and efficiently. Even a sizable market entrant may find that building a parallel distribution system is too daunting a task. The other option is using a distribution approach totally different from that of the competition to develop a competitive advantage. A new approach will have to be carefully analyzed and tested against the cultural, political, and legal environments in which it is to be introduced.

In some cases, all feasible channels may be blocked by domestic competitors through contractual agreements or other means. U.S. suppliers of soda ash, which is used in glass, steel, and chemical products, have not been able to penetrate the Japanese market even though they offer a price advantage. The reason is the cartel-like condition developed by the Japan Soda Industry Association, which allegedly sets import levels, specifies which local trading company is to deal with each U.S. supplier, and buys the imports at lower U.S. prices for resale by its members at higher Japanese prices. Efforts by U.S. producers to distribute directly or through smaller, unaffiliated traders have faced strong resistance. The end users and traders have feared alienating the domestic producers, on whom their business depends. That resistance is changing, mainly due to grassroots demand for lower prices. Quite often, however, U.S. firms contributed to the problem by attempting to market products poorly designed for Japanese tastes through retail outlets out of sync with Japanese lifestyles.

Managing Internal Factors. Company objectives and corporate needs must be served by channel design, specific profit or market share goals, or simply a management desire to use particular channels. One of the most expedient methods of market development is partnerships. But some firms will eschew local market partnerships fearing they will lose control.

Partnerships can be undertaken, however, if appropriate controls are in place to secure expansion with relatively little investment, an approach coffee retailer Starbucks uses worldwide, for example. It creates exclusive supply arrangements with partners such as cruise lines, bookstores, and hotels to develop new channels. It partners with local entrepreneurs to open new country markets. And the company partners with manufacturers to develop new products, such as working with Red Hook Brewery to design a coffee-enhanced dark beer. Starbucks benefits from four key success factors:

- Investing very little capital, less than 5 percent of revenue, in international expansion.
- Shifting all business risk to local partners.
- Licensing allows stricter control over all operations than does franchising (e.g., parent company consultants visit each store once a month).
- Getting regulatory and cultural expertise on, for instance, product adaptations from local partners.[2]

The channel decision, once made, might change as the company's market presence grows and its products advance toward the maturity stages of their life cycles. If expansion is too rapid and the adjustments made to local market conditions too extensive, a major marketing asset—standardization and economies of scale and scope—can be lost.

The nature of the product, its *character*, will have an impact on the design of the distribution system. Generally, the more specialized, expensive, bulky, or perishable the product and the more after-sale service it may require, the more likely the supply chain will be relatively short. Staple items, such as soap, tend to have longer supply chains.

The type of channel chosen must match the product's positioning. And changes in overall market conditions, such as currency fluctuations, may require changes in distribution as well. An increase in the value of the billing currency may cause a repositioning of the marketed product as a luxury item, necessitating an appropriate channel (such as an upper-grade department store) for its distribution.

Rules of thumb aside, particular products may be distributed in a number of ways even to the same target audience. In Japan, for example, soap manufacturers usually distribute through large wholesalers then to retailers. But some soap manufacturers use two, or perhaps three wholesale layers to ensure the most intensive type of distribution.

Capital requirements and the marketer's financial strength will determine the type of channel and the basis on which channel relationships will be built. The stronger the marketer's finances, the more able the firm is to establish channels it either owns or controls. Intermediaries' requirements for beginning inventories, selling on a consignment basis, preferential loans, and need for training all will have an impact. For example, an industrial goods manufacturer may find that potential distributors in a particular country lack the capability of servicing the product. The marketer then has two options: set up an elaborate training program at headquarters or regionally or set up company-owned service centers to help distributors. Either approach will require a significant investment.

Closely related to the capital dimension is *cost*: the expenditure incurred in maintaining a channel once it is established. Cooperative advertising is an example. Costs will vary over the life cycle of a relationship with a particular channel member as well as over the life cycle of the products marketed. And costs will vary in terms of the relative power of the manufacturer vis-à-vis its intermediaries. Concentrated distribution systems erode the marketing strength of manufacturers.

Costs may also be incurred by protecting the company's distributors against adverse market conditions. A number of U.S. manufacturers helped their distributors maintain competitive prices through subsidies when the exchange rate for the U.S. dollar caused pricing problems. Extra financing aid has been extended to distributors that have been hit with competitive adversity. Such support, although often high in monetary cost, is usually a wise investment in maintaining strong manufacturer-distributor relationships.

The number of areas in which the marketer's products are represented and the quality of that representation determine *coverage*. Marketers use three approaches:

1. Intensive coverage, which calls for distributing the product through the largest number of different types of intermediaries and the largest number of individual intermediaries of each type.
2. Selective coverage, which entails choosing a select number of intermediaries for each area to be penetrated.
3. Exclusive coverage, which involves only one entity in a market.

Generally, intensive and selective coverage call for longer supply chains using different types of intermediaries, usually wholesalers and agents. Exclusive distribution is conducive to more direct sales and provides the advantage of a close, well-coordinated relationship, quite possibly with a larger distributor having more influence in the local market. Some goods, such as ethnic products, have geographically concentrated markets allowing for more intensive distribution with a more direct channel.

A company typically enters a market with one local distributor, but as volume expands, the distribution base often has to be adjusted. Expanding distribution too quickly may cause problems, however. Overextending to meet overoptimistic sales forecasts is one problem. So is the tendency of expansion to add channel types inconsistent with the product's original positioning: expanding distribution from specialty outlets to mass distribution, for instance. The impact on channel relations may be significant if existing dealers perceive loss of sales as a result of such a move. This may be remedied by keeping the product lines in mass-distribution outlets different or possibly developing a different brand for the new channels.

Using intermediaries will automatically lead to some loss of manufacturer *control* over marketing. The looser the relationship between marketer and intermediary, the less control the marketer can exert. The longer the channel, the more difficult it becomes for the marketer to have a final say in pricing, promotion, and the types of outlets in which the product will be made available. In the initial stages of internationalization or specific market entry, an intermediary's specialized knowledge and working relationships are needed, but as exporters' experience base and sales in the market increase, many opt to establish their own sales offices.

The type of product or service marketed influences the control decision. In the case of industrial and high-technology products, control will be easier to exert because intermediaries depend on the marketer for new products and service. Where the firm's marketing strategy calls for a high level of service, it uses integrated channels to ensure that the service does get performed.

Exercising control causes more conflict within distribution channels than any other factor. Marketers need to be sensitive and careful in communicating with foreign intermediaries about the company's intentions and the need for certain control measures. These might include the marketer's need to be the sole source of advertising copy or to be in charge of all product-modification activities. Generally, the more control the marketer wishes to have, the more cost is involved in securing that control.

Continuity is key. Channel design decisions are the most long-term of the marketing mix decisions, and the wrong choices will haunt an international marketing effort. Nurturing continuity rests heavily on the marketer because foreign distributors may have a more short-term view of the relationship. For example, Japanese wholesalers believe that it is important for manufacturers to follow up initial success with continuous improvement of the product. If such improvements are not forthcoming, competitors are likely to enter the market with similar, lower-priced products, and the wholesalers of the imported product will turn to the Japanese suppliers.

Continuity is also expressed through visible market commitment. Industries abroad may be quite conservative; distributors will not generally support an outsider until they are sure it is in the market to stay. Companies have made prominent investments, such as securing a listing on a local stock exchange or setting up a locally staffed sales subsidiary to prove they are serious in staying.

The supply chain depends on *communication*, making it an important channel design issue. Internationally, the distance that is perceived to exist between a buyer and a seller has multiple aspects in business-to-business markets, all of which must be considered when determining whether to use intermediaries and, if used, what types. For example, socially and culturally, any two entities in a distribution relationship may not be familiar with each other's ways of operating. Similarly, the time and geographic distance result in challenges in establishing contact and in the actual delivery of products and services.[3]

Communication, if bungled, can breed resentment among intermediaries. Proper communication involves not only the passage of information between channel members but also a better understanding of each party's needs and goals. This can be achieved through personal visits, exchange of personnel, or distribution advisory councils. Consisting of members from all channel participants, advisory councils meet regularly to discuss opportunities and problems that may have arisen.

Choosing Intermediaries

Types Available. Two basic decisions are involved in choosing the type of intermediaries—*distributors and agents*— to serve a particular market. First, the marketer must determine the type of relationship to have with intermediaries:

- A distributor will purchase the product and will therefore exercise more independence than an agency. Distributors are typically organized along product lines and provide the international marketer with complete marketing services.
- Agents have less freedom of movement than distributors because they operate on a commission basis and do not usually physically handle the goods. This, in turn, allows the marketer control to make sure, for example, that the customer gets the most recent and appropriate product version.

In addition to the business implications, the choice of type will have legal implications in terms of the agreements to which the intermediary can commit its principal and the ease of termination of the agreement.

The international marketer also must decide whether to utilize *indirect exporting, direct exporting,* or *integrated distribution* to penetrate a foreign market:[4]

- Indirect exporting requires dealing with another domestic firm that acts as a sales intermediary for the marketer, often taking over the international side of the marketer's operations. The benefits, especially in the short term, are that the exporter can use someone else's international channels without having to pay to set them up. But there may be long-term concerns in using this strategy if the marketer wants to actively and aggressively get into the markets itself. Indirect exporting is only practiced by firms very early on in their internationalization process.
- With direct exporting, the marketer takes direct responsibility for its products abroad by either selling directly to the foreign customer or finding a local representative to sell its products in the market.
- Integrated distribution requires the marketer to make an investment—such as a sales office, a warehouse, or assembly facility—in the foreign market to indicate long-term commitment. It entails more financial risk than direct or indirect exporting.

Where to Find Them. A poor choice of channel members will set an international marketing program back for years once the damage is done. Sometimes small exporters succeed passively, choosing from distributors that contact them. The initial contact may result from an advertisement or from a trade show contact. The marketer's best interest, however, is in taking an active role with a careful planning process. Understand market conditions, the company's needs, and what it can reasonably expect from a distributor. Both governmental and private agencies can assist the marketer in locating intermediary candidates.

- The U.S. Department of Commerce and various government agencies have various services available that, for modest fees, help export-minded companies find suitable foreign representation.
- DOC's Trade Opportunities Program (TOP) matches product interests of over 70,000 foreign buyers with those indicated by its U.S. subscribers.
- The Country Directories of International Contacts (CDIC) provide the names and contact information for directories of importers, agents, trade associations, and government agencies on a country-by-country basis. Both TOP and CDIC are available from DOC's Economics and Statistics Administration (www.stat-usa.gov) Web site.

The U.S. government also provides ways a marketer can indicate interest in international markets.

- The *U.S. Exporters Yellow Pages* (www.myexports.com) is a free directory that includes information and display advertisements on more than 17,000 U.S. companies interested in exporting.
- *Commercial News USA* (www.cnewsusa.com) is a catalog-magazine featuring advertisements by U.S. producers distributed worldwide 12 times each year.

Two U.S. government services are specifically designed for locating foreign representatives.

- The Agent/Distributor Service (ADS) locates foreign firms interested in export proposals submitted by U.S. firms and determines their willingness to correspond with the U.S. firm. Both U.S. and foreign commercial service posts abroad supply information on up to six representatives who meet these requirements.
- The International Company Profile (ICP) is a valuable service (www.icpcredit.com), especially when the screening of potential candidates takes place in markets where reliable data are not readily available. ICPs provide a trade profile of specific foreign firms. They also provide a general narrative report on the reliability of the foreign firm.

Individual state agencies provide similar services, all available online.

The easiest approach for the firm seeking intermediaries is to consult trade directories for *private sources* of help. Country and regional business directories such as Kompass for Europe (www.kompass.com), Bottin International for worldwide (www.bottin.fr), and the Japan Trade Directory (www.jetro.go.jp) are good places to start. Company lists by country and line of business can be ordered from Dun & Bradstreet (www.dnb.com), Reuben H. Donnelly (www.rhdonnelly.com), and Kelly's Directory (www.kellys.co.uk). Telephone directories, especially the yellow page sections or editions, can provide distributor lists. For Telex directories, more information is available at www.who.de/telex.pdf. Although not detailed, these listings will give addresses and an indication of the products sold.

The firm can ask its facilitating agencies—such as banks, advertising agencies, shipping lines, and airlines—for information. All these have substantial international information networks that are part of the value-added service they provide clients. The marketer can take an even more direct approach by advertising in traditional media and online to solicit representation. In addition, trade fairs are an important forum to meet and learn about potential distributors. The marketer may also deal directly with contacts from previous applications, launch new mail solicitations, use its own sales organization for the search, or communicate with existing customers to find prospective distributors. The latter may happen after a number of initial unsolicited sales to a market, causing the firm to want to enter the market on a more formal basis. If resources permit, the international marketer can use outside service agencies or consultants to generate a list of prospective representatives.

Screening. Although the criteria for screening candidate intermediaries (or assessing current ones) will differ in detail by industry, product category, market conditions, and the marketers' needs, a generic checklist can be a starting point. Criteria used include sales and marketing factors (such as knowledge of market and coverage), product and service factors (such as product expertise and quality of sales personnel), and management factors (such as previous success and commitment to proposed relationship).[5]

The financial *performance* and standing of the candidate is critical. Is it making money and does it have enough resources to perform necessary marketing tasks and assume customer credit risks? Financial reports are not always complete or reliable, or they may lend themselves to interpretation differences, pointing to a need for third-party opinion. Many Latin American intermediaries lack adequate capital, a situation that can lead to more time spent managing credit than managing marketing strategy.

Evaluate the distributor's current product lines along four dimensions: competitiveness, compatibility, complementary nature, and quality. Quite often, international marketers find that the most desirable distributors in a given market are already handling competitive products and are therefore unavailable. In that case, the marketer can look for an equally qualified distributor handling related products. The complementary nature of products may be of interest to both parties, especially in industrial markets, where ultimate customers may be in the market for complete systems or one-stop shopping. The quality match for products is important for product positioning reasons; a high-quality product may suffer unduly from a questionable distributor reputation. The number of product lines handled gives the marketer an indication of the level of effort to expect from the distributor. Some distributors are interested in carrying as many products and product lines as possible to enhance their own standing, but they have the time and the willingness to actively sell only those that bring the best compensation.

Also check the candidate's physical facilities for handling the product. This is essential particularly for products that may be subject to quality changes, such as food products. The assessment should also include the candidate's marketing materials, including a possible Web site, for adequacy and appropriateness.

The distributor's market coverage must be examined: not only the territory covered and the number of market segments served, but also how well those markets are served. The characteristics of the sales force and the number of sales offices are good quantitative indicators. To study the quality of the distributor's market coverage, the marketer can check whether salespeople call on executives, engineers, and operating people or concentrates mainly on purchasing agents. In some areas of the world, the marketer has to make sure that two distributors will not end up having territorial overlaps, which can lead to unnecessary conflict.

The distributor's reputation for *professionalism* must be checked. This rather abstract measure takes its value from a number of variables that all should help the marketer forecast fit and effectiveness. The distributor's customers, suppliers, facilitating agencies, competitors, and other members of the local business community should be contacted for information on the business conduct of the distributor in such areas as buyer-seller relations and ethical behavior. This effort will shed light on variables that may be important only in certain parts of the world, such as political clout, which is essential in certain developing countries.

Determine the candidate's business goals, what the distributor expects to get from the relationship, and where the international marketer fits into those plans. Because a channel relationship is long term, the distributor's views on future expansion of the product line or its distribution should be understood. And how much capability can the distributor give, or need to receive, in meeting the marketing tasks the exporter expects?

Finally, the marketer should determine the distributor's overall attitude toward cooperation and commitment to the marketer. An effective way of testing a distributor's attitude and weeding out the less interested candidates is to ask the distributor to develop or assist in developing a local marketing plan. This endeavor will reveal potential problem areas and will spell out which party is to perform the various marketing functions.

Although the initial screening can take place at the marketer's offices, the three to five finalists should be visited, their facilities inspected, and their various constituents in the market interviewed. A number of other critical data sources are important for firms without the resources for on-site inspection. The distributor's suppliers or firms not in direct competition can provide in-depth information. A bona fide candidate will also provide information through a local bank. Credit reports are available through the National Association of Credit Management, Dun & Bradstreet, and local credit reporting agencies.

When the international marketer has found a suitable intermediary, the parties sign a foreign sales agreement. The agreement can be relatively simple, but given the numerous differences in the market environments, certain elements are essential. The checklist prepared by *Business International* in Exhibit 12.2 is the most comprehensive in stipulating the nature of the contract and the respective rights and responsibilities of the marketer and the distributor.

Contract duration is important, especially when an agreement is signed with a new distributor. In general, distribution agreements should be for a specified, relatively short period (one or two years). The initial contract with a new distributor should stipulate a trial period of either three or six months, possibly with minimum purchase requirements. Duration should be determined with an eye on the local laws and their stipulations on distributor agreements and terminations.

Geographic boundaries for the distributor should be determined with care, especially by smaller firms. Future expansion of the product market might be complicated if a distributor claims rights to certain territories. The marketer should retain the right to distribute products independently, reserving the right to deal directly with certain customers. For example, many marketers maintain a dual distribution system, dealing directly with certain large accounts. This type of arrangement should be explicitly stated in the agreement. Transshipments, sales to customers outside the agreed-upon territory or customer type, have to be explicitly prohibited to prevent the occurrence of parallel importation.

Payment methods must be spelled out, stipulating methods of payment as well as how the distributor or agent is to draw compensation. Distributors derive compensation from various discounts, such as the functional discount, whereas agents earn a specific commission percentage of net sales, such as 15 percent. Given the volatility of currency markets, the agreement should also state the currency to be used. The international marketer also needs to make sure that none of the compensation forwarded to the distributor is in violation of the Foreign Corrupt Practices Act in American law or the OECD guidelines. A violation occurs if a foreign official receives a payment in exchange for business favors, depending on the nature of the action sought. So-called grease or facilitating payments, such as a small fee to expedite paperwork through customs, are not considered violations.

Product and conditions of sale need to be agreed on. The products or product lines included should be stipulated, as well as the functions and responsibilities of the intermediary in terms of carrying the goods in inventory, providing service in conjunction with them, and promoting them. Conditions of sale determine which party is to be responsible for some of the expenses involved, which will in turn have an effect on the price to the distributor. These conditions include credit and shipment terms.

Communication standards between the parties must be stipulated in the agreement if a marketer-distributor relationship is to succeed. The marketer should have access to all information concerning the marketing of his or her products in the distributor's territory, including past records, present situation assessments, and marketing research concerning the future. Formal communication channels should be specified for formal grievances. The contract should require protecting the confidentiality of the information provided by either party and protect the intellectual property rights involved.

Exhibit 12.2:
Elements of a Distributor Agreement

A. Basic Components
    1. Parties to the agreement
    2. Statement that the contract supersedes all previous agreements
    3. Duration of the agreement (perhaps a three- or six-month trial period)
    4. Territory:
        a. Exclusive, nonexclusive, sole
        b. Manufacturer's right to sell direct at reduced or no commission to local government and old customers
    5. Products covered
    6. Expression of intent to comply with government regulations
    7. Clauses limiting sales forbidden by U.S. Export Controls or practices forbidden by the Foreign Corrupt Practices Act
B. Manufacturer's Rights
    1. Arbitration:
        a. If possible, in the manufacturer's country
        b. If not, before international Chamber of Commerce or American Arbitration Association, or using the London Court of Arbitration rules
        c. Definition of rules to be applied (e.g., in selecting the arbitration panel)
        d. Assurance that award will be binding in the distributor's country
    2. Jurisdiction that of the manufacturer's country (the signing completed at home); if not possible, a neutral site such as Sweden or Switzerland
    3. Termination conditions (e.g., no indemnification if due notice given)
    4. Clarification of tax liabilities
    5. Payment and discount terms
    6. Conditions for delivery of goods
    7. Nonliability for late delivery beyond manufacturer's reasonable control
    8. Limitation on manufacturer's responsibility to provide information
    9. Waiver of manufacturer's responsibility to keep lines manufactured outside the United States (e.g., licensees) outside of covered territory
  10. Right to change prices, terms, and conditions at any time
  11. Right of manufacturer or agent to visit territory and inspect books
  12. Right to repurchase stock
  13. Option to refuse or alter distributor's orders
  14. Training of distributor personnel in the United States subject to:
        a. Practicality
        b. Costs to be paid by the distributor
        c. Waiver of manufacturer's responsibility for U.S. immigration approval

C. Distributor's Limitations and Duties
  1. No disclosure of confidential information
  2. Limitation of distributor's right to assign contract
  3. Limitation of distributor's position as legal agent of manufacturer
  4. Penalty clause for late payment
  5. Limitation of right to handle competing lines
  6. Placement of responsibility for obtaining customs clearance
  7. Distributor to publicize designation as authorized representative in defined area
  8. Requirement to move all signs or evidence identifying distributor with manufacturer if relationship ends
  9. Acknowledgment by distributor of manufacturer's ownership of trademark, trade names, patents
  10. Information to be supplied by the distributor:
      a. Sales reports
      b. Names of active prospects
      c. Government regulations dealing with imports
      d. Competitive products and competitors' activities
      e. Price at which goods are sold
      f. Complete data on other lines carried (on request)
  11. Information to be supplied by distributor on purchasers
  12. Accounting methods to be used by distributor
  13. Requirement to display products appropriately
  14. Duties concerning promotional efforts
  15. Limitation of distributor's right to grant unapproved warranties, make excessive claims
  16. Clarification of responsibility arising from claims and warranties
  17. Responsibility of distributor to provide repair and other services
  18. Responsibility to maintain suitable place of business
  19. Responsibility to supply all prospective customers
  20. Understanding that certain sales approaches and sales literature must be approved by manufacturer
  21. Prohibition of manufacture or alteration of products
  22. Requirement to maintain adequate stock, spare parts
  23. Requirement that inventory be surrendered in event of a dispute that is pending in court
  24. Prohibition of transshipments

SOURCE: "Elements of a Distributor Agreement," *Business International,* March 29, 1963, 23–24. Reprinted with permission from *Business International.* Updated by Ilkka Ronkainen with executive interviews in October 2002 and February 2003.

MANAGING CHANNEL RELATIONSHIPS

A channel relationship is like a marriage; it brings together two independent entities that have shared goals. For the relationship to work, each party must be open about its expectations and openly communicate changes perceived in the other's behavior that might be contrary to the agreement. The greater the partnership, the more likely the marketing success.

Overcoming Obstacles

Conflicts will surface, ranging from small grievances such as billing errors to major ones—rivalry over channel duties, perhaps—but the partners should be able to manage disagreements. Sometimes, a third party might cause trouble, such as gray market intermediaries (a company that produces or purchases authentic and legitimately manufactured trademark items abroad but imports or diverts those items to the United States by bypassing designated channels competing with legitimate importers and exclusive distributors. Nevertheless, the international marketer must solve the problem and manage the relationship for the long term. Even if an exporter enjoys a seller's market and can get away with unduly pressuring intermediaries, environmental conditions could change and the insensitive exporter suddenly find itself abandoned by the marketing partners it needs.

Typical Complications. Three types of complications can bedevil the foreign market distribution relationship: ownership; geographic, cultural, and economic distance; and different rules of law.[6] Rather than just complain, both parties need to take strong action to remedy them. Often, the major step is acknowledging that differences do indeed exist.

Ownership is different in international marketing, where manufacturers and distributors are usually independent entities. Distributors typically carry the products of more than one manufacturer and judge products by their ability to generate revenue without added expense. The international marketer, in order to receive disproportionate attention for its concerns, might offer both monetary and psychological rewards.

Both parties can bridge the *distance* between themselves—whether it is geographic, psychological, economic, or a combination—through effective two-way communication. This should go beyond normal routine business communication to include innovative ways of sharing pertinent information. The international marketer may place one person in charge of distributor-related communications or put into effect an interpenetration strategy—that is, an exchange of personnel so that both organizations gain further insight into the other.

The partners must manage cross-cultural differences in their belief systems and behaviors. For example, does one partner's culture expect individualism and acting in self-interest while the other partner expects everyone to honor a collective good?

Economic distance manifests itself in exchange rates, for example, when rate instability requires flexibility in handling unforeseen fluctuations. For example, U.S. motorcycle maker and exporter Harley Davidson instituted a system of risk sharing in which it will maintain a single foreign currency price as long as the spot exchange rate does not move beyond a mutually agreed-upon rate. Should it happen, Harley Davidson and the distributor would share the costs or benefits of the change.

In many markets *laws and regulations* may contribute to discord by restricting manufacturer control. In the European Union, for instance, the international marketer cannot prevent a distributor from reexporting products to customers in another member country, even though the marketer has another distributor in that market. The only remedy is to include the necessary stipulations in the distributor agreement, for example, a clause prohibiting transshipments.

Most of the criteria used in selecting intermediaries can be used to evaluate existing intermediaries and guide changes in the supply chain when needed. But channel adjustment is nothing to take lightly. Shifting to different channels, eliminating some intermediaries, or changing the duties and compensation of current intermediaries will cause major disruptions in the marketing program. The question is, How long and how deep will those disruptions be?

Coping with Gray Markets. Gray markets, or parallel importation, refer to authentic and legitimately manufactured trademark items that are produced and purchased abroad but imported or diverted to the United States by bypassing designated channels. Gray market products vary from inexpensive consumer goods such as chewing gum to expensive capital goods such as excavation equipment.

Various conditions allow unauthorized resellers to exist. The most important are price segmentation and exchange rate fluctuations. Competitive conditions may require the international marketer to sell essentially the same product at different prices in different markets or to different customers. Because many products are priced higher in, for example, the United States, a gray marketer can purchase them in Europe or the Far East and offer discounts between 10 and 40 percent below list price when reselling them in the U.S. market. In some cases, product shortages create gray markets. At one time, many U.S. computer manufacturers had to turn to gray marketers to secure their supply of memory semiconductors lest their production lines grind to a halt. However, in these cases, the gray market goods typically cost more than those usually available through authorized suppliers. In other cases when there are multiple production sites for the same product, gray markets can emerge due to negative perceptions about the country of origin.

Opponents and supporters of gray market practices disagree on whether the central issue is price or trade rights.

Detractors argue that:

- The gray market unduly hurts legitimate trademark owners.
- Without protection, trademark owners will have little incentive to invest in product development.
- Gray marketers will "free ride" and take unfair advantage of the trademark owners' marketing and promotional activities.
- Parallel imports can deceive consumers by not meeting product standards or their normal expectations of after-sale service.
- Gray market goods can severely undercut local marketing plans, erode long-term brand images, eat up costly promotion funds, and sour manufacturer-intermediary relations.

Proponents of parallel importation approach the issue from an altogether different point of view. They argue for their right to "free trade" by pointing to manufacturers that are both overproducing and overpricing in some markets. The main beneficiaries, they say, are consumers who benefit from lower prices and discount distributors, with whom some of the manufacturers do not want to deal and who have now, because of gray markets, found a profitable market niche.

In response to the challenge, manufacturers have chosen various approaches to combat gray marketing.

Despite a Supreme Court ruling in 1988 legitimizing gray markets in the United States, foreign manufacturers, U.S. companies manufacturing abroad, and authorized retailers have continued to fight the practice. In 1991, the U.S. Customs Service enacted a new rule blocking parallel channel importation of trademarked goods that have been authorized for manufacture and sale abroad by U.S. trademark holders. Parallel importing of goods of foreign manufacturers will not be affected. Meanwhile courts have shown little sympathy for cases involving deception, when the gray goods aren't what the customer was told to expect. For example, Lever Brothers won a long case to stop discounters from selling Sunlight brand dishwashing detergent, produced for the British market, in the United States. Because tap water is generally harder in Britain, formulation of the product there is different from Lever's U.S. version, which produces more lather. Lever reported lost sales and complaints from customers who bought the British brand and were disappointed.[7]

The solution for the most part lies with the contractual relationships that tie businesses together. In almost all cases of gray marketing, someone in the authorized channel violates the agreements signed. One of the standard manufacturers' responses is disenfranchising violators. Tracking down offenders is quite expensive and time consuming, however. Some of the gray marketers can be added to the authorized dealer network if mutually acceptable terms can be reached, thereby increasing control of the channel of distribution.[8]

A one-price policy can eliminate one of the main reasons for gray markets. This means choosing the most efficient of the distribution channels through which to market the product, but it may also mean selling at the lowest price to all customers regardless of location and size. A meaningful one-price strategy must also include a way to reward the providers of additional services, such as warranty repair, in the channel.

Other manufacturer counterstrategies have included producing different versions of products for different markets. Manufacturers also fight back by warning consumers against buying gray market goods, which manufacturers will not cover with their warranties. Some gray marketers, however, provide their own warranty-related service and guarantees.

Terminating Relationships. Many reasons might justify terminating a channel relationship, but the most typical are changes in the international marketer's distribution approach—establishing a sales office, for instance—or poor performance by the intermediary.

Channel relationships go through what has been called the "international distribution life cycle." Over time, the manufacturer's marketing capabilities increase while a distributor's ability and willingness to grow the manufacturer's business in that market decreases. When a producer expands its market presence, it may expect more of a distributor's effort than the distributor is willing to make available.[9] Furthermore, with expansion, the manufacturer may want to expand its product line to items that the distributor is neither interested in nor able to support. In some cases, intermediaries may not be interested in growing the business beyond a certain point (e.g., due to progressive taxation in the country) or pursue as aggressively as the principal may expect (i.e., being more of an order-taker than an order-getter). As a marketer's operations expand, it may want to start coordinating operations across markets for efficiency and customer-service reasons or to cater to global accounts. It will need to control distribution to a degree that independent intermediaries are not willing to accept or requiring a level of service that they may not be able to deliver.

On the other hand, the marketer should recognize at the outset that the relationship between a principal and an intermediary goes through phases that can be managed for mutual benefit. The partnership does not need to end. Going into the distributor relationship with eyes wide open means following these guidelines:[10]

1. Select distributors; don't let them select you.
2. Look for distributors capable of developing markets, rather than those with just a few customer contacts.
3. Treat local distributors as long-term partners, not temporary market-entry vehicles.
4. Support market entry by committing money, managers, and proven marketing ideas.
5. Maintain control over marketing strategy from the start.
6. Make sure distributors provide detailed market and financial performance data.
7. Build links among national distributors at the earliest opportunity.

If structural changes do require termination, the marketer must proceed carefully, understanding the effect it will have on the intermediary, and communicate openly to make the transition smoothly. For example, the intermediary can be compensated for investments made, and major customers can be visited jointly to assure them that service will be uninterrupted.

Termination conditions are one of the most important considerations in the distributor agreement, because the just causes for termination vary and the penalties for the international marketer may be substantial. Just causes include fraud or deceit, damage to the other party's interest, or failure to comply with contract obligations concerning minimum inventory requirements or minimum sales levels. These must be spelled out carefully because local courts are often favorably disposed toward local businesses. In some countries, termination may be time consuming and expensive, or not even be possible.

In the manufacturer-distributor "marriage," prenuptial agreements are essential. The time to think about termination is before the overseas distribution agreement is signed. It is especially prudent to find out what local laws say about termination and to check what type of experience other firms have had in the particular country. Careful preparation can allow the exporter to negotiate a termination without litigation. If the distributor's performance is unsatisfactory, careful documentation and clearly defined performance measures may help show that the distributor has more to gain by going quietly than by fighting.

GLOBAL LOGISTICS

Except for Saudi wheat, Big Macs sold in Saudi Arabia are made entirely from foreign ingredients: beef patties from Spain, sauce from the United States, Mexican onions and sesame seeds, Brazilian oil and sugar, and packaging from Germany. The world's giant fast-food chain, a premier model of global sourcing, consolidates warehousing and distribution so that all the materials of the uniform Big Mac can come together, however far-flung producers and distributors may be. McDonald's "cracks the global supply chain to create a borderless environment," said its global logistics manager.

To keep McDonald's restaurants in 120 countries and their 40 million customers per day in continuous supply, the company has become one of the world's largest buyers of beef and other ingredients for its products. In large markets the company sources its ingredients locally, while in small markets like Saudi Arabia, McDonald's uses its distribution system so that items like beef patties can be supplied almost anywhere in the world. The benefits of this type of supply chain management for global retailers like McDonald's are a stable source of supply and protection against currency exchange risk.

In new markets, McDonald's slashes costs by switching from importing to local manufacturing. Local production is not just cheap but also helps insulate the company from exchange rate changes. In Russia, for example, McDonald's has set up local companies to supply everything from pickles to construction materials for its restaurants. Because of local sourcing, McDonald's says, its Russian operations remain profitable in spite of slower sales due to an economic slowdown.[11]

Inside Global Supply Chain Management

A hallmark of the truly global firm is how it serves widely dispersed customer locations with global sourcing. Logistics, the complex of strategies and services that move physical goods into and out of the firm around the world, is the tool employed. In an era of new trade opportunities opening around the globe where infrastructures suffer from major shortcomings, competent logistics management is more important than ever before.

A systems approach links traditionally separate logistics components and orchestrates the performance, quality, and timing of the entire supply chain. Logistics management coordinates tools such as just-in-time (JIT) delivery to reduce inventory cost, electronic data interchange (EDI) for more efficient order processing, and early supplier involvement (ESI) for better planning. Often, firms concentrate on their core competencies and rely on outsourcing alliances to provide the logistics. For example, a firm can choose to focus on manufacturing and leave all aspects of order filling and delivery to an outside provider. By working closely with customers such as retailers, firms develop efficient customer response (ECR) systems, which track sales activity on the retail level. As a result, manufacturers can precisely coordinate production in response to actual shelf replenishment needs.

Three Concepts. Supply chain management, recognized as a distinct and growing executive discipline, is rooted in three notions that govern its approach to global business: the systems concept, the total cost concept, and the trade-off concept. Together they control the processes linking suppliers at one end of a company's supply chain and the ultimate buyer at the other end.

The systems concept recognizes that materials flows within and outside of the firm are so extensive and complex that they can be considered only in the context of their interaction. Instead of each corporate function, supplier, and customer operating with the goal of individual optimization, the systems concept stipulates that some components may have to work suboptimally to maximize the benefits of the system as a whole. For the systems concept to work, information flows and partnership trust are critical.

The total cost concept is a logical outgrowth of the systems concept, using cost as the premier performance metric. Logistics system members need to understand the true costs of their operations using activity-based costing (ABC), itself a management discipline for identifying and allocating often elusive indirect as well as direct costs. In the international arena, total cost includes the often considerable impact of national tax policies and exchange rate risk. Management's objective becomes after-tax profit maximization rather than minimizing total cost.[12]

The trade-off concept recognizes the interactions among system components: how changing one affects the performance and costs of other. For example, locating a warehouse near customers might reduce the cost of transportation, but a new warehouse generates new costs. A lean inventory will save storage and financing costs but possibly require additional emergency shipment costs.

New Competitive Dimensions. Logistics costs, comprising from 10 to 30 percent of the total landed cost of an international order,[13] are the last frontier of cost reduction for most international marketers. Companies have already achieved many of the cost reductions that are possible in global venture financing and production; they are now beginning to look at international logistics as a competitive tool that promises to be dynamic, even explosive, in the years to come. It is fair to say that logistics may well become the key dimension by which firms distinguish themselves internationally.

Technological advances and progress in communication systems and information-processing capabilities are particularly significant in designing and managing logistics systems globally. But, while most industrialized countries can offer the technological infrastructure and business practices for computer-to-computer exchange of business information and close supply chain coordination, such conditions hardly exist everywhere. Comparing Russia and the United States illustrates the problem. In the U.S. economy, the total cost of distribution is close to 11 percent of GDP. Russia—battling space constraints, poor lines of supply, nonexistent distribution and service centers, limited rolling stock, insufficient transportation systems, and little understanding of logistics management—finds distribution cost remaining well above 30 percent of GDP.

Unlike domestic operations, where experience and extensive benchmarks guide management judgment, international logistics managers frequently depend on educated guesses to determine the steps required to obtain a desired service level. Variations and lack of familiarity with locale create uncertainty that can't be overcome by applying domestic-market solutions. International survival requires understanding the differences of the international logistics field:

- Distance adds longer lead times, more safety inventory, and generally more opportunities for things to go wrong.
- Currency variation requires contingency planning.
- Crossing borders is a task replete with challenges unknown to domestic shippers and usually requires the help of specialized intermediaries.
- Transportation modes might differ significantly not only in getting overseas but also in shipping within local markets where infrastructure, freight services, and the overall reliability of transit could bear little resemblance to one's home market.

Let's examine some of these dimensions closer—others are discussed elsewhere in this book—particularly transportation, inventory, storage and packaging issues and the inevitable paperwork trails they generate.

Shipping the Goods. International marketers can count on an established transportation network in industrialized nations. But elsewhere, they may well find variations. Some countries might have excellent inbound and outbound transportation systems but weak transportation links within the country. This is particularly true in former colonies, where the original transportation systems were designed to maximize the extractive potential of the countries. In such instances, shipping to the market may be easy, but distribution within the market may be very difficult and time consuming. Local infrastructures must be studied: rail and trucking systems, pipelines (including future routings), and water-borne transportation. Extreme variations also exist in the frequency of transportation services. For example, a ship may not visit a particular port for weeks or even months. Sometimes, only carriers with particular characteristics, such as small size, will serve a given location.

Mistakes can be costly, as one food processing company learned when it built a pineapple cannery at the mouth of a river in Mexico. The company planned to float the ripe fruit on barges down to the cannery from the plantations upstream. But to its dismay, the firm discovered that at harvest time the river current was far too strong for barge traffic. Because no other feasible alternative method of transportation existed, it closed the plant and sold the new equipment for a fraction of its original cost.[14]

Ocean shipping, an important transportation mode for international trade, is handled by liner service, bulk service, and tramp or charter service. Liner service offers regularly scheduled passage on established routes. Bulk service mainly provides contractual services for individual voyages or for prolonged periods of time. Tramp service is available for irregular routes and is scheduled only on demand.

The most common ships used are conventional (break-bulk) cargo vessels, container ships, and roll-on-roll-off (RO-RO) vessels. Conventional cargo vessels are useful for oversized and unusual cargoes but may be less efficient in their port operations. Container ships carry standardized containers that greatly facilitate the loading and unloading of cargo and intermodal transfers. As a result, the ship spends less time in port. RO-RO vessels are essentially oceangoing ferries. Trucks can drive onto built-in ramps and roll off at the destination. Another vessel is the LASH (lighter aboard ship) vessel:

Barges stored on the ship are lowered at the point of destination, ready to operate along inland waterways and shallow water.

The availability of a certain type of vessel, however, does not automatically mean that it can be used. The greatest constraint in international ocean shipping is the lack of ports and port services. For example, modern container ships cannot use some ports because the local equipment is unable to handle the traffic. Local governments might not have the money to invest in port facilities, or they might keep ports small to limit imports. Increasingly, however, nations recognize the importance of appropriate port structures. Investing in leading-edge port technology can also provide a competitive edge for a country seeking foreign investment.

Airfreight is available to and from most countries, including developing nations where operating a national airline is often a matter of national prestige. Airfreight volume has grown tremendously. High-value items are more likely to be shipped by air, particularly if they have a high weight-to-volume ratio. Perishables and other items requiring a short transit time, such as emergency repair parts for a customer, are airfreight candidates as well.

Choosing Shipping Modes. In choosing the appropriate mode of transportation, the manager must consider the performance of each on four dimensions: transit time, predictability, cost, and noneconomic factors.

Transit time, ranging from 45 days for an ocean shipment to 24 hours via airfreight, obviously will have a major impact on the overall logistical operations of the firm. A short transit time may reduce the need for an overseas depot, facilitate emergency shipments, and allow the company to maintain smaller overseas inventories, cutting financial requirements.

Predictability is critical to freight service quality. While ocean and airfreight service can suffer delays, a delay of one day for airfreight tends to be seen as much more severe and "unreliable" than the same delay for ocean freight. However, delays tend to be shorter in absolute time for air shipments. As a result, arrival time via air is more predictable, facilitating smaller inventory safety stocks and more precise delivery times for customers. If inadequate port facilities exist, airfreight may again be the better alternative; unloading oceangoing vessels is more cumbersome and time-consuming than for planes. Finally, merchandise shipped via air is likely to suffer less loss and damage from movement. Once the merchandise arrives, it is more likely to be ready for immediate delivery—a facet that also enhances predictability.

International transportation service prices are usually priced on the basis of both the *costs* of the service provided and value of the service to the shipper. Price becomes a function of market demand and the monopolistic power of the carrier. Because of the high value of the products shipped by air, airfreight is often priced according to the value of the service. To keep costs down, a shipper can join groups such as shippers associations, which give the shipper more leverage in negotiations. Alternatively, a shipper can decide to mix modes of transportation in order to reduce overall cost and time delays. For example, air can handle part of the shipment route, while truck or ship can cover another portion.

Most important, however, are the company's overall logistical needs and the importance of merchandise arriving on time, which will be different for regular garments than for high-fashion dresses, for instance. The effect of transportation cost on price and the need for product availability abroad must also be considered. For example, some firms may wish to use airfreight as a new tool for aggressive market expansion. Airfreight may also be considered a good way to begin operations in new markets without making sizable investments for warehouses and distribution centers. Simply comparing transportation modes on the basis of price alone is insufficient.

Noneconomic factors often influence the choice. The transportation sector nationally and internationally benefits and suffers from heavy government involvement. Governments might own carriers or heavily subsidize them, pressuring shippers to use national carriers even if more economical alternatives exist. Government cargoes are most likely to require such preferential treatment. Restrictions are not limited to developing countries. For example, in the United States, all government cargo and all official government travelers must use national flag carriers when available.

The Paperwork. Documentation for international shipments is universally perceived as so complicated, especially by smaller firms, that it becomes a trade barrier requiring dozens of person-hours per shipment. Standardization efforts such as the U.S. Standard Master for International Trade have simplified the process somewhat, as has regional cooperation such as the European Union. A trucker used to need two pounds of documents to carry a shipment from Amsterdam to Lisbon. Now, the requirement is just a single piece of paper. Increasingly, electronic data transfer is replacing paperwork to speed the process.

Few international marketers, especially small or medium-sized firms and those new to exporting, are familiar with the many and varied details involved in transportation. These may include arranging for shipment from the factory, transferring from train to vessel, securing of rates and space on vessels, clearing customs, stowing, delivery at the port of destination to docks, clearance through local customs, and finally, delivery to the buyer. Larger exporters have a separate department or staff to secure transportation services and proper documentation, whereas smaller firms rely on support agencies for this work.

In the simplest form of exporting, the only documents needed are a bill of lading and an export declaration. Most exports fit under a general license, which is a generalized authorization consisting simply of a number to be shown on the documents. Certain goods and data require a special validated license for export. For importation, the basic documents are a bill of lading and an invoice. And, in light of the need for increased homeland security, since December 2002 the U.S. Customs Service requires importers to provide advance notice of cargo designated for the United States as it's loaded in foreign ports.

Typical documents needed for an international shipment are:[15]

I.   Documents Required by the U.S. Government
     A. Shipper's export declaration
     B. Export license
     C. Cargo presentation declaration (for imports)
II. Commercial Documents
     A. Commercial invoice
     B. Packing list
     C. Inland bill of lading
     D. Dock receipt
     E. Bill of lading or airway bill
     F. Insurance policies or certificates
     G. Shipper's declaration for dangerous goods
III. Import Documents
     A. Import license
     B. Foreign exchange license
     C. Certificate of origin
     D. Consular invoice
     E. Customs invoice

Shipper's export declarations state proper authorization for export and serves as a means for government data collection efforts.

Packing lists, if used, detail the contents, the gross and net weights, and the dimensions of each package. Some shipments, such as corrosives, flammables, and poisons, require a shipper's declaration for dangerous goods. Because of global terrorism, shippers increasingly use such lists, having to provide them to ports of destination well in advance.

Government licenses, such as *import licenses,* may be required for certain types or amounts of particular goods in certain countries. *Foreign exchange licenses* allow the importer to secure the needed hard currency to pay for the shipment. The exporter has to provide the importer with the data needed to obtain these licenses from government authorities and should make sure, before the actual shipment, that the importer has indeed secured the documents.

Bills of lading are the most important documents to the shipper, the carrier, and the buyer. They acknowledge receipt of the goods, they represent the basic contract between the shipper and the carrier, and they are evidence of title to the goods for collection by the purchaser. Various types of bills of lading exist such as the inland bill of lading: a contract between the inland carrier and the shipper. Bills of lading may be negotiable instruments in that they may be endorsed to other parties (order bill) or may be non-negotiable (straight).

Dock receipts and *warehouse receipts* are issued prior to the bill of lading when the international marketer is responsible for moving the goods to the U.S. port of export or a warehouse.

Collection documents must also be produced and always include a *commercial invoice* (a detailed description of the transaction), possibly a *consular invoice* (required by certain countries for data collection purposes), and perhaps a *certificate of origin* (required by certain countries to ensure correct tariffs).

Insurance documents are produced when stipulated by the transaction.

Dealing with customs authorities anywhere in the world requires experience and preparation. Improper or missing documents can easily lead to difficulties that will delay payment or even prevent it. If a customs service seizes the merchandise, delays can be measured in weeks and may end up in a total financial loss for the particular shipment.

Support services can help move the goods. An *international freight forwarder* acts as an agent for the international marketer in moving cargo to the overseas destination. The forwarder advises the marketer on shipping documentation and packing costs and will prepare and review the documents to ensure that they are in order. Forwarders will also book the necessary space aboard a carrier. They will make necessary arrangements to clear outbound goods with customs and, after clearance, forward the documents either to the customer or to the paying bank. A customs *broker* serves as an agent for an importer with authority to clear inbound goods through customs and ship them on to their destination. These functions are performed for a fee. National customs authorities often regulate customs brokers.

Managing Inventories. Inventories tie up corporate funds. Multinational manufacturers increasingly use just-in-time inventory policies to minimize inventory needs, often expecting suppliers to manage the process. Internationally, currency exchange rates compound inventory management complexity. The firm can make use of currency fluctuations by either reducing or increasing its inventory to obtain a corporate benefit. International inventory management should therefore be flexible. The level of inventory is determined by three factors: the order cycle time, desired customer service levels, and use of inventories as a strategic tool.

Order cycle time is the total time that passes between the placement of an order and the receipt of the merchandise. Order transmission, order filling, packing and preparation for shipment, and transportation can easily approach a hundred days or more. Large inventories may have to be maintained both domestically and internationally to bridge these time gaps. Cycle times are more likely to be inconsistent internationally, adding to the need for inventory safety stocks.

The international marketer should attempt to reduce order cycle time and increase its consistency without an increase in total costs. This objective can be accomplished by altering methods of transportation, changing inventory locations, or improving any of the other components of the order cycle time, such as the way orders are transmitted. By shifting order placement to direct computer-order entry, for example, a firm can reduce the order cycle time substantially. The shift to such a new system can be very expensive, however, and difficult to implement with partners who are limited in their information technology capabilities.

Customer service levels determine inventory requirements, but domestic standards might be inappropriate abroad. Customer expectations need to be understood in each market. Some customers will be prepared to pay a premium for speed, others may put a higher value on flexibility, and another group may see low cost as the most important issue. Flexibility and speed are expensive, so it is wasteful to supply them to customers who do not value them highly.

International inventories can be used as a *strategic tool* to finesse currency valuation changes or hedge against inflation. By increasing inventories before an imminent devaluation of a currency, instead of holding cash, the corporation reduces its exposure to devaluation losses. In case of high inflation, large inventories can provide an important inflation hedge. In such circumstances, the international inventory manager must balance the cost of large inventories with the benefits accruing from hedging against inflation or devaluation. Many countries, for example, charge a property tax on stored goods.

Warehouse location decisions must balance the cost of storage facilities against the flexibility of storage close to markets worldwide. Available facilities will vary; public storage is widely available in some countries, but such facilities may be scarce in others. Also, the standards and quality of facilities abroad vary. As a result, the company might need to invest directly in warehouse facilities.

Foreign trade zones can have a major effect on international logistics because they are considered, for purposes of tariff treatment, to be outside the customs territory of the country within which they are located. They are special areas and can be used for warehousing, packaging, inspection, labeling, exhibition, assembly, fabrication, or transshipment of imports without burdening the firm with duties. In some countries, the benefits derived from lower factor costs, such as labor or energy, may be offset by high duties and tariffs. Foreign trade zones eliminate the impact of duties from the location decision.

Firms can also make use of sharp differentials in production factor costs by locating close to another country's border. For instance, the maquiladora program between the United States and Mexico permits firms to carry out their labor-intensive operations in Mexico while sourcing raw materials or component parts from the United States, free of Mexican tariffs. Subsequently, the semifinished or assembled products are shipped to the U.S. market and are assessed duties only for the foreign labor component.

One country that has used trade zones very successfully for its own economic development is China. Through the creation of special economic zones in which there are no tariffs, substantial tax incentives, and low prices for land and labor, the government has attracted many foreign investors bringing in billions of dollars. These investors have brought new equipment, technology, and managerial know-how and have therefore substantially increased the local economic prosperity.

Both parties to the arrangement benefit from foreign trade zones. The government maintaining the trade zone achieves increased employment. The firm using the trade zone obtains a spearhead in or close to the foreign market without incurring all of the costs customarily associated with such an activity. As a result, goods can be reassembled and large shipments can be broken down into smaller units. Also, goods can be repackaged when packaging weight becomes part of the duty assessment. Finally, goods can be given domestic "made-in" status if assembled in the foreign trade zone. Thus, duties may be payable only on the imported materials and component parts rather than on the labor that is used to finish the product. Whenever you examine use of a trade zone, you must keep the additional cost of storage, handling, and transportation in mind.

Global Packaging Issues. Packaging gets the merchandise to the ultimate destination in a safe, maintainable, and presentable condition, but packaging that is adequate for domestic shipping may be inadequate for international transportation. The vessel carrying the goods and loading/unloading stress can take their toll. By law, the shipper takes responsibility for appropriate packaging.

Packaging decisions must take into account *varied conditions* in environments such as climate. When the ultimate destination is very humid or particularly cold, the exporter must make special provisions to prevent damage to the product. The task becomes even more challenging when dramatic climate changes occur during a shipment. A firm in Taiwan that shipped drinking glasses packed in straw to the Middle East learned the hard way. The drier Middle Eastern climate dried out the straw protection. The glasses were broken by the time they reached their destination.[16]

Packaging issues also need to be closely linked to the storage properties of the product, the weight of packaging material, and, lest one forget, the customer's need. Customers might have limits on the size or weight of packages they can handle. Although the packaging of a product is often used as a form of display, international shipment packaging can rarely serve the dual purpose of protection and display. Double packaging may be necessary. The display package is for future use at the point of destination; another package surrounds it for protective purposes.

Containerization offers one solution to the packaging problem. Intermodal containers—large metal boxes that fit on trucks, ships, railroad cars, and airplanes—ease the frequent transfer of goods in international shipments and produce greater safety, security, and perhaps less expensive shipping rates. Container traffic is heavily dependent on the existence of appropriate handling facilities and the quality of inland transportation. In some countries, rules for the handling of containers may be designed to maintain employment. For example, U.S. union rules obligate shippers to withhold containers from firms that do not employ members of the International Longshoreman Association for loading and unloading containers within a 50-mile radius of Atlantic or Gulf ports.

Managing Logistics Operations

One can argue persuasively for coordinating international logistics at corporate headquarters, lest subsidiaries optimize their individual operations to the overall detriment of the company. But when headquarters exerts control, it must also take responsibility for its decisions. Ill will may arise if local managers are appraised and rewarded on the basis of performance they do not control. To avoid internal problems, reporting should be centralized in, for example, the vice president for international logistics, who becomes the objective final arbiter of the company's priorities. Of course, that individual should also be in charge of determining appropriate rewards for all parties involved. Such centralized logistics decision making can boost profitability significantly.

An alternative to the centralized international logistics system is the "decentralized full profit center model." If each subsidiary is managed as a profit center, each carries the full responsibility for its performance, which can lead to greater local management satisfaction. However, there is a trade-off: unless the firm is regarded as a global account by service providers, it could lose the substantial benefits of centralized logistics. Once products are within a specific market, however, increased input from local logistics operations should be expected and encouraged.

Contract Logistics. International firms increasingly choose to outsource their logistics, which is usually considered not a core competency of the firm and thus best left to experts. The relatively new industry of contract logistics services booked $60.8 billion revenue in 2001, according to consultants Armstrong & Associates. Principal attractions include cost, convenience, and superior technology. Logistics providers can offer unique skills, including inventory and returns management, contract warehousing, manufacturing support, dedicated contract carriage, custom packaging, and technical support.

Services vary in scope. Some providers use their own assets in physical transportation; others subcontract out portions of the job. Still others concentrate on developing systems and databases or consulting on administrative matters. In many instances, the partnership consists of working closely with established transport providers such as Federal Express or UPS.

One of the greatest benefits of contracting out the logistics function in a foreign market is the ability to take advantage of an in-place network complete with resources and experience. On the other hand, diminished supply chain control is one of the main arguments against using contract logistics. However, that need not happen. The control and responsibility toward the customer should remain with the firm, even though operations may move outside.

Common-sense rules ensure smooth relations with a third-party provider. Communications must be clear and concise from the outset. Expectations, especially regarding data availability and accuracy, should be put in writing and closely monitored. Any agreement should contain alternative plans, preferably pretested, and a comprehensive exit plan. The third-party provider must understand the unique needs of its client, and the client should monitor activities.

Reverse Logistics. Environmental laws and customer returns are difficult to honor without a logistics plan. Because laws and regulations differ across the world, the firm needs to be responsive to a wide variety of requirements. Reverse distribution systems ensure that the firm not only delivers the product to the market but also can retrieve it from the market for subsequent use, recycling, or disposal. The ability to develop such reverse logistics is becoming a key determinant for market acceptance and profitability.

Society is beginning to recognize that retrieval should not be limited to short-term consumer goods, such as bottles. Rather, it may be even more important to retrieve and dispose of long-lived capital goods, such as cars, refrigerators, air conditioners, and industrial goods, with the least possible burden on the environment. Increasingly, governments are establishing rules that hold the manufacturer responsible for the ultimate disposal of the product at the end of its economic life. In Germany, for example, car manufacturers have to take back their used vehicles for dismantling and recycling. The European Union has required member states to implement a similar program with the End-of-Life Vehicle Directive.

According to the Reverse Logistics Executive Council, U.S. firms pay more than an estimated $35 billion annually for handling, transportation, and processing of returned products. Disposition management, administration time, and the cost of converting unproductive returns into productive assets are extra. The design of such long-term systems across the world may well be one of the key challenges and opportunities for the logistician and will require close collaboration with all other functions in the firm.

Environmental issues are increasingly critical in global trade. Shippers of oil or other potentially hazardous materials, for instance, are expected to use carriers with excellent safety records and safeguards in place, such as double-hulled ships. Society may even expect corporate involvement in choosing the route, and the routes of return flows, that the shipment will travel, preferring routes that are not near ecologically important and sensitive zones.

In the packaging field, government and social organizations increasingly expect companies to minimize their use of packing materials, and to use more environmentally sound materials. Customers increasingly set their own standards for suppliers, or embrace ISO 14000, an international standard specific to environmental practices.

E-BUSINESS AND WORLD TRADE

The majority of exporters still see a Web site as a marketing and advertising tool yet to be expanded to order-taking capabilities, but that is changing rapidly. The collapse of the late 1990s dot-com mania aside, e-commerce (selling on the Web) and e-business (automation throughout the supply chain) will grow explosively in the century's first decade. While the U.S. accounts for the majority of e-commerce activity, the non-U.S. portion, particularly in Western Europe, is expected to grow rapidly as business communities attempt to catch up. However, there might continue to be resistance in developing countries, which cannot afford investments in electronic infrastructure.

The benefits of e-business are potentially huge. It eliminates costly and error-prone paperwork and can speed up the whole order-filling and shipping process. Automation also provides effective information systems for better planning and tracking for shippers, importers, and foreign customers.

Beyond the Web, marketers will find themselves constantly challenged by technology and by other new, marketing capabilities. Global marketers even now must stay abreast of these key e-business applications:[17] (1) global supply chain management; (2) e-procurement; (3) e-fulfillment; (4) web-enabled product design and development; (5) global branding; (6) global account management; (7) global "centers of excellence"; (8) knowledge management portals and horizontal communities; (9) global talent pools; and (10) e-learning and e-training.

Channels New and Old

Many companies willing to embrace e-commerce will not have to do it on their own. "Hub" sites (also known as "portals," "virtual malls," or "digital intermediaries") have started to bring together buyers, sellers, distributors, and transaction payment processors into large electronic marketplaces. Hubs open up supplier relationships for smaller companies and those outside of the buyer's domestic market:

- GE's Trading Process Network (www.tpnregister.com) allows GE production and purchasing facilities around the world to quickly find and purchase products from approved suppliers electronically.
- Pitney Bowes' suppliers need only Internet access and a standard Web browser to be electronically linked to the manufacturer's supply system to see how many of their products are on hand and how many will be needed in the future. Its VendorSite even includes data that small suppliers can use for production planning.
- Covisint, the global e-business exchange supported by leading automakers, promises suppliers who join that they can compress planning cycles, increase efficiency and asset utilization, and realize greater profits.

Despite short-term setbacks, hubs will become prominent virtual marketplaces worldwide, particularly for trading commodities, routine repurchases, and strong brand name products. Concurrently, multinationals will expand their private hubs on key corporate customers' intranet systems to facilitate centralized buying from any customer site worldwide.

As new intermediaries appear, traditional channels will fight to survive. While the e-business disintermediation threat has not met initial expectations—customer buying preferences and logistical needs still call for "bricks" as well as "clicks"—pure information brokerage functions are the first imperiled by technology's ability to give all buyers complete market information. Travel agents appear atop the hit list, and stockbrokers appeared imperiled amidst the hype over discount online brokers.

Although today's e-business trends are appearing almost exclusively in the industrialized world, they will spread globally in very little time. Another large piece of the global e-business puzzle is how societies adopt or resist the free flow of information itself. Open societies wrestle with restrictions (such as those designed to protect children) while protecting free speech rights. Closed societies face the threat of electronic information dissemination sidestepping authoritarian gatekeepers. How the Chinese manage their precarious, if not unsustainable, balance between authoritarian government and growing ranks of Web-using, educated, and affluent citizens portends much about the future of e-business around the world.

Competitive Table Stakes

Customers worldwide will demand "24/7" access. Marketers can cope with response and delivery challenges by outsourcing services or by including regional warehouses in their international distribution networks.

Those who perform well will enjoy substantial competitive advantages when customers become more comfortable doing business online, although the growth rate of online transactions is hardly a given. Even in the United States, very few consumers who use the Web to choose products actually place orders online. Although about 55 percent of automobile buyers examine cars online, less than 1 percent actually purchase online, for example.[18] But as online e-business becomes an established option for customers, it will no longer be a discretionary option for manufacturers; online marketing will be a requirement for survival.

Global Obstacles and Opportunities

Some pessimists argue that the World Wide Web does not live up to its name, since it is mostly a tool for the United States and Europe. To optimists, emerging markets provide a chance to try out new approaches where existing systems and practices don't get in the way. In many of the emerging markets, especially Asia and Latin America, both GM and Ford have factories that are more flexible and will allow build-to-order programs and innovative online retailing methods.[19]

Firms must be sensitive to the governmental role in e-commerce as well as in traditional import and export regulation. No real consensus or uniformity exists on the taxation of e-commerce, especially in the case of cross-border transactions. Until more firm legal precedents are established, international marketers should be aware of their potential tax liabilities and prepare for them.

Issues of security and privacy will continue to be active areas of concern for everyone. While the private sector argues for the highest database safeguards, governments, especially in the United States, insist on having access to data that could reveal criminal behavior and terrorist plans. Consumer activists demand greater individual control over the use of personal information. Amid the political debate, an international group of executives has united to oppose Internet taxes and restrictions on data exports. This group, calling itself the Global Business Dialogue on Electronic Commerce (www.gbde.org), has pushed for the adoption of a "seal of approval" for Web sites that protect consumer privacy. It has also advocated third-party arbitration in solving e-commerce disputes.

Privacy advocates applaud European Union regulations allowing individuals to review and limit personal data exchanged commercially. U.S. firms engaging in direct marketing overseas have had to adapt to the European Union's stringent requirements. The European Union blocks transmission of data to countries if their domestic legislation is not seen to provide an adequate level of protection. The issue between the United States and the European Union will most likely be settled by multinational corporate giants taking the lead in adopting global privacy policies that become de facto, if not de jure, standards. It seems clear that some supervision is needed to ensure fairness and privacy. What is unclear is who should conduct such supervision—domestic governments, international organizations such as the WTO, or a newly formed supranational group.

Intellectual property is another sector in legal and technological turmoil. Technologies permit instantaneous and flawless copying and distribution—authorized or not—of copyrighted material such as publications, records, and films. Despite legislation to protect copyright owners—the Digital Millennium Copyright Act enacted in the Unites States in 1999 is likely to be just an opening salvo in the war between intellectual property owners and users—traditional intermediaries between artists and fans face a fight for survival. If artists can deliver their works directly to customers, what will be the role of music and book publishers and dealers?

FUTURITIES

Innovative distribution approaches will determine new ways of serving markets. For example, television through QVC has already created a $2.2 billion shopping mall available in more than 60 million homes. The Internet offers new distribution alternatives, imperiling the survival of intermediaries who have relied on serving poorly informed buyers. Aside from the late 1990s' dot-com naiveté, exciting innovations emerged and ever newer ideas beckon from the horizon. For example, refrigerators will report directly to grocery store computers that they are running low on supplies and require a home delivery billed to the customer's account. On the business-to-business level, large buyers with sophisticated inventory tracking and reordering systems increasingly expect suppliers to plug into their networks to enable benefits such as just-in-time (JIT) supply, customized production, and direct order entry around the globe. E-commerce and e-business will continue to revolutionize channel management, leaving vulnerable those marketers, international and domestic alike, which do not make the effort to master them.

NOTES

1. F. H. Katayama, "Japan's Big Mac," *Fortune,* September 15, 1986, 114–120.
2. Denise Incandela, Kathleen L. McLaughlin, and Christiana Smith Shi, "Retailers to the World," *The McKinsey Quarterly* 35 (Number 3, 1999): 84–97. See also http://www.starbucks.com.
3. David Ford, "Buyer/Seller Relationships in International Industrial Markets," *Industrial Marketing Management* 13 (May 1984): 101–112.
4. "Market Entry Strategy," *Business America,* March 25, 1991, 12–17; Frank Reynolds, "How to Capture the Flag," *Exporter* 3 (October 1991): 27–28.
5. Franklin R. Root, *Foreign Market Entry Strategies* (New York: American Management Association, 1983), 74–75.
6. Phillip J. Rosson, "Success Factors in Manufacturer–Overseas Distributor Relationships in International Marketing," in *International Marketing Management,* ed. Erdener Kaynak (New York: Praeger Publishing, 1984), 91–107.
7. "Brand Battles," *International Business,* April 1993, 83.
8. For a comprehensive discussion on remedies, see Robert E. Weigand, "Parallel Import Channel—Options for Preserving Territorial Integrity," *Columbia Journal of World Business* 26 (Spring 1991): 53–60, and S. Tamer Cavusgil and Ed Sikora, "How Multinationals Can Counter Gray Market Imports," *Columbia Journal of World Business* 23 (Winter 1988): 75–85.
9. David J. Arnold, "Seven Rules of International Distribution," *Harvard Business Review* (November-December 2000).
10. David J. Arnold, "Seven Rules of International Distribution," *Harvard Business Review* (November-December 2000).
11. Aviva Freudmann, "Supplying Big Macs: A Lesson in Logistics," *Journal of Commerce,* May 19, 1999, 3A; and Carol Matlack, "Betting on a New Label: Made in Russia," *Business Week,* April 12, 1999, 122E6.
12. Paul T. Nelson and Gadi Toledano, "Challenges for International Logistics Management," *Journal of Business Logistics* 1 (Number 2, 1979): 7.
13. R. T. Hise, "The Implications of Time-Based Competition on International Logistics Strategies," *Business Horizons* (September/October 1995): 39–45.
14. David A. Ricks, *Blunders in International Business* (Oxford, England: Blackwell Publishers, 2000), 16.
15. See: Dun & Bradstreet, *Exporter's Encyclopedia* (New York: Dun & Bradstreet, 1985); and Marta Ortiz-Buonafina, *Profitable Export Marketing* (Englewood Cliffs, NJ: Prentice-Hall, 1984), 218–246; and www.ams.usda.gov/international.
16. David A. Ricks, *Blunders in International Business* (Oxford, England: Blackwell Publishers, 2000), 27.
17. S. Tamer Cavusgil, "Extending the Reach of E-Business," *Marketing Management* 11 (March/April 2002): 24–29.
18. Arvind Rangaswamy, presentation to Penn State eBusiness Research Center May 9, 2002 Academic Workshop.
19. "GM Tests E-Commerce Plans in Emerging Markets," *The Wall Street Journal,* October 25, 1999, B6.

13

International Negotiation and Communication

How and where you promote says more than meets the eye . . . or ear.

Effective communication as a cornerstone of marketing becomes even more important in the international arena. Whether it is a question of generating promotional campaigns or negotiating to set up a marketing system, the international marketer needs to understand what pleases or displeases the target audience.

For example, American businesspeople should avoid U.S.-centric references in some cultures, especially self-congratulatory ones, which are perceived as arrogant. Sports metaphors might not communicate properly, depending on the culture. In France, for example, don't cite a baseball analogy; relate sports metaphors to World Cup soccer, especially French successes. Additionally, international marketers should study the business styles of their counterparts in foreign markets. One study found that the style of French negotiators was the most aggressive of 13 diverse cultural groups analyzed.[1]

Effective communication is particularly important in international marketing because of the geographic and psychological distances that separate a firm from its intermediaries and customers. Most communication is verbal, but nonverbal communication and the symbolism within silent languages must also be considered because they often create challenges for international marketers.

This chapter examines the communication processes, tools, and services involved in intercultural negotiations and marketing communications programs for exporters and for global marketers. Because the exporter's alternatives may be limited by the entry mode and by resources available, its tools and the challenges are quite different from those of the multinational firm.

INTERNATIONAL NEGOTIATING

When American international marketing managers travel abroad to do business, they are frequently shocked to discover the extent to which the many variables of foreign behavior and custom complicate their efforts. One of these differences is negotiation. The process of negotiation in most countries differs from that in the United States, requiring U.S.-based international marketing managers to adjust their approaches to establishing rapport, information exchange, persuasion, and concession making if they are to be successful in dealing with their clients and partners, such as intermediaries.

The level of adjustment depends on how well the parties to a negotiation understand each other's cultures. But subtleties can complicate that otherwise straightforward advice. In China, for example, the ideal negotiator is someone who has an established relationship with the Chinese and is trusted by them. But, Chinese-Americans or overseas Chinese may be less effective in leading a negotiation. Where the Chinese are often willing to make an exception for visitors, they will expect ethnic Chinese to accept the Chinese way of doing things. The ideal team would, therefore, include a non-Chinese who understands the culture and an ethnic-Chinese individual. Together, the two can play "good guy–bad guy" roles and resist unreasonable demands.[2] If neither party is familiar with the counterpart's culture, they should turn to outside facilitators.

Negotiation Stages

The process of international business negotiations can be divided into four stages: the offer, informal meetings, strategy formulation, and negotiations.[3] Culture will influence which stages are most important and how long it will take to complete a deal—one session or prolonged talks for weeks. In Northern Europe, for example, the Protestant tradition and indoor culture tend to emphasize the technical, the numerical, and the tested. Negotiators make careful prenegotiation preparations. In contrast, Southern Europe, with its Catholic background and open-air lifestyle, tends to favor personal networks, social contexts, and flair. Meetings in the South are often longer, but the total decision process may be faster.[4]

Offers. The offer stage allows the two parties to assess each other's needs and degree of commitment. Background factors of the parties, such as objectives, and the overall atmosphere, such as a spirit of cooperation, set the initial expectations for negotiations. For example, many European buyers may be skittish about dealing with a U.S. exporter, given the reputation U.S. companies have in some quarters for failing to be persistent in making a sale or running away when business environmental factors turn sour.

Informal Meetings. Informal meetings, held after the buyer has received the offer and often conducted in casual settings, bring parties together to discuss the terms and get acquainted. In many parts of the world—Asia, the Middle East, Southern Europe, and Latin America—informal meetings often make or break the deal. Foreign buyers may want to feel that they are doing business with someone who is sympathetic and trustworthy. For example, U.S. exporters to Kuwait rank the strength of the business relationship ahead of price as the critical variable driving buying decisions.[5] In some cases, it may be necessary to use facilitators (such as consultants or agents) to establish the contact.

Strategies. Both parties have to formulate strategies for formal negotiations. This means not only careful review of the offer itself but also preparation for the give-and-take of the negotiations. For example, research studies have found that competitive bargainers can take advantage of U.S. and Canadian English-speaking negotiators,[6] who are more trusting than other cultural groups.[7] Therefore, the behaviors of clients and partners bear close watching. In the case of governmental buyers, for instance, it is imperative to realize that public-sector needs may not necessarily fit into a business-rational mold. In any talks, negotiators may not necessarily behave as expected; for example, the negotiating partner may adjust behavior to the visitor's culture.

Formal Talks and Gambits. The actual face-to-face negotiations and the approach used in them will depend on the cultural background and business traditions prevailing in different countries. The most commonly used are the competitive and collaborative approaches.[8] In a competitive strategy, the negotiator is concerned mainly about a favorable outcome at the expense of the other party, while in the collaborative approach focus is on mutual needs, especially in the long term. For example, an exporter accepting a proposal that goes beyond what can be realistically delivered (in the hopes of market entry or renegotiations later) will lose in the long term. To deliver on the contract, the exporter may be tempted to cut corners in product quality or delivery, eventually leading to conflict with the buyer.

The choice of location for the negotiations plays a role in the outcome as well. Many negotiators prefer a neutral site. This may not always work, for reasons of resources or parties' perceptions of the importance of the deal. The host does enjoy many advantages, such as lower psychological risk due to familiar surroundings. Guests may run the risk of culture shock and being away from professional and personal support systems. These pressures are multiplied if the host chooses to manipulate the situation with delays or additional demands. Visiting teams are less likely to walk out; as a matter of fact, the pressure is on them to make concessions. However, despite the challenges of being a guest, the visitor has a chance to see first-hand the counterpart's facilities and resources, and to experience culture in that market. In addition, visiting a partner, present or potential, shows commitment to the effort.[9]

Foreign Negotiation Tips

A combination of attitudes, expectations, and habitual behavior influences negotiation style.[10] Although some of the following recommendations may not square with approaches used at home, they may allow the negotiator to adjust to the style of the host-country negotiators.

Teamwork. Using specialists will strengthen the team substantially and allow for all points of view to receive proper attention. Further, observing negotiations can be valuable training experience for less-experienced participants. Whereas Western teams may average 2 to 4 people, a Chinese negotiating team may consist of up to 10 people.[11] A study of how U.S. purchasing professionals conduct negotiations abroad revealed that while the vast majority believed a small team (2 to 5 individuals) was ideal, they also said their international counterparts often outnumbered their teams.[12]

Leave intragroup disagreements at the door. Show one team face during negotiations, handling disputes among team members privately.

Traditions and Customs. Consultants and local representatives can help international negotiation neophytes to understand status relationships and business procedures abroad. For example, in highly structured societies such as Korea, people pay great respect to age and position. What seem like simple rituals can cause problems if misunderstood. No first encounter in Asia is complete without an exchange of business cards. Both hands should be used to present and receive cards, and respect should be shown by reading them carefully. One side should be translated into the language of the host country.

Language. Ideally, the international marketing manager should be able to speak the customer's language, but that is not always possible. Using interpreters allows for longer response time and a more careful articulation of arguments. If English is being used, a native speaker should avoid both jargon and idiomatic expressions, avoid complex sentences, and speak slowly and enunciate clearly.

An ideal interpreter also briefs the negotiator on cultural dimensions, such as body language, before any meetings. For example, sitting in what may be perceived as a comfortable position in North America or Europe may be seen by the Chinese as showing a lack of control of one's body and, therefore, of one's mind.

Authority Limits. Negotiators from North America and Europe are often expected to have full authority when they negotiate in the Far East, although their local counterparts seldom if ever do. Announcing that the negotiators do not have the final authority to conclude the contract may be perceived negatively; however, if it is used as a tactic to probe the motives of the buyer, it can be quite effective. It is important to verify who does have that authority and what challenges may be faced in getting that decision.

Patience. In many countries such as China, business negotiations may take three times the amount of time that they do in the United States and Europe. Showing impatience in countries such as Brazil or Thailand may prolong negotiations rather than speed them up. Also, U.S. executives tend to start relatively close to what they consider a fair price in their negotiations, whereas Chinese negotiators may start with "unreasonable" demands and a rigid posture.[13]

Ethics. The attitudes and values of foreign negotiators may be quite different from those that a U.S. marketing executive is accustomed to. Being tricky can be valued in some parts of the world, but be frowned on elsewhere. For example, Western negotiators may be taken aback by last-minute changes or concession requests by Russian negotiators.

Silence. To negotiate effectively abroad, a marketer needs to read all types of communication correctly. U.S. businesspeople often interpret inaction and silence as a negative sign. As a result, Japanese executives tend to expect to use those ploys to win lower prices or sweeter deals. Finns may sit through a meeting expressionless, hands folded and not moving much. There is nothing necessarily negative about this; they show respect to the speaker with their focused, dedicated listening.[14]

Persistence. Insisting on answers and an outcome may be seen as a threat by negotiating partners abroad. In some markets, negotiations are seen as a means of establishing long-term commercial relations, not as an event with winners and losers. Confrontations are to be avoided because minds cannot be changed at the negotiation table; this has to be done informally. Confrontations also might cause a counterpart to lose face, considered a serious insult throughout the Far East.

Big Picture. Negotiators should avoid concessions until all issues have been discussed because they grant unnecessary benefits to their counterparts. Concessions traditionally come at the end of bargaining. This is especially true in terms of price negotiations. If price is agreed on too quickly, the counterpart may want to insist on too many extras for that price.

Agreements. Understanding what constitutes an agreement will vary from one market to another. In many parts of the world, legal contracts are still not needed; referring to legal counsel may indicate that the relationship is in trouble. For the Chinese, the written agreement exists mostly for the convenience of their Western partners and represents an agenda on which to base the development of the relationship.

When an agreement is reached, it is critical that both parties leave with a clear understanding of the terms. This may entail only the relatively straightforward act of signing a written distributor agreement, but in the case of large-scale projects, details must be explored and spelled out. In contracts that call for cooperative efforts, the responsibilities of each partner must be clearly specified. Otherwise, obligations that were expected to be the duty of one contracting party may result in costs to the other. For example, foreign principal contractors may be held responsible for delays caused by the inability of local subcontractors (whom the client might require) to deliver on schedule.

INTERNATIONAL MARCOM

The international marketing manager has the responsibility of formulating a marketing communications strategy for the company and its products and services. The first step is determining the offering features and benefits to communicate to the export market. Constant market monitoring and a large enough budget to sustain a competitive, if not superior, marketplace "share of voice" are essential commitments. Token efforts in heavily competitive markets will not satisfy a growth strategy, all other elements of the marketing mix being equal. In some cases, an exporter will have to limit marketing communications to one country, even one area, at a time to achieve its goals with the available budget.

International campaigns require patient investment to generate awareness, knowledge, liking, preference, and favorable purchase intentions for a product or brand in a market before the payback begins. The process might take years; payback periods of one or two years cannot be realistically expected in most markets.

For many exporters, a critical factor is supporting the intermediary. Whether a distributor is willing to contribute a $3 million media budget or a few thousand dollars makes a big difference. In some cases, intermediaries take a leading role in the promotion of the product in a market. In most cases, however, the exporter should retain some control of the campaign rather than allow intermediaries or sales offices a free hand in the various markets operated. In cases where the locally based intermediaries are small and may not have the resources to engage in promotional efforts, the exporter may suggest dealer participation programs. In exchange for including the intermediaries' names in promotional material without any expense to them—for example, in announcing a sweepstakes—the exporter may request increased volume purchases from the intermediaries.

Although markets may be dissimilar, common themes and common objectives need to be maintained by individual market campaigns. Many exporters and multinational marketers provide advertising graphics, layout templates, and written copy for local translation to distributors and local country subsidiaries. Although many exporters do not exert pressure to conform, overseas distributors take advantage of annual meetings to discuss promotional practices with their head office counterparts.

Strategic Mix

The promotional mix consists of the tools the international marketer can use to form a total communications program for targeted markets. The tools include:

1. Personal selling: The process of assisting and persuading a prospect to buy a product or service or to act on an idea through use of person-to-person communication with intermediaries and/or final customers.
2. Advertising: Any form of impersonal presentation of ideas, goods,

or services by an identified sponsor, with predominant use made of mass communication or paid media, such as print, broadcast, or electronic media, or direct communication that is aimed at individual business-to-business customers or ultimate consumers using computer technology and databases.

3. Publicity: Any form of nonpaid, commercially significant news or editorial comment about ideas, products, or institutions.

4. Sales promotion: Direct inducements that provide extra product value or incentive to the sales force, intermediaries, or ultimate consumers.

5. Sponsorship: The practice of promoting the interests of the company by associating it with a specific event (typically sports or culture) or a cause (typically a charity or a social interest).

6. Packaging: Unique colors and shapes—known in U.S. law as "trade dress"—can play a promotional role.

The marketer must choose either a "push" or "pull" basic communication strategy. Push strategies sell products into the distribution channels, reasoning that distributors will push the goods at the final buyers. Personal selling and trade-oriented sales promotion play a leading role in the process. Pull strategies are designed to work at the customer end of the distribution channel by creating demand that pulls product through the channels. The mass communication tools of advertising and publicity play a major role in generating customer preference and demand.

The type and number of customers influences the balance of the promotional mix. In business and government markets with relatively few but larger customers making complex, big-ticket purchases, personal selling with its substantially higher cost per contact is the preferred tool. Advertising to business buyers generally plays a support role, building general awareness of a marketer and its brands and soliciting sales leads from interested prospects. In consumer markets, such one-on-one contact usually isn't practical, so marketers expect mass communication through advertising and publicity to generate demand.

Direct marketing via the mail, telephone, and the Internet can serve push and pull strategies alike. Promoting to individual consumers or business buyers believed to have greater-than-average interest in a product category can be efficient and effective depending on campaign objectives. And, direct marketing proponents eagerly point out, managers can compare direct marketing campaign costs and results directly to monitor and improve their performance over time.

International Communications Tools

The main communications tools exporters use to communicate with the foreign marketplace from their domestic base are business and trade journals, directories, direct advertising, the Internet, trade shows, and personal selling.

If the exporter's strategy calls for a major promotional effort in a market, it is advisable either to use a domestic agency with extensive operations in the intended market or to use a local agency and work closely with the company's local representatives in media and message choices. Later in this chapter we discuss global client-agency partnerships for the multinational marketer.

Because the client's relationship with advertising agencies should be close, it may be helpful if the exporter's domestic agency has an affiliate or local office in the target foreign market. The management and coordination functions can be performed by the agency at home, while the affiliate can execute the program as it seems appropriate in that market. An exporter, if it has a sufficient budget, may ask its domestic agency to set up a branch overseas.

Some exporters, especially those that have a more significant presence overseas, leave the choice of the agency to local managers. If a local agency is to be chosen, the exporter must make sure that coordination and cooperation between the agency and the exporter's domestic agency can be achieved.

Periodicals. Many varied general business and trade publications are available to the exporter. Some, such as *Business Week, Fortune, The Economist, The Wall Street Journal,* and *The Financial Times,* are standard information sources worldwide. Extensions of these are their regional editions; for example, *The Asian Wall Street Journal* or *Business Week—Europe.*

Trade publications (known formally as "specialized business publications") can be classified as: "horizontal," which cater to a particular job function cutting across industry lines, such as *Purchasing World* or *Industrial Distribution;* and "vertical" because they deal with several management functions within the same industry—*Chemical Engineering* or *International Hospital Supplies,* for example. These periodicals are global, regional, or country-specific in their approaches. Many U.S.-based publications are available in national language editions, with some offering regional editions for specific export markets—for example, the Spanish edition of *Feed Management,* titled *Alimentos Balanceados Para Animales.*

Government-sponsored publications often offer promotion potential. For example, *Commercial News USA* (www.cnewsusa.com), published by the U.S. Department of Commerce, is an effective medium for the marketer interested in making itself and its products known worldwide for a modest sum. It is distributed only overseas for free through U.S. embassies and consulates in more than 150 countries.

Directories. Directories provide effective venues for advertising abroad. Many markets feature exporter yellow pages, some of which offer online versions in addition to the traditional print ones. For example, myexports.com (formerly the *U.S. Exporters' Yellow Pages*), cosponsored by the U.S. Department of Commerce, offers U.S. firms a means to promote their businesses worldwide at no cost (if they just want to be listed) and at low cost for an advertisement or link to their e-mail or home page.

Some of directories are country-specific. For example, BellSouth's *Guia Internacional* (www.guiaexport.bellsouth.com) allows exporters to showcase their products to over 200,000 Latin American and Caribbean importers. A number of online directories, such as Internet International Business Exchange (www.imex.com), provide the exporter the opportunity to have banner ads (i.e., ads placed on frequently visited Web sites) for $250 to $1,000 a month. The appendix to Chapter 9 lists a number of representative online export-information directories.

Media Costs. The two main concerns when selecting media are reaching the appropriate target audience(s) and doing so efficiently as measured by the cost per thousand (often called simply "CPM" in advertising circles) of a medium's audience. If the exporter is in a position to define the target audience clearly (for example, in terms of demographics or product-related variables), the choice of media will be easier.

CPM doesn't tell the full story, however. Marketers should understand how media work synergistically. For example, advertisements in publications and directories may have the function of driving customers and prospects to the exporter's Web site.

Standard Rate & Data Service (www.srds.com) is a premier source for international media buyers. SRDS provides a complete list of international publications in the International Section of the Business Publication, along with circulation information for the United Kingdom, Italy, France, Austria, Switzerland, Germany, Mexico, and Canada.

Outside those areas, the exporter has to rely on the assistance of publishers or local representatives. The simplest approach may be to use U.S. publishers, in which the exporter may have more confidence in terms of rates and circulation data. If a more localized approach is needed, a regional edition or national publication can be considered. Before selecting an unfamiliar journal, the marketer should analyze its content and overall quality of presentation.

Direct Marketing. Direct marketing uses advertising via mail, email, or telephone to communicate individually with a prospect. In effect, it is personal selling without the expense of the sales call, but without the face-to-face impact as well. This category of communication tool also includes direct response and Internet advertising which are designed to build direct marketing databases (e.g., direct mail lists) with the names of interested prospects responding to media advertising.

Direct mail is by far the dominant direct-marketing medium because of its flexibility, personalization opportunities, and relatively low cost. Its success depends on the attractiveness of the *offer* and the accuracy and appropriateness of the *mailing lists* used—two elements that savvy marketers constantly test and refine. But unlike the United States and Canada where a thriving list management industry offers mailers a myriad of well-documented, high-quality database choices, international business communities rarely match that standard. However, more and better lists are surfacing in Asia, Latin America, and the Middle East. In addition, reliable, economical, global postal service has become available.

Even when mailing lists are available, they may not be as up-to-date or as precise as the U.S. marketer needs or is accustomed to. In China, for example, lists are available to send literature directly to factories, ministries, professional societies, research institutes, and universities. However, such mailings can be extremely costly and produce few results. An effective and efficient direct-mail campaign requires extensive market-by-market planning of materials, format, and mode of mailing.

Catalogs are typically distributed to overseas customers through direct mail, although many catalogs have online versions as well. Their function is to make the exporter's name known, generate requests for further information, stimulate orders, and serve as a reminder between transactions. Catalogs are particularly useful for reaching qualified technical specialists. In many markets, especially the developing ones, people may be starving for technology information and will share any mailings they receive. A very small investment can reach many potential end users. However, the key to effective market penetration is a local address to assuage the fears of customers unwilling to send money to a foreign location.

Traditional direct mail is undergoing many innovations and major changes. New types of mail services (e.g., the Mexican Post Office's Buzon Espresso) will enable companies to deal more efficiently with customers who buy through catalogs or electronic means. New electronic media will assume an increasing share in the direct-marketing area. However, direct marketing will continue to grow as a function of its targetability, its measurability, and the responsiveness of consumers to direct marketing efforts.

In the past, U.S. marketers thought that country-specific offices were almost essential to bringing their companies closer to overseas customers. Now with functioning telecommunication systems and deregulation in the industry, telemarketing (including sales, customer service, and help-desk-related support) is flourishing throughout the world. A growing number of countries in Latin America, Asia, and Europe are experiencing growth in this area as consumers are becoming more accustomed to calling toll-free numbers and more willing to receive calls from marketers.

Some exporters see the use of *inbound telemarketing call centers* as a preliminary step to entering an international market with a deeper presence such as a sales office. Locating call centers around the globe depends on a variety of issues, such as the product's distribution, fulfillment logistics, the criticality of a local presence, language, the ability to handle calls from various time zones, and other capabilities. Costa Rica is the choice for Central and Latin American call center operations, Australia for the Asia-Pacific, and Singapore for Asia itself, while Belgium, Holland, Ireland, and Portugal are leading locations in Europe.[15] If only one center is used in Europe, for example, access to a multilingual work force is a major factor in selecting the location. Advanced routing capabilities send calls to native language-speaking inbound telemarketing representatives depending on the inbound call's country of origin.

Call center activity has developed more slowly in Asia than it has in North America and Europe, mostly because of infrastructure and cultural resistance to new forms of communicating with business. However, new customer relationship management technologies are helping to overcome such resistance. Database marketing allows the creation of an individual relationship with each customer or prospect. For example, at the time a call is received, a call center operator will know a customer's background with the company or overall purchasing habits.

Internet Marketing. As we noted in Chapter 12, the Internet and its World Wide Web have become powerful marketing tools only beginning to have what will be a profound influence on the way customers, marketers, and distributors exchange goods and, more important, information about those goods and related services. At the most basic level of that process, the Internet is a communications medium replete with information sharing capabilities. Unlike noninteractive media, the Web site can close sales. Nowadays, a Web site is an essential part of one's business presence, especially in the industrialized world. Lacking a Web site can convey a negative image.

Of course, the Web site should serve the marketer's overall strategy and dovetail into the marketer's complete promotional mix. A site for appearance's sake underutilizes the medium's potential. And it leaves a company vulnerable to rivals. Remember that on the Web, your competitors anywhere in the world are just one click away.

The well-designed site enables the company to increase its presence in the marketplace, providing information customers need to make buying decisions on a "24/7" basis. A highly interactive Web site can provide tailored pages (e.g., different languages) and product solutions, allowing customers to serve themselves when and where they choose. The site could help cut the marketer's overall promotion costs.

Naturally, the exporter must have the necessary capacity to serve all interested customers through the Web site, especially if there is an increase in interest and demand. Capacity should include the important dimension of after-sales service. Also provide an online forum for customers where they can exchange news and views about your products while you watch, learn, and respond, if necessary, to incorrect information and misperceptions. A forum can help spark product development and design ideas. More important, showing customers that the company cares about their views will build loyalty.

In addition to communications with customers, the Internet communicates with internal constituents. Exporters may have part of their Web sites set up with detailed product and price information that only their agents, representatives, or distributors can access. The exporter can notify everyone concerned simultaneously when changes occur.

The Internet can act as a more traditional communications medium as well. Purchasing *banner advertising* that appears on sites likely to draw your target audiences' interest is similar to purchasing advertising space in their favorite print publications. But rather than having to telephone or return in-ad coupons to ask for information by mail or fax, interested prospects can click on the banner ad and move directly to the advertiser's Web site. The effectiveness of banner advertising is a matter of much debate in online marketing circles, indicating that it is not likely to be a centerpiece of most exporter's media mix. But growing use of the medium, particularly in less-developed markets just now coming online, and rapidly improving technology make all bets about the future uncertain. The wise marketer watches his target audiences' Web usage closely.

While English-only Web sites can deliver information and support to some international customers, having local-language sites and registering with local search engines demonstrate appropriate market and cultural sensitivity. The choice of languages will depend on the target audience. The most popular languages, besides English, are French, Spanish, German, Japanese, and Chinese. For some, a dialect must be specified; for example, Spanish has three main variants: European, Mexican, and South American. The exporter also needs to determine which pages have to be modified. Pages that emphasize marketing, sales, and corporate identity are normally the ones chosen.[16]

While the exporter's local Web sites may—and for global product or service offerings, should— be quite similar in terms of aesthetics and design, adjustments should also be made for such dimensions as depth of product line and level of market presence. Customers who are familiar with the Internet may access information about products and services before purchasing them and may visit sites in several countries. Second-generation technology is increasing the interactivity of advertising on the Web. Given that individuals around the world have different information needs, varying levels of company and product familiarity, and different user capabilities, exporters can adjust their Web sites' content and develop paths tailored to each group of customers or even to an individual customer.

Finally, online communications strategy should also include provisions for technological development in target markets. For example, a full-color site with lots of text will not be legible or attractive on the monochrome screens of smart phones using WAP (wireless application protocol) technology, which is growing in popularity. And complex Web pages that nonetheless download at acceptable speeds in the U.S. or Europe might become frustrating bottlenecks in countries with less-developed telephone and broadband capacity, angering customers.

PERSONAL SELLING TO EXPORT MARKETS

Personal selling is the most effective of the promotional tools available to the marketer. Although its costs per contact are high, personal selling provides immediate feedback on customer reaction as well as information on markets. The degree to which the exporting firm is involved internationally influences the nature of its personal selling effort.[17]

Selling Indirect Exports

An indirect exporter typically sells to domestically based export intermediaries. That keeps investment and selling costs low but affords little control over sales abroad and little knowledge of markets abroad. This may change somewhat if the marketer becomes party to an ETC with other similar producers. Even in that case, the ETC will have its own sales force and exposure to the effort may be limited. Any learning that takes place is indirect; for example, the intermediary may advise the marketer of product adaptation requirements to enhance sales.

Selling Direct Exports

A direct exporter typically sells to intermediaries and other distributors in their home markets, though that does not provide direct contact with ultimate buyers. The exporter must provide basic selling aids such as product specification and data literature, catalogs, advertising assistance, the results of product testing, and demonstrated performance information—everything needed to support the intermediaries' sales forces.

To help ensure that the exporter-intermediary interaction will work:[18]

1. Know the sales scene: Often what works in the exporter's home market will not work somewhere else, particularly in compensation methods. In U.S. firms, incentives and commission play a significant role, while in most other markets salaries comprise the major share of compensation. The best way to approach this is to study the salary structures and incentive plans in other competitive organizations in the market in question.
2. Research the customer: Customer behavior will vary across markets, meaning the sales effort must adjust as well. ECA International, which sells marketing information worldwide based on a membership concept (companies purchase memberships to both participate in information gathering and receive appropriate data), found that its partners' sales forces could not sell the concept in Asia. Customers wanted instead to purchase information piece by piece. Only after research and modification of the sales effort was ECA able to sell the membership idea to customers.
3. Work with the culture: Realistic objectives have to be set for

salespeople based on their cultural expectations, especially in setting goals and quotas. Cultural sensitivity should extend to interactions with the intermediary's sales force—in training situations, for example. In some cultures, such as those in Asia, the exporter is expected to act as a teacher and more or less dictate how things are done. In some others, such as in Northern Europe, training sessions should be conducted in a seminar-like atmosphere of give-and-take.

4. Learn from your local representatives: If the sales force perceives a lack of fit between the marketer's product and the market, as well as an inability to do anything about it, the result will be demotivating. Given its close contact with customers, a local sales force is an asset to the exporter. Beyond daily feedback, the exporter is wise to undertake two additional approaches to exploit the experience of local salespeople. First, the exporter should have a program by which local salespeople can visit the exporter's operations and interact with the staff. If the exporter is active in multiple markets of the same region, it is advisable to develop ways to put salespeople in charge of the exporter's products in different markets to exchange ideas and best practices. Naturally, the exporter should make regular periodic visits to markets entered.

Selling Integrated Exports

An integrated exporter has direct contact with customers, internalizing the sales effort through either a sales office in the target market or home office direct contact with the buyer. The exporter assumes more cost and risk but generates much more market knowledge and the ability to manage the customer relationship.

The role of personal selling is greatest when the exporter sells directly to the end user or to governmental agencies, such as foreign trade organizations. Firms selling products with high price tags (such as Boeing commercial aircraft) or companies selling to monopsonies (single-buyer markets) must rely heavily on person-to-person communication, oral presentations, and direct-marketing efforts, perhaps supported by corporate advertising and publicity so that prospects know something positive about the exporter in advance.

The exporter might link the sales effort to customers through sales force automation tools, call center technology, customer service departments, and the Internet. Ensure that such tools do not generate unfavorable perceptions, as they might in some cultures that place a very high value on personal relationships. Localizing tools to market language and culture can help.

Establishing a local sales presence does not have to mean dropping intermediaries; the exporter's salespeople may be dedicated to supporting intermediaries' sales efforts. At this stage, expatriate sales personnel, especially those needed to manage the effort locally or regionally, may be used. The benefits of expatriates are their better understanding of the company and its products, and their ability to transfer best practices to the local operation. With expatriate management, the exporter can exercise a high amount of control over the sales function. Customers may also see the sales office and its expatriate staff as a long-term commitment to the market. The challenges lie mostly in the fit of the chosen individual to the new situation. The cost of having expatriate staff is considerable, approximately 2.5 times the cost at home, and the availability of suitable talent may be a problem, especially if the exporting organization is relatively small.[19]

Trade Shows

Akin to personal selling, marketing goods and services at trade shows (also called "trade fairs" and "exhibitions") is a European tradition that dates back to 1240 AD. After sales forces, trade shows are one of the most significant cost items in marketing budgets. Although they are usually associated with industrial firms, some consumer products firms use exhibitions as well.

Typically, a trade show is an event at which manufacturers, distributors, and other vendors display their products or describe their services to current and prospective customers, suppliers, other business associates, and the press. Whether an exporter should participate in a trade show depends largely on the type of business relationship it wants to develop with a particular country. More than 16,000 trade shows create an annual $50 billion in business worldwide.[20] A company looking only for one-time or short-term sales might find the expense prohibitive, but a firm looking for long-term involvement may find the investment worthwhile.

Participation Pluses. Arguments in favor of trade show participation include:

1. Trade fairs provide an excellent opportunity to introduce, promote, and demonstrate new products to many prospects efficiently.
2. An appearance at a show produces goodwill and periodic

customer and prospect contact. Beyond the impact of displaying specific products, many firms place strong emphasis on "waving the company flag" against competition. The show also boosts the morale of company salespeople and distributors.

3. A show is a cost-effective way to solicit and screen candidate intermediaries for the firm, especially in a new market.

4. Show attendance is one of the best ways to contact government officials and decision makers, especially in China. For example, participation in the Chinese Export Commodities Fair, which is held twice a year in Guangzhou, China, is "expected" by the host government.

5. Trade fairs provide an excellent chance for market research and collecting competitive intelligence. The exporter is able to view most rivals at the same time and to test comparative buyer reactions. Trade fairs provide one of the most inexpensive ways of obtaining evaluative data on the effectiveness of a promotional campaign.

6. Exporters are able to reach a sizable number of sales prospects in a brief time period at a reasonable cost per contact. More than 86 percent of all attendees of the average trade show are buying influencers (managers some responsibility for purchasing products and services). Of equal significance is the fact that trade show visitors are there because they have a specific interest in the exhibits.[21]

7. A show can be a good place to find suppliers.

Participation Minuses. On the other hand, the following are among the reasons exporters cite for not participating in trade fairs:

1. High costs are a problem, though participating in events sponsored by the U.S. Department of Commerce or exhibiting at U.S. trade centers or export development offices can be less expensive. An exporter can also lower costs by sharing expenses with distributors or representatives. Further, the costs of closing a sale through trade shows are estimated to be much lower than for a sale closed through personal representation.

2. Difficulty in choosing the right trade fairs. Many firms rely on suggestions from their foreign distributors on which fairs to attend and what specifically to exhibit. Caterpillar, for example, usually allows its foreign dealers to make the selections for themselves. In markets where conditions are more restricted for exporters, such as China, Caterpillar in effect serves as the dealer and participates itself.

3. Larger exporters with multiple divisions face the problem of

coordination. Several divisions may be required to participate in the same fair under the company banner. Similarly, coordination is required with distributors and agents if joint participation is desired, which requires joint planning.

Planning Essentials. Trade show participation extends beyond just the cost of placing and staffing an exhibit. Marketers should promote their show appearance in advance and invite key prospects to visit, perhaps with the help of incentives, not only the booth but also a nearby hospitality suite conducive to negotiations. Exhibitors also need systems for evaluating post-show performance and tracking qualified sales leads.

Exporters may participate in general or specialized industry trade shows. General trade fairs are held in Hannover, Germany, and Milan, Italy. An example of a specialized one is Retail Solutions, a four-day trade show on store automation held in London.

Participants planning to exhibit at large trade shows may elect to do so independently or as part of a national pavilion. For small and medium-sized companies, reduced cost and ease of arrangements are significant benefits of group pavilions, which are often part of governmental export promotion programs. Even foreign government assistance may be available; for example, the Japanese External Trade Organization (JETRO) helps non-Japanese companies participate in the country's two largest trade shows.

Other promotional events that the exporter can use are trade missions, seminar missions, solo exhibitions, video/catalog exhibitions, and virtual trade shows:

- Trade missions can be U.S. specialized trade missions or industry-organized, government-approved (IOGA) trade missions, both of which aim at expanding the sales of U.S. goods and services and establishing agencies and representation abroad. The U.S. Department of Commerce offers assistance with both objectives.
- Seminar missions are events in which a local organization invites 8 to 10 firms to participate in a one- to four-day forum, during which the team members conduct generic discussions on technological issues. Forums are designed to share information, with promotion taking at most a soft-sell approach. The exporters follow up by individual meetings with end users, government agencies, research institutions, and other potentially useful contacts. Individual firms may introduce themselves to certain markets by proposing a technical seminar there. Synopses of several alternative proposed lectures, together with company details and the qualifications of the speakers, must be forwarded to the proper body,

which will circulate the proposals to interested organizations and coordinate all the arrangements. The major drawback is the time required to arrange for such a seminar, which may be as much as a year.

- Solo exhibitions are generally limited to one, or at the most, a few product themes and are held only when market conditions warrant them.
- Video/catalog exhibitions allow exporters to publicize their products at low cost. They consist of 20 to 35 product presentations on videotapes, each lasting 5 to 10 minutes. They provide the advantage of actually showing the product in use to potential customers.
- Virtual trade shows enable exporters to promote their products and services over the Internet and to have an electronic presence without actually attending a trade show. The virtual show sponsor collects and forwards sales leads to participating companies. The show itself remains available on the Web for a specified time such as a year. The U.S. Department of Commerce maintains its BuyUSA Web portal (www.buyusa.com) for U.S. suppliers and international companies to conduct searches, create online contact lists, and promote themselves free of charge.

MANAGING COMMUNICATIONS GLOBALLY

The general requirements of effective marketing communications apply to the multinational corporation, of course, although the multinational copes with challenges beyond those of the exporter. The technology is in place for global communication efforts, but difficult challenges still remain in the form of cultural, economic, ethnic, regulatory, and demographic differences in the various countries and regions. Whether orchestrating a multidomestic collection of semiautonomous subsidiaries or implementing a truly global strategy of a worldwide entity providing local variations, the firm must balance centralized vs. decentralized communications factors. To what degree must a unit adhere to global themes and positioning? How much central control can be exerted without eroding the local units' initiative? Balance is the heart of successfully thinking globally while acting locally.

Worldwide Sales Forces

The personal selling principles and practices discussed earlier in this chapter certainly apply to global marketers' sales forces. But the issues are not so much about selling through international trade intermediaries as they are country subsidiary direct sales to consumers or to dealers and resellers. Selling is usually part of every product and service marketing mix, if only to complete a process begun by advertising.

In some cases, a multinational sales force may be truly international. Boeing and Northrop-Grumman salespeople engage in sales efforts around the world from their domestic bases, for example. However, most of those companies' personal selling is handled by subsidiaries with varying degrees of headquarters' involvement. When selling to well-defined prospects is a prime marketing tool worldwide, headquarters should ensure a coordinated effort across markets. But when distribution is intensive, channels are long, or markets have tradition-oriented distribution, headquarters' role should be less pronounced and should concentrate mostly on offering help and guidance.[22]

Foreign companies entering the Japanese market face challenges in establishing a sales force. Recruitment poses the first major problem, since well-established and usually local entities have an advantage in attracting personnel. Foreign companies therefore have entered into joint ventures or distribution agreements to obtain a sales force. Companies can also expect to invest more in training and organizational culture-building activities than in the United States. These may bring long-term advantages in fostering loyalty to the company.[23]

To deal with the globalization of customers, marketers have extended national account management programs across countries, typically for the most important customers.[24] AT&T, for example, distinguishes between international and global customers and provides the global customers with special services including a single point of contact for domestic and international operations.

Worldwide Marcom

The steps in planning global communications are familiar requirements: determining audiences, setting program objectives, allocating budgets, choosing media, designing creative strategies, implementing the program, and measuring its effectiveness. But the rules of engagement are at times quite different for globally integrated marketing than for single-market efforts.

Audiences. Global marketers face multiple audiences in addition to customers. Suppliers, intermediaries, governments, local communities, bankers and creditors, media organizations, shareholders, and employees are all stakeholders with which a global marketer should communicate. Some campaigns may target multiple audiences simultaneously. Corporate advertising buffs up the company image and that of its constituent products with investors, supply-chain partners, regulators, and employees, as well as with customers, for instance. Its objectives are often to increase awareness, reposition the company, or combat myths or misconceptions. And branding studies by the American Productivity and Quality Center find that strong brand promotion energizes employee identification with the firm as well as moves goods. Such effects can particularly benefit a company's foreign subsidiaries that employ local personnel.

Logic argues for identifying multimarket target audience similarities so a communication program can be more efficient. Savvy marketers research audiences for common economic expectations, product needs, demographics, income, education, and other variables. Corporate advertising supporting their more traditional product-specific efforts might be particularly efficient when packaged as a global image campaign employing appeals to social issues or other topics that resonate with several countries' audiences.

Campaign Objectives. A critical step for any campaign global or domestic is setting clearly defined, measurable objectives. Without them, the marketer has little idea about the campaign's eventual success and how to improve upon it. Simply declaring an objective as "increasing sales" hardly sets a target level the organization can aim at.

Objectives should be hierarchical—global, regional, and local—with those set at the local level being the most specific in terms of expected revenue increases, improved market share, better distribution penetration, more favorable opinion-leader attitudes, or whatever objectives are appropriate. Marketers at global headquarters and local subsidiaries should work together to ensure that local programs respond to local marketing opportunities while serving global communications goals. Although some campaigns, especially global ones, may have more headquarters involvement than usual, local input is still quite important, especially to ensure that local organizations carry out the plan as expected.

Budgets. The promotional budget links established objectives with media, message, and control decisions. Ideally, the budget would be set as a response to the objectives to be met, but resource constraints get in the way. Many marketers use an objective and task method, the preferred approach in any venue, which sets a budget in terms of the marketing effects to be achieved (such as maintaining a competitively adequate "share of voice") and then leavens the total by the money actually available. Merely setting budgets as some management ordained or historical percentage of sales, though widely practiced, is poor practice because marketing programs generate sales, not the other way around.

Budgets can also be used as a global control mechanism if headquarters retains final budget approval. In these cases, headquarters decision makers must have a clear understanding of cost and market differences to be able to make rational decisions.

Media Strategies. Target audience characteristics, campaign objectives, and the budget form the basis for the choice between media vehicles and the development of a media schedule. The major factors determining the choice of the media vehicles to be used are (1) the availability of vehicles in a given market, (2) the product or service itself, and (3) media habits of the intended audience.

Media availability and spending vary dramatically around the world, with the United States spending more money on advertising than most of the other major advertising nations combined. Other major spenders are Japan, the United Kingdom, Germany, Canada, and France. Some Latin American nations have the heaviest concentration of their advertising in television, while print media reign supreme in some Scandinavian lands. Cable and satellite enhance TV penetration in affluent markets, while radio remains a strong medium in many developing markets. Outdoor and transit advertising, cinema advertising, and, of course, the Internet also vie for ad dollars in many foreign markets. On the horizon in developed nations: interactive telephone and TV.

The multinational marketer developing a global media program faces plenty of homework market by market. A medium popular in one country might well be significantly less important in a nearby land. Currency exchange rate fluctuations further complicate media planning. Some countries such as Mexico offer the "French plan," which gives rate protection for advertisers who pay for television spots a year in advance.

The major problems affecting media availability and planning involve conflicting national regulations. Conditions do vary from country to country, and ads must comply with national regulation. Even within the European Union there is no uniform legal standard. Most European countries either observe the Code of Advertising Practice of the International Chamber of Commerce or base their guidelines on it. Some of the regulations include limits on the amount of time available for advertisements. In Italy, for example, the state-owned and commercial TV channels have different maximum advertising limits.

Other regulations affect presentation. In Italy, strict separation between programs and commercials is almost a universal requirement, preventing U.S.-style sponsored programs. Restrictions on items such as comparative claims and gender stereotypes are prevalent; for example, Germany prohibits the use of superlatives such as "best."

Until recently, with few exceptions, most nations have been very successful in controlling advertising that enters their borders. When commercials were not allowed on the state-run stations, advertisers in Belgium had been accustomed to placing their ads on the Luxembourg station. Radio Luxembourg has traditionally been used to beam messages to the United Kingdom. By the beginning of the century, however, approximately half of the homes in Europe had access to additional television broadcasts through either cable or direct satellite, limiting national boundary restrictions.

The implications of this to global marketers are significant. The viewer's choice will be expanded, leading to competition among government-run public channels, competing state channels from neighboring countries, private channels, and pan-European channels. This means that marketers need to make sure that advertising works not only within markets but across countries as well. As a consequence, media buying will become more challenging.

Widely differing restrictions on how products can be advertised frustrate many a global marketer and advertising agency. Agencies often have to produce several separate versions of a campaign to comply with various national regulations. Consumer protection in general has dominated the regulatory scene since the 1980s, and changing and standardizing these regulations, even in an area like the European Union, is difficult. Tobacco, alcohol, and pharmaceutical products undergo the most regulation in Europe.

Certain products are subject to special rules. In the United Kingdom, for example, advertisers cannot show a real person applying an underarm deodorant; the way around this problem is to show an animated person applying the product. What is and is not allowable is very much a reflection of the country imposing the rules. Explicit advertisements of contraceptives are commonplace in Sweden, for example, but far less frequent in most parts of the world.

Beyond the traditional media, the international marketer may also consider product placement in movies, TV shows, games, or Web sites. In some markets, it might be an effective method of attracting attention due to constraints on traditional media. In China, for example, most commercials on Chinese state-run television are played back-to-back in 10-minute segments, making it difficult for any 30-second ad to stand out from the clutter. Soap operas, such as "Love Talks," have been found to be an effective way to get to the burgeoning middle class in the world's most populous country.[25]

A major objective of media strategy is to reach the target audience with a minimum of waste circulation. That means identifying key audience characteristics. Were conditions ideal—and they seldom are in international markets—the media strategist would have data on media circulation, audience characteristics, and advertising exposure. But in many cases, advertisers have found circulation figures to be unreliable or even fabricated.

A related issue is the way some governments try to protect their own national media from foreign ones. In Canada, for example, the government prevents foreign publishers from selling space to Canadian advertisers in so-called split-run editions that, in effect, have Canadian readers but no local content.

Media vehicles that have target audiences on at least three continents and for which the media buying takes place through a centralized office are generally considered to be *global media.*

Global media have traditionally been print publications that, in addition to the worldwide edition, have provided advertisers the option of using regional editions. For example, *Time* provides more than 100 editions, enabling advertisers to reach a particular country, continent, or the world. In print media, global vehicles include dailies such as *International Herald Tribune,* weeklies such as *The Economist,* and monthlies such as *National Geographic.* Included on the broadcast side are BBC Worldwide TV, CNN, the Discovery Channel, and MTV.

Major consumer advertising categories dominate advertising in global media, particularly airlines, financial services, telecommunications, automobiles, and tobacco. In choosing global media, media buyers consider the three most important media characteristics: targetability, client-compatible editorial, and editorial quality. Some global publications have found that some parts of the globe are more appealing to advertisers than others; at times they eliminate editions that do not generate sufficient advertiser interest.

In broadcast media, panregional radio stations have been joined by television as a result of satellite technology. The pan-European satellite channels, such as Sky Channel and Super Channel, were conceived from the very beginning as advertising media. Many observers are skeptical about the potential of these channels, especially in the short term, because of the challenges of developing a cross-cultural following in often highly nationalistic markets. Pan-European channels have had to cut back, for instance, while native language satellite channels like Tele 5 in France and RTL Plus in

Germany have increased their viewership. The launch of STAR TV has increased the use of regional advertising campaigns in Asia. The other alternative to broadcast TV showing immediate promise is cable television with channels that cater to universal segments with converging tastes, such as MTV, Animal Planet, or the Cartoon Network.

The Internet provides the international marketer with a truly global medium. One simple way of getting started is to choose a few key languages for the Web site. For example, Gillette decided to add German and Japanese to its Mach 3 razor Web site after studying the number of Internet users in those countries.[26] If the marketer elects to have a global site and region-specific sites, they all should have a similar look, especially in terms of the level of sophistication. Another method is to join forces with Internet service providers and advertise on their portals.

Creative Strategies. The writers and art directors in charge of the creative strategy—what your message says—must have a clear idea of the characteristics of the target audience. That can be a challenge in foreign markets, particularly understanding customer motivations. How will customers perceive the product? Does it meet a need, real or imagined, physical or emotional? Can customers use the product given local customs and conditions? Do market conditions allow a product to be positioned as a differentiated brand?

The ideal situation in developing message strategy is to have a world brand—a product that is manufactured, packaged, and positioned the same around the world. Companies that have been successful with the global approach have shown flexibility in the execution of the campaigns. The creative strategy may be global, but overseas subsidiaries then tailor the message to suit local market conditions, regulations, and nuances. Localizing global ideas can be achieved through various tactics, such as adopting a modular approach (e.g., some common parts, some localized) or localizing international symbols (e.g., using the same creative approach but with local spokespeople).

Marketers may develop a modular approach that uses multiple broadcast and print ads from which country organizations can choose the most appropriate for their operations. This can provide local operations with cost savings and allow them to use their budgets on tactical campaigns (which may also be developed around the global idea). For example, the "Membership Has Its Privileges" campaign of American Express, which has run in 24 countries on TV and 3 more in print, was adjusted in some markets to make sure that "privileges" did not have a snob or elitist appeal, especially in countries with a strong caste or class system.

Product-related regulations will affect advertising messages as well. When the General Mills Toy Group's European subsidiary launched a product line related to G.I. Joe-type war toys and soldiers, it had to develop two television commercials, a general version for most European countries and another for countries that bar advertisements for products with military or violent themes. As a result, in the version running in Germany, Holland, and Belgium, Jeeps replaced the toy tanks, and guns were removed from the hands of the toy soldiers. Other countries, such as the United Kingdom, do not allow children to appear in advertisements.

Marketers may also want to localize their international symbols. Some of the most effective global advertising campaigns capitalized on the popularity of pop music worldwide and used well-known artists in the commercials, such as Tina Turner for Pepsi. In some versions, local stars have been included with the international stars to localize the campaign.

Aesthetics play a role in localizing campaigns. The global marketer does not want to chance the censoring of the company's ads or risk offending customers. For example, even though importers of perfumes into Saudi Arabia want to use the same campaigns as are used in Europe, they occasionally have to make adjustments dictated by moral standards. In one case, the European version shows a man's hand clutching a perfume bottle and a woman's hand seizing his bare forearm. In the Saudi Arabian version, the man's arm is clothed in a dark suit sleeve, and the woman's hand is merely brushing his hand.

The environmental influences that call for local modifications, or in some cases totally unique approaches, are culture, economic development, and lifestyles.

Of the cultural variables, language is most apparent in its influence on promotional campaigns. The European Union alone has 11 languages: English, Finnish, French, German, Dutch, Danish, Italian, Greek, Spanish, Swedish, and Portuguese. Advertisers in the Arab world have sometimes found that the voices in a TV commercial speak in the wrong Arabic dialect.

The challenge of language is often most pronounced in translating themes. For example, Coca-Cola's worldwide theme "Can't Beat the Feeling" is the equivalent of "I Feel Coke" in Japan, "Unique Sensation" in Italy, and "The Feeling of Life" in Chile. In Germany, where no translation really worked, the original English language theme was used. One way of getting around this is to have no copy or very little copy and to use innovative approaches, such as pantomime. Using any type of symbolism will naturally require adequate copy testing to determine how the target market perceives the message.

The stage of economic development—and therefore the potential demand for and degree of awareness of the product—may vary and differentiate the message from one market to another. Whereas developed markets may require persuasive messages (to combat other alternatives), a developing market may require a purely informative campaign. Campaigns may also have to be dramatically adjusted to cater to lifestyle differences in regions that are demographically quite similar. For example, N. W. Ayer's Bahamas tourism campaign for the European market emphasized clean water, beaches, and air. The exceptions are in Germany, where it focuses on sports activities, and in the United Kingdom, where it features humor.

Unique market conditions may require localized approaches. Although IBM has used global campaigns (the Little Tramp campaign, for example), it has also used major local campaigns in Japan and Europe for specific purposes. In Japan, it used a popular television star in poster and door-board ads to tell viewers, "Friends, the time is ripe" (for buying an IBM personal computer). The campaign was designed to bolster the idea that the machine represents a class act from America. At the same time, IBM was trying to overcome a problem in Europe of being perceived as "too American." Stressing that IBM is actually a "European company," an advertising campaign told of IBM's large factories, research facilities, and tax-paying subsidiaries within the European Union.

Managing Global Marcom. Many multinational corporations are staffed and equipped to perform the full range of promotional activities. But in most cases global or domestic, they will rely on the outside expertise of advertising agencies and other promotion services companies such as media buyers and specialty marketing firms. In the organization of promotional efforts, a company faces two basic issues: the type of outside services to use and how to establish decision-making authority for promotional efforts. Given the greater uncertainty of foreign markets, the answers are especially critical for the global marketer.

Of all the outside promotion-related services, advertising agencies are by far the most significant. Agencies form world groups for better coverage. Global firms such as Omnicom, WPP Group, and Interpublic Group own agency subsidiaries that have offices worldwide, such as Ogilvy & Mather, J. Walter Thompson, Brouillard Communications, Hill and Knowlton, and other venerable names. Other groups have more limited networks of branch offices and often rely on alliances to fill in gaps in their worldwide market coverage. Some predict that the whole industry will be concentrated into a few huge multinational agencies. Agencies with networks too small to compete have become prime takeover targets in the creation of worldwide mega-agencies, as agencies fear they will lose or never have a shot at desirable accounts unless they can handle world brands.

Using an agency with a worldwide network is common. It ensures consistency and aids coordination, especially when the global marketer's operations are decentralized. It also makes the exchange of ideas easier and may therefore lead, for example, to wider application of a modification or a new idea. Agency network coverage is a major factor, not so much for cost savings but for having a firm's strategic partner agencies in enough of the right markets. Major realignments of client-agency relationships have occurred due to mergers and to clients reassessing their own strategies with global or regional approaches.

The main concern about using global mega-agencies is client conflict. With only a few giant agencies to choose from, the global marketer may end up with the same agency as a main competitor. The mega-agencies believe they can meet any objections by structuring their companies as rigidly separate, watertight agency networks under the umbrella of a holding group such as Interpublic.

Government regulation helps to preserve local agencies. In Peru, for example, a law mandates that any commercial aired on Peruvian television must be 100 percent nationally produced. Local agencies also tend to forge ties with foreign agencies for better coverage and customer service and thus become part of the general globalization effort.

Overall, agencies are adjusting their operations to centrally run client operations. Many accounts are now handled by a lead agency, usually in the country where the client is based. More agencies are establishing strong international supervisors for global accounts, who can overrule local agencies and make personnel changes. Some agencies have set up specialty units specifically for managing clients' global campaigns.

In the past, many multinational corporations allowed local subsidiaries to make advertising decisions entirely on their own. Others gave subsidiaries an approved list of agencies and some guidance. Still others allowed local decisions subject only to headquarters' approval. Now the trend is toward centralization of all advertising decisions, including those concerning the creative product.

The options for allocating decision-making authority range from complete centralization to decentralization. With complete centralization, headquarters claims to have all the right answers and has adequate power to impose its decisions on all of its operating units. Decentralization involves relaxing most of the controls over foreign affiliates and allowing them to pursue their own promotional approaches.

Of 40 multinational marketers recently surveyed by *Advertising Age*, 26 percent have centralized their advertising strategies, citing as their rationale the search for economies of scale, synergies, and brand consistency. About a third, 34 percent, of the companies favor decentralization with regional input. This approach benefits from proximity to market, flexibility, cultural sensitivity, and faster response time. The largest group of marketers uses central coordination with local input.

The important question is not who should make decisions but how advertising quality can be improved at the local level. One prescription for gaining approval in multinational corporations is an eight-step interactive approach using coordinated decentralization, striving for flexible execution of a common strategy.[27]

The approach, illustrated in Exhibit 13.1, maintains strong central control but at the same time capitalizes on the greatest asset of the individual markets—market knowledge. Interaction between the central authority and the local levels takes place at every single stage of the planning process. The central authority is charged with finding the commonalties in the data provided by the individual market areas. This procedure will avoid one of the most common problems associated with acceptance of plans—the NIH syndrome (not invented here)—by allowing for local participation by the eventual implementers.

Measuring Effectiveness. Retailing legend John Wanamaker famously said, "I know half the money I spend on advertising is wasted. Now, if I only knew which half." The fact is, however, that advertising effectiveness can be measured in many ways: customer awareness, response, recall, attitudes, intentions, and executive judgment. The metrics vary in precision and in the degree they can be linked to the company's eventual profit. But as a practical matter, what matters most are metrics that satisfy the managers in charge. As another department store manager put it, according to advertising lore, "We know our newspaper ads work if customers are lined up in the morning to get in for the big sale."

The technical side of these measurement efforts does not differ from that in the domestic market, but the conditions are different. Very often, syndicated audience research services, such as A.C. Nielsen, are not available to the global marketer. If available, their quality may not be at an acceptable level.

Exhibit 13.1: Coordinated Approach to Pan-Regional Campaign Development

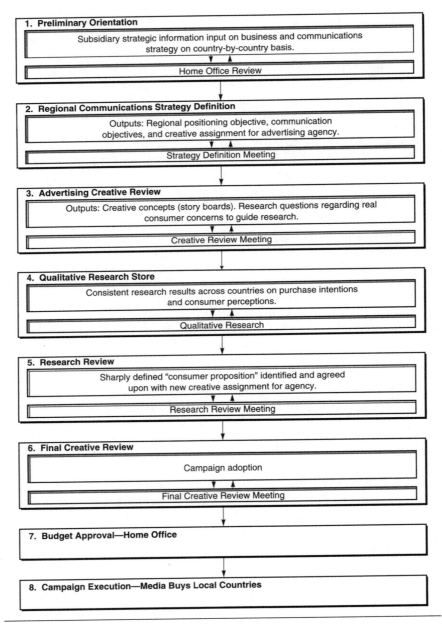

1. Preliminary Orientation

Subsidiary strategic information input on business and communications strategy on country-by-country basis.

Home Office Review

2. Regional Communications Strategy Definition

Outputs: Regional positioning objective, communication objectives, and creative assignment for advertising agency.

Strategy Definition Meeting

3. Advertising Creative Review

Outputs: Creative concepts (story boards). Research questions regarding real consumer concerns to guide research.

Creative Review Meeting

4. Qualitative Research Store

Consistent research results across countries on purchase intentions and consumer perceptions.

Qualitative Research

5. Research Review

Sharply defined "consumer proposition" identified and agreed upon with new creative assignment for agency.

Research Review Meeting

6. Final Creative Review

Campaign adoption

Final Creative Review Meeting

7. Budget Approval—Home Office

8. Campaign Execution—Media Buys Local Countries

SOURCE: David A. Hanni, John K. Ryans, Jr., and Ivan R. Vernon, "Coordinating International Advertising: The Goodyear Case Revisited for Latin America," *Journal of International Marketing* 3 (Number 2, 1995): 83–98.

Testing is also quite expensive and may not be undertaken in the smaller markets. Compared with costs in the U.S. market, marketers expect proportionally greater research costs overseas. The big marcom research challenge now is caused by the increase in global and regional campaigns. Comprehensive and reliable measures of campaigns for a mass European market, for example, are difficult because audience measurement techniques and analysis differ for each country. Advertisers are pushing for universally accepted parameters to compare audiences in one country to those in another.

Additional Marcom Tools

Sales Promotion. Sales promotion has been used as the catchall term for promotion that does not classify as advertising, personal selling, or publicity. Sales promotion directed at consumers involves such activities as couponing, sampling, premiums, consumer education and demonstration activities, cents-off packs, point-of-purchase materials, and direct mail. The use of sales promotions as alternatives to and as support for advertising has grown worldwide. The appeal is related to several factors: the cost and clutter of media advertising, simpler targeting of customers compared with advertising, and easier tracking of promotional effectiveness; for example, coupon returns provide a clear measure of effectiveness.

For sales promotion to be effective, the campaign planned by manufacturers or their agencies must gain the dealer support—i.e., the support of local retailers. Coupons from consumers, for example, have to be redeemed and sent to the manufacturer or to the company handling the promotion. A.C. Nielsen tried to introduce cents-off coupons in Chile and ran into trouble with the nation's supermarket union, which notified its members that it opposed the project and recommended that coupons not be accepted. The main complaint was that an intermediary, like Nielsen, would unnecessarily raise costs and thus the prices to be charged to consumers. Also, some critics felt that coupons would limit individual negotiations because Chileans often bargain for their purchases.

Sales promotion tools fall under varying government regulations generally designed to control the use of gifts, premiums, and contests as sales inducements. A particular type or size of incentive may be permissible in one market but illegal in another. The Scandinavian countries present the greatest difficulties in this respect because every promotion has to be approved by a government body. In France and the Netherlands, for instance, a gift cannot be worth more than a token amount, making certain promotions virtually impossible. Although sweepstakes and competitions are allowed in most of Western Europe, to insist on receiving proofs of purchase as a condition of entry is not permitted in Germany.

In the province of Quebec, advertisers must pay a tax on the value of the prizes they offer in a contest, whether the prize is a trip, money, or a car. The amount of the tax depends on the geographical extent of the contest. If it is open only to residents of Quebec, the tax is 10 percent, if open to all of Canada, 3 percent, if worldwide, 1 percent. Subtle distinctions apply in the regulations between a premium and a prize. As an example, the Manic soccer team was involved with both McDonald's and Provigo Food stores. The team offered a dollar off the price of four tickets, and the stubs could be cashed for a special at McDonald's. Provigo was involved in a contest offering a year's supply of groceries. The Manic-McDonald's offer was a premium that involved no special tax; Provigo, however, was taxed because it was involved in a contest. According to the regulation, a premium is available to everyone, whereas a prize is available to a certain number of people among those who participate.

Regulations such as those make truly global sales promotions rare and difficult to launch. Although only a few multinational brands have been promoted on a multiterritory basis, the approach can work for products such as soft drinks, liquor, airlines, credit cards, and jeans, which span cultural divides. Naturally, local laws and cultural differences have to be taken into account at the planning stage. Although many of the promotions may be funded centrally, they will be implemented differently in each market so that they can be tied with the local company's other promotional activities.

Public Relations. Public relations is the marketing communications function charged with executing programs to earn public understanding and acceptance for the company, which means both internal and external communication. The function can further be divided into proactive and reactive forms.

Especially in multinational corporations, internal communication, or *internal public relations*—is important to create an appropriate corporate culture. The Japanese have perfected this in achieving a *wa* (we) spirit. Everyone in an organization is, in one way or another, in marketing and will require additional information on issues not necessarily related to his or her day-to-day functions.

A basic part of most internal programs is the employee publication produced and edited typically by the company's public relations or advertising department and usually provided in both hard copy and electronic format. Some have foreign language versions. More often, each affiliate publishes its own employee publication. The better this vehicle can satisfy the information needs of employees, the less they will have to rely on others, especially informal sources such as the grapevine. Audiovisual media in the form of emails, films, videotapes, slides, and videoconferencing are being used, especially for training and indoctrination purposes. Some of the materials that are used internally can be provided to other publics as well; for example, booklets, manuals, and handbooks are provided to employees, distributors, and visitors to the company.

External public relations can have many audiences: mainly customers and prospects but also investors, government regulators, community opinion and political leaders, suppliers, and the general public. It can be a critical function for foreign firms competing against companies with strong local identities. External campaigns can include corporate symbols, corporate advertising, customer relations programs, cause-related and event-related marketing, and publicity. Publicity is particularly important because it's perceived as more trustworthy than advertising.

Handling crises when unanticipated developments strike requires reactive public relations—often called *crisis communications*—including anticipating and countering criticism. Crisis management is becoming a more formal function in companies with specially assigned task forces ready to step in if problems arise. In general, companies must adopt policies that will allow them to effectively respond to pressure and criticism, which will continue to surface. Effective crisis management policies have the following traits:

- Openness about corporate activities, with a focus on how these activities enhance social and economic performance.
- Preparedness to utilize the tremendous power of the multinational corporation in a responsible manner and, in the case of pressure, to counter criticisms swiftly.
- Integrity, which often means that the marketer must avoid not only actual wrongdoing but the mere appearance of it.
- Clarity, which will help ameliorate hostility if a common language is used with those pressuring the corporation.[28]

Reasonable critics understand that the marketer cannot compromise the bottom line, but complications arise over cross-border cultural misunderstandings. In one notable instance, the Interfaith Center on Corporate Responsibility urged Colgate-Palmolive to stop marketing Darkie toothpaste under that brand name in Asia because of the term's offensiveness elsewhere in the world. Colgate sold Darkie toothpaste in Thailand, Hong Kong, Singapore, Malaysia, and Taiwan packaged in a box that featured a likeness of Al Jolson in blackface. Colgate-Palmolive redid the package and changed the brand name to Darlie. In recent years, American human rights activists have called multinational and even domestic-only marketers to task for allegedly exploiting foreign labor employed by their suppliers

The company can handle public relations itself, or through an outside agency. Many advertising agencies have their own PR capabilities or are affiliated with major agencies. The PR field also sports a long list of specialist agencies whose services range from press agentry to lobbying governmental officials foreign and domestic. Product support PR may work best with a strong component of control at the local level and a local PR firm, while crisis management—given the potential for worldwide adverse impact—most often should be controlled from a global center.[29] Thus, global marketers funnel short-term projects to single offices and their agencies for their local expertise while maintaining contact with the global agencies for their worldwide reach when a universal message is needed.

Sponsorship Marketing. Sponsorship involves the marketer's investment in events or causes. Sporting and cultural events receive the most corporate sponsorship spending, creating revenue streams that have become crucial parts of event economics, such as the financing supporting the Olympic Games. In return for healthy fees paid, usually to achieve an exclusive sponsorship in a product category, marketers associate themselves with positive strategic images, strong fan appeal, and unprecedented global reach as achieved by the Olympics and the World Cup quadrennial extravaganza.

The risk is that an event may become embroiled in controversy and hurt sponsors' images. Also "ambush marketers" cut corners on event trademarks and coverage rights. During the 1996 Atlanta Olympic Games, some official sponsors' competitors garnered a higher profile than the sponsors themselves. Pepsi built stands outside venues and plastered the town with signs. Nike secured large amounts of radio and TV time. Fuji bought billboards on the route from the airport into downtown Atlanta. None contributed anything to the International Olympic Committee during that time.[30]

Cause-related marketing is a combination of public relations, sales promotion, and corporate philanthropy. This activity should not be developed randomly but as an integrated social vision and a planned long-term social policy. For instance, Unilever's Funfit Program for its Persil washing powder brand in Europe creates resource packs for teachers and has helped to boost children's fitness through physical education lessons. Microsoft launched an information technology Web site in Singapore that donated one cent to local charities for each page hit within the site. Building favorable community relations is "Food for the soul of the organization."

FUTURITIES

Advances in international communications will have a profound impact on marketers. Entire industries are becoming more footloose in their operations—i.e., less tied to their current location in their interaction with markets. Service industries lead the trend because by easily bridging distances, they are mainly concerned about the right to operate rather than the right to establish a physical presence. Why build a large bank or insurance edifice and combat local regulations if a computer linkage with the customer will do? Best Western Hotels in the United States has channeled its entire reservation system through a toll-free number serviced out of the prison system in Utah. Companies could as easily concentrate their communications activities in other countries, and increasing numbers of them do, hiring telephone personnel or data entry staff from services based in areas where educated labor is available at relatively low cost. For manufacturers, staffs in different countries talk together and also can share pictures and data on their computer screens. These simultaneous interactions with different parts of the world will strengthen research and development efforts. Faster knowledge transfer will allow for the concentration of product expertise, increased division of labor, and a proliferation of global operations.

NOTES

1. John L. Graham, "Vis-à-Vis International Business Negotiations," in *International Business Negotiations,* Jean-Claude D. Usunier and Pervez N. Ghauri, ed. (London: The Dryden Press, 1996), chapter 7; "Negotiating in Europe," *Hemispheres,* July 1994, 43–47.
2. Arnold Pachtman, "Getting to 'Hao!'" *International Business* (July/August 1998): 24–26.
3. Pervez N. Ghauri, "Guidelines for International Business Negotiations," *International Marketing Review* 4 (Autumn 1986): 72–82.
4. "Negotiating in Europe," *Hemispheres,* July 1994, 43–47.
5. V. J. Rehberg, "Kuwait: Reality Sets In," *Export Today* 7 (December 1991): 56–58.
6. Nancy J. Adler, John L. Graham, and Theodore Schwarz Gehrke, "Business Negotiations in Canada, Mexico, and the United States," *Journal of Business Research* 15 (1987): 411–429.
7. D.L. Harnett and L.L. Cummings, *Bargaining Behavior: An International Study* (Houston, TX: Dame Publications, 1980), 231.
8. Claude Cellich, "Negotiations for Export Business: Elements for Success," *International Trade Forum* 9 (Number 4, 1995): 20–27.
9. Jackie Mayfield, Milton Mayfield, Drew Martin, and Paul Herbig, "How Location

Impacts International Business Negotiations," *Review of Business* 19 (Winter 1998): 21–24.

10. Adapted from J. L. Graham and R. A. Herberger, Jr., *"Negotiators Abroad—Don't Shoot from the Hip,"* Harvard Business Review 61 (July–August 1983): 160–168.

11. Sally Stewart and Charles F. Keown, "Talking with the Dragon: Negotiating in the People's Republic of China," *Columbia Journal of World Business* 24 (Fall 1989): 68–72.

12. Hokey Min and William P. Galle, "International Negotiation Strategies of U.S. Purchasing Professionals," *International Journal of Purchasing and Materials Management* 29 (Summer 1993): 41–53.

13. Berry J. Kesselman and Bryan Batson, "China: Clause and Effect," *Export Today* 12 (June 1996): 18–26.

14. Richard D. Lewis, *When Cultures Collide* (London: Nicholas Brealey Publishing, 1996), chapter 17.

15. Sam Bloomfield, "Reach Out and Touch Someone Far, Far Away," *World Trade,* April 1999, 80–84.

16. Gerry Dempsey, "A Hands-On Guide for Multilingual Web Sites," *World Trade,* September 1999, 68–70.

17. Adapted from Reijo Luostarinen and Lawrence Welch, *International Operations of the Firm* (Helsinki, Finland: Helsinki School of Economics, 1990), ch. 1.

18. Charlene Solomon, "Managing an Overseas Sales Force," *World Trade,* April 1999, S4–S6.

19. For a detailed discussion of the expatriate phenomenon, see Michael R. Czinkota, Ilkka A. Ronkainen, and Michael H. Moffett, *International Business: 2000 Update* (Fort Worth, TX: The Dryden Press, 2000), chapter 20.

20. Kathleen V. Schmidt, "Trading Plätze," *Marketing News,* July 19, 1999, 11.

21. "Taking Advantage of Trade Fairs for Maximum Sales Impact," *Business International,* October 12, 1987, 321–323.

22. John S. Hill, Richard R. Still, and Unal O Boya, "Managing the Multinational Sales Force," *International Marketing Review* 8 (1991): 19–31.

23. John L. Graham, Shigeru Ichikawa, and Yao Apasu, "Managing Your Sales in Japan," *Euro-Asia Business Review* 6 (January 1987): 37–40.

24. G. S. Yip and T. L. Madsen, "Global Account Management: The New Frontier in Relationship Marketing," *International Marketing Review* 13 (Number 3, 1996): 24–42.

25. "Chinese TV Discovers Product Placement," *The Wall Street Journal,* January 26, 2000, B12.

26. "The Internet," *Advertising Age International,* June 1999, 42.

27. Dean M. Peebles, John K. Ryans, and Ivan R. Vernon, "Coordinating International Advertising," *Journal of Marketing* 42 (January 1978): 28–34.

28. Oliver Williams, "Who Cast the First Stone?" *Harvard Business Review* 62 (September–October 1984): 151–160.

29. Michael Carberry, "Global Public Relations," keynote speech at Public Relations Association of Puerto Rico's Annual Convention, San Juan, September 17, 1993.

30. "Olympic Torch Burns Sponsors' Fingers," *Financial Times,* Dec.13, 1999, 6.

14

Organizing for Global Marketing

Balancing your international enterprise.

A legendary marketing company, Procter & Gamble, put globalization at the heart of its ongoing corporate restructuring thrust, code named Organization 2005. P&G recognizes that there is a big difference between selling products in 140 countries around the world and truly planning and managing lines of business on a global basis.

There are five key elements to Organization 2005:

1. Global business units (GBUs): P&G is moving from four business units based on geographic regions to four GBUs based on product lines. This will drive greater innovation and speed by centering global strategy and profit responsibility on brands, rather than on geographics.

2. Market development organizations (MDOs): The company is establishing eight MDO regions that will tailor global programs to local markets and develop marketing strategies to build P&G's entire business on superior local consumer and customer knowledge.

3. Global business services (GBS): GBS brings business activities such as accounting, human resource systems, order management, and information technology into a single global organization to provide these services to all P&G business units at best-in-class quality, cost, and speed.

4. Corporate functions: P&G has redefined the role of corporate staff. Most have moved into new business units, with the remaining staff refocused on developing cutting-edge new knowledge and serving corporate needs. For example, the company decentralized its 3,600-person information technology department so that 97 percent of its members now work in P&G's individual product, market, and business teams or are part of GBS, which provides shared services such as infrastructure to P&G units. The remaining 3 percent are still in corporate IT. In addition, 54 "change agents" have been assigned to work across the 7 GBUs to lead cultural and business change by helping teams work

together more effectively through greater use of IT, real-time collaboration tools in particular.

5. Culture: Changes to P&G's culture should create an environment that produces bolder, mind-stretching goals and plans, bigger innovations, and greater speed. For example, the reward system has been redesigned to better link executive compensation with new business goals and results.

A good example of P&G's use of collaborative technology is a product called Swiffer, a dust sweeper with disposal cloths electrostatically charged to attract dust and dirt. Swiffer, which was introduced to the market in August 1999, represents collaboration among multiple P&G product groups, including paper and chemicals. Swiffer took just 18 months to go from test market to global availability. In the past, when a product was introduced, it might have taken years for it to be available worldwide, since management in each region was responsible for the product's launch there, including everything from test marketing to getting products onto retailers' shelves. Collaborative technologies, including chat rooms on the company's intranet, are transforming the company's conservative culture to one that encourages employees to be candid, test boundaries, and take chances.[1]

As companies evolve from purely domestic entities to multinationals, their organizational structure and control systems must change to reflect new strategies. With growth comes diversity in terms of products and services, geographic markets, and personnel, leading to a set of challenges for the company. Two critical issues are basic to addressing these challenges:

- The type of organization that provides the best framework for developing worldwide strategies while at the same time maintaining flexibility with respect to individual markets and operations.
- The type and degree of control to be exercised from headquarters to maximize total effort.

Organizational structures and control systems have to be adjusted as market conditions change.

STAGES OF GLOBAL OPERATIONS

The basic configurations of international organizations correspond to those of purely domestic ones, but the greater the degree of internationalization, the more complex the structures can become.

The types of structures that companies use to manage foreign activities can be divided into three stages or categories based on the degree of internationalization:

1. Little or no formal organizational recognition of international activities of the firm: This category ranges from domestic operations handling an occasional international transaction on an ad hoc basis to separate export departments.
2. International division: Firms in this category recognize the ever-growing importance of international involvement.
3. Global organizations: These can be structured by product, area, function, process, customer, or combination thereof.

As worldwide competition has increased dramatically in many industries, the latest organizational response is networked global organizations in which heavy flows of technology, personnel, and communication take place between strategically interdependent units to establish greater global integration. The ability to identify and disseminate best practices throughout the organization is an important competitive advantage for global companies.

Little or No Formal Organization

Much of this has been described previously in the book, so we'll just summarize a few key points here. In the early stages of a company's international involvement, the share of international operations in the sales and profits of the corporation is initially so minor that no organizational adjustment takes place. The company conducts transactions episodically through a resident expert or a facilitating agent, such as a freight forwarder. As international demand grows and interest within the firm increases, management sets up a separate export entity, either an internal department or subdepartment or independent outside export management company that becomes the de facto export department of the firm. Such an indirect approach to international involvement means the firm accumulates very little experience of its own.

As the firm becomes more involved in foreign markets, the export department structure becomes obsolete and is replaced by joint ventures or direct foreign investment, which require those involved to have functional experience. The firm therefore typically establishes an international division. There are several variations possible at this stage, but what is most important is that the amount of coordination and control required quickly establishes the need for a more formal international organization in the firm.

The International Division

The international division centralizes in one entity, with or without separate incorporation, all of the responsibility for international activities at the same organizational level as domestic operations. The approach aims to eliminate a possible bias against international operations that may exist if domestic divisions are allowed to independently serve international customers. The international division concentrates international expertise, information flows concerning foreign market opportunities, and authority over international activities and foreign subsidiaries. However, manufacturing and other related functions remain with the domestic divisions in order to take advantage of economies of scale.

To avoid situations in which the international division is at a disadvantage in competing for production, personnel, and corporate services, companies need to coordinate their respective domestic and international operations. Coordination can be achieved through a joint staff or by requiring domestic and international divisions to interact in strategic planning and to submit the plans to headquarters. Further, many corporations require and encourage frequent interaction between domestic and international personnel to discuss common challenges in areas such as product planning. Coordination is also important because domestic operations may be organized along product or functional lines, whereas international divisions are geographically oriented.

International divisions best serve firms with few products that do not vary significantly in terms of their environmental sensitivity, and when international sales and profits are still insignificant compared with those of the domestic divisions.[2] Companies may outgrow their international divisions as their international sales grow in significance, diversity, and complexity. European companies used international divisions far less than their U.S. counterparts due to the relatively small size of their domestic markets. Philips Electronics, for example, would have never grown to its current prominence by relying on the Dutch market alone.

While international divisions were popular among U.S. companies in the 1970s and 1980s, globalization of markets and the increased share of overseas sales have made international divisions less suitable than global structures. For example, Loctite, a leading marketer of sealants, adhesives, and coatings, moved from having an international division to a global structure in which the company is managed by market channel (e.g., industrial automotive and electronics industry), to enable Loctite employees to combine efforts and expertise worldwide.[3]

Global Organizational Structures

Global structures have grown out of competitive necessity. In many industries, competition is on a global basis, with the result that companies must have a high degree of reactive capability.

Companies can choose among six basic types of global structures as their product diversity, market diversity, and foreign sales volume expand:

1. Global product structure, in which product divisions are responsible for all manufacturing and marketing worldwide.
2. Global area structure, in which geographic divisions are responsible for all manufacture and marketing in their respective areas.
3. Global functional structure, in which the functional areas (such as production, marketing, finance, and personnel) are responsible for the worldwide operations of their own functional areas.
4. Global customer structure, in which operations are structured based on distinct worldwide customer groups.
5. Mixed—or hybrid—structure, which may combine the other alternatives.
6. Matrix structure, which integrates the various approaches already discussed and allows the company to exercise specialized control by more than one type of headquarters unit (e.g., functional expertise and customer group knowledge) simultaneously across the globe.

Product Structure. The product structure is the one most used by multinational corporations. This approach gives worldwide responsibility to strategic business units organized by product lines. Each product division has its own headquarters and foreign subsidiary operations. Most consumer product firms utilize some form of this approach, mainly because of the diversity of their products.

One of the major benefits of the product approach is improved cost efficiency through centralized manufacturing facilities. This is crucial in industries in which competitive position is determined by world market share, which in turn is often determined by the degree to which manufacturing is rationalized.[4]

Adaptation to this approach may cause problems because it is usually accompanied by consolidation of operations and plant closings. A good example is Black & Decker, which rationalized many of its operations in its worldwide competitive effort against Makita, the Japanese power tool manufacturer. Similarly, Goodyear reorganized itself into a single global organization with a complete business team approach for tires and general products. Tightening worldwide competition largely prompted the move.[5] In a similar move, Ford merged its large and culturally distinct European and North American auto operations by vehicle platform type to make more efficient use of its engineering and product development resources against rapidly globalizing rivals.[6] One team of engineers for worldwide markets designed the Ford Focus, Ford's compact car introduced in 1999.

Another benefit of the product-line orientation is the ability to balance the functional inputs needed by a product and to react quickly to product-specific problems in the marketplace. Even smaller brands receive individual attention. Product-specific attention is important because products vary in terms of the adaptation they need for different foreign markets. All in all, the product approach ideally develops a global strategic focus in response to global competition.

At the same time, however, this structure fragments international expertise within the firm because a central pool of international experience no longer exists. The structure assumes that managers will have adequate regional experience or advice to allow them to make balanced decisions. Coordination of activities among the various product groups operating in the same markets is crucial to avoid unnecessary duplication of basic tasks. For some of these tasks, such as market research, special staff functions may be created and then hired by the product divisions when needed. Also, if product managers lack an appreciation for the international dimension, they may focus their attention on only the larger markets, often with emphasis on the domestic markets, and fail to take the long-term view.

Area Structure. The second most frequently adopted approach is the area structure. The firm is organized on the basis of geographical areas; for example, operations may be divided into those dealing with North America, the Far East, Latin America, and Europe. Individual country subsidiaries report to the regional divisions.

Regional aggregation may play a major role in this structure. Many multinational corporations have located their European headquarters in Brussels, for example, where the European Union has its headquarters. The inevitability of a North American trading bloc led to the creation of Campbell Soup Co.'s North American division, which replaced the U.S. operation as the power center of the company.[7] Similarly, 3M Co. reorganized to capitalize on regional trends in Europe and North America. In Europe, for instance, 3M formed European Business Centers (EBCs) focused on reaching the pan-European marketplace more efficiently. Each of the EBCs operates along product rather than geographic lines, and each is responsible for its business functions throughout Europe.[8]

The driver of the choice can also be cultural similarity, such as in the case of Asia, or historic connections between countries, such as in the case of combining Europe with the Middle East and Africa. Ideally, the company gives no special preference to the region in which it locates its headquarters. Central staffs provide coordination support for worldwide planning and control activities performed at headquarters.

The area approach follows the marketing concept most closely because individual areas and markets are given concentrated attention. If market conditions with respect to product acceptance and operating conditions vary dramatically, the area approach is the one to choose. Companies opting for this alternative typically have relatively narrow product lines with similar end uses and end users. However, expertise is most needed in adapting the product and its marketing to local market conditions. Once again, to avoid duplication of effort in product management and in functional areas, staff specialists—for product categories, for example—may be used.

Some marketers may feel that going into a global product structure may be too much too quickly and opt, therefore, to have a regional organization for planning and reporting purposes. The objective may also be to keep profit or sales centers of similar size at similar levels in the corporate hierarchy. If a group of countries has small sales compared with other country operations, they can be consolidated into a region. The benefits of a regional operation and regional headquarters are more efficient coordination of programs across the region (as opposed to globally), a management more sensitized to country-market operations in the region, and the ability for the region's voice to be heard more clearly at global headquarters (as compared to what an individual, especially smaller, country operation could achieve).[9]

Without appropriate coordination from the staff, essential information and experience may not be transferred from one regional entity to another. Also, if the company expands in terms of product lines, and if end markets begin to diversify, the area structure may become inappropriate.

Functional Structure. Of all the global organization approaches, the functional structure is the simplest from the administrative viewpoint because it emphasizes the basic tasks of the firm such as manufacturing, sales, and research and development. A vice president of, say, production, heads world production operations at all subsidiaries. So does the vice president of sales, etc. This approach works best when both products and customers are relatively few and similar in nature. Because coordination is typically the key problem, staff functions have been created to interact between the functional areas. Otherwise, the company's marketing and regional expertise may not be exploited to the fullest extent.

A variation of this approach is one that uses processes as a basis for structure. The process structure is common in the energy and mining industries, where one corporate entity may be in charge of exploration worldwide and another may be responsible for the actual mining operation.

Customer Structure. Firms may also organize their operations using the customer structure, especially if the customer groups they serve are dramatically different—for example, consumers versus businesses versus governments. The product may be the same, but the buying processes of the various customer groups may differ. Catering to these diverse groups may require specialists in particular divisions. One type of customer that typically receives such special attention is government, where bidding characterizes procurement and price plays a larger role than when businesses are the buyers.

Mixed Structure. Mixed, or hybrid, organizations also exist combining two or more organizational dimensions simultaneously. The approach permits management to focus on products, areas, or functions, as needed, with, say, product groups and customer groups at headquarters both exercising control over some subsidiaries. This approach may occur in a transitory period after a merger or an acquisition, or it may come about because of a unique customer group or product line (such as military hardware). It may also provide a useful structure before the implementation of the matrix structure.[10]

Organization structures are, of course, never as clear-cut and simple as described here. Whatever the basic format, product, region, function, and customer management must be accommodated. One alternative, for example, might be an initial product structure that would eventually have regional groupings. Another alternative might be an initial area structure with eventual product groupings. However, in the long term, coordination and control across such structures become tedious.

Matrix Structure. In an attempt to facilitate planning, organizing, and controlling interdependent businesses, critical resources, strategies, and geographic regions, many multinational corporations have adopted the matrix structure. The matrix structure probably allows a corporation to best meet the challenges of global markets: to be global and local, big and small, decentralized with centralized reporting by allowing the optimizing of businesses globally and maximizing performance in every country of operation. Organizational matrices integrate the various approaches already discussed and allow the company to exercise specialized control by more than one type of headquarters unit (e.g., functional expertise and customer group knowledge) simultaneously across the globe. A corporate culture of teamwork and cooperation is essential to matrix organization success.

Philips Electronics provides an example. It established a complex organization in response to its complicated mix of varying market and product characteristics. It formed 7 product divisions (which it then divided into 60 product groups) to rationalize manufacturing for continent-wide markets rather than lines of products for individual markets. Philips has 3 general types of country organizations:

- In "key" markets, such as the United States, France, and Japan, product divisions manage their own marketing as well as manufacturing.
- In "local business" countries, such as Nigeria and Peru, the organizations function as importers from product divisions, and if manufacturing occurs, it is purely for the local market.
- In "large" markets, such as Brazil, Spain, and Taiwan, a hybrid arrangement is used depending on the size and situation.

Philips's product divisions and the national subsidiaries interact together in a matrix-like configuration with the product divisions responsible for the globalization dimension and the national subsidiaries responsible for local representation and coordination of common areas of interest, such as recruiting. The matrix structure manager has functional, product, and resource managers as direct reports. The approach is based on team building and multiple command, each team specializing in its own area of expertise. It provides a mechanism for cooperation between country managers, business managers, and functional managers on a worldwide basis through increased communication, control, and attention to balance in the organization.

However, the matrix requires sensitive, well-trained middle managers who can cope with problems that arise from reporting to two bosses—such as a product line manager and an area manager. For example, every management unit may have some sort of multidimensional reporting relationship, which may cross functional, regional, or operational lines. On a regional basis, group managers in Europe, for example, report administratively to a vice president of operations for Europe. But functionally they report to group vice presidents at global headquarters.

Many companies have found the matrix structure problematic. The dual reporting channel easily causes conflict; complex issues are forced into a two-dimensional decision framework; and even minor issues may have to be resolved through committee discussion. Ideally, managers should solve problems themselves through formal and informal communication; however, physical and psychic distance often make that impossible. Especially when competitive conditions require quick reaction, the matrix, with its inherent complexity, may slow the company's reaction. As a result, the authority has started to shift in many organizations from area to product although the matrix may still officially be used.

DEVELOPING AND IMPLEMENTING THE GLOBAL PLAN

Once the organizational framework is in place, the company must implement its global marketing strategy. Structures themselves do not indicate where the authority for decision making and control rests within the organization nor will they reveal the level of coordination between units. Degrees of coordination are, from highest to lowest levels of control:

- Central control: No national structures.
- Central direction: Central functional heads have line authority over national functions.
- Central coordination: Central staff functions in coordinating role.
- Coordinating mechanisms: Formal committees and systems.
- Informal cooperation: Functional meetings and exchange of information.
- National autonomy: No coordination between decentralized units, which may even compete in export markets.[11]

It is rare to find companies exercising either of the two extreme options.

Loci of Control

In decentralized systems, controls are relatively loose and simple, and the flows between headquarters and subsidiaries are mainly financial: Each subsidiary operates as a profit center. Allowing maximum flexibility at the country-market level takes advantage of the fact that subsidiary management knows its market and can react to changes quickly. Problems of motivation and acceptance are avoided when decision makers are also the implementers of the strategy.

Firms are typically neither totally centralized nor totally decentralized. Some functions, such as finance, lend themselves to more centralized decision making, whereas other functions, such as promotional decisions, lend themselves to far less. Research and development is typically centralized in terms of both decision making and location, especially when basic research work is involved. Partly because of governmental pressures, some companies have added R&D functions on a regional or local basis. In many cases, however, variations in decision making are product and market based; for example, global decision making for pricing and local decisions for service and delivery.

Influential Factors. The organizational structure and locus of decision making in multinational corporations are determined by a number of factors. They include:

- The degree of involvement in international operations.
- The businesses in which the firm is engaged.
- The size and importance of the markets.
- The human resource capability of the firm.[12]

The effect of the degree of involvement on structure and decision making was discussed earlier in the chapter. With low degrees of involvement by the parent company, subsidiaries can enjoy high degrees of autonomy as long as they meet their profit targets. The same situation can occur in even the most globally involved companies, but within a different framework. As an example, consider Philips USA, which generates 20 percent of the company's worldwide sales. Even more important, it serves a market that is on the leading edge of digital media development. Therefore, it enjoys an independent status in terms of local policy setting and managerial practices but is nevertheless within the parent company's planning and control system.

The firm's country of origin and the political history of the area can also affect organizational structure and decision making. For example, Swiss-based Nestlé, with only 3 to 4 percent of its sales in its small domestic market, has traditionally had a highly decentralized organization. Moreover, events of the past 90 years, particularly during the two world wars, have often forced subsidiaries of European-based companies to act independently in order to survive.

The type and variety of products marketed will have an effect on organizational decisions. Companies that market consumer products typically have product organizations with high degrees of decentralization, allowing for maximum local flexibility. On the other hand, companies that market technologically sophisticated products, such as General Electric's turbines, display centralized organizations with worldwide product responsibilities. Even in matrix organizations, one of the dimensions may be granted more say in decisions; for example, at Dow Chemical, geographical managers have the strongest voice.

Going global has recently meant transferring the world headquarters of important business units abroad. For example, Philips has moved the headquarters of several of its global business units to the United States, including taking its Digital Video Group, Optimal Storage, and Flat Panel Display activities to Silicon Valley. Apart from situations that require the development of an area structure, the characteristics of certain markets or regions may require separate arrangements for the firm. For many Japanese and European companies, the North American market has been granted such attention with, for example, direct organizational links to top management at headquarters.

The human factor in any organization is critical. Managers both at headquarters and in the subsidiaries must bridge the physical and psychic distances separating them. If subsidiaries have competent managers who rarely need to consult headquarters about their problems, they may be granted high degrees of autonomy. In the case of global organizations, subsidiary management must understand the corporate culture because subsidiaries must sometimes make decisions that meet the long-term objectives of the firm as a whole but that are not optimal for the local market.

Coordinated Decentralization. On the other hand, many multinational companies faced with global competitive threats and opportunities have adopted global strategy formulation, which by definition requires some degree of centralization. What has emerged as a result can be called coordinated decentralization. This means that overall corporate strategy is provided from headquarters, but subsidiaries are free to implement it within the range established in consultation between headquarters and the subsidiaries.

However, moving into this new mode may raise significant challenges. Among these systemic difficulties are a lack of widespread commitment to dismantling traditional national structures, driven by an inadequate understanding of the larger, global forces at work. Power barriers—especially if the personal roles of national managers are under threat of being consolidated into regional organizations—can lead to proposals being challenged without valid reason. Finally, some organizational initiatives (such as multicultural teams or corporate chat rooms) may be jeopardized by the fact that people do not have the necessary skills (e.g., language ability) or that an infrastructure (e.g., intranet) does not exist in an appropriate format.[13]

One particular case is of special interest. Organizationally, the forces of globalization are changing the country manager's role significantly. With profit-and-loss responsibility, oversight of multiple functions, and the benefit of distance from headquarters, country managers typically had enjoyed considerable decision-making autonomy as well as entrepreneurial initiative. Today, however, many companies have to emphasize the product dimension of the product-geography matrix, which means that the power has to shift at least to some extent from country managers to worldwide strategic business unit and product line managers. Many of the previously local decisions are now subordinated to global strategic moves. Therefore, the future country manager will have to have diverse skills (such as government relations and managing entrepreneurial teamwork) and wear many hats in balancing the needs of the operation for which the manager is directly responsible with those of the entire region or strategic business unit.[14] To emphasize the importance of the global/regional dimension in the country manager's portfolio, many companies have tied the country manager's compensation to the way the company performs globally or regionally, not just in the market for which the manager is responsible.

"Glocal" Organizations. No international structure is ideal, and some experts challenge the wisdom of even looking for an ideal. They have called attention to new processes that, in a given structure, would develop new perspectives and attitudes to reflect and respond to complex demands of the opposite forces of global integration and local responsiveness. Rather than a question of which structural alternative is best, the question is thus one of how best to take into account the different perspectives of various corporate entities when making decisions. In structural terms, nothing may change. Philips still has its basic matrix structure, for example, yet major changes have occurred in internal relations. The basic change was from a decentralized federation model—headquarters is the hub to which subsidiaries report exclusively—to a networked global organization in which subsidiaries report to headquarters but also coordinate activities directly with each other. The term "glocal" has been coined to describe the approach.[15]

Companies that have adopted the glocal approach have added three strengths to their organizations:[16]

1. Development and communication of a clear corporate vision that guides individuals wherever they may work in the organization. Examples include Johnson & Johnson's corporate credo of customer focus and NEC's C&C (computers and communication).
2. Effective management of human resource tools to broaden individual perspectives and develop employee identification with corporate goals. This develops global managers who can find opportunities in spite of environmental challenges and creates a global perspective among country managers.
3. Integration of individual thinking and activities into the broad corporate agenda, overcoming the "not-invented-here" syndrome to co-opt possibly isolated, even adversarial managers.

The glocal network avoids the problems of duplication of effort, inefficiency, and resistance to ideas developed elsewhere by giving subsidiaries the latitude, encouragement, and tools to pursue local business development within the framework of the global strategy. Headquarters considers each unit as a source of ideas, skills, capabilities, and knowledge that can be utilized for the benefit of the entire organization. This means that the subsidiaries must be upgraded from the role of implementation and adaptation to that of contribution and partnership in the development and execution of worldwide strategies. Efficient plants may be converted into international production centers, innovative R&D units may become centers of excellence (and thus role models), and leading subsidiary groups may be given a leadership role in developing new strategies for the entire corporation.

Promoting Internal Cooperation

Global marketing in today's environment means moving ideas as well as goods around the world. Teaching is one of the ways to do that, in programs ranging from senior executive-level workshops to company-wide employee training. Many companies emphasize teachable points of view: explanations of what a person knows and believes about how to succeed in his or her business.[17] For example, General Electric's Jack Welch coined the term "boundarylessness" to describe the way people can act without regard to status or functional loyalty and look for better ideas from anywhere. The top leadership of GE spends considerable time at training centers, interacting with up-and-comers from all over the company. Each training class is given a real, current company problem to solve, and the reports can be career makers or breakers.

A number of benefits arise from this approach. A powerful,

teachable point of view can reach the entire company within a reasonable period by having students become teachers themselves. At PepsiCo, the CEO passed his teachable point on to 110 executives, who then passed it on to 20,000 people within 18 months. Secondly, participants in teaching situations are encouraged to maintain the international networks they develop during the sessions.

Teachers do not necessarily need to be top managers. They can be specialists in an area of critical educational need such as e-commerce.

International Teams. Another method to promote internal cooperation for global marketing is through international teams or councils. In the case of a new product or program an international team of managers may be assembled to develop strategy. Although final direction may come from headquarters, the input has included information on local conditions, and implementation of the strategy is enhanced because local managers were involved from the beginning. This approach has worked even in cases that, offhand, would seem impossible because of market differences. Both Procter & Gamble and Henkel have successfully introduced pan-European brands for which strategy was developed by European strategy teams. These teams consisted of local managers and staff personnel to smooth eventual implementation and to avoid unnecessarily long and disruptive discussion about the fit of a new product to individual markets.

On a broader and longer-term basis, companies use councils to share best practices, an idea that may have saved money or time or a process that is more efficient than existing ones. Most professionals at the leading global marketing companies are members of multiple councils.

While technology has made teamwork of this kind possible wherever the individual participants may be, technology alone may not bring about the desired results. "High-tech" approaches inherently mean "low touch," sometimes at the expense of results. Human relationships are still paramount. A common purpose is what binds team members to a particular task. It can only be achieved through trust and attained through face-to-face meetings. At the start of its model 777 project, for instance, Boeing brought members of the design team from a dozen different countries to Everett, Washington, giving them the opportunity to work together for up to 18 months. Beyond learning to function effectively within the company's project management system, they also shared experiences that, in turn, engendered a level of trust between individuals that later enabled them to overcome obstacles raised by physical separation. The result was a design and launch in 40 percent less time than for comparable projects.

Communication Tools. The term network also implies two-way communications between headquarters and subsidiaries and between subsidiaries themselves. While this communication can take the form of newsletters or regular and periodic meetings of appropriate personnel, new technologies are allowing marketers to link far-flung entities and eliminate traditional barriers of time and distance.

Intranets integrate a company's information assets into a single and accessible system using Internet-based technologies such as email, newsgroups, and the World Wide Web. For example, employees at Levi Strauss & Co. can join an electronic discussion group with colleagues around the world, watch the latest Levi's commercials, or comment on the latest marketing program or plan.[18] "Let's Chat about the Business" emails go out at Ford every Friday at 5 P.M. to about 100,000 employees to share as much information as possible throughout the company and encourage dialogue. In many companies, the annual videotaped greeting from management has been replaced by regular and frequent emails (called e-briefs at GE). The benefits of intranets are:

- Increased productivity in that there is no longer lag time between an idea and the information needed to implement it.
- Enhanced knowledge capital that is constantly updated and upgraded.
- Facilitated teamwork enabling online communication at insignificant expense.
- Incorporation of best practices at a moment's notice by allowing marketing managers and sales personnel to make up-to-the-minute decisions anywhere in the world.

Country Subsidiaries' Roles

Country organizations should be treated as a source of supply as much as a source of demand. Quite often, however, headquarters managers see their own roles as the coordinators of key decisions and controllers of resources and perceive subsidiaries as implementers and adapters of global strategy in their respective local markets. Furthermore, all country organizations may be seen as the same. This view severely limits the utilization of the firm's resources by not using country organizations as resources and by depriving country managers of possibilities of exercising their creativity.

Exhibit 14.1: Country Organization Roles

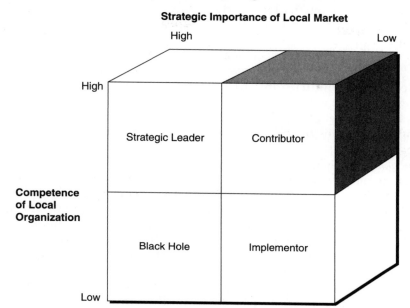

Strategic Importance of Local Market

The role that a particular country organization can play depends naturally on that market's overall strategic importance as well as the competencies of its organization. From these criteria, four different roles emerge, as shown in Exhibit 14.1.

The *strategic leader* role can be played by a highly competent national subsidiary located in a strategically critical market. The country organization serves as a partner of headquarters in developing and implementing strategy. Procter & Gamble's Eurobrand teams, which analyze opportunities for greater product and marketing program standardization, are chaired by a brand manager from a "lead country."[19]

A *contributor* is a country organization with a distinctive competence, such as product development. Increasingly, country organizations are the source of new products. These range from IBM's breakthrough in superconductivity research, generated in its Zurich lab, to low-end innovations like Procter & Gamble's liquid Tide, made with a fabric-softening compound also developed in Europe.[20] Similarly, country organizations may be assigned as worldwide centers of excellence for a particular product category, for example, ABB Strömberg in Finland for electric drives, a category for which it is a recognized world leader.[21]

Implementers provide the critical mass for the international marketing effort. These country organizations may exist in smaller, less-developed countries in which corporate commitment to market development is less. Although most entities are given this role, it should not be slighted: Implementers provide the opportunity to capture economies of scale and scope that are the basis of a global strategy.

The *black hole* is a situation of weak competence in a strategically important market. In some cases, firms may bide their time, using their presence in a major market as an observation post to keep up with developments before making a major thrust for entry. Often, however, the black hole needs to be filled and fixed. In strategically important markets such as the European Union, local presence is considered necessary for maintaining the company's overall global competitiveness and, in some cases, to anticipate competitive moves in other markets. One of the major ways of building local organization competence is to enter into strategic alliances.

Whether the relationship between headquarters and country organizations is loose or tight control or somewhere in between, country subsidiaries need enough operating independence to cater to local needs and to provide motivation to the country managers. For example, an implementer should provide input in the development of a regional or a global strategy or program. Strategy formulation should ensure that appropriate implementation can be achieved at the country level.

Characteristics of Success

The networked approach is not a structural adaptation but a procedural one that requires a change in management mentality. Adjustment is primarily in the coordination and control functions of the firm. While there is still considerable disagreement about which approaches work, some measures have been shown to correlate with success.

A McKinsey & Co. survey of chief executive officers of 43 leading U.S. consumer companies shed light on organizational features that distinguish internationally successful companies. Companies were classified as more or less successful compared to their specific industry average, using international sales and profit growth over the

1986–91 period as the most important indicators of success. Survey results indicated distinctive traits correlating with high performance in international markets, strengths companies can develop to enhance prospects for international success:

- Differentiate treatment of international subsidiaries.
- Let product managers in subsidiaries report to the country general manager.
- Have a worldwide management development program.
- Make international experience a condition for promotion to top management.
- Have a more multinational management group.
- Support international managers with global electronic networking capabilities.
- Have overseas R&D centers.
- Remain open to organizational change and continuous self-renewal.

In general, successful companies globally coordinate their international decision making, with more central direction than less successful competitors. This difference is most marked in brand positioning, package design, and price setting. The one notable exception is an increasing tendency to decentralize product development.[22]

CONTROL THAT FITS THE MISSION

Controls influence the behavior and performance of organization members to meet their goals. Controls focus on actions to verify and correct actions that differ from established plans. Within an organization, control serves as an integrating mechanism. Controls are designed to reduce uncertainty, increase predictability, and ensure that behaviors originating in separate parts of the organization are compatible and in support of common organizational goals despite physical, psychic, and temporal distances.[23] On the one hand, headquarters needs information to ensure that international activities contribute maximum benefit to the overall organization. On the other hand, controls should not be construed as a code of law and allowed to stifle local initiative.

Types of Controls

Most organizations display some administrative flexibility, as demonstrated by variations in the application of management directives, corporate objectives, or measurement systems. A distinction should be made, however, between variations that have emerged by design and those that are the result of autonomy. The one is the result of management decision, whereas the other has typically grown without central direction and is based on emerging practices. In both instances, some type of control will be exercised. Here, we are concerned only with controls that are the result of headquarters initiative rather than consequences of tolerated practices. Firms that wait for self-emerging controls often find that such an orientation may lead to rapid international growth but may eventually result in problems in areas of product-line performance, program coordination, and strategic planning.[24]

Benchmarking Best Practices. Whatever the system, it is important in today's competitive environment to have internal benchmarking to relay organizational learning and share best practices throughout the corporate system. That avoids the costs of reinventing solutions that have already been discovered. "International Best Practices Exchange," the article in Exhibit 14.2 describes that knowledge transfer process.

Three critical features are necessary in sharing best practices. First, there needs to be a device for organizational memory. For example, at Xerox, contributors to solutions can send their ideas to an electronic library where they are indexed and provided to potential adopters in the corporate family. Second, best practices must be updated and adjusted to new situations. For example, best practices adopted by the company's Chinese office will be modified and customized, and this learning should then become part of the database. Finally, best practices must be legitimized. This calls for a shared understanding that exchanging knowledge across units is valued in the organization and that these systems are important mechanisms for knowledge exchange. An assessment of how effectively employees share information with colleagues and utilize the databases can also be included in employee performance evaluations.

In the design of the control system, a major decision concerns the object of control. Two major objects are typically identified: output and behavior.[25] Output controls consist of balance sheets, sales data, production data, product line growth, or a performance review of personnel. Managers accumulate measures of output at regular intervals and send them from the foreign operation to headquarters, where they are compared to the plan or budget. Behavioral controls require exerting influence over behavior after, or ideally before, it leads to action. This influence can be achieved, for example, by

Exhibit 14.2: International Best Practices Exchange

As growing competitive pressures challenge many global firms, strategies to improve the transfer of best practices across geographically dispersed units and time zones becomes critical. The premise is that a company with the same product range targeting the same markets pan-regionally should be able to use knowledge gained in one market throughout the organization. The fact is, however, that companies use only 20 percent of their most precious resources—knowledge, in the form of technical information, market data, internal know-how, and processes and procedures. Trying to transfer best practices internationally amplifies the problem even more.

U.K.-based copier maker Xerox (formerly Rank Xerox), with more than 60 subsidiaries, has been working hard to make better use of its knowledge corporatewide. A 35-person group identified nine practices that could be applied throughout the group. These ranged from the way the Australian subsidiary retains customers to Italy's method of gathering competitive intelligence to a procedure for handling new major accounts in Spain. These practices were thought to be easier to "sell" to other operating companies, were considered easy to implement, and would provide a good return on investment.

Three countries were much quicker introducing new products successfully than others. In the case of France, this was related to the training given to employees. The subsidiary gave its sales staff three days of hands-on practice, including competitive benchmarking. Before they attended the course, salespeople were given reading materials and were tested when they arrived. Those remaining were evaluated again at the end of the course, and performance reports were sent to their managers.

The difficult task is to achieve buy-in from the other country organizations. Six months might be spent in making detailed presentations of the best practices to all the companies and an additional three years helping them implement the needed changes. It is imperative that the country manager is behind the proposal in each subsidiary's case. However, implementation cannot be left to the country organizations after the concept has been presented. This may result in the dilution of both time and urgency and the creation of country-specific customization that negates comparisons and jeopardizes the success of the change. In Xerox's case, executives were pleased with the $400 million savings achieved once half the recommendations had been adopted by half of the organization.

SOURCE: Michael McGann, "Chase Harnesses Data with Lotus Notes," Bank Systems and Technology 34 (May 1997): 38; "Rank Xerox Aims at Sharing Knowledge," *Crossborder Monitor* (September 18, 1996): 8; and "World-Wise: Effective Networking Distinguishes These 25 Global Companies," *Computerworld* (August 26, 1996): 7.

providing sales manuals to subsidiary personnel or by fitting new employees into the corporate culture.

Instruments of Control. To institute either of these measures, corporate officials must choose instruments of control. The general alternatives are bureaucratic/formalized control or cultural control.[26] Bureaucratic controls consist of a limited and explicit set of regulations and rules that outline desired levels of performance. Cultural controls, on the other hand, are much less formal and are the result of shared beliefs and expectations among the members of an organization.

The elements of bureaucratic/formalized controls are an international budgeting and planning system, a functional reporting system, and policy manuals used to direct functional performance. Budgets are short-term guidelines in such areas as investment, cash, and personnel, while plans refer to formal long-range programs with more than a one-year horizon. The budgeting and planning process is the major control instrument in headquarters-subsidiary relationships. Although systems and their execution vary, the goal is to achieve the best fit possible with the objectives and characteristics of the firm and its environment.

Budgeting time frames are typically one year because budgets are tied to the accounting systems of the company. Long-range plans, on the other hand, extend over periods of 2 to 10 years, and their content is more qualitative and judgmental in nature than that of budgets. Shorter periods, such as 2 years, are the norm because of the uncertainty of diverse foreign environments. Although firms strive for uniformity, this may be comparable to trying to design a suit to fit the average person. The budget and planning processes themselves follow formal schedules.

Functional reports are another output control instrument used by multinational corporations. The structure and elements of these reports are typically highly standardized to allow for consolidation at the headquarters level. Standard report types—according to a survey of 117 American, German, and Japanese multinational firms—are:[27]

- Balance sheet
- Profit-and-loss statement
- Production output
- Market share
- Cash and credit statement
- Inventory levels
- Sales per product
- Performance review of personnel
- Report on local economic and political conditions

Because the frequency and types of reports to be furnished by subsidiaries are likely to increase due to globalization, it is essential that subsidiaries see the rationale for these often time-consuming tasks. Two approaches, used in tandem, can facilitate the process: participation and feedback. Involving the authors of reports in their ultimate use serves to avoid the perception at subsidiary levels that reports are "art for art's sake." When this is not possible, feedback about results and consequences is an alternative.

On the behavioral front, headquarters may want to guide the way in which subsidiaries make decisions and implement agreed-upon strategies. U.S.-based multinational companies, relying heavily on manuals for all major functions, tend to be far more formal than their Japanese and European counterparts.[28] The manuals are for functions such as personnel policies for recruitment, training, motivation, and dismissal. The use of policy manuals as a control instrument correlates with the level of reports required from subsidiaries.

In countries other than the United States, multinationals put less emphasis on formal controls, which are viewed as rigid and too quantitatively oriented. Rather, the emphasis is on *corporate values and culture*, and evaluations are based on the extent to which an individual or entity fits in. Cultural controls require an extensive socialization process, and informal, personal interaction is central to the process. Substantial resources must be spent to train the individual to share the corporate culture, "the way things are done at the company."

For example, to build common vision and values, managers at Matsushita spend a substantial amount of their first months in what the company calls "cultural and spiritual training." They study the company credo, the "Seven Spirits of Matsushita," and the philosophy of the founder, Konosuke Matsushita. Then they learn how to translate these internalized lessons into daily behavior and operational decisions. Although more prevalent in Japanese organizations, many Western entities have similar programs such as Philips' "organization cohesion training" and Unilever's "indoctrination."[29] This corporate acculturation will be critical for managers asked to accept the possible transfers of best practices within the organization.

The primary instruments of cultural control are the careful selection and training of corporate personnel and the institution of self-control. The choice of cultural controls rather than bureaucratic controls can be justified if the company enjoys a low turnover rate. Cultural controls are thus applied, for example, when companies offer lifetime or long-term employment, as many Japanese firms do.

In selecting home-country nationals and, to some extent, third-country nationals, multinational companies are exercising cultural control. They assume that these managers have already internalized the norms and values of the company and that they tend to run a country operation with a more global view. In some cases, the use of headquarters personnel to ensure uniformity in decision making may be advisable; for example, for the position of financial officer, Volvo uses a home-country national. Expatriates are used in subsidiaries not only for control purposes but also for initiating change and to develop local talent. Companies control the efforts of management specifically through compensation, promotion, and replacement policies.

When the expatriate corps is small, headquarters can exercise control through other means. Management training programs for overseas managers as well as visits to headquarters will indoctrinate individuals to the company's way of doing things. Similarly, visits to subsidiaries by headquarters teams will promote a sense of belonging. These may be on a formal basis, as for a strategy audit, or less formal—for example, to launch a new product. Some innovative global marketers assemble temporary teams of their best talent to build local skills. IBM, for example, drafted 50 engineers from its facilities in Italy, Japan, New York, and North Carolina to run three-week to six-month training courses on all operations carried on at its Shenzhen facility in China. After the trainers left the country, they stayed in touch by email, so whenever the Chinese managers have a problem, they know they can reach someone for help. The continuation of support has been as important as the training itself.[30]

Corporations rarely use one pure control mechanism. Rather, they emphasize both quantitative and qualitative measures. Corporations are likely, however, to place different levels of emphasis on the types of performance measures and on the way the measures are used.

Exercising Control

Within most corporations, different functional areas follow different guidelines, depending on their characteristics and needs. For example, marketing controls rely more on behavioral dimensions than do manufacturing or finance metrics. Yet differentiation is sometimes based less on appropriateness than on personality. One researcher hypothesized that manufacturing subsidiaries are controlled more intensively than sales subsidiaries because production more readily lends itself to centralized direction, and technicians and engineers adhere more firmly to standards and regulations than do salespeople.[31]

Quantitative Pluses and Minuses. In their international operations, U.S.-based multinational corporations place major emphasis on obtaining quantitative data. Although this allows for good centralized comparisons against standards and benchmarks, or cross-comparisons between different corporate units, the approach has its drawbacks. In the international environment, additional dimensions—such as inflation, differing rates of taxation, and exchange rate fluctuations—may distort the performance evaluation of any given individual or organizational unit.

For the global corporation, measuring whether a business unit in a particular country is earning a superior return on investment relative to risk may be irrelevant to the contribution an investment may make worldwide or to the long-term results of the firm. In the short term, the return may even be negative. Therefore, the quantitative control mechanism might inappropriately indicate reward or punishment. Standardizing the information received may be difficult if the environment fluctuates and requires frequent and major adaptations. Further complicating the issue is the fact that, although routine quantitative information may be collected monthly or at least quarterly, environmental information that fills in the picture behind the numbers may be acquired annually, or "now and then," or only when crisis looms on the horizon.

To design a control system that is acceptable not only to headquarters but also to the organization and individuals abroad, a firm must take great care to use only relevant data. The more behaviorally based and culture-oriented controls are, the more care that needs to be taken.[32]

Sensible Control. In designing a control system, management must weigh the costs of establishing and maintaining it against the benefits gained. Any control system will require investing in a management structure and systems design. As an example, consider the costs associated with cultural controls: Personal interaction, use of expatriates, and training programs are all quite expensive. Yet these expenses may be justified in savings through lower employee turnover, an extensive worldwide information system, and a potentially improved control system.

The impact goes beyond the administrative component. If controls are erroneous or too time consuming, they can distort operations. And time spent on reporting takes time from other tasks. When managers consider reports marginally useful, they aren't motivated to prepare them. A parsimonious design is important. The control system should collect all the information required and trigger all the intervention necessary, but it should not create a situation that resembles a puppeteer pulling strings.

The impact of the environment must also be taken into account when designing controls. First, the control system should measure only factors over which the organization has control. Rewards or sanctions make little sense if they are based on effects that may be relevant for overall corporate performance but over which the subsidiary has no influence, such as prices. Neglecting the importance of individual performance metrics would send the wrong signals and severely demotivate personnel.

Also, control systems should harmonize with local regulations and customs. In some cases, however, corporate behavioral controls have to counter unacceptable local customs even when it hurts the bottom line, such as when a subsidiary operates in markets where unauthorized facilitating payments are a common business practice.

FUTURITIES

It has long been accepted that entrepreneurship at all levels of an organization is a critical driver of success. Managing knowledge is the strategic imperative for developing the spirit of entrepreneurship at all levels of globally involved companies. Country units cannot be mere implementors of a centrally developed strategy; nor can they be the only organizational forum for stimulating this spirit globally. Exploiting entrepreneurship across corresponding units in different markets is equally important. Furthermore, knowledge can be disseminated upward—from the local or country unit back to the central headquarters. In brief, the organizational flows of knowledge transfer should include up, down, and sideways.

Many inherent barriers exist against the interactions necessary for new approaches to knowledge exchange, ranging from a lack of systems and skills to communicate throughout the organization system to fundamental structures that favor central decision making and stifle country-unit initiatives. Technology has assisted in overcoming communication barriers through the use of Intranets, which establish the credibility of country organizations and lead to acknowledging the rationale for differentiation of roles for these units. As a result of these developments, centers of excellence have grown up to exploit and enhance existing capabilities and to leverage the resulting resources across multiple markets, not simply within individual markets. For example, having an innovation center in India for the development of environmentally friendly packaging or efficient energy systems provides a base for the transfer of knowledge to similar emerging and developing markets. In addition, development work done at such centers may easily lead to transfer of technologies and ideas back to the developed markets the company operates in.

While technologies may have solved some of the challenges of communication and education and overseas experience may have generated the skills and sensitivities need to overcome these challenges, the "headquarters-knows-best" mindset must change before knowledge transfer can be fully exploited. Most marketers agree that local adjustments are important in developing of marketing strategy but have not seen the need for similar internal adjustments.[33]

NOTES

1. Sources: P&G Jump-Starts Corporate Change," *Internetweek,* November 1, 1999, 30; "All around the World," *Traffic World,* October 11, 1999, 22–24; "Organization 2005 Drive for Accelerated Growth Enters Next Phase," P&G News Releases, June 9, 1999, 1–5; and "Procter & Gamble Moves Forward with Reorganization," *Chemical Market Reporter,* February 1, 1999, 12.
2. Richard D. Robinson, *Internationalization of Business: An Introduction* (Hinsdale, IL: The Dryden Press, 1984), 84.
3. See http://www.loctite.com/about/global_reach.html, and "How Loctite Prospers with 3-Man Global HQ, Strong Country Managers," *Business International,* May 2, 1988, 129–130.
4. William H. Davidson and Philippe Haspeslagh, "Shaping a Global Product Organization," *Harvard Business Review* 59 (March–April 1982): 69–76.
5. "How Goodyear Sharpened Organization and Production for a Tough World Market," *Business International,* January 16, 1989, 11–14.
6. "Red Alert at Ford," *Business Week,* December 2, 1996, 38–39.
7. B. Saporito, "Campbell Soup Gets Piping Hot," *Fortune,* Sept. 9, 1991, 94–98.
8. 3M Co. 1998 Annual Report, 1–3.
9. John D. Daniels, "Bridging National and Global Marketing Strategies through Regional Operations," *International Marketing Review* 4 (Autumn 1987): 29–44; Philippe Lasserre, "Regional Headquarters: The Spearhead for Asia Pacific Markets," *Long Range Planning* 29 (February 1996): 30–37.
10. Daniel Robey, *Designing Organizations: A Macro Perspective* (Homewood, IL: Irwin, 1982), 327.
11. N. Blackwell, J. P. Bizet, P. Child, and D. Hensley, "Creating European Organizations That Work," *The McKinsey Quarterly* 27 (No. 2, 1991): 376.
12. Rodman Drake and Lee M. Caudill, "Management of the Large Multinational: Trends and Future Challenges," *Business Horizons* 24 (May–June 1981): 83–91.
13. N. Blackwell, J. P. Bizet, P. Child, and D. Hensley, "Creating European Organizations That Work," *The McKinsey Quarterly* 27 (No. 2, 1991): 376–385.
14. J. A. Quelch and H. Bloom, "The Return of the Country Manager," *McKinsey Quarterly* 33 (No. 2, 1996): 31–43; J. I. Martinez and J. A. Quelch, "Country

Managers: The Next Generation," *International Marketing Review* 13 (No. 3, 1996): 43–55.

15. Thomas Gross, Ernie Turner, and Lars Cederholm, "Building Teams for Global Operations," *Management Review,* June 1987, 32–36.

16. C. A. Bartlett and S. Ghoshal, "Matrix Management: Not a Structure, a Frame of Mind," *Harvard Business Review* 68 (July–August 1990): 138–145.

17. *Noel Tichy, "The Teachable Point of View: A Primer,"* Harvard Business Review 77 (March–April 1999): 82–83.

18. "Internet Software Poses Big Threat to Notes, IBM's Stake in Lotus," *The Wall Street Journal,* November 7, 1995, A1–5.

19. John A. Quelch and Edward J. Hoff, "Customizing Global Marketing," *Harvard Business Review* 64 (May–June 1986): 59–68.

20. Richard I. Kirkland, "Entering a New Age of Boundless Competition," *Fortune,* March 14, 1988, 18–22.

21. "Percy Barnevik's Global Crusade," *Business Week Enterprise* 1993, 204–211.

22. Adapted from Ingo Theuerkauf, David Ernst, and Amir Mahini, "Think Local, Organize . . . ?" *International Marketing Review* 13 (Number 3, 1996): 7–12.

23. W. G. Egelhoff, "Patterns of Control in U.S., U.K., and European Multinational Corporations," *Journal of International Business Studies* 15 (Fall 1984): 73–83.

24. William H. Davidson, "Administrative Orientation and International Performance," *Journal of International Business Studies* 15 (Fall 1984): 11–23.

25. William G. Ouchi, "The Relationship between Organizational Structure and Organizational Control," *Administrative Science Quarterly* 22 (March 1977): 95–112.

26. B. R. Baliga and A. M. Jaeger, "Multinational Corporations: Control Systems and Delegation Issues," *Journal of International Business Studies* 15 (Fall 1984): 25–40.

27. Anant R. Negandhi and Martin Welge, *Beyond Theory Z* (Greenwich, CT: JAI Press, 1984), 18.

28. Anant R. Negandhi and Martin Welge, *Beyond Theory Z* (Greenwich, CT: JAI Press, 1984), 16.

29. C. A. Bartlett and S. Ghoshal, "Matrix Management: Not a Structure, a Frame of Mind," *Harvard Business Review* 68 (July–August 1990): 138–145.

30. Tsun-Yan Hsieh, Johanne La Voie, and Robert A. P. Samek, "Think Global, Hire Local," *The McKinsey Quarterly* 35 (Number 4, 1999): 92–101.

31. R. J. Alsegg, *Control Relationships between American Corporations and Their European Subsidiaries,* AMA Research Study No. 107 (New York: American Management Association, 1971), 7.

32. Hans Schoellhammer, "Decision-Making and Intra-Organizational Conflicts in Multinational Companies," presented at the Symposium on Management of Headquarter-Subsidiary Relationships in Transnational Corporations, Stockholm School of Economics, June 2–4, 1980.

33. For related articles see J. Birkinshaw and N. Hood, "Unleash Innovation in Foreign Subsidiaries," *Harvard Business Review* 79 (March 2001): 131–138; and J. Birkinshaw and T. Sheehan, "Managing the Knowledge Life Cycle," *Sloan Management Review* 44, 1 (2002): 75–83.

15

Twenty-First Century Trade Globalists

International marketers are the vanguard
of the American empire of ideals.

At the start of the twenty-first century, the new trade globalist stands at a fork in the road of international marketing. Will global firms, in concert with governments and multinational agencies, use the lessons of recent years to improve trade's positive contributions, reform its worst abuses, and empower the world through market forces? Or will developed markets and the mainstream trade establishment muddle along with their protectionist and parochial views, retard their own growth, and ignore the poverty and plight of billions of people?

Though we hope for the former and doubt the latter scenario will be as bad as some globalization critics contend, we expect unsettled times for the world economy as the first decade of the twenty-first century unfolds. Neither path at the fork in the road will become an automatic or default choice. By helping to improve the efficiency and effectiveness of international marketing, we believe that this book makes a contribution to an informed debate and, hopefully, encourages the development and use of market forces and market signals.

The ongoing major imbalances of international trade flows, the protection of intellectual property, and the need to incorporate new participants from emerging and less-developed markets will be key concerns in the international trade framework. A primary question will be whether the World Trade Organization (WTO) can accommodate and resolve these new challenges. Multilateral trade negotiations are essential to attaining the ultimate goal of world trade: free markets in which labor, land, capital and technology—leavened by doses of human compassion—achieve their most productive uses in every country.

At the start of the century, we see signs pointing to each direction.

THE OPTIMISTS' PATH

The September 11, 2001 disasters have made the developed world more aware and, hopefully, more determined to grapple with the concerns of world citizens everywhere, including those in developing and less-developed nations. Pledges of more foreign aid and realistic international loan assistance indicate that the leaders of the richest nations recognize the need for collective assistance in a troubled world.

The Age of "Common Sense"

Greater attention to trade and trade experience in corporate suites and the nation's schools of management indicate how American business is recognizing the importance of global commerce. At Georgetown University's McDonough School of Business, our international marketing team has systematically tracked the activities of international firms for more than two decades.

In listening to the world, it appears to us that, in partial response to the attacks of September 11, 2001, a new global age of common sense and shared visions is emerging, characterized by five key dimensions:

1. A common sense of vulnerability: What happened in New York and Washington D.C. can occur at any location around the globe.
2. A common sense of outrage: The attacks did not engender moral ambivalence, at least not among multinational businesspeople.
3. A renewed global common sense of collaboration: Ever since the demise of the Soviet Union, there has been, even among those nations closely allied with the U.S., a reluctance to appreciate a joint direction or a common interest. But the 2000s promise a new understanding of the need to work together, to identify mutual goals, and to have a vision of a future with substantial commonalities. On the business side in foreign exchange, for instance, firms are reviving risk-sharing agreements through which corporations share the positive and negative effects of any major currency movements.
4. A politics of common sense: The rigid claims that used to characterize export controls, for example, have yielded to more simple and direct questions about technology trade. Closer collaboration among partner countries has actually relaxed export control policies as it tightened the net to deny questionable exports to dubious customers. Another example of common sense is the fast-track trade negotiation authority Congress conferred on the

president in 2002. On the international level, the round of trade talks agreed to in Doha indicates a willingness to tackle the tough trade issues such as agricultural subsidies, dumping regulations, property rights, and investment rules.

5. A common sense of shared concerns: For quite some time when addressing global issues, marketers and policymakers worldwide emphasized their local concerns, special quirks, and homegrown idiosyncrasies. They focused on all the things that make us different and possibly separate us. In the age of the new trade globalist, however, we need to concentrate on the issues that make us behave alike, that bring us together, and that strengthen the bonds between us. We need to give new currency to the term *mankind* and re-prioritize objectives such as life, liberty, and the pursuit of happiness with new appreciation and vigor.

Marketers' Initiatives

America's international marketers are changing their behavior in response to the trade trends around them. Our research finds major changes—though not all of them are expansive from a globalist's viewpoint—occurring in four key areas.

First is international customer management. Rather than just selling wherever possible, firms now focus much more than before on where to sell what to whom. Managers are developing a greater appreciation for the type and degree of risk exposure that certain regions of the world offer. Some of the leading risk factors can be the policies of home and host governments, exchange rate fluctuations, or economic turmoil.

Firms are increasingly considering the development of trade portfolios that allocate effort and limits in different regions of the world. Such portfolios are intended to achieve two goals. Limits of dependence on any region or customer are designed to reduce a firm's exposure in case of conflict or unexpected interruptions. Systematic development of markets is then used to balance existing exposure, to diversify a firm's risk, and to offer a fallback position.

There is also a greater scrutiny now of the alternative opportunities presented by foreign direct investment and exporting.

Foreign direct investment demonstrates the long-term nature of a firm's objectives and makes use of local advantages. It also facilitates collaboration and reduces some of the firm's exposure to the vagaries of border-crossing transactions. At the same time, however, it renders the firm vulnerable to the effects of government policies and any divergence between home and host country. Some firms are beginning to look beyond the strict economic dimensions of foreign direct investment and are considering it as a tool to signal that there is an area or a partner one has full confidence in and to demonstrate commitment. Such a relationship focus may well trigger more support from host government agencies.

Exporting will in the near term remain the principal tool of international expansion for firms new to the global market or those highly concerned about international risk. Exporting gives a firm much broader and quicker coverage of world markets with the ability to respond nimbly to changes. Risks are lower, but costs due to transshipment and transaction expenses tend to be higher, affecting the competitiveness of a venture.

Even though they consider an export orientation to be less risky, many firms are not as aggressive as they used to be in seeking new business or new accounts. This seems to be a reflection of the new desire to deal with established customers, with "people we know and with whom we have developed a feeling of trust." While firms typically tend to pursue multiple avenues of internationalization, an export approach currently appears to be the preferred method of new market entry.

Second is international people management because greater scrutiny also extends to corporate employees. Without necessarily differentiating between American and foreign applicants for employment, firms now take a much closer look at credentials and claims of past achievements and activities. Some U.S. firms, though very globally oriented, are becoming much more cautious in their hiring practices when it comes to foreign nationals. Because it becomes more difficult to control someone's access to information once that person is inside the organization, these firms appear to have made clear-cut decisions, rightly or wrongly, to not consider nationals from highly controversial countries for employment.

At the same time, the issue of culture and diversity among employees has taken on a much greater importance within firms. Managers who had previously only focused on the bottom line with a theme of "who cares about culture?" now have developed a much greater understanding and appreciation for the differences among employees. It is now more likely that senior management accepts the fact that things may be done differently in other nations and that some of these practices may require adapting one's own approaches.

Third is international production management. Manufacturers are devoting more scrutiny to where and how they produce. Increased concerns by members of the supply chain now make it imperative to identify and manage dependence on international inputs. A domestic source simply provides a greater feeling of comfort and fewer worries about supply interruptions or other problems.

And some buyers now treat country-of-origin declarations as political flags, rejecting products from specific regions, such as textile imports from Pakistan, we have been told.

On balance, relationship marketing and network building count more than ever. Buyers put a premium on dealing with known, long-term suppliers. Increasingly, suppliers from abroad may have to be recommended by other customers and demonstrate their ability to plan for and cope with contingencies before their products are even considered.

Fourth is international logistics management. Closely related to production concerns are logistics and supply chain matters. Companies have already accepted that the international pipeline has slowed down. Customary steps simply will take longer for the foreseeable future. However, the structure of the pipeline and the scrutiny given to the materials going through it have become much more important. Security measures at border crossings take longer since September 11. There is a desire and need for expanding the security bubble around a shipment and people long before they reach home shores, leading to a much more aggressive collaborative outreach by firms and governments around the world. And what used to be lip service paid to an organization's internal security is now a matter of top management attention. Firms also need to demonstrate, often to government authorities and insurance companies, how much more security-minded they have become.

THE PESSIMISTS' PATH

The trade picture has its dark side. Despite the sentiments of public officials and executive survey results we are hearing, the actual behavioral record has not been encouraging. Long-standing distrust of foreign commitments still stalks the capitals of the world, making it sometimes difficult to dismiss some policy maneuvers—in sectors such as steel or agriculture, for instance—as required tactics only in the short term. If trade relations cannot be continued on a multilateral basis, bilateral agreements and narrowly focused protectionism will increase on a global scale. International trade volume might even decline.

Growing protests over labor exploitation, job exporting, rapacious environmental policies, and discrimination against developing exports increasingly raise questions about the value and morality of the trade precepts guiding the world since World War II. Critics claim free trade as practiced only means the other guy should open his markets. Governments keep trying to have it both ways, protectionism at home and free markets everywhere else. Critics contend that trade restrictions cost poor nations $100 billion a year, twice as much as they receive in aid.[1] World market forces without adjustments and accommodations for LDCs and the developing world—gradually easing their adjustment into market-driven trade—could perpetuate poverty, famine, and terrorism.

Import barriers aren't the only problem. Multinational corporation direct investments often fail to provide all the benefits host countries think they will get. Too much profit repatriation, too little tax remittance, too much labor exploitation, and too much effort expended wooing investments bleed the advantages out of them. By bringing technology and skills to a country, direct investment can squeeze homegrown innovators and suppliers out of the market or expose them to competition they cannot yet handle.

EMPIRE: PRO AND CON

Between these positive and negative views of free trade and its effect on a new world order, the realities of unsettled trends and contradictions are what we've really inherited from terrorism, recession, and reduced expectations. Perhaps too little has been thought of late about a twenty-first century American "empire" in the making, a *Pax Americana* of U.S.-enforced—and presumably U.S.-defined—peace and prosperity.

At its best, most benign implication, *Pax Americana* describes a world of harmony and humility, with democratic institutions—modeled on America, of course—leading a world transformation rooted in free trade, market economics, and democratic principles. An American peace can offer a new perspective for international investment. In his theory of the international product life cycle, Raymond Vernon of Harvard University presaged global innovation and production.[2] His thinking for many years supported the belief that investment, production, and therefore wealth would eventually spread to all nations, resulting in lower-cost products and a broader manufacturing base. However, for quite some time now, the cycle has not continued but has stalled in China and Vietnam. Most nations in Africa and many other developing countries have yet to benefit.

Firms tell us that risk, prevailing uncertainty, and productivity limitations have made them reluctant to expand in these areas. Were there a substantial increase in stability, accompanied by local institutions desiring peace and economic development, the international product life cycle might extend to those less developed nations. Today's trickle of investment and purchasing could become a torrent in search of new opportunities. Those concerned with enforcing the peace in regions that might breed terrorists would be well served to consider peace a key instrument for growth and prosperity in disadvantaged nations.

But, lest we forget, power and benevolence do not automatically go hand in hand. It was protectionism that allowed the U.S. economy to survive the predations of the British Empire, the same empire said to have presided over late nineteenth-century famines in China, India, and Africa that killed 50 million people.[3] Think also about the outcome of the Punic Wars between the Roman Empire and Carthage during their trade disputes. Two thousand years later, the once-glorious city of Carthage is still in ruins.

But "empire" need not mean bullying. It does bear reminding that the United States, for example, prohibits irresponsible pharmaceutical testing abroad, even if legal in another country. It was the United States which after lengthy and agonizing debates chose the location where to bury nuclear waste, the choice being not some far away territory of adversaries, but a domestic location. One wonders what some of the prior world powers would have inflicted on their foes or even allies. There is virtue at work!

THE MARKETING VANGUARD

Since command economies have failed so spectacularly around the world, it is clear that the private sector, individual companies, and their executives drive economic policies and the components that constitute American world leadership. Ultimately, companies' collective decisions—watched over by regulators who enforce the rules of the game—determine public policy in concert with the voters who are also their employees and stockholders.

That means marketers—the people in charge of creating the customers essential to profitability—are the vanguard of trade leadership. And because everyone in a firm with customer-related responsibilities is a marketer, many have a role in international trade—from the CEO negotiating foreign deals to the multilingual receptionist helping visiting traders feel more at home. In order to work appropriately for the stakeholders of a firm, an aspiring corporate manager in the United States must have a world view and take part in global commerce. Fortunately, the available marketing tools and techniques are better than ever.

Beyond the tools, there has been major progress in the responsibility of firms on a global level. Of course, globalization adds to the pressures on managers, and some—as headlines in the U.S., Europe, and Japan attest—have responded by taking shortcuts and using smoke and mirrors. Make no mistake; nefarious business practices need to be identified, terminated, and the executives punished. Quick, ongoing, and public action by the industrialized nations is essential for world acceptance of globalization and market forces.

As proponents of the market-based system, we are "selling" the world on two key issues. One is the benefit of market forces that results from the interplay of supply and demand. This interplay in turn uses price signals instead of government fiat to adjust activities, thrives on competition, and works within an environment of respect for profitability and private property. In exchange for the chance to earn profits, investors allocate resources to the most productive and efficient uses.

The second key proposition concerns the trust between managers and investors. In return for high compensation, the nonowner managerial class must provide the absentee owners and other stakeholders with their best efforts to preserve and increase stakeholders' benefits.

The key to making it work is managerial and corporate virtue, vision, and veracity. Unless the world can believe in what firms and managers say and do, it will be hard, nay impossible, to forge a global commitment between those doing the marketing and the ones being marketed to. It is therefore of vital interest to the proponents of globalization to ensure that corruption, bribery, lack of transparency, and misleading stakeholders are relegated to the scrap heap of history. If its negotiations of trading rules are to make sense, the World Trade Organization must take steps to preserve the acceptance of markets and management around the world. A commitment to transparency, responsiveness, long-term thinking, and truthfulness will be essential to achieve this objective.

This book has given you a comprehensive review of the strategies, tactics, tools, and institutions that power world trade, particularly for marketers orchestrating their own global corporate "empires." Specific policy prescriptions and recommended business strategies are an ever-moving target. So stay informed. But the enduring truth remains that what each marketer does in his or her micro-level choices contributes to the macro success or failure of American worldwide leadership.

The times are new, but the inspiration for how we should shoulder that leadership is not. Go back two millennia and consider how St. Paul, also called the thirteenth Apostle, handled his marketing